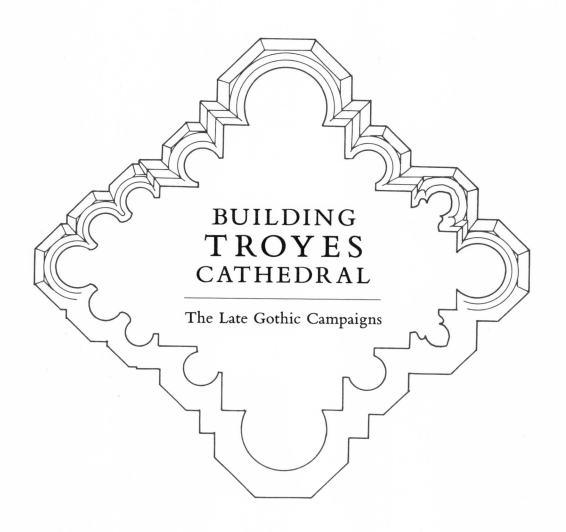

BUILDING
TROYES
CATHEDRAL

The Late Gothic Campaigns

STEPHEN MURRAY

INDIANA UNIVERSITY PRESS

BUILDING TROYES CATHEDRAL

CATHEDRAL

The Late Gothic Campaigns

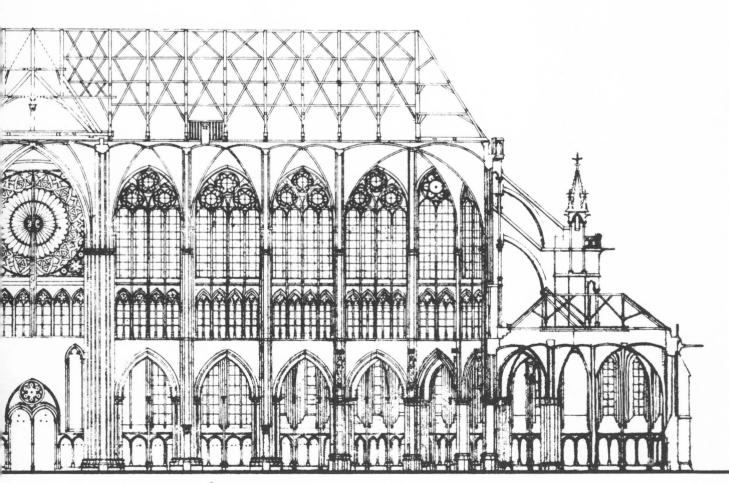

BLOOMINGTON & INDIANAPOLIS

Published with the assistance of the J. Paul Getty Trust and the
Millard Meiss Publication Fund of the College Art Association of America.

Drawings on the title and epigraph pages are by André Droesch.
Chapter openings are Gothic initials used at Troyes by Jean Lecoq.

Manufactured in the United States of America

Library of Congress Cataloging-in-Publication Data

Murray, Stephen, 1945–
  Building Troyes Cathedral.

  Bibliography: p.
  Includes index.
   1. Cathédrale de Saint-Pierre-et-Saint-Paul
(Troyes, France) 2. Architecture, Gothic—France—
Troyes. 3. Troyes (France)—Buildings, structures,
etc. I. Title.
NA5551.T744M87 1986   726'.6'0944331   85-45744
ISBN 0-253-31277-9

1 2 3 4 5 90 89 88 87

For the people of Troyes

"Publier les comptes des proviseurs, ce serait donc faire connaître cette glorieuse époque où tous, grands et petits, bourgeois et pauvres artisans, animés par la foi, venaient si puissamment contribuer à l'érection de ces cathédrales qui ravissent notre imagination. . . .

A. ASSIER, *Comptes de l'oeuvre de l'église de Troyes*, 1855.

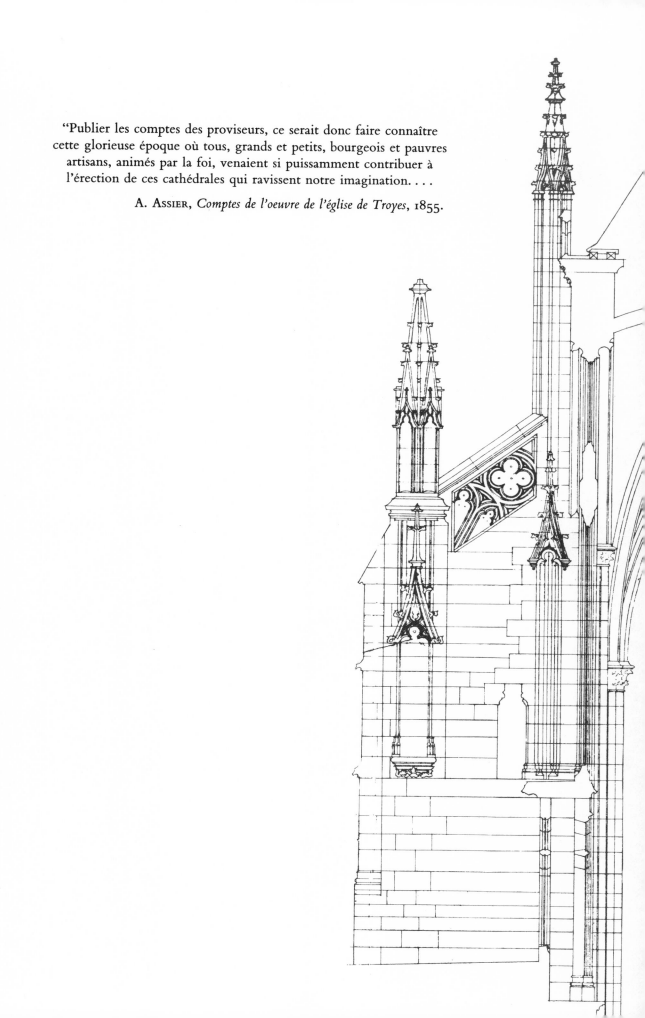

CONTENT

PREFACE AND ACKNOWLEDGMENTS   XVII

I. INTRODUCTION: THE UNFINISHED CATHEDRAL, 1200–1290   I
II. CONSERVATISM AND INNOVATION, MISTAKES
AND DISASTER, 1290–1390   18
III. MAINTENANCE, REPAIR, AND EMBELLISHMENT, 1390–1450   44
IV. THE LATE GOTHIC MASTERS OF THE NAVE, 1450–1502   61
V. MARTIN CHAMBIGES, *SUPREMUS ARTIFEX*, 1502–1532   87
CONCLUSION   110

Illustrations follow page 60

APPENDIX A. HANDLIST OF FABRIC ACCOUNTS   113
APPENDIX B. SELECTED TEXTS   116
APPENDIX C. ANALYSES OF THE WORKSHOP AND REVENUES   199
APPENDIX D. DESCRIPTION AND CHRONOLOGY OF
THE FLYING BUTTRESSES OF THE NAVE   216

NOTES   227
SELECTED BIBLIOGRAPHY   245
INDEX   251

Illustrations

Illustrations are of Troyes Cathedral unless otherwise indicated.

1. Plan of the medieval city of Troyes (E. Chapin, *Les villes de foires*)
2. Plan of Troyes Cathedral
   a) *Bâtiments de France* plan
   b) Chronology and grid system of reference. Chronology of choir after N. Bongartz, *Die frühen Bauteile*
3. Plan of the frontispiece
4. Simplified schemes to show the dimensional relationships in the frontispiece.
   a) Plan
   b) Elevation
5. Section of nave at division 5
6. Simplified plan and elevation of one bay of the vault of the central vessel
7a. Section of upper nave pier at D 2
7b. Section of upper nave pier at D 5
8. Moulding profiles of the jambs of the clerestory windows
9. Interior of west towers, section of attached pier
10. Interior of west towers, section of free-standing pier
11. Interior of nave, section of pier B 1
12. Interior of nave, section of pier E 1
13. Interior of nave, section of pier D 2
14. Interior of nave, section of pier C 5
15. Interior of nave, section of pier D 5
16. Interior of nave, section of pier E 5
17. Interior of nave, section of pier F 5
18. Interior of nave, section of pier C 6 (crossing)
19. Interior of nave, arch and rib profiles
    a) Main arcade, bay 5–6
    b) Aisle, transverse arch, bay 5–6
    c) Lateral chapel, bay 5–6

Note: the illustrations are arranged with the drawings first, then photographs, proceeding from exterior to interior; west to east; general view before details; lower parts before upper; north to south. All photographs and drawings are by the author unless otherwise indicated.

   d) Diagonal rib, bay 5-6

   e) Diagonal rib, west end of the nave.

20. Base mouldings of piers, comparative profiles

   a) Pier C 6

   b) Pier C 5

   c) Pier C 3

   d) Troyes, Saint-Urbain, south transept, east side

   e) Pier B 2

21. Design for a rose window of the type employed by Martin Chambiges

22. Elements of the design vocabulary of Late Gothic

   a) Ogee

   b) Fillet

   c) Soufflet

   d) Mouchette

   e) Rotated or inscribed squares

   f) Inscribed hexagons

23. Restoration drawing of the spur at D E 1 by the architect Selmersheim, 1889

24. The nave in its provisional state, 1390–1450, section

25. The nave in its provisional state, 1390–1450, longitudinal elevation

26. Master Bleuet's plan for the west façade

27. Nave, campaigns of construction, 1450–1500

28. Beauvais Cathedral, chronology of the transepts

29. Beauvais Cathedral, section of smaller pier type in transept

30. Beauvais, Saint-Etienne, section of pier in choir aisle

31. Beauvais, Saint-Etienne, section of pier in main arcade of choir

32. Senlis Cathedral, section of sixteenth-century pier in transept

33. Nineteenth-century lithograph of the cathedral, C. Fichot (photograph by M. Vuillemin)

34. West façade (M. Vuillemin)

35. West façade, oblique view

36. West façade, center portal, embrasures and jambs

37. Nave, north side, looking east

38. Troyes, Vauluisant Museum, cork model of the cathedral

39. Chapel N 4, by Anthoine Colas, c. 1456

40. Nave, south side, tracery of chapel S 4, by Anthoine Colas, c. 1456

41. Nave, north side, three eastern lateral chapels, N 1–3, completed early fourteenth century

42. Chapel N 5, by the workshop of Chambiges, c. 1521

43. North transept façade, begun c. 1210–1220; rose c. 1400; decorative buttresses and ogee arch by Anthoine Colas, 1462–1463

44. General view of roof of nave and transept, showing flying buttresses

45. General view of upper nave, south side

46. Upper nave, west gable by Jehançon Garnache, 1492

47. Upper nave, south side, spur at D E 1 by Anthoine Colas and Jehançon Garnache, completed 1492, restored by Selmersheim, 1889
48. Upper nave, south side, general view of flyers, looking east
49. Upper nave, north side, view of flyers and clerestory, looking east
50. Upper nave, north side, upper flyer at B C 2 by Jehançon Garnache, 1492–1493, abutting pier by Anthoine Colas, 1470s
51. Upper nave, south side, upper flyer at D E 2 by Jehançon Garnache, 1493–1494, abutting pier by Anthoine Colas, 1470s
52. Upper nave, north side, pier C 4
    a) Lower part
    b) Upper part
53. Upper nave, south side, pier D 4
    a) Lower part
    b) Upper part
54. Upper nave, north side, outer upright of flying buttress at A 5, detail of attached pinnacle.
55. Upper nave, north side, flying buttress at A B C 5
    a) General view
    b) Upper flyer
56. Upper nave, north side, pier C 5
    a) Lower part
    b) Upper part
57. Upper nave, south side, pier D 5
    a) Lower part
    b) Upper part
58. Upper nave, south side, flying buttress at D E F 5
    a) General view, showing change in inclination in upper flyer
    b) Upper flyer
59. Upper nave, north side, clerestory window at C 3 4 by Jehançon Garnache, 1499–1500, type A
60. Upper nave, south side, clerestory window at D 1 2 by Jehançon Garnache, 1498–1499, type A
61. Upper nave, north side, clerestory window at C 2 3 by Jehançon Garnache, 1499–1500, type B
62. Upper nave, south side, clerestory window at D 5 6 by Jehançon Garnache, 1497–1498, type C
63. Upper transept, west side of north arm, flyer at B 5 6
64. Interior, general view looking east (M. Vuillemin)
65. Interior nave, north side, looking east
66. Interior nave, south side, looking east
67. Interior, eastern bays of nave; crossing and choir (Courtauld Institute)
68. Interior, eastern bays of nave seen from south nave aisle (Courtauld Institute)
69. Interior, eastern bays of nave seen from north nave aisle (Courtauld Institute)

70. Interior, eastern bays of nave and west side of south transept (Courtauld Institute)

71. Interior, west side of south transept

72. Interior, east side of north transept

73. Interior, general view of choir (Courtauld Institute)

74. Interior, general view of northern choir aisles looking east (Courtauld Institute)

75. Interior, general view of northern nave aisles, looking east (Courtauld Institute)

76. Interior west towers, south side, free-standing pier designed by Pierre Chambiges, 1530s

77. Interior nave, south aisles looking west showing junction with west façade scheme

78. Interior nave, north aisles, pier B 1, designed by Master Bleuet, 1455 and constructed by Anthoine Colas; capitals by Colas

79. Interior nave, base of pier C 1, designed and constructed by Jaquet le Vachier, 1452–1453

80. Interior nave, south aisles, pier E 1, designed and constructed by Anthoine Colas, after 1468

81. Interior nave, south aisles, base of pier D 2, designed and constructed by Jaquet le Vachier, 1452–1453

82. Interior nave, southern lateral chapel S 4, southwest corner, chapel designed and constructed by Jaquet le Vachier, c. 1452–1453

83. Interior nave, northern lateral chapel N 2, lower wall, early fourteenth century

84. Interior nave, south arcade, base of pier C 5, c. 1270s, by "the Saint-Urbain Master"

85. Interior nave, north aisles, pier C 1, showing capital, arches, and vault by Anthoine Colas, late 1450s to early 1470s

86. Interior nave, south arcade, pier D 1, capital probably begun by itinerant Flemish artist and finished by Anthoine Colas, 1455–1456

87. Interior nave, northern lateral chapel N 4, east end of arch in the chapel mouth, showing corbel added by Anthoine Colas to accommodate inner mouldings of the arch

88. Interior nave, north arcade, capital of pier C 2, 1370s

89. Interior nave, south arcade, capital of pier D 2, by Anthoine Colas, 1450s

90. Interior nave, south aisles, pier E 2 from the east, pier and capital by Jaquet le Vachier, early 1450s, vaults by Anthoine Colas, early 1460s

91. Interior nave, south aisles, pier F 2 and chapel wall from the east. Pier, capital and vault springers by Jaquet le Vachier, early 1450s, vaults by Anthoine Colas, early 1460s

92. Interior nave, north aisles, pier and capital at A 4, early fourteenth century

93. Interior nave, detail of triforium on north side, bay C 1 2 (left) and C 2 3 (right) by Anthoine Colas and Jehançon Garnache, 1470s to 1490s

94. Interior nave, capitals of high vault of central vessel
a) C 1, by Anthoine Colas, 1470s
b) D 1, by Anthoine Colas, 1470s
c) C 2, by Anthoine Colas, 1470s
d) D 2, by Anthoine Colas, 1470s

    e) C 3, by Jehançon Garnache, 1485

    f) D 3, by Jaquet le Vachier, 1483–1484

    g) C 4, c. 1360s–1370s

    h) D 4, c. 1360s

    i) C 5, c. 1340s–1350s

    j) D 5, c. 1340s–1350s

    k) C 6, early fourteenth century

95. Interior nave, upper north side, high capital at C 1 with springer placed for diagonal rib by Colas but discontinued by Garnache

96. Interior nave, upper south side, high vault springers at D 4, showing dislocation in window mouldings

97. Interior nave, general view of the high vaults installed by Jehançon Garnache, 1496–1498

98. Beauvais Cathedral, exterior of south transept façade, lower parts (to balustrade under the rose) by Martin Chambiges, 1500–1532, upper parts 1540s–1550s

99. Beauvais Cathedral, interior of north transept, general view, looking east

100. Beauvais Cathedral, interior of north transept, base of pier C 4, by Martin Chambiges, soon after 1510

101. Beauvais Cathedral, interior of north transept, chapel vault, soon before 1517

102. Beauvais Cathedral, interior of south transept, chapel vault, c. 1520s

103. Beauvais, Saint-Etienne, interior choir, south elevation

104. Beauvais, Saint-Etienne, interior choir, north aisles, pier base

105. Beauvais, Saint-Etienne, interior of sepulchre chapel to north of choir (present baptismal chapel), detail of vault

106. Melun, Saint-Aspais, exterior of choir, east end, portal (Arch. phot./S.P.A.D.E.M., Paris/V.A.G.A., New York, 1986)

107. Paris, Ecole des Beaux Arts, fragment from the Hôtel le Gendre

108. Paris, Notre-Dame, interior choir, south aisles, pier base, c. 1300

109. Paris, Saint-Germain l'Auxerrois, interior of west porch, northern bay

110. Paris, SS. Gervais and Protais, interior choir, general view

111. Paris, Saint-Jacques de la Boucherie, tower

112. Paris, Saint-Merry, interior nave, west end, pier base

113. Paris, Sainte-Chapelle, exterior west façade, detail of rose window

114. Senlis Cathedral, south transept façade

115. Senlis Cathedral, interior south transept, pier base by Pierre Chambiges

116. Sens Cathedral, north transept façade, by Martin Chambiges and Huges Cuvelier, first decades 16th century

117. Sens Cathedral, south transept façade, begun late 13th century, completed by Martin Chambiges and Huges Cuvelier, 1489–c. 1500

118. Troyes, Saint-Jean au Marché, north side of choir

119. Troyes, Saint-Urbain, choir, detail of pier base

120. Troyes, Saint-Urbain, choir

Preface and Acknowledgments

This book has been through several stages of metamorphosis before reaching its present form. My interest in Troyes Cathedral was first kindled as a result of my Master's Essay for the Courtauld Institute on some unpublished fabric accounts that had found their way to the British Library. Eric Stone, my tutor at Keble College, Oxford, had introduced me to the mysteries of the medieval manorial account, and when my interests turned to cathedral building, Howard Colvin of Saint John's College suggested that I should look at the Troyes accounts. Christopher Hohler gave me far more help than I ever realized at the time and Peter Kidson directed my doctoral dissertation on the most famous of the masons who worked at Troyes Cathedral, Martin Chambiges.

While engaged in field work at Troyes I met Norbert Bongartz, who was preparing a doctoral dissertation on the choir of the cathedral, and I learned much from my collaboration with him. We decided to publish the cathedral in a two-volume monograph which was to appear in France. My colleague at Indiana University, Theodore Bowie, kindly translated my text into French for this publication, and also offered many editorial suggestions. When the difficulties with the two-volume French publication finally became insuperable, Norbert Bongartz went ahead with the publication of his own work in a German edition (*Die frühen Bauteile der Kathedrale in Troyes. Architekturgeschichtliche Monographie*, Hochschul-Verlag, Stuttgart, 1979). I then rewrote my own book in English, transforming it from an "archaeological" monograph into a work intended for a wider audience. In order to make my contribution on the Late Gothic parts of Troyes Cathedral a self-contained monograph, I have summarized the early history of the construction in the first chapter on the Unfinished Cathedral.

In my research on Troyes Cathedral I have faced a major problem in the real embarrassment of riches. The written sources are so copious that I can only hope to present a small fraction of them in the texts I have transcribed in Appendix B. These transcribed texts should be seen as the work of an Art Historian—in other words, while always striving for accuracy, I do not pretend to give a critical edition of the texts. Thus, where several versions of the same text exist I recognize the fact (see Appendix A) but I only chose to transcribe one of them.

J.-M. Roger, archivist of the *Archives départementales de l'Aube*, took a keen interest in my work and helped me to avoid innumerable errors in my transcriptions. I should hasten to add that I take full responsibility for any errors that remain. I have also received help with my texts from Emanuel Mickel, Garth McCavana, and Christopher Crockett.

A host of other people have helped me with their encouragement and interest: Carl Barnes, Caroline Bruzelius, François Bucher, William Clark, Walter Leedy, Marilyn Schmitt, Lon Shelby, and many others. Indiana University has provided me with a summer faculty fellowship and various travel grants. George M. Wilson, then Dean of Research and Graduate Development at Indiana University, did the magic necessary to make possible my two summer schools held in Troyes in 1973 and 1974. I owe much to the students who participated in these sessions.

I remember with particular gratitude and affection my friends in Troyes: abbé M. Mathat of the Maison Notre-Dame-en-Ile; Mgr. Marsat, vicar general; F. Bibolet of the municipal library; S. Morisseau, former architect of the *Bâtiments de France*, and his collaborator, A. Droesch. Mlle. J. Launay, Director of *Vie en Champagne*, was a source of inspiration and inspired criticism. The prolonged periods I have spent in Troyes have generally been a source of great enrichment for me, and for this reason I dedicate this book, with respect, to the people of Troyes, who have every reason to be proud of their cathedral.

My wife, Grainne, participated in the inception of this work in the campaigns of measuring completed in 1971 and 1972 for the Ph.D. dissertation, and she bore with me through the long period that ensued before this material reached its final form, frequently suggesting that I should get back to what was really important to me—the publication of my work on Troyes.

BUILDING
TROYES
CATHEDRAL

The Late Gothic Campaigns

I

Introduction: The Unfinished Cathedral, 1200–1290

 OR MORE THAN THREE CENTURIES (C. 1200 to mid 1500s) the city of Troyes was dominated by the still unfinished bulk of the Gothic cathedral of Saints Peter and Paul.[1] For generations the clergy—bishops and canons—worried over the planning of the great enterprise; for generations artisans toiled over the unfinished walls. During the early years of construction Troyes was the capital city favored by the powerful counts of Champagne and bustled with the activity of the annual fairs. Long before the cathedral was completed, however, the dynasty of the counts was extinct, the importance of the fairs had waned, and the surrounding countryside was devastated by the troops and brigands involved in the Hundred Years War. The completion of the cathedral was only possible in the period of recovery that followed the end of hostilities.

The planning and construction of the cathedral were obviously affected by a wide range of factors—the liturgical and aesthetic demands of the clergy, the balance of political power, the source and nature of funding and the vicissitudes of the flow of cash to the fabric. However, the stones of the cathedral were not shaped by abstract historical "forces": they were chiselled by masons. Knowledge of the working practices of medieval masons is somewhat scanty. The major problem faced by scholars in this field is to relate the references to individual masters found in the scattered written sources to the buildings (many of them lost)

for which they were responsible.[2] The study of Troyes Cathedral provides a rare opportunity for the correlation of evidence derived from the written sources with a study of the building itself. Thus, it will be possible to establish the identity of most of the leading master masons, to understand the organization of the workshop, to illustrate some of the construction methods used and the nature of the decision-making process, and to identify the sources of funding. Above all, it will be possible to add a new dimension to our understanding of the sequence of style discernible in the building. This new dimension will be gained when we turn away from the understanding of style purely as a neo-Platonic phenomenon divorced from human agency, and concentrate instead upon the builders themselves.

Our study is rendered possible through the survival of a considerable body of written evidence. Comparable evidence is lacking for the great cathedrals of the period of the creation and flowering of the Gothic style—cathedrals such as Chartres, Soissons, Bourges, Reims, and Amiens. We know the names of the master masons of Reims and Amiens Cathedrals, but the exact definition of the *oeuvre* of Robert de Luzarches or Jean d'Orbais has thus far eluded us.[3]

Given the dependence of the present study upon the primary written sources, and given the relative paucity of such sources in the High Gothic period, it follows that our main focus will be upon the Late Gothic campaigns at Troyes. The prime written source is the building account or fabric account.[4] A sequence of such accounts survives from the period shortly before 1300 through to the late Middle Ages. The earliest accounts are somewhat laconic, offering few details about the work in progress, and the sequence is punctuated by extensive gaps. However, by the mid fourteenth century the amount of information contained in each account is quite extensive and fewer lacunae exist. Moreover, the information given in the account can be supplemented through reference to the records of the deliberations of the chapter, starting in 1361. It will be found that the clergy frequently discussed problems relating to the construction of the cathedral, and that contracts with the masons were sometimes recorded in the minutes kept for each meeting.[5]

Each fabric account comprises a series of items of receipt with a grand total, followed by a similar series of items of expense, also with a grand total. At the end of the account it is computed whether the receipts exceeded the expenses, and if so the agent(s) rendering the account will enter the surplus as the first item of receipt in the following year's account. If the opposite situation existed, and the expenses exceeded the receipts, then the deficit will be entered as the first item of expense the following year.

The agents rendering the account were generally canons, one or more, of the cathedral chapter. It was the task of these canons, the *proviseurs*, to keep accurate weekly lists of receipts and expenses, and to enter them at the end of the fiscal year in the fabric account, according to a fairly rigid formula.[6] Written in Latin on the parchment pages of a codex, the earliest accounts bear witness to the difficulties of finding an appropriate vocabulary in Latin for the various parts of the building. Thus, in referring to scaffolding or to the stones of a vault, the *proviseurs* found themselves using French words (*les allours; les pendans*), and by the 1370s they were content to lapse into the vernacular altogether—the last account in Latin is for 1373–74. Similarly, by the late fourteenth century the use of parchment was abandoned in favor of paper.

Much can be learned about the artisans involved in the construction of the cathedral from the records of the names and salaries of the masons, carpenters, glaziers, etc., currently on the payroll.[7] Many of the workers were manual laborers, undertaking unskilled tasks, but also to be found are the names of the elite master masons and carpenters who were responsible for planning and design. The record of the artisans' names would be kept in the weekly lists of expenses, since these lists might serve as a proof that the payment of the salary had actually been made. The *proviseurs* at Troyes were unusually scrupulous in transcribing the names of the artisans and some details of their work into the final fair copy of the account that was to be scrutinized by the auditors.[8] Thus, while most of the weekly lists of wages have been lost, the accounts themselves can furnish a wealth of information about the identity of the builders and the sequence of construction at the cathedral.

The fabric accounts of Troyes Cathedral are of such incomparable richness that they deserve to be published in full, but such a publication would demand a bulky series of volumes and would attract a limited audience.[9] It is the intention of the present study to provide the reader with two different means of access to some of the key material in these accounts. The first method may be understood as a kind of longitudinal survey of the evidence on a year-by-year basis. Thus, Appendix B provides key texts relating to the identification of the masons and other artisans, the definition of the work in hand, and, where possible, techniques and methods of construction. The second method involves a series of analytical charts documenting the state of the fabric fund and the composition of the workshop at certain key moments; see Appendix C.

We have provided a brief introduction to the fabric accounts; what now of the building itself? Troyes Cathedral is a five aisled basilica intersected by a transept (Fig. 2). The central vessel, with vaults rising some twenty-eight meters above the pavement, is approximately twice as high as it is wide, a proportion that conveys a general sense of moderation and stability (Figs. 64–73).[10] The impression of relative horizontality in the spatial economy of the interior is enhanced by views through the broad arches of the main arcade into the double aisles that continue along the entire length of the church. The outer and inner aisles are of approximately the same height and take on the appearance of spacious hall churches (Figs. 74–75).

To the east the three straight bays of the choir swing into a seven bay hemicycle of sophisticated design. A simple-minded approach to the planning of the eastern termination of a Gothic cathedral can produce an abrupt transition from straight bays to hemicycle. The designers of the Troyes choir have avoided this through the choice of a hemicycle vault pattern that links the eastern semi-circle

3

with a transitional straight bay. Moreover, the crown of radiating chapels is wrapped around the hemicycle and envelops the eastern straight bays of the choir. From the exterior the tall vessel of the central choir looks as if it has been inserted into the surrounding circlet of chapels (Fig. 33).

The easternmost bays of the outer aisle of the choir form shallow diagonally placed chapels similar to those found at Saint-Yved at Braine.[11] The other chapels project deeply outward from the ambulatory passage and are boldly articulated with a high degree of mural relief. On the south side the place of the chapel at the base of the hemicycle has been taken by the rectangular sacristy/treasury complex. The way in which the radiating chapels flow around the east end of the choir to link the hemicycle with the body of the choir allows us to catch a glimpse of a master designer of great wit and genius.

To the west, the three bays of the body of the choir open into a crossing whose aisleless transept arms extend outward for three bays. Both transept façades are pierced with portals, the northern one opening on to the *Rue de la Cité* and the southern one to the bishop's court. The upper part of each façade is glazed with an enormous rose window inscribed inside a rectangular cage of tracery.[12]

West of the crossing the nave marches five full bays, then comes a narrow space effecting an awkward transition into the massive masonry of the west end. As defined earlier, the double aisles continue down the full length of the nave, giving a five-aisled composition terminated somewhat abruptly in a three-segment west façade scheme. The five chapels opening from the outer aisle on each side of the nave add considerably to the expansive horizontality of this part of the building.

The general organization of the superstructure is similar throughout. The bays are defined as vertical slices of space by means of substantial bundles of five shafts rising unbroken from the pavement to the quadripartite vaults.[13] Stocky compound piers support an arcade whose considerable thickness (about 1.20m.) is masked by means of multiple mouldings. The middle level of the elevation is a glazed triforium whose sill projects at a point somewhat less than halfway up the elevation. In the triforium two skins of tracery are separated by the space of a mural passage.[14] The outer skin is glazed and the inner one, set on the same plane as the arcade wall, is composed of open tracery. The triforium is linked with the clerestory by means of continuous mullions. The clerestory windows, occupying the entire space between the upper piers and glazed with stained glass of deeply saturated color, are truly the glory of this cathedral. Indeed, the structure seems to have been designed as an appropriate receptacle for stained glass—the clerestory is relatively low and visually accessible; the triforium is glazed, and the double aisles allow the beholder to gain a vantage point in the outer aisle where the clerestory window of the opposite wall is comfortably framed in the arch of the arcade (Figs. 68 & 69).

The same pervasive horizontality that dominates the interior space is also expressed in the exterior massing of the cathedral (Fig. 33). In the choir this is the result of the deep projection of the radiating chapels beyond the mass of the superstructure. The absence of a lean-to roof over the aisles and chapels also serves to emphasize the autonomy of the lower horizontal mass. Because of the glazed triforium the aisle roofs cannot butt up against the central vessel, but instead are arranged with two sloping surfaces and a crest down the middle.[15] As we consider the exterior forms of the choir, we cannot help noticing the existence of two very clearly distinct campaigns of construction—the radiating chapels with their narrow lancets and absence of tracery contrast sharply with the broad clerestory windows with their screens of decorative tracery. Although the clerestory was finished in the 1240s it lacks the bristling gables and pinnacles characteristic of other works of this period. The extraordinarily ugly flying buttresses of the choir date entirely from the mid nineteenth century.[16]

The horizontal mass of the cathedral, broken by the gabled arms of the transept, continues down the five bays of the nave (Fig. 45). In the lower nave the exterior wall of the five lateral chapels flanking the nave forms an unbroken gabled screen of decorative stonework, tracery, and stained glass. The intensity of the decoration of the nave chapels contrasts sharply with the restrained quality of the rest of the exterior (Fig. 37).

The uprights for the flying buttresses of the nave are embodied in the massive masonry forming the divisions between the chapels. The visual unity of the upper nave results from its stylistic homogeneity (late fifteenth century) and the emphatic termination of the five bays at the western gable.

The western frontispiece, constructed in the sixteenth century, surprises us with its great mass and exuberant decoration (Figs. 34 & 35). The five-aisled basilica is expressed in its west façade in a three segment composition that is so distinct from the body of the church as to remind us of a *Westwerk*. At Troyes two towers were intended (the *Tour Saint Pierre* on the north and the *Tour Saint Paul* on the south) but only the northern one was finished.[17]

As a postscript to this brief physical description of the cathedral, we should note the ubiquitous signs of structural distress. Such distress is manifested in three ways—in piers and buttresses bowed outward by the thrust of arches and vaults (crossing piers, transept arms, transept façades); in the obvious evidence of rebuilding necessitated by structural failure (upper choir, south transept façade), and in the record of repeated collapses and rebuilds found in the written sources. It is partly as a result of certain chronic structural difficulties that the construction dragged on for three and a half centuries.

Despite all these problems, the cathedral constitutes a formidable and truly beautiful unity—a glimpse of a vision of the Heavenly Kingdom and a testimony to the extraordinary faith of its builders. It also bears witness to the marshalling of limited funds for the construction as a series of discernible building campaigns. In this context a "campaign" may be understood as a unified phase of construction embodying a coherent and unified vocabulary of forms. A particular master mason might have his own vision of the completed cathedral, and he would choose his

5

architectural forms in relation to this vision. However, it is also important to recognize the constraints placed upon a master mason by the existing parts of the building. In order to avoid interrupting the unity of the building a master will often continue to employ the design elements of a previous generation. Although we can find the work of at least fifteen named master masons and three unnamed masters in the cathedral, we cannot find eighteen different types of architecture. In a general sense, it is convenient to recognize seven different campaigns in the cathedral (Fig. 2b). It will be seen that two of them embodied a distinct clash between conflicting visions. These seven campaigns fall into two major phases of effort. The first three campaigns can be found in the thirteenth century choir and transept, and the last three in the nave and west façade completed in the fifteenth and sixteenth centuries. The fourth campaign embodied in the first (eastern) bays of the nave and parts of the upper transept is the most enigmatic, involving conflicting visions and a prolonged period of construction extending from the late thirteenth century to the late fourteenth century.

For the first three campaigns we have little documentary evidence. Thus, an understanding of the thirteenth century work on the choir will rest primarily upon evidence of a stylistic or archaeological kind. For the remaining four campaigns, however, the fabric accounts and other written sources will allow us to understand the construction of the cathedral more fully as an historical process.

The fabric accounts provide the names of the master masons and the building embodies these masters' work. How, then, is it possible to relate the two, recognizing the identity of a named master in a particular part of the building? This may be done by matching the topographical indications provided in the accounts with the physical characteristics of the cathedral and its site. Thus, we read much in the accounts concerning the maintenance of a great provisional wall which closed in the west end of the unfinished nave. An analysis of the plinths of the piers of the nave will reveal that the first three bays belong to a unified phase of construction, and that the bases of the remaining two bays are later. Inspection of the transverse arches of the aisles at division 3 indicates that the west sides of these arches are somewhat weathered: it is thus quite certain that the provisional wall existed at this point and that the western sides of the arches had been left outside the wall and exposed to the weather.[18] Another important landmark of the site was the old bell tower at the west end of the nave of the former cathedral, which was being progressively demolished to make way for the Gothic structure. Work said to be near the *gros clocher* can thus be located to the west end of the nave. Work said to be near the *grand clocher*, on the other hand, would be at the other end of the nave near the tower which formerly crowned the transept crossing.[19] Work said to be taking place "toward the road" will be on the north side of the cathedral, the road in question being the *Rue de la Cité*, while "on the side of the bishop's court" signifies the south side. References can also be found to work "near the well," the well in question being beside pier D 2 in the south arcade of the nave.

Through the correlation of the written with the physical evidence it is possible to add a new dimension to our understanding of the process of construction. The evidence from Troyes reveals that this process was a highly complex one, involving frequent pauses to reconsider appropriate strategy, frequent appeals for outside help, and frequent setbacks. These setbacks included the necessity to demolish existing work which had been completed, but which had become obsolete owing to changes of plan (as in 1508) as well as the disappearance of parts of the building through collapse.

The material from Troyes casts significant light upon the problem of artistic identity in Gothic design. Much has been written on the subject of "The Medieval Mason."[20] At Troyes it is possible to refine this concern and to ask, "which mason?" One encounters enormous differences between master masons working at Troyes within the same general time period. Jaquet le Vachier, for example, active from 1450 to 1455, was a fumbling and highly conservative designer, superseded because of his inability to solve major design problems and to carve appropriate capitals. On the other hand, Martin Chambiges (active after 1502) was a leading master, respected for his opinion on structural matters, and an inventive designer of piers, portals, tracery, vaults, and all the refinements of a tasteful Late Gothic building. If such differences could exist within a relatively short time span at the same building site, it goes without saying that we may expect similarly wide variations of practice across the various regions of France and the centuries of Gothic.

The story of Troyes Cathedral will provoke an exploration of aspects of regionalism in Gothic architecture. At the beginning of construction Troyes was a flourishing architectural center; later, however, local invention had been eclipsed by centers elsewhere, notably the Ile-de-France, Picardy, and northern Champagne.[21] When, in the mid fifteenth century, it was necessary to draft a design for the west end of Troyes Cathedral, local masters could not supply the answers and an appeal was made to the master mason of Reims Cathedral. Faced with this major problem, our Late Gothic master, Bleuet by name, made a most significant reply: go and look at the western frontispieces of the cathedrals of Reims and Amiens and Notre-Dame of Paris, and base your own design upon these prototypes (Appendix B, 1455, 6). This dependence of a fifteenth century master upon thirteenth century prototypes can obviously tell us much about the relationship of what we call "Late Gothic" to "High Gothic."

Similarly, the written evidence allows us to test existing suppositions about artistic personality in Gothic architectural design. Some writers have considered that a master might have a particular set of forms that he would employ over a working life that might extend for decades. However, the evidence from Troyes does not necessarily support such a hypothesis. Certain masters are found (Anthoine Colas, for example) who are apt to take on the character of a chameleon.[22]

Material from the Troyes fabric accounts was exploited by P. Piétresson de Saint-Aubin in order to prepare a most valuable study of the quarry industry.[23]

Through most of the period of the construction of the cathedral masons were sent from the cathedral workshop to cut blocks of stone in one of the quarries supplying hard limestone. The verb for this preliminary cutting is *traire* or *assemiler*, as opposed to *tailler*, the final chiselling. The quarries were located in three different areas: directly to the south of Troyes at a distance of fifty to sixty kilometers (Tonnerre, Tanlay, Lezinnes, etc.); to the southeast at a distance of thirty to forty kilometers (Bourguignons, Polisot, etc.) and to the northeast at a distance of some eighty kilometers (Savonnières, Aulnois, etc.). The chapter owned several quarries (for example, one given in 1208 by the count of Bar-sur-Seine) but most of the stone had to be purchased. Transport was arranged by contract with local carters—a cart was capable of carrying about fifteen cubic feet of stone. The cost of the transport by far exceeded the cost of the extraction of the stone. Limited use was made of water transport (by the Seine, from Bar-sur-Seine). Much of the stone came along the ancient Roman road from Tonnerre. The great expense of long-distance transportation led to the frequent use of the soft local chalk, quarried just outside the city walls at Point-Sainte-Marie, Sainte-Maure, and many other sites. The fabric accounts provide details as to the shifting relationship between the cathedral workshop and the quarries. Thus, in the 1490s the final chiselling (*tailler*) of certain key parts of the flying buttresses was undertaken down at the quarry (Appendix B, 1495–96, 2 & 3). An extraordinary revolution took place in the early sixteenth century with the appointment of Martin Chambiges as master of the workshop. Instead of sending masons to the quarry to *assemiler*, it was decided to send very precise instructions together with templates (Appendix B, 1507–8, 1; 1508–9, 7).

Evidence from the fabric accounts will allow us to determine how long it took to construct a great window or a vault. Of particular interest is the demonstration that the vaults constructed at Troyes in the late Middle Ages were centered over mounds of the local clay soil, humped up to give the severies the necessary domical shape.[24] Thus, in constructing each vault large quantities of "masoning earth" (*terre à maçonner*) were purchased (Appendix B, 1496–97, 11).

Study of the fabric accounts will allow us to dismiss or qualify three powerful local legends. All cathedrals tend to gather such legends and Troyes is no exception. For centuries it has been believed that the English played some key role in the construction.[25] However, the accounts do not record the names of any great donors of English origin or the participation of English artisans in the workshop. It will be seen, however, that the allies of the English in the early fifteenth century, the Burgundians, did make an impact on the construction. The dukes of Burgundy were generous patrons of the fabric, and the choice of a master mason from Brussels in 1383 may have resulted from the close relations between the bishops of Troyes and the dukes. Second, there is a powerful local legend that the cathedral was constructed on wooden piles. However, the fabric account for the work of founding the western piers of the nave reveals quite clearly that although the use of such piles had been discussed, the foundations are entirely of masonry,

8

and extend to a depth of twenty-six feet. The lower part of the foundation is chalk and the upper part (the top four feet) is limestone (Appendix B, 1451–52, 3 & 4). The third local legend involves a great ramp of earth constructed between the hill at Montgueaux and the cathedral in order to raise the stones into place. The fabric accounts make frequent references to cranes or lifting gear for raising the stones (for example, Appendix B, 1452–53) and the purchase of earth was not to make a ramp, but to bed the stones of the vaults.

In reviewing the written evidence one constantly returns to problems caused by the unfinished state of the cathedral: provisional roofs or screens that leak or threaten to blow away in the wind; gutters that cannot carry the rain water away; children climbing over unfinished pillars. The solution to the latter problem was to wrap the pillar in briars—the medieval equivalent of barbed wire (Appendix B, 1506–7, 8). The most significant problem caused by the unfinished state of the cathedral was the tendency of unsupported piers to rotate outward, propelled by an already existing arch or vault, and not yet supported by the as-yet-unbuilt adjacent bay.[26] The builders of Troyes Cathedral had frequent recourse to provisional props, either of wood or stone, in order to solve this problem. It will be seen that the use of such props at the west end of the unfinished nave caused very major problems in the sequence of construction.

We are so used to the interpretation of the medieval cathedral as the embodiment of sublime neo-Platonic Idea that it comes as something of a relief to find that its builders were human, capable of indecision and even error.[27] Such indecision accompanied the construction of the nave flyers, and in 1494 the bishop and chapter initiated a discussion of the grave question as to whether the nave flyers should be built first, with their tendency to push the building inward, or whether the high vaults should have precedence, threatening to push the building outward (Appendix B, 1494–95, 4 & 6).

Troyes had more than its fair share of collapses: the upper choir in 1228, the crossing tower in 1365, the upper nave and north transept rose in 1389. In 1700 the rebuilt crossing tower was struck by lightning and the cathedral roof was consumed in the ensuing fire, causing the massive statue of Saint Michael on the west gable to topple backward, crashing through the vaults and crushing several workers in the nave below. Few casualties are recorded for the medieval campaigns of construction at Troyes. One example may be given of the death of an artisan in line of duty, Colin Millet, through the collapse of a provisional flying buttress in 1531 (Appendix B, 1530–31, 3). We are told that his attempt to de-center the flyer was somewhat premature. Between the major collapses at Troyes there was a constant struggle to keep the unfinished building aloft, concentrating particularly upon the area of the upper transept arms, which had a disturbing tendency to settle outward. Some of these problems were caused by the use of the local chalk stone in the foundations and in exposed parts of the building.[28] In the foundations the chalk turned to paste owing to the dampness of the soil, necessitating major campaigns of restoration (particularly on the choir) in the nineteenth century.[29]

9

Exposed to the weather, the chalk was subject to water penetration and to the destructive effects of frost.[30] It is open to question as to whether the use of defective material was the fault of the masons, or of the under-budgeted administrators of the fabric. To the masons' account, however, must be placed the various design faults that contributed to the weakness of the building. These faults included the use of a roofing system over the aisles of the choir and the nave that was incapable of evacuating the accumulation of rain water and snow. The roofs in question were in the form of a series of pyramid-like structures, designed to let the light penetrate to the reverse side of the glazed triforium (Fig. 38).[31] Such roofs obviously drain inward as well as outward and excellent gutters are necessary in order to lead the accumulated rain water away from the inner part of the roof system (the gutter running outside the triforium). The gutters running between the pyramidal roofs did not have enough of an inclination to ensure a vigorous flow of water, and were subject to blockage by countless acts of God—for example, the accumulation of debris, snow, or dead pigeons—and the blocked gutter would then spill its load on top of the aisle vaults beneath.[32]

Other mistakes were of a more structural nature. They included the excessive reduction of the mass of key structural elements such as the buttresses of the transept façades and the upper piers of the nave as well as the use of a type of flying buttress that was too flimsy to meet the outward thrust of the high vaults. The faulty flyers were reviewed in an expertise in 1362, some twenty years before the collapse of the upper nave.

Thus, the multiple disasters encountered at Troyes were the result of certain structural weaknesses in the cathedral, use of inappropriate materials (chalk), and inadequate maintenance. The number of artisans on the payroll at any given time was generally limited, and progress was relatively slow. It is precisely because of these problems that we are able to discover so much about the construction that dragged on into a period where extensive documentation is available. Troyes Cathedral thus belongs to a fairly sizeable category of French churches begun in the early to mid thirteenth century but not finished until the close of the Middle Ages.[33]

This general situation resulted from the deteriorating economic and political framework of France in the late thirteenth and early fourteenth centuries: war, decline of commerce, depopulation, famines, and epidemics. One also has to take into account the local circumstances of the bishop and chapter, the patrons of the cathedral. In the early Middle Ages the bishop would often dominate the economic, political, and judicial life of the city over which he presided.[34] The city of Troyes had developed from the *castrum* of *Augustobona*, the Roman city built on a relatively high spot in the marshes of the river Seine at the point of crossing of a major road, from Lyon to Boulogne.[35] The walls of the *cité* were rebuilt during the period of Viking raids. The interior of the *cité* was divided by two main roads, the more important of which was later to become the *Rue de la Cité*.

The cathedral was located in the southeastern part of the *cité*, with its east end toward the wall (Fig. 1).[36]

Whereas in neighboring cities such as Meaux and Châlons-sur-Marne the bishop remained a dominant force throughout the Middle Ages, in Troyes a powerful rival established himself in the very area of the *cité* itself: the count of Champagne.[37] In the mid tenth century Bishop Anségise attempted to assert the episcopal power to dominate the city and the surrounding area, but this attempt was blocked through the efforts of Count Robert, son of Herbert of Vermandois.[38] Anségise was forced to flee and when he returned with an army to defend his claims he was defeated. He was able to resume his spiritual and ecclesiastical powers, but secular authority in Troyes was retained by the counts. In the eleventh century and up until around 1150 the bishops of Troyes were chosen by the counts of Champagne who also conferred upon the bishop and chapter the jurisdictional powers they held in Troyes.[39] The chapter thus exercised justice over the cloister as well as the *bourg* of Saint Denis to the east of the *cité*. The counts retained control over the minting of coins.

The *cité* was dominated by religious establishments: in addition to the cathedral, the bishop's palace, the canons' houses, the monastery of Saint-Loup, and the priory of Saint-Quentin and Saint-Jean-en-Chastel were all located within the walls.

The thriving suburb that developed in the eleventh and twelfth centuries to the southwest of the old *cité* was entirely under the domination of the counts of Champagne, not the bishops of Troyes.[40] It was in this part of the city that the famous fairs of Champagne took place, the *foire chaude de Saint Jean* in June-July and the *foire froide de Saint Remi* in October-November.[41] The importance of these fairs in the life of Troyes is expressed in the naming of two of the major parishes in honor of Saint-Jean and Saint-Remi. The fairs flourished thanks to the protection provided by the counts, who profited from various tolls levied upon transactions carried out at the fair.[42] Merchants came to the fair with a variety of different currencies and money changing was a major operation. A mass of charters regulated the practice of money changing in Troyes and the tables of the money changers were rented out by agents of the count, who also determined the general arrangement of the stalls. The profits from the tolls levied on the fairs were considerable, and the greatest count of the twelfth century, Henry the Liberal, was a generous patron of the churches and religious establishments of Troyes and the surrounding area.[43] Unfortunately for the cathedral of Troyes, he chose to direct his *largesse* elsewhere, toward his own collegiate church of Saint-Etienne, for example.[44] Henry the Liberal had very poor relations with the higher clergy of his county, including the bishops of Châlons, Langres, and Meaux as well as Mathieu, bishop of Troyes.[45]

Count Henry's difficulties with Bishop Mathieu reflect the more independent stance adopted by the bishops of the second half of the twelfth century including Hatton (1122–1145) and Henri de Carinthie (1145–1169).[46] This movement toward independence came to a crescendo in the period just before the construction of the Gothic cathedral. In 1171–1172 Bishop Mathieu successfully challenged the claim of the canons of Saint-Etienne to enjoy freedom from episcopal jurisdiction, and in 1177 the same bishop had the episcopal temporalities confirmed by King Louis VII. It has been claimed that this confirmation marks "the beginning of the emancipation of the bishops of Troyes from the power of the counts."[47] The construction of a magnificent Gothic cathedral should obviously be seen in the context of this movement toward emancipation.

The growth of commerce and industry in the twelfth century led to the flowering of cities and the old feudal relationships were transformed, many *seigneurs* finding it to their advantage to allow their townspeople to form a commune. This would involve the abandonment on the part of the *seigneur* of the right to exact arbitrary taxation. However, the *seigneur* might gain from property taxes, and would reap enormous benefits from a mass of tolls applied to the commercial and industrial activities of the members of the commune. The very success of the fairs held at Troyes and the administrative framework which developed along with these fairs may have tended to retard the development of communal institutions in the city. Whereas elsewhere communes developed as early as the late eleventh and twelfth centuries, in Troyes a commune was not granted by the counts until 1230, and it remained in existence for a period of only about ten years.[48] Whereas in certain cities (Beauvais, for example, where the bishop was also count) revenues from the tolls applied to commerce and industry might be available to help with the expenses of constructing the cathedral, at Troyes this does not seem to have been the case. The bishop and chapter of the cathedral would only gain in an indirect way from the dramatic growth of the city. In the period around 1300 the episcopal revenue from his holdings around Troyes and Méry-sur-Seine was estimated at 5,500 pounds—a fairly modest sum. In the seventeenth century episcopal revenue was estimated at 7,953 pounds.[49]

The old cathedral of Troyes had been burned in the fire which consumed part of the city in 1188.[50] Little is known of the pre-Gothic cathedral—it is generally believed that it had been built under Bishop Milo in the years soon before 1000. The old structure was a basilica with a projecting transept and a western bell tower.[51] It seems certain that the old cathedral was damaged rather than destroyed in the fire, since construction work on the new choir was delayed for a dozen years or more. It is probable that as much of the old building as possible was preserved and that demolition took place on a piecemeal basis, from east to west. The old bell tower (*gros clocher*) survived until 1532.

It had been assumed that the starting date for the campaigns of construction on the Gothic choir was provided by the acquisition in 1208 of land beyond the old wall of the *cité* for the construction of the axial chapel.[52] Norbert Bongartz, however, has recently demonstrated that the construction of the choir was begun at the base of the radiating chapels and that the axial chapel was the last to have been undertaken.[53] It is probable that this work on the hemicycle and radiating chapels was directed by a local master, since the planning of this part of the building reflects elements derived from Notre-Dame-en-Vaux at Châlons-sur-Marne and the cathedral of Meaux.[54] The three-story elevation and the diagonal placement employed in the radiating chapels may be derived from the churches at Braine and Orbais.[55] The radiating chapels and the main piers of the hemicycle embody the first of the seven personal visions evident in the cathedral.

As construction progressed, however, this distinctly local flavor was lost; Bongartz has suggested that a second master, probably from the Ile-de-France, may have assumed direction around 1210 and constructed the straight bays of the choir (Fig. 74) and the lower parts of the transept arms and crossing. In the exterior of the building a clear break is visible at the base of the system of radiating chapels. In the straight bays of the choir the total height of the windows is increased and window tracery is introduced. The second master was also responsible for the piers of the aisles and the main arcade of the choir. It is noticeable that he increased the mass of the main piers and the thickness of the arcade wall. This second master was familiar with the great achievements of High Gothic, especially Chartres Cathedral, as is reflected in the type of piers used in the choir aisles (*piliers cantonnés*) and in the overall proportions of the central vessel. Reims Cathedral was also a major source of influence upon this second master, as is revealed in the introduction of window tracery in the windows of the choir aisles. The appearance of a master mason from the Ile-de-France coincided with a period when the county was falling increasingly under the domination of the Capetian kings.[56]

The choir was nearing completion when the building was damaged by a whirlwind in 1228. It is probable that a third master (also from the Ile-de-France) was already in control of the workshop by the 1220s. This third master went on to construct the triforium and upper parts of the choir in a style which closely resembles the thirteenth century work at the abbey church of Saint-Denis, to the north of Paris (Fig. 73).[57] The middle level of the Troyes choir (the triforium) is no longer a dark arcaded band (as at Chartres, Reims, or Soissons) but has windows let into the exterior wall. The triforium is rather tall in relation to the arcade and clerestory, and the two upper levels of the elevation (triforium and clerestory) are linked together vertically,[58] each bay containing four units. At triforium level each of the four units is subdivided into two lancets with trilobed arches. The major units are topped by trefoils, placed with the apex downward. This delicate tracery composition is placed on the same plane as the clerestory, each unit of which comprises four lancets grouped in pairs, the composition topped by three great oculi. The upper choir at Troyes is an expression of an aesthetic where brittle two-dimensional tracery compositions dominate, where subtle elisions link various parts of the building that had previously been left separate and where mass has been reduced to a minimum. This emphasis on delicate forms and reduction of mass may also be observed in the original flying buttresses of the choir (Fig. 33).[59] Following in the tradition of the collegiate church of Saint-

Quentin and Auxerre Cathedral, these flyers comprised tracery panels linking the lower supporting arch with the upper rim.[60] The head of the lower arch was placed at a level corresponding to the capitals of the clerestory windows and the upper rim reached almost to the top of the clerestory wall. Not only was the construction extremely light, but it is also evident that a considerable gap existed between the upper and lower supports. Moreover, it is clear that the original clerestory piers of the upper choir were weakened through the existence of openings pierced at the level of the clerestory passage. Evidence of blocked passages can still be seen in the upper piers on the east side of the transept arms. These piers of inadequate cross section and inadequately buttressed by the flyers had already started to buckle outward in the Middle Ages.[61] They were entirely replaced in the nineteenth century.

Two important points should be stressed in connection with the general significance of the design of the Troyes upper choir. First, it is clear that in certain respects, structural security has been compromised in favor of optical effect. The upper piers of the choir were badly distorted before the nineteenth century restorers of the cathedral saw fit to demolish this part of the building and rebuild it. Second, it is important to emphasize that the general effect of the upper choir was one sought after by two or more centuries of later builders at Troyes. It offered a model from which the Late Gothic masters were unable to escape. In seeking to mimic the optical effects of the upper choir certain Late Gothic master masons fell into the trap of reproducing the same defective structural members, notably the flimsy upper piers and flying buttresses.

The campaign of construction that included the rebuilding of the upper choir after the collapse in 1228 embodies the third vision evident in the choir of Troyes Cathedral. The choir was complete by the middle decades of the thirteenth century.

The transept had been begun by the second master (1210–1220s) who laid out the lower walls and began the piers on the west sides of the transept arms. The upper parts of the two inner bays on the east side of the transept arms were completed in the same campaign as the upper choir (1230s–1240s) (Fig. 72). In the outer bays of the eastern elevation of the transept arms and in the upper parts of the façades and the upper parts of the western sides of the transept arms the designers of the cathedral began to modify the well-established forms of the choir (Figs. 70 & 71). In the triforium, quatrefoils replace trefoils and the western clerestory windows bear witness to a restless striving toward new forms.

If we were to impose simple stylistic labels upon the three campaigns of construction embodied in the choir and eastern side of the transept of Troyes Cathedral, we might apply the epithet "Early Gothic" or "Regional Gothic" to the radiating chapels, "High Gothic" to the work of the second master in the straight bays of the choir and lower transept, and "Parisian Rayonnant" to the third master who was responsible for the upper choir and eastern side of the two inner bays of the transept arms. Each of these phases was the expression of a powerful personal vision, first, a distinctly Champenois arrangement, followed by two imported styles. In the upper west walls of the transept arms and in the early work on the nave, we see the beginnings of the transition to Late Gothic. This is the fourth campaign alluded to at an earlier point; it will be the subject of the following chapter.

Given the prolonged period of construction necessary for the completion of the choir and the beginnings of work on the nave (1200 to c. 1290) it is hard to escape the conclusion that the fabric of Troyes Cathedral received inadequate financial support from the bishop and chapter. Whereas the twelfth century bishops at Troyes had been recruited from the ranks of the local aristocracy, this was no longer the case in the thirteenth century. Bishop Garnier de Trainel, who presided over the beginnings of construction, was a member of the local aristocracy but he was absent during the early years of construction, participating in the Fourth Crusade.[62] His successor, Herveus, a doctor from the Sorbonne, was not a local man, and this set the pattern to be followed throughout the rest of the thirteenth century.

The organization of the construction effort was certainly the affair of the cathedral chapter but it is impossible to determine whether the canons supported the fabric through funds derived from their prebends.[63] It is certain that they refrained from doing so in the fourteenth century (see Chapter II) but in the burst of enthusiasm engendered by the start of the new enterprise it is possible that the clergy might have seen their way to making a regular contribution to the fabric in the first years of construction.[64]

The only firm evidence that survives regarding the funding of the early campaigns is to be found in a sequence of indulgences granting a certain number of days' remission from purgatory in return for financial contributions to the fabric. Such indulgences were granted in 1213, 1215, 1228, 1229, 1240, and 1263.[65] We can gain very little specific information from these documents concerning the state of the building or the financial arrangements of the fabric. In the indulgence dated 1213 reference is made to the lack of other resources for the fabric and in 1215 the lavish (expensive) quality of the new work is mentioned.[66] The documents of 1228 and 1229 refer to the splendor of the new work, to the lack of resources, and to the disastrous storm which had caused the ruin of the new choir.[67] The later documents repeat the standard phraseology on the lack of funds and the expense of the new work.

In the absence of specific information from fabric accounts it is quite impossible to determine what proportion (if any) of the receipts came from fixed contributions from the bishop and chapter, from indulgences, or from other sources. The sheer number of indulgences does suggest, however, that the fabric fund was heavily dependent upon this kind of income. Such a source of revenue would be highly sensitive to disruptions of a political or economic nature. A landowner whose crops had been burned by an invading army is unlikely to purchase the spiritual benefits of an indulgence. The first part of the thirteenth century saw the peace of Champagne disrupted and widespread devastation through civil war.[68] The reign of Count Henry I, the Liberal (1152–1181), was a period of peaceful prosperity, but the last decades of the twelfth century and early thirteenth century saw a period of crisis for the dynasty of the counts of Champagne. Count Henry II (1181–1197) was a minor during the early part of his reign and absent on crusade in the second part. The crusading zeal of Count Henry II and his successor Thibaut III cost Champagne very dearly. Whereas Henry the Liberal had spent his surplus income at home in the form of lavish ecclesiastical endowments, much of this wealth was now being exported. Henry II levied a heavy aid on his county just before his departure.[69] While in the Holy Land he married the queen of Jerusalem, by whom he had two daughters. The validity of this marriage was not recognized in the west and a dangerous succession problem was created for the future.

Thibaut III (1197–1201), Henry II's brother, spent most of his brief reign in the Holy Land.[70] At the time of his premature death no male heir existed; his son, Thibaut (Thibaut IV, "le Chansonnier"), was born posthumously. A powerful group of Champenois nobles sided with the daughters of Henry II against the regency of Blanche of Navarre, the widow of Thibaut III. King Philip Augustus seized the opportunity to tighten his control over Champagne, and Blanche was forced to purchase royal recognition and support through a succession of very expensive treaties.[71] The cash necessary to buy this recognition was raised through massive aids imposed upon the major cities of the county.[72] Civil war broke out in 1215 and lasted for more than three years.

Thibaut IV achieved majority in 1222. The early part of his reign saw a devastating invasion of Champagne by a league of barons angry with the count for a variety of reasons.[73] The invasion led to widespread destruction of towns and countryside. In 1229 Thibaut was forced to burn several of his own towns to prevent them from falling into the hands of the enemy. It is interesting to remark that the great collapse of the choir (1228) took place one year before the invasion of Champagne by the league of barons.

The destruction caused by the movement of hostile armies and the taxes levied to cover the costs of the war must have affected the ability of the faithful of the diocese to contribute to the fabric of the cathedral. These are the circumstances that led to the repeated indulgences and to the use of the relics owned by the cathedral in quests to raise additional funds.

The stock of precious relics owned by the bishop and chapter of Troyes Cathedral was enriched through several important acquisitions made in Constantinople by Bishop Garnier de Trainel (died 1205).[74] The body of Saint Helen of Athyra was one of many relics sent to the West after the conquest of Constantinople in 1204. An envoy was dispatched from Troyes to the Byzantine capital to find out more details about the life of the little-known saint, and came back to Troyes with a *Vita* alleged to be by Saint John Chrysostom.[75] It seems that the clergy at Troyes, aware of the potential financial gain to be made from the possession of a relic of great popular appeal, did their best to promote the cult of the saint.[76] In 1260 the feast of Saint Helen was initiated, and two years later Pope Urban IV granted an indulgence of one year to all those visiting the cathedral on the feast of Saint Peter or Saint Helen (May 4). As an encouragement to potential donors, the miracle-working prowess of the saint was emphasized in one of the clerestory windows of the upper choir.[77]

Viollet-le-Duc, the great nineteenth century champion of Gothic architecture, recognized a category of cathedrals where limited financial resources had led to cost-cutting, particularly in the invisible part of the building, the foundations.[78] He placed Troyes Cathedral in the first rank of such monuments, remarking, however, on the considerable scale and the great beauty of the work. The factors that lay behind the financial exigency of the bishop and chapter are closely associated with the peculiar characteristics of the formation of the city and the history of Champagne in the thirteenth century. The unfinished cathedral was an eloquent testimony to a situation where the clergy were unable to lend substantial support to the fabric fund. This situation will be amply documented in the following chapter.

II
Conservatism and Innovation, Mistakes and Disaster, 1290–1390

HE UNFINISHED CATHEDRAL OF Troyes, a massive construction project begun with limited resources around 1200, was still far from complete after almost a century's efforts. The written sources that survive for the campaigns of construction after 1290 allow us to form a much clearer picture of the organization and chronology of construction. It will be seen that with the choir and eastern sides of the transept arms complete, work had reached the eastern bays of the nave and the west sides and upper parts of the transept.

In the decades after 1290 an attempt was made to complete three bays of the nave up to the high vaults and to erect a tower over the transept crossing. Both these projects were doomed to failure—the tower collapsed in 1365, the upper nave in 1389, and the north transept rose window immediately afterwards. These are the disasters alluded to in our chapter heading. The parts of the building completed in this period are in a style that we might term "advanced Rayonnant." In other words they draw heavily upon forms developed in the decades between the 1230s and the 1260s.

We are in the fourth of the seven phases defined in our first chapter—a phase involving an uneasy dialogue between modernization and the power of existing forms. Logistical factors produced another kind of dialogue in these years. In order to complete the upper transept it was necessary to rush ahead with the early work on the nave to provide the supports for the flying buttresses against the western sides of the transept arms. Thus, it is no surprise to find that similar forms (especially window tracery) were developed in these two different parts of the building. The clergy were thus forced to overextend themselves on construction efforts in two areas (nave and upper transept) at a time when the economic life of the city was reaching a precarious state.

What were the factors underlying the economic difficulties of the decades around 1300? During the thirteenth century the fairs of Champagne had undergone various significant changes.[1] They had begun as a local market for the buying and selling of textiles and agricultural products, but had developed an international dimension with the participation of Flemish and Italian merchants and bankers. Wool and woven products passed south and Mediterranean goods and spices found their way north. In the second half of the thirteenth century, however, the exchange of products became less important and the fairs were increasingly dominated by exchanges of currency and by banking operations, which continued to flourish until the first decades of the fourteenth century. Historians have suggested a variety of reasons for the remarkably rapid decline that ensued.[2] The nature of international banking was changing and becoming less peripatetic with the growth of the great Italian banking houses. Contemporaries saw excessive royal spending and taxes as a major factor behind the decline of the fairs. The development of rival cities such as Nîmes and Paris certainly did not help the situation. The Franco-Flemish war interrupted commerce—for example, in 1315 Louis X forbade Flemish merchants and bankers access to the fairs of Champagne, and the Italians were excluded a little later. The development of maritime routes between Flanders and Italy was also a factor, as were the industrialization of Italy and changes in the precious metals market.

The fairs had flourished thanks to the protection and personal interest of the counts of Champagne. When Count Henry III died in 1274 in Pamplona he left a daughter named Jeanne.[3] A marriage with a son of Edward I of England had been contemplated, but this plan was abandoned in favor of Philip, second son of Philip III, king of France (1270–1285). The wedding took place in 1284 and the subsequent death of the king and his eldest son led to the accession of Philip IV as king of France in 1285. In this way the county of Champagne was absorbed into the kingdom of France. The historian of the counts of Champagne, d'Arbois de Jubainville, concluded his last chapter with the words, "From this time onward, the county, reduced to the level of a simple province, ceased to have a life of its own."[4] This is obviously something of an overstatement, and it is important to stress that the damaging results of the absorption of Champagne arose not so much through the event per se but more through the circumstances that attended it. The historian of the city of Troyes, T. Boutiot, commented, "By law, Champagne was united with the Crown; in fact it was dismembered to the profit of the great vassals of the king of France who commanded the parties opposed to the king. . . . "[5] Four powerful groups held major territorial stakes in the county; the

Conservatism and Innovation, Mistakes and Disaster, 1290–1390

house of Navarre (as a result of the marriage of Count Thibaut III to Blanche de Navarre); the English (through the marriage of Count Henry III's widow, Blanche d'Artois, to Edmund, count of Lancaster); the Capetian and Valois monarchs of France; and the dukes of Burgundy.[6] The dukes of Burgundy gained a position of preeminence in the county through the marriage of King Louis X (died 1316), the son of Jeanne of Champagne, to Marguerite of Burgundy. A complex series of treaties left Duke Eudes IV of Burgundy in possession of a number of important cantons in the immediate vicinity of Troyes.

While discussing the problems of the years around 1300, it is necessary to mention a bizarre interlude in the fortunes of the clergy of the diocese—the trial of Bishop Guichard (1299–1317).[7] Guichard's meteoric rise from monk to prior of Saint-Ayoul in Provins, abbot of Montier-la-Celle, and bishop of Troyes resulted from the favor of Blanche, countess of Champagne and mother-in-law of King Philip IV. As bishop of Troyes he behaved in an extraordinary manner and eventually alienated his former protectors. In the struggle between the king of France and Boniface VIII the bishop favored the pope and this certainly contributed to his downfall. The first set of charges brought against him, including sedition, assassination, forgery, and alchemy, were dropped in 1302, but soon afterward a new case was made against the bishop. This time the charges included murder through sorcery: specifically, he was accused of having baptized and burned a wax effigy of the queen. He spent many years in prison before his principal accuser, Noffo-Dei, admitted that the charges were false. Noffo-Dei had also denounced the leading Knights Templar who were burned in 1311. The bishop was fortunate to have escaped a similar fate. He died in 1317, leaving considerable debts incurred, no doubt, through the prolonged trials.

Guichard was succeeded as bishop by Jean d'Auxois, Guillaume Méchin, Jean de Cherchemont, Jean d'Aubigny, and Jean II d'Auxois. With the next bishop, Henri de Poitiers (1353–1370), the worst effects of the Hundred Years War were being felt in Troyes and the surrounding area. The same period saw the spate of peasant uprisings known as the Jacquerie and the beginnings of the ravages of the Black Death. The years around 1350 were undoubtedly quite disastrous for the city of Troyes. The French defeat in the battle of Poitiers (1356) led to the imposition of heavy taxes to raise money for the ransom of the captured French king and also desperate (and expensive) attempts to bring the city fortifications up to date.[8] Owing to the extensive Burgundian, Navarrais, and Lancastrian holdings in Champagne, the countryside was overrun by a range of different foreign troops. Pont-sur-Seine and Nogent were held by the notorious Eustache d' Aubrecicourt and five hundred mercenaries. In 1358 the English and Navarrais seized the bishop's château at Aix-en-Othe and attempted to capture Troyes. Bishop Henri de Poitiers (1353–1370), who was also captain and governer of Troyes, together with Brokars de Fenestrange, the Count of Vaudémont, and other Champenois seigneurs, undertook a counterattack against Eustache d' Aubrecicourt and scored a notable victory at the battle of Nogent (June 23, 1359).[9] The French returned to Troyes with their

BUILDING TROYES CATHEDRAL

booty and the release of Eustache d' Aubrecicourt was negotiated by the English for a considerable ransom.

The effect of war, disease, and high taxation upon the city of Troyes may be assessed through reference to the report made by the royal commissioners who visited the city in 1375.[10] They reported that the number of taxable hearths in the city had diminished, and that the inhabitants, unable to meet the heavy taxes levied to pay ransoms, raise armies, and maintain fortifications, were abandoning their city. They estimated that the city had paid 500 francs (equal in value to pounds) for aids and 30,000 pounds for defense.

In 1379 the English were in Champagne again, and the defense of Troyes was organized by the Duke of Burgundy. After the treaty of Brétigny (1360) King Charles V had established his brother, the Duke of Burgundy, as his lieutenant in certain key cities in Champagne, including Troyes. English troops, led by the Duke of Buckingham, were unable to take the city in 1380.[11]

When one reads of the misery and destruction of the period, as recounted by the local historian, Boutiot, one is somewhat surprised to find that the fabric fund of the cathedral received a steady, if limited, flow of cash and that the administrators of the fabric continued to entertain ideas of completing the unfinished nave of the cathedral until a major disaster, the collapse of the nave (in 1389), forced them to put the idea out of their heads.[12] The documents suggest that the construction of the cathedral in this period was almost entirely the concern of the chapter. Contracts with masons were between the mason and the chapter, without mention of the bishop, and the two *proviseurs* who administered the fabric were generally canons, although after 1387 one of them was considered to be responsible to the bishop.[13]

What kinds of income were available for cathedral construction? In general terms, we may distinguish between two main types of income: one might be termed "regular funds" and the other "irregular." Regular income would result from a commitment made by one of the patrons of the cathedral (bishop or chapter) to set aside a certain part of their annual income for the use of the fabric fund. Such a situation can be found at the beginning of work on Beauvais Cathedral in 1225, when the bishop and chapter both committed one tenth of their income to the fabric fund for a ten year period.[14] However, it has been seen that the bishop of Troyes could not have hoped to command a flow of cash sufficient to allow him to play a comparable role. Similarly, the income of the chapter was not sufficient to allow it to bear a substantial part of the cost of construction. A canon would receive his income from two different sources, from the cash and grain derived from the holdings of land and rights enjoyed by the chapter (the prebend) and from the distributions made during certain offices.[15] It has been calculated that a prebend was worth about 20 pounds and 15 sous per annum in the years around 1400 and this calculation is corroborated by the receipt of 20 pounds recorded in the fabric account for 1366–67 resulting from the gift of a prebend from the canon Pierre d'Arbois. In addition to his prebend a canon would

Conservatism and Innovation, Mistakes and Disaster, 1290–1390

receive distributions made during certain offices, including the sums of money paid at the anniversary of the death of certain pious donors. The value of the distributions amounted to about 45 pounds in the period around 1400, giving each canon a total income of 65 pounds per annum. It is interesting to find that Henry de Bruisselles, master mason of the workshop in the 1380s, earned precisely 65 pounds per annum. Thus, the life of a medieval canon at Troyes was hardly an opulent one. We should also refer to the indulgence of Pope Nicholas V in 1451 (see Appendix B) that dwells at some length upon the inability of the clergy to support the construction with funds derived from their prebends.

We thus come to the second kind of income (irregular funds), derived from voluntary contributions. Such contributions might be made on an occasional basis by one or other of the patrons of the cathedral (bishop or chapter) or by some other outside patron: king, duke of Burgundy, or local seigneur. They might also be placed in collecting boxes located in the cathedral or in other churches in the city. In addition, quests were made for the fabric both inside and outside the diocese of Troyes. However, it is necessary to remember that the distinction between "regular" funds and "voluntary" contributions might not have seemed so clear to the fourteenth century mind. Thus, if an indulgence were announced for the profit of the fabric fund, the potential donor might be constrained to make a contribution in order to enjoy the spiritual benefits that would accrue. A similar situation would arise if it were announced, for example, that all offerings made at a particular mass would be devoted to the fabric. The medieval quest would also probably impose a certain spiritual obligation upon the potential donor. It has been demonstrated that the clergy of Troyes did their best to promote the cult of certain saints whose relics were in the possession of the cathedral, notably Saint Helen of Athyra.[16] Given the thaumaturgical power of this saint, contributions to the fabric made in connection with the display of her relics should not be considered as purely "voluntary."

The fabric accounts will allow us to plot the overall fortune of the fabric in the fourteenth century, and to identify the sources of income. In Appendix C the figures for the income and expenses of the fabric have been arranged in the form of a graph. It is necessary to alert the reader to the fact that a situation where we see a constant growth in the income of the fabric will not necessarily indicate that new revenues are being found. This situation might also result if major expenses are not being incurred, and the unspent balance is being carried over to add to the following year's income. When we study the chart for the gross figures from the receipts and expenses for this period given in Appendix C, we will note that income exceeded expenses in all but one year, 1389, the year of the collapse of the nave. The degree of fluctuation was much higher in the later period (1370–1390), when major campaigns of construction had ceased and the efforts of the workshop were concentrated upon the choir screen. In the early part of our period (1290s–1340s), when major construction was under way on the eastern bays of the nave, the degree of fluctuation was much less. Receipts and expenses moved somewhat

TABLE 1:

Receipts of the fabric, 1294–1301, to the nearest pound *tournois*

	1294	1294–95	1295–96	1296–97	1297–98	1298–99	1299–1300	1300–1
1.	—	17	52	65	120	83	16	70
2.	88	106	99	112	87	97	108	117
3.	—	43	42	42	22	45	44	44
4.	20	114	95	88	83	87	83	—
5.	28	18	20	72	21	48	27	28
6.	—	1	1	1	4	4	1	2
7.	—	—	3	—	—	—	2	3
Totals	136	299	312	380	338	364	281	264

1. From last year
2. Quests in diocese (by deanery)
3. Quests outside the diocese
4. Collecting boxes (including relics)
5. Legacies
6. Rents
7. Extraordinary

in harmony one with another: in other words, increased income in any given year
was matched by increased expense. This observation moves us to raise the question
as to whether construction was planned carefully in relation to anticipated income,
or whether the opposite situation applied, where funds could be raised to cover
the anticipated cost of the current year's construction.

The evidence suggests that the latter situation applied. When expenses increased sharply because of the collapse of the nave in 1389, income soared. This
event could hardly have been planned in advance and the necessary funds raised to
cover anticipated expense. Our hypothesis that construction needs provided the
driving force, and that funds could be raised to cover an emergency situation, is
confirmed by the study of the sources of income, shown in Table 1. The *proviseurs*,
Johannes, archdeacon of Sainte-Margerie (later cantor) and Odo de Toriaco,
canon, have arranged the items of receipt under seven categories.[17] In seven of the
eight years for which we have information, money collected from quests inside
the diocese of Troyes constituted the largest source. This money was collected in
the various deaneries that made up the diocese: the deanery of Arcis-sur-Aube
(to the north of Troyes) consistently ranked first, exceeding by far the deanery of
Troyes itself.[18] The accounts do not give any information as to how the money
was collected, except that letters were issued in connection with the quests—
an item for the expense of copying these letters is sometimes included in the fabric
account.

Conservatism and Innovation, Mistakes and Disaster, 1290–1390

The second largest item was the money from the collecting boxes. This total sum is broken down into about six categories of receipts: from a box in the choir; from the *archa reliquarium*, a collecting box associated with the relics of the cathedral; from the relics of Saint Helen and Saint Mastidia on their feast days; from the collecting boxes (*de bustiis*) opened on the day of the great synod;[19] and from the relics (i.e., other than the two female saints). Saint Helen could be relied on to bring in 6 to 7 pounds per year in the 1290s, but her companion Mastidia was somewhat less reliable, sometimes producing sums of about one pound and often nothing. The largest item under "boxes" was simply entered as *de bustiis*—from the boxes opened on synod day. This item remained at such a steady level as to make one wonder whether the office of collector had not been farmed out for a fixed annual rent.

It will be noticed that the items of receipt for the 1290s do not include any contributions from the bishop or chapter, either on a regular basis or as an occasional gift.[20] On the contrary, the *proviseurs* make it clear that the bishop and chapter have both been guilty of diverting funds away from the fabric. Thus, the money from the collecting box in the choir was not being received after 1295 because it had been diverted by the chapter. Bishop Jean de Nanteuil (1269–1298) had laid hands on a sum of money raised from the carrying of the relics of Saint Helen, but on his death he repented of his act and ordered his executors to return the money to the fabric.[21] Jean's successor was the infamous Guichard, who immediately took possession of the money from the *archa reliquarium* and other income from the relics.[22] Unfortunately the lacuna in the series of fabric accounts after 1301 prevents us from finding out whether the *proviseurs* were successful in wresting these moneys away from the bishop and chapter.

As shown in Table 2 the *proviseurs* from 1333 to 1340, Johannes de Auxeyo, cantor, and Obertus de Placentia, canon, have rearranged the items of receipt, including the revenues from quests inside the diocese together with quests outside the diocese, to give six main categories. As in the 1290s, quests constitute the largest single item. The accounts bear witness to a determined attempt to expand the external quests. It is clear that the position of questor was farmed out to agents who paid a fixed annual payment. The fabric now received funds from a surprisingly wide range of pilgrimage centers including Rome (Sanctus Spiritus), Saint-Loup-du-Naud, Paris, Sens, and Saint-Anthoine, Reims. Three different questors collected money from the diocese of Troyes during these years: Johannes de Villeta, Guillelmus, and Theobaldus—the money from this source ranging from thirty to sixty pounds. The proceeds of the collecting boxes opened on the day of the great synod constitute the largest item in this category, amounting to as much as eighty pounds (1339–40). Also included is the money placed in the *archa reliquarium* and other income from the relics. The separate entries for the processions of Saint Helen and Saint Mastidia have now been abandoned.

The category *de troncho chori*, from the box in the choir, is of particular interest. In fact, the money placed in the collecting box in the choir was only one

TABLE 2:

Receipts of the fabric, 1333–1340, to the nearest pound *tournois*

	1333–34	1334–35	1335–36	1336–37	1337–38	1338–39	1339–40
1.	50	46	110	118	43	56	105
2.	92	100	74	75	70	73	83
3.	32	14	30	61	76	20	21
4.	148	138	183	178	198	192	211
5.	2	2	2	2	1	2	2
6.	–	–	21	5	–	19	21
Totals	324	300	419	439	388	361	443

1. From last year
2. From the box in the choir
3. Legacies
4. Quests
5. Rents
6. Extraordinary

of a number of items included in this part of the account. Also included was money derived from anniversaries or remembrances of pious donors, now defunct. A distribution would be made to those present, the cash and grain being derived from rents purchased by the donor and given to the chapter. It is clear that in the period between 1301 and 1330 the decision had been made to divert some of the proceeds of these anniversaries toward the fabric. Also diverted from the great chamber were the payments made on the occasions of meetings of the general chapter and some of the distributions normally received by canons at certain offices (*pro cothidiano*). Some confusion is apparent in the record-keeping for these years, and the *proviseurs* admit to the fact when they recognize that the item *de troncho chori* has been expanded to include extraneous sources. The account for 1338–39 recognizes the new dimension of this category, *de troncho chori, sive a camera et celerio per cedulas*—from the collecting box in the choir, or from the chamber and the cellarer (as indicated) by receipt.[23]

These details, tedious though they may seem, are most important for our understanding of the problem faced by the *proviseurs* in collecting money for the construction of the cathedral and in accounting for it. The situation was changing, and yet the *proviseurs* were attempting to fit the new facts into the well established framework of the account. The change may be understood in terms of the need to find additional regular funds: in other words, sources that had previously been received by other accounting agencies of the chapter (the great chamber and the cellar), but which were now being diverted toward the fabric.

By the 1360s the accounting system had responded to these changes, and the account for 1366–67 specifies no less than twenty items of receipt. The new items include anniversaries paid by a donor for annual remembrance of a deceased person; a sum payable at each general meeting of the chapter; a sum payable at the nomination of a new canon for his cope,[24] and weekly collections for the fabric made at the mass of the Holy Spirit. The list of receipts looks impressive, but when we compare the overall income in 1366–67 with that of 1296–97, we find little increase in the regular sources of revenue. The main factor behind the higher income in 1366–67 was the subsidy granted by King Charles V (128 pounds, 6 sous, 8 deniers) and the gift of the fruits of a prebend by the canon Pierre d'Arbois (20 pounds, 19 sous).

Occasional gifts were also significant in the following year's account, 1367–68 and included a donation of 60 pounds, 8 sous, 6 deniers from the dean and chapter but nothing from the bishop. For the first time in 1372–73, we find the item for funerals (*pailles des morts*). The account for the same year includes sums received from the confraternities of Saints Savinien and Peter and Paul. These confraternities were composed of lay people dedicated to raising funds for the fabric. The account for 1389–90 reveals yet another new form of receipt, the annual rent from houses donated to the fabric by one Pierre de Verdun.

One forms the distinct impression that in light of the dismal economic circumstances and the absence of funds drawn from the regular revenues of the bishop or chapter, the administrators of the fabric were attempting to bolster their funds with additional sources of income. The records of the deliberations of the chapter (beginning in 1361) reveal a general decline in capitular revenues as a result of war and disease.[25] As we will see when we turn to the sequence of construction of the cathedral, this was a particularly disastrous period, with a major expertise held in 1362 and the collapse of the crossing tower in 1365.

It is significant to note that the reorganization of the fabric fund in the first half of the fourteenth century reflects certain profound changes in the framework of municipal government.[26] In the late thirteenth century the inhabitants of Troyes had enjoyed the right to elect a representative known as a *voyeur* who advised the agents of the count on the use of the various tolls and dues paid, for example, at the city gates and for the maintenance of defense. Under the pressure of the disasters of the 1340s and 1350s and the need for large sums of money for defense, a new system developed in this period—a period when Henri de Poitiers, bishop of Troyes, was also governor of the city. The new system allowed for a much greater role for the inhabitants who now elected representatives (clergy and lay people) to a municipal council (*conseil municipal*). This body is first mentioned in the 1350s. These developments would certainly produce an enhanced interest in the accountability of the agents who disposed of the money raised through taxation. This greater interest in accountability is expressed in the new format for the cathedral fabric accounts first seen in the 1360s.

The reform of the fabric fund, begun after 1301 and institutionalized by the 1360s, provided the format to be followed through the rest of the Middle Ages. Despite this reform, however, the immediate problem remained: a major part

26

of the income came from irregular sources that were liable to be adversely affected by the economic disruptions of the time. It was only possible to meet the major crises of the fabric through the generosity of outside patrons. In 1389–90 when a major portion of the upper nave collapsed the bishop and chapter both made donations to the fabric: 40 pounds from the former and 300 pounds from the latter. The duke of Burgundy made a gift of 100 pounds in the same year. The donations of the bishop and chapter were of a once-only nature; in the year immediately following we find 200 pounds donated by the king, 50 pounds from the pope, and 386 pounds from the bourgeois of the city of Troyes, but nothing more from the bishop and chapter.

Can we now relate the situation defined above to the sequence of construction in the cathedral? In particular, can we go beyond the formula, "have money, can build; have no money, cannot build," in order to demonstrate ways in which the form of the building is related to problems in the cash flow feeding the fabric fund? In order to answer these exciting questions, we have to address a third, rather more prosaic one: just how far had construction reached at Troyes by the decades around 1300?

The existing scholarship on Troyes provides a fairly wide range of dates for the early work on the nave, from the 1260s to the 1360s.[27] The earliest fabric accounts date from the 1290s, but they are laconic in the extreme, consisting of a list of items of income and expense, with little in the way of specific topographical information.[28] Several items in the accounts of this period refer to bells (Appendix B, hereafter referred to as "B," 1294, item 2; 1295–96, item 1; 1299–1300, item 1), and we even find a reference to work on a bell tower (B, 1296–97, 2), but there is nothing to allow us to establish whether the tower in question was the transept crossing tower (generally called the *grand clocher*) or the great tower that had existed to the west of the old cathedral and which survived until around 1530. This latter tower was known as the *gros clocher*. There is an inherent probability, however, that the former tower was involved. It collapsed in 1365, and it must have been constructed in the decades around 1300, in association with work on the upper parts of the transept arms.[29] It is probable that the construction of the lower part of the first three bays of the nave would have accompanied the completion of the upper parts of the transept and the crossing vault.

The fabric accounts for 1294 to 1301 record a prodigious quantity of masonry work in the form of weekly wages to masons, carpenters, roofers, and glaziers[30] as well as extensive purchases of materials (Table 3). In 1299–1300 no stone was purchased. It is probable that exterior work was being carried out in this year on the roof, since slates and tiles had been purchased in the previous year. Many entries refer to the construction of vaults (B, 1294, 1; 1294–95, 1, 2, 3, & 4; 1295–96, 2). The allusion to "pillars over the vaults" (1294–95, 2) is most interesting, since it suggests that aisle vaults are involved, and not the vaults of the central vessel. The reference to the painting of certain vaults indicates that at least one bay of vaulting was now complete. Although it is highly probable that the vaults

Conservatism and Innovation, Mistakes and Disaster, 1290–1390

TABLE 3:

Expenses of the fabric, 1294–1301, artisans and stone

Year	For masons, carpenters, and other artisans			For building stone from Angy		
	pounds	sous	deniers	pounds	sous	deniers
1294	35	10	8	14	18	0
1294–95	85	19	1	46	18	0
1295–96	132	9	3	34	16	4
1296–97	163	9	3½	48	10	4
1297–98	159	6	4	59	19	3
1298–99	133	14	11½	151	14	1
1299–1300	168	11	10			
1300–1	160	9	5½			

in question are the aisle vaults at the east end of the nave, the fabric accounts are not specific enough to allow us to rule out other possibilities. We may be sure, however, that in the last years of the episcopate of Jean de Nanteuil (1269–1298) and in the early years of Bishop Guichard (1299–1317) substantial masonry work was under way, and that this work was under the direction of a Master Henricus, described as *magister fabrice*, and that vaults and a bell tower were involved. It is impossible to establish how long Master Henricus remained as master mason, owing to the lack of evidence for the years before 1294 or after 1301. In certain years between 1294 and 1301 he received a payment for going to the quarry to supervise the extraction of stone at Angy, near Tonnerre in Burgundy.

A series of accounts from the 1330s (Table 4) is equally ambiguous. Roofing work was undertaken on the nave in 1333–34 and in 1335–36, but this could equally well have been on the unfinished roof of the first bays of the new nave, or on the roof of the old nave, which was not yet entirely destroyed. There are other references to the construction of a bell tower (B, 1335–36, 2). The construction of an engine to lift a great bell indicates that the tower was complete and that the bells were being installed (1336–37). We also find references to certain new vaults, whose location is not specified (1336–37, 2).

The master mason directing the work throughout the 1330s was Master Jacobus, identifiable through the entry of an item of expense for the purchase of his robe trimmed with fur (B, 1333–34).

The last account in this series (1339–40) is the first to provide details of the workshop led by Master Jacobus, who was paid two sous per day. It can be seen in the chart given in Appendix C that this was a relatively large workshop, only slightly smaller than the one responsible for the construction of the upper nave in the 1490s. The only possible location for the "new vaults" constructed in the

TABLE 4:

Expenses of the fabric, 1333–1340, artisans and materials

Year	For masons' wages and materials			For building stone			Timber			Roofers and carpenters		
	p.	s.	d.	p.	s.	d.	p.	s.	d.	p.	s.	d.
1333–34	162	11	2	93	19	1				8	1	6
1334–35	124	0	3	14	0	0				7	18	0
1335–36	128	3	6	61	8	2	35	12	6	28	8	1
1336–37	146	2	4	38	9	10				81	3	5
1337–38	152	13	10	100	0	0				42	19	11
1338–39	111	8	8	74	9	8				34	12	1
1339–40	151	9	6	66	17	2						

1330s is in the upper transept, since the nave aisle vaults belong to the 1290s and the first high vault of the nave to the 1350s. Whereas in the 1290s the carpenters and roofers had been included with the masons, it is now possible to distinguish them.

In addition to the fabric accounts we have another kind of written evidence which will help us to fix the chronology of the campaigns of construction on the cathedral in the years around 1300, namely the foundation of the altars in the first chapels of the nave.[31] In this context, the word "foundation" does not refer to the masonry footings of the building, or to anything involving the physical fabric of the structure. The word is used to convey the meaning of endowment: thus, the foundation of an altar implies the donation of property or rents in order to endow a chaplaincy and distributions to those attending certain offices. The chaplain would receive a stipend derived from the initial gift, and in return for the stipend, he would be expected to say the offices at the altar at times which are usually specified in the charter of foundation. As far as the construction of the building is concerned, this type of source must obviously be used with great caution, since it is possible to endow an altar long after the construction of the building was complete, or, conversely, before the appropriate part of the cathedral has been constructed. The latter situation is illustrated in the nave chapels of Troyes Cathedral. In 1373 Bishop Jean Braque authorized the canon Dreux (also rendered Drouin or Droyn) de la Marche (d. 1381) to found an altar for the celebration of a mass which he had instituted.[32] However, the chapel which bore his name in the cathedral was not constructed until the early sixteenth century. This apparent enigma is explained by the fact that the chapel that bore the name of Dreux de la Marche originally existed in a small chamber to the south of the old west bell tower until the demolition of the tower around 1530, at which time the chapel was translated to its permanent location in the nave.[33]

Conservatism and Innovation, Mistakes and Disaster, 1290–1390

Thus, we must consider the evidence relating to the foundation of chapels as essentially circumstantial in nature. The accumulation of a bulk of circumstantial evidence, can, however, be most convincing, and this is the case in connection with our first nave chapels: four of the six earliest nave chapels (the lateral chapels at the east end of the nave) can be associated with foundations made in the early years of the fourteenth century. On the south side of the nave the second chapel (Nativity and Assumption of the Virgin) was founded by the dean, Henri de la Noue, in 1305,[34] and the foundation of the third chapel (Saint Louis) is documented in a charter of 1309.[35] On the north side the first chapel (Saint Michael) was founded in 1325 by the archdeacon Jacques de Basson,[36] while the third chapel (Conception and Madeleine) is associated with names of Jacques and Girard de la Noue: the knight Jacques de la Noue founded the feast of the Conception in 1326.[37]

All of the evidence summarized above has been of a circumstantial nature. Beginning in 1362, however, our texts provide some more specific details relating to the fabric of the cathedral. Of particular importance is the record of a visit made to the cathedral by an outside master mason, Pierre Faisant, in the year 1362, and the charter of King Charles V, dated August 31, 1365, according certain concessions to the chapter in order to raise funds for the reconstruction of the recently collapsed tower over the transept crossing.[38]

The record of the visit of 1362 has been preserved in the register of the deliberations of the chapter. It is one of the most instructive documents that we have for this period, not only inasmuch as it relates to the particular situation at Troyes, but also in the light it casts on cathedral construction in general (B, 1362). The concerns expressed by the visiting master bear witness to a workshop facing enormous difficulties resulting from the unfinished state of the cathedral, inadequate maintenance, and general lack of expertise on the part of the local builders. These problems were exacerbated by certain aspects of the design of the building, notably the form of the aisle roofs that made it hard for the rain water to escape from the gutters. Thus, we find that the gutters around the choir aisles were leaking (B, 1362, 1); that the entablatures were crumbling (2); that it was necessary to repoint the balustrades and gutters at the level of the clerestory, because the water was overflowing and running down the walls (6); that the joints in the upper passageways were leaking and that the water was running down inside the walls (7); and that the four gutters of the bell tower were in need of repair (8). This leakage of water around the base of the tower (probably the crossing tower) almost certainly contributed to the collapse of this tower in 1365. Similarly, the saturation of the stone by water overflowing from the gutters, combined with the destructive effects of winter frost, may have contributed to the collapse of the nave in 1389.

Three items in the record of the visit relate not to questions of maintenance but to structural problems resulting from the design of the flying buttresses, which were alleged to be faulty. Two of the flyers mentioned in the text may be located in the choir, one near the bishop's chapel (indicating the south side); item 5 locates the other faulty flyer in question near the house of the great archdeacon, which suggests the north side.[39]

The remarks of the visitor, Pierre Faisant, on the subject of the "new work" of Master Jehan de Torvoie are of the highest interest (B, 1362, 4). Pierre Faisant reminds us a little of William of Sens at Canterbury.[40] In both cases, the visiting expert attempted first of all to allay the fears of the prospective patron, but then went on to propose a radical solution. Thus, Pierre Faisant, having examined the new work of Jehan de Torvoie, reported that there was no problem except that (and here comes the bombshell) the flyers had been placed too high! He specified that the upper flyer was involved, and that it would be necessary to demolish it as far as the "pinnacles that move from the angles" and then to rebuild it, using the old masonry as far as possible.

It is obviously most important to locate the faulty flyers and the "new work" of Jehan de Torvoie. Only one attempt has ever been made, this by Mgr. Roserot, who suggested that the term "upper flyer" described a double unit as at Reims or Soissons, with two flyers situated directly one over the other.[41] The present flying buttress system of the choir has two flyers, one placed directly over the other, but we have to remember that this arrangement in its entirety dates only from the nineteenth century. The medieval flyers of Troyes Cathedral comprised a unit formed of a lower supporting arch and an upper rim, linked by tracery panels (Figs. 33 & 34). The double aisles of the choir and nave necessitated two units, a lower one over the outer aisle, and an upper one over the inner aisle. It is this upper unit (i.e., over the inner aisle) to which the text refers.

It is unlikely that the flyers of the choir were involved, since they had been in place since the mid-thirteenth century, and could hardly have been considered "new work." Moreover, the text relating to the flyer on the south of the choir specifies that only one unit was affected. The only possible area for the "new work" of Jehan de Torvoie is in the upper nave. The faulty flyers were almost certainly at the extreme east end of the nave, adjacent to the transept. The upper flyers here spring from an upright which supports two such flyers, one against the upper transept and the other against the first bay of the nave (Figs. 44, 48, 55 & 58a). The two upper flyers form an angle, and a pinnacle rises from the upright, just as specified in the text. Finally, and most important, an analysis of the building at this point will demonstrate that a remodeling has taken place, and that the height of the upper flyers has been reduced. Two different solutions have been applied in order to achieve the desired reduction in height (Fig. 5). On the north side the upper and lower flyers were rebuilt at a slightly lower level, retaining the original angle of incline in the unit (Fig. 55). The upper rim of the lower flyer no longer engages on the moulding of the upright. The reduction of the height of the top rim of the upper unit is also apparent in the way that the tracery panels have been interrupted. On the south side, on the other hand, the lower flyer was left intact, and the upper unit was entirely rebuilt, but its angle of incline was

Conservatism and Innovation, Mistakes and Disaster, 1290–1390

reduced in order to achieve a slightly lower level of abutment (Fig. 58). It is readily apparent that the upper and lower flyers no longer form a continuous straight line. Thus, the easternmost flyers of the nave have the three required characteristics: an upper and a lower unit; an angle formed between two flyers, and evidence of a rebuilding to reduce their height.

We will shortly review the fabric accounts for the period immediately after the visit of Pierre Faisant in order to document the work of reconstruction on these flyers. First, however, we will skip several years of the construction sequence in order to look ahead to the collapse of the nave twenty-seven years after the visit, in 1389. The name of the inept master who had constructed the faulty flyers, Jehan de Torvoie, was still remembered in the workshop, and the collapse was attributed to his defective work. Specifically, the collapse was said to have taken place because of the fall of a great window frame (*forme*) constructed by Jehan de Torvoie in the upper nave (B, 1389–90, 3). Earlier writers have tended to minimize the importance of this collapse. It has been suggested that the word *forme* should be read as *ferme*, a wooden beam in the roof.[42] The word is definitely *forme*, however, and the idea that Jehan de Torvoie had built the clerestory windows at the east end of the nave is fully in accord with the evidence that he had constructed the flyers in the same area. If flyers were in place, then it is reasonable to assume that vaults had also been constructed. This supposition is confirmed by an analysis of the upper piers at the east end of the nave. Whereas the upper western piers have not suffered any significant deformation as a result of the outward thrust of the vaults, piers C 4 and C 5 on the north side and D 4 and D 5 on the south have been pushed outward.[43] This deformation is especially evident in the two piers on the north side, up to a height of about two meters above the clerestory passage (Fig. 56). Above this level, the piers have been rebuilt, and recover a vertical axis. The successive campaigns of reconstruction on the upper piers and flying buttresses are somewhat complex, and have been summarized in Appendix D. The deformation of the four eastern piers of the nave cannot have been the result of the outward thrust of the existing vaults (constructed in the late fifteenth century), since, if this were the case, all of the piers would have been equally deformed. The eastern piers have been deformed by the construction of vaults that were inadequately buttressed—the faulty flyers of Jehan de Torvoie. The combination of poorly planned flyers and frost damage resulting from inadequate maintenance led to the collapse of the upper nave in 1389. This was a major event, involving two high vaults.

What happened to the unfortunate Jehan de Torvoie after the visiting master had found his work on the upper nave to be defective? He was almost certainly terminated, since we find no mention of his name in connection with the position of master mason of the workshop in the records after 1362.[44]

On July 12, 1365, the bishop and chapter signed a contract with a certain Master Thomas to continue the work, with the help of three other masons, who seem to have worked as a team: Michelin de Jonchery, Michelin Hardiot, and

Jehan Thierry (B. 1365).[45] As far as the surviving documents show, Master Thomas contributed little to the campaigns of construction. His work was probably confined to the repair of the defective parts of the building specified in the expertise of 1362. Soon afterward, the attention of the bishop and chapter was diverted by yet another disaster, the collapse of the bell tower over the transept crossing. Was Jehan de Torvoie blamed for this event too? The texts do not provide any evidence allowing us to reconstruct the circumstances attending the disaster, although Pierre Faisant, the visiting expert, had remarked that the four gutters around the tower were defective. The crossing tower was probably a wooden one and its collapse (on August 13, 1365) inflicted limited damage upon the body of the church (B, 1366–67).

As indicated earlier, Master Thomas did not survive for long after 1365.[46] A new contract made soon after the collapse, names a team of three masons as joint masters of the workshop.[47] Michelin de Jonchery, Jehan Thierry, and Michelin Hardiot had previously occupied a secondary position in the workshop of Master Thomas. The tone of the contract, so soon after the collapse of the tower, is severe (B, 1366). Whereas the earlier contract with Master Thomas had begun by specifying the salary, and had gone on in rather vague terms to prohibit him from working elsewhere, the new contract specified that the chapter could give one month's notice, and that the masons were financially responsible for any defective work.

The fabric accounts for the succeeding years allow us to follow the work of the three master masons specified in the contract. The damage inflicted on the vaults of the lateral chapels by the collapse of the bell tower was repaired and work continued on certain "great arches" and "small arches" (B, 1366–67, 3, 4, & 5). The pillars between the great and small arches are also mentioned (B, 1366–67, 4). In 1366–67, the work is concentrated in two locations, on the south side of the choir, near the treasury, and in the other part of the church, near the *grenier* (B, 1366–67, 1 & 4). The arches (great and small) and the piers cannot have been interior elements, since the arches of the nave aisles date uniformly from the period around 1300. The elements defined in the texts (large arch, pillar, small arch) correspond to the elements of the flying buttress; the large flyer over the inner aisle, the intermediary upright (*culée*), and the small flyer over the outer aisle. The supposition that flying buttresses were involved, and not interior arches and pillars, is confirmed by the fact that the work led to damage on the roofs, which then had to be repaired (B, 1367–68, 4). These were the roofs of the aisles and chapels below the flyers.

The work on the flyers was said to be in two locations, one on the south side of the choir, and the other near the *grenier*. We remember that Pierre Faisant had recommended that a flyer on the south side of the choir was to be rebuilt, but what of the *grenier*? Fortunately a passage in our fabric account allows us to locate the *grenier* to the south side of the nave, just outside the third chapel (B, 1367–68, 3). This location is also confirmed in the existing plans of the cathedral

33

complex prior to the transformations of the nineteenth century.[48] We may be fairly certain that we are dealing with a flying buttress at bay division 3 or 4.

A lacuna in the series of surviving fabric accounts prevents us from following the work of our team of three master masons any further, but we may be fairly sure that they continued with the work of repair and the reconstruction of the faulty parts of the building associated with the name of Jehan de Torvoie. This done, it would be possible to resume the "new work," moving away from the completed eastern bays of the nave in a westerly direction.

A fabric account survives for the year 1372–73.[49] In this account we find mention of the foundation of a new pillar. This pillar cannot have been the upright of a flying buttress, since its foundation involved the digging of a hole in the ground. It is evident that an additional pier in the north arcade of the nave was constructed at a date well after the first three bays which had been built in the years around 1300. Pier C 2 is similar in form to these earlier piers, but the capital has foliage wrapped around it, not springing out of it, as we find in earlier capitals (Fig. 88). It is also noticeable that pier C 2 is excessively weathered, as though it had been left exposed to the rain and frost for a considerable period of time. With the three eastern bays of the nave complete and closed in with a provisional wall at division 3, this pier must have been left exposed outside for about a century (between 1373 and 1470s).[50]

The accounts for the years after 1372 are missing, but the extracts from these lost accounts published by Gadan in the mid nineteenth century reveal that the windows on the west side of the north transept were being glazed (B, 1375–76).[51]

It is clear that the early campaigns of construction on the nave in the decades after 1300 were conceived as a series of vertical slices, with each bay of the cathedral brought right up to the level of the high vaults. The first two bays of the nave had certainly been completed in this way, and the foundation of pier C 2 indicated that preparations were being made to lay out the lower parts of bay 2–3 prior to completing the upper parts of 3–4.

The immediate prospect of finishing the nave was again snatched away through a new set of structural problems in the completed parts of the building. Worries over the structural security of the cathedral are reflected in an invitation sent to the celebrated outside expert Drouet de Dammartin, master mason of Charles V and of the duke of Berry (B, 1379–80, 2).[52] The attention of the visiting master was directed primarily at the rose of the south transept façade, although the entire building was also inspected. The fabric account for this year indicates that the team of masons was no longer active.

The repairs to the rose were completed by the following year (1380–81), and from this date for a period of about seventy years (until 1450) the chapter was unable even to contemplate the completion of the nave. On the contrary, the resources of the fabric were diverted toward the construction of a stone choir screen (the *jubé*, to be discussed in the next chapter) and to repair work of considerable urgency, necessary to ensure the stability of the nave.

With all efforts directed toward the completion of the choir screen, it is probable that the envelope of the building was neglected. Several passages in the fabric accounts of the 1380s report ominous symptoms. In 1381–82 the roof was struck by lightning, and as it was being repaired, it caught fire. In 1383–84 a major wooden beam in the roof broke (B, 1383–84, 2). Deformation in the area of the upper crossing is suggested by the construction of a provisional chalk flyer against the crossing (B, 1387–88, 1). This flyer was probably placed inside one of the easternmost clerestory windows of the nave in order to prevent the great arches of the crossing from pushing the western crossing piers outward. Mention is made of a second arch inside a window (B, 1389–90, 2), and later the arches were raised up a little higher (B, 1390–91, 2). These arches against the western piers of the crossing remained in place until 1486–87, when they were demolished in order to make way for the final work of completion on the upper nave (B, 1486–87, 2).

Finally, at Christmas 1389, the nave collapsed because of the fall of an upper window, that is to say, one of the clerestory windows, presumably in the eastern bay of the nave (B, 1389–90, 4). This year's account mentions the placing of a wooden prop to support a pillar (buttress?) of chalk existing inside a window built by Jehan de Torvoie. This pillar or buttress was almost certainly the chalk buttress against the crossing, inside one of the easternmost clerestory windows (bay 5–6). The window was in a dangerous state, and it was necessary to prop up one of the flanking piers (B, 1389–90, 2). Damage inflicted upon the aisle roofs in the course of this work confirms that we are dealing with pillars projecting up above the aisle roofs at clerestory level. In spite of this urgent repair work, the nave collapsed because (we are told) of the failure of one of the enclosing arches of the clerestory. Soon after the collapse of the upper nave, the rose window of the north transept fell out (B, 1389–90, 5).

An emergency team of some thirty laborers was recruited in January 1390 to clear away the timber and stone. The masons, under the direction of Henry de Bruisselles, continued work on the choir screen until June 1390, at which time they were transferred to work on the nave (B, 1389–90, 1). Certain piers had to be partially demolished and rebuilt in order to install a new low-level provisional roof, as will be seen in Chapter III.[53]

A summary of the conclusions to be derived from the written evidence for the period 1290–1390 would be in order before turning to a more exhaustive study of the elements of the building itself. In the 1290s we found Master Henricus directing masonry work on the cathedral. Vaults were under construction (probably of the eastern bays of the nave aisles), and work was undertaken on bells and a bell tower, perhaps the crossing tower. In the 1330s Master Jacobus directed construction of vaults (transept?) and bell tower. Master Jehan de Torvoie was active in the period before 1362, and it is quite clear that he built the upper parts (clerestory windows, flyers, and vaults) of the eastern bay of the nave. Jehan de Torvoie's work was found to be defective (1362) and Master Thomas was hired to

Conservatism and Innovation, Mistakes and Disaster, 1290–1390

undertake the work of modification and repair. This work was delayed by the collapse of the crossing tower (1365) and the death of Thomas. His former subordinates, Michelin de Jonchery, Michelin Hardiot, and Jehan Thierry, rebuilt the defective flyers of the eastern bays of the nave, and founded a new pier (pier C 2, in 1372) in order to continue the work into the western bays of the nave. These efforts were interrupted by the desire to start work on a new choir screen (1382) and by the collapse of the upper nave and north transept rose (1389). Since we know that the upper parts of the eastern bays of the nave were under construction in the 1340s and 1350s, it is reasonable to suppose that the lower parts of the eastern nave and the upper transept were built in the decades around 1300, and that they embodied the work of Masters Henricus and Jacobus (1290s–1330s). This supposition is in accord with the evidence from the foundation of the first chapels of the nave, and the dating of the stained glass of the same chapels.[54]

The dating of the early work in the nave on the basis of written evidence is particularly important given the element of conservatism apparent in the work and the dependence upon earlier models. In general terms, we will see that the master masons drew their ideas from four main sources: the much earlier work on the central vessel of the choir (work that had been completed almost a century before); the more recent work on the upper transept arms of Troyes Cathedral; and two major outside sources: the collegiate church of Saint-Urbain situated just to the west of the cathedral, and the cathedral of Notre-Dame in Paris.[55]

At a superficial glance, the nave of Troyes Cathedral appears fairly uniform: five bays composed of a central vessel made up of three levels, matching those of the transept and choir, vaulted with quadripartite rib vaults (Figs. 2, 5, & 64–70). The central vessel is flanked by double aisles on each side and lateral chapels are placed between the exterior buttresses.

The use of the double aisle in the nave is, of course, relatively infrequent. The main source was certainly Notre-Dame of Paris, which also provided the inspiration for the lateral chapels placed between the buttresses. Whereas at Paris these chapels were an afterthought, at Troyes they are integral with the nave, although their presence had not been anticipated by the designer(s) of the transept, as is revealed by the awkwardly canted wall of the easternmost chapel. The pulling of the buttresses into the interior space rather than allowing them to protrude on the outside lends to the composition the streamlined look of Late Gothic (Fig. 38).

The overall proportions of the nave, matching those of the choir, correspond to an aesthetic more appropriate for High Gothic or Rayonnant than for Late Gothic (Fig. 67). The proportion of the central vessel is roughly that of two squares placed one on top of the other (width of central vessel, 13.90m.; height, 28m.) (Fig. 5). The inner aisle also has cubic proportions (width, 6.00m.; height of abaci, 6.00m.). Interestingly, the outer aisle is somewhat wider than the inner one, and its vaults are a little higher.[56]

This preoccupation with squares reflects mid thirteenth century thinking. We find similar schemes in the work of Pierre de Montreuil, in the post–1231 campaigns at Saint-Denis, and in the choir of Beauvais Cathedral.[57] Impossible for Masters Henricus and Jacobus at Troyes to capture the special effects favored by their contemporaries: soaring arcades with enhanced spatial continuity with the aisles and reduced clerestories.

If Masters Henricus, Jacobus, Thomas, Michelin Hardiot, Michelin de Jonchery, Jehan Thierry, Jehan de Torvoie, and the others found it impossible to escape from the powerful forces of conservatism in the overall design of the plan and elevation for the nave of Troyes Cathedral, were they any more innovative in their design of individual elements: piers, mouldings, window tracery, and the like?

The Rayonnant architecture of the upper choir provided the "classic" statement from which subsequent generations found it impossible to escape. It has been seen that the eastern sides of the transept arms, finished at about the same time as the choir, embodied the same type of elevation (Fig. 72).[58] On the western sides of the transept arms, although the piers belong to the period around 1220, the profile of the arches of the transept arcade is similar to that found in the nave. Above arcade level in the triforium and clerestory an uncomfortable sequence of innovations is evident (Figs. 70 & 71). In each transept arm the triforium was installed from the outer bays moving toward the crossing. Thus, the two outer bays have tracery forms embodying quatrefoils resembling the outermost bays on the east side of the transept, whereas adjacent to the western crossing piers the capitals have been omitted from the triforium and much more sophisticated moulding forms have been used.[59]

In the clerestory level of the western side of the north transept the two outermost windows have simple rounded mullions whereas the window adjacent to the crossing has mullions with multiple shafts. In the corresponding windows on the south side the central window is the oldest, with simple rounded mullions, whereas the other two windows have multiple shafts (Fig. 71). Experiments were also made in the patterns of the window tracery in the clerestory (Fig. 44). The three windows in the west side of the south transept look less fully developed, with three oculi surmounting three lancets. A similar pattern occurs in the central window on the west side of the north transept, but the two other windows embody a more complex pattern of interlocking lancets. The harmonious relationship between the triforium and clerestory has been entirely lost in the two bays flanking the western crossing piers.

The main vaults of the transept arms are quadripartite with keystones bearing both foliage decoration and figurative elements. The vault of the crossing has an enormous pierced keystone decorated with foliage and a star pattern formed of ribs, tiercerons, and liernes (Fig. 67). It is highly probable that the vaults were installed only after the construction of the transept roof and the crossing tower. The reference to "new vaults" in 1336–37 very likely refers to the vaults of the

37

transept arms. The star vault should be dated around 1340, although it was restored after the fire and collapse of the crossing tower in 1700.[60]

It is evident that a dialogue has taken place between the development of the forms of the upper west sides of the transept arms and in the first three bays of the nave. This dialogue resulted from structural and logistical factors—the nave had to be begun in order to provide the necessary support for the upper west sides of the transept arms and to allow the installation of the transept vaults. The western side of the transept also provided an ideal arena for experimentation with new forms destined for use in the nave.

The original intention for the beginning of work on the nave involved the foundation of the piers of the main arcade. Thus, the lower parts of the two piers of the main arcade on the north side of the nave (piers C 4 and C 5) are of a form quite different from all the others (Figs. 14, 69, & 84). The bases of the piers in question lack the octagonal raft of the other nave piers. Moreover, whereas the other nave piers have square plinths for each of the shafts, these two piers have octagonal plinths continuing right down to the level of the pavement. In the lowest part of the eastern of the two piers, C 5, almond shaped shafts have been placed to receive the diagonal ribs. The use of such sharpened forms in the pier reveals the intention to bring the support more fully into accord with the forms of the arches and ribs. We thus have a step toward the elimination of the capital—a step that had been taken in the workshop of the collegiate church of Saint-Urbain, Troyes, begun in the 1260s. The pier bases in the cathedral bear a strong resemblance to the bases found in the collegiate church (Figs. 84 & 119). The "Saint-Urbain Master" only began two piers at the cathedral, however, before the decision was made to found all the piers of the main arcade and aisles of the first three bays of the nave using forms that were much more archaic (Figs. 15, 16, 17, & 75).

As already noticed, the nave of Troyes Cathedral has double aisles and lateral chapels placed between the stumps of the flying buttresses, much like Notre-Dame of Paris. Whereas the lateral chapels of Notre-Dame were constructed on a piece-meal basis as an afterthought, the first three chapels flanking the north and south aisles of the Troyes nave were constructed as a single campaign in perfect unity of style, simultaneously with the corresponding bays of the nave.[61]

It is quite clear that lateral chapels were not intended in the Troyes nave when the lower parts of the transept were laid out. A window had been placed in each of the transept bays opening into the space where the line of chapels exists and this window has been blocked and the first chapel on each side has been canted outward in order to gain the necessary depth.[62] The exterior forms of the first three nave chapels are quite different from any of the earlier parts of the cathedral (Figs. 33, 37, & 41). Since the buttresses are enclosed inside the building, embodied in the walls dividing the chapels, the exterior wall can remain quite flat. The lowest part of the wall, entirely unarticulated, is capped by the heavily projecting moulding of the window sill. The divisions between the chapels, projecting very slightly, sit on top of this sill. In their lowest parts the divisions are simple flat pilasters, but higher up the front edge of the diagonal pinnacle of the flying buttress upright is allowed to appear. These dividing pilasters frame three chapels on each side. The chapel windows are framed with straight sided gables projecting up above the top of the wall and enclosing trefoils.[63] The general composition was derived from the clerestory of the choir of Saint-Urbain, Troyes (Fig. 120).

The gables of the cathedral chapels break the pervasive horizontality of the cathedral exterior and emphasize the individuality of each separate chapel. This seems entirely appropriate given the fact that while the cathedral is the expression of the collective piety of clergy and people, the chapels were the expression of the piety of individual donors. These donors gave the funds necessary to found the altar, and in return they enjoyed the right to a tomb inside the chapel[64]—in other words, we are dealing with chantry chapels.

Two different kinds of tracery pattern can be found in the first nave chapels. The narrow windows of the easternmost unit on each side enclose three lancets topped by three oculi (Fig. 41).[65] The central lancet reaches up into the gap between two oculi to give a hint of an incipient ogee. The mullions have simple rounded front edges. The tracery pattern was derived from the windows in the apse of Saint-Urbain (Fig. 120). The forms in the cathedral, however, seem more primitive, lacking the fluency of the work in the collegiate church, where the designers were poised at the point of discovery of the logic of the double-curved tracery pattern. Very similar forms can also be found in four of the windows in the clerestory on the west side of the cathedral transept (Fig. 44).

The windows of the next two chapels on each side of the nave resemble the two windows of the north transept that have a pattern where interlocking lancets form three main units (Figs. 41 & 44). The chapel windows seem more fully developed than the transept windows, but this may be simply the result of the fact that in the chapels the three major units are further subdivided to make six lancets. In the chapels the trefoils and quatrefoils placed in the interstices are unframed; elements of the tracery are prismatic (sharp-edged) and the major mullions have multiple shafts.

The interior forms of the chapels are entirely dependent upon the nave chapels of Notre-Dame of Paris—specifically, the three chapels at the east end of the north aisles, sometimes attributed to Pierre de Montreuil.[66] Instead of a socle arcade to articulate the lowest part of the chapel wall we find a two-dimensional scheme. Around the lowest part of the wall runs a shallow bench which receives the bases of mullions running directly up into the window tracery (Fig. 83). Similar mullions on the solid east and west walls of the chapels ascend to form blind tracery panels capped by trilobed forms. The space of each chapel is thus defined by a brittle spider's web of mullions and tracery. The vertical linkage of wall and window reflects Parisian taste, especially as reflected in the work of Pierre de Montreuil.

39

It is not surprising to find that these delicately linear compositions are lit by windows filled with stained glass which is much less saturated with color than in the choir. Lafond, who dated this glass to the period just after 1300 (a date which is entirely consistent with the foundations of the altars reviewed earlier) remarked on its conservative quality.[67] Thus, we might have expected more grisaille and less colored glass. The compositions are made up of a series of panels enclosing individual figures or abbreviated scenes. It is amusing to recognize in the architecture forms that strongly resemble the exterior façades of the chapels themselves.[68]

Thus, in the chapels we find a new kind of architecture, refined in its forms and more brilliantly lit than the choir. As we move away from the lateral chapels toward the central vessel of the nave, however, the architecture becomes heavier. The piers dividing the double aisles of the nave are a completely revised version of the equivalent units in the choir (Figs. 16, 74, & 75). The latter units are octagonal *piliers cantonnés*, derived, no doubt, from Chartres. In the Troyes nave the octagonal units have been transformed into squares. Each pier receives a similar load of transverse arches and ribs on all four sides, and thus it is entirely appropriate that the plan of the pier should be a symmetrical one. The piers in the chapel mouths are based upon a similar plan, modified because of the special position adossed to the solid masonry of the chapel walls (Figs. 17 & 75). One is struck by the extremely conservative aspect of the bases of these piers. Many significant changes had been made in the design of pier bases in the previous half century. Octagons and hexagons had found increasing favor in the plinths, and the base moulding was often run together with a lower moulding that flares outward in the shape of a trumpet bell. A pier base inserted in the south aisle of the choir of Notre-Dame at Paris around 1300 exemplifies these changes (Fig. 108). The Troyes base mouldings comprise an upper and lower torus (rim) without a scotia (groove) in the fashion approved for the second part of the thirteenth century (Fig. 20 a & b). However, there is no trumpet bell moulding nor any use of hexagons. The plinths are all square, and the entire composition sits atop an octagonal raft very much like that found in the thirteenth-century crossing piers (Fig. 18).

The capitals of the piers, on the other hand, have hexagonal abaci (Figs. 75 & 92). The first use of hexagonal abaci in Troyes Cathedral can be pinpointed to the campaign on the upper choir that followed the collapse of 1228—in other words at a date in the 1230s or the 1240s. The sharpened form of the hexagon is in perfect accord with the reduction of the mass of the transverse arches and ribs in the nave aisles which are somewhat slimmer than their counterparts in the choir. The sculptured foliage of the capitals is made up of semi-naturalistic forms springing out of the body of the capital. A favorite type is a thick, fleshy leaf resembling a water plant.

The piers of the main arcade are a direct copy of the choir piers except that the thickness of the pier on the north-south axis has been increased, while the east-west thickness has been diminished (Fig. 15). The pier provides triple shafts for the arches of the main arcade and the aisles and a bundle of five shafts to ascend to the arches and ribs of the high vaults and to the clerestory window arches. The plinths of the piers are square and an octagonal raft is present.

Supported by the piers of the main arcade and aisles are quadripartite rib vaults (Fig. 75). In the arches and ribs we find the appearance of a new form of moulding (new for the cathedral workshop): a square-nosed fillet which forms the outer orders of transverse arches (Fig. 19).[69] The choir had used an almond shape in this context. Once again, we must give credit to the fertile environment of the Saint-Urbain workshop for the appearance of the square-nosed fillet in Troyes. The vaults of the aisles and chapels have keystones with finely chiselled foliage. The keystones are somewhat higher than the crests of the transverse arches, lending to the vault a slightly domical character. The severies are also slightly humped up so that each severy takes on the character of a shallow domical vault. This is less true in the nave lateral chapels where the entire vault resembles a barrel vault with its axis running north-south.

When we turn away from the aisles and chapels in order to examine the central vessel of the nave (Fig. 69), we find that although the high vaults and the tracery of the clerestory and triforium are uniformly Late Gothic (1470s–1490s), we can nevertheless detect signs of early work extending up as far as the capitals of the high vaults in three piers on the north and south sides, enclosing two bays of the upper nave (the western crossing piers and the two adjacent piers C 5, C 4, D 5 and D 4)(Fig. 94). The high capitals of these piers bear a general resemblance to the aisle capitals, having tufts of foliage springing directly out from their bodies. The abaci are hexagonal, as in the choir. These capitals are easily distinguishable from the Late Gothic capitals of the three western bays of the nave, which have strands of foliage wrapped around the body of each capital. Evidence that the early work on the eastern bays of the nave was carried up at least to the high capitals and beyond is also visible in the interrupted mouldings of the window frame. On the north side (D 4 and D 5) the break occurs at a higher level corresponding with the capital of the enclosing arch of the window (Fig. 96).

The tracery of the triforium was installed by Masters Anthoine Colas and Jehançon Garnache in the 1470s and 1480s.[70] Nevertheless, it is important to note the evidence of an earlier triforium in the form of the mullion bases attached to the main piers in the three eastern bays of the nave (Fig. 69). Several variations on the form of the bases are apparent.[71] Was the tracery of the triforium already installed in the fourteenth century, matching the three double lancets used in each bay on the east side of the transept? Was this early triforium demolished in the collapse of the upper nave that took place in 1389? No firm answers are available to these questions, although we will see that the textual evidence suggests that one bay of a pre-collapse triforium may have survived in the east end of the south side of the nave.

On the exterior of the upper nave, the uprights of the flying buttresses adjacent to the transept (at division 5) were clearly built with the eastern bays of

Conservatism and Innovation, Mistakes and Disaster, 1290–1390

the nave aisles (Fig. 54). The complex chronology of the construction of the flying buttresses of the Troyes nave has been summarized in Appendix D. The flyers constructed against the first bay of the nave by Jehan de Torvoie in the 1350s were copies of the flyers of the choir, with openwork tracery panels linking a lower supporting arch and an upper rim. These flyers were rebuilt in the 1360s, however, and partially demolished after the collapse of the nave in 1389, and then reconstructed by Jehançon Garnache in the 1490s.

We have learned about the mistakes made in the construction of the Troyes nave (faulty flying buttresses, use of chalk instead of hard stone, failure to undertake necessary maintenance) and about the disaster of 1389 (the collapse of the upper nave) from the written sources, which have also helped provide a chronology for the initial campaign of construction. In light of this chronology, the forms of the nave (piers, vaults, etc.) seem somewhat conservative—or, expressed in a different way, the masons responsible for the work were heavily influenced by the need to match the forms of the transept and choir. In reproducing these older forms, the masons of the nave built into their work some of the inherent structural weaknesses of the Rayonnant design of the upper choir: a tendency to reduce mass to a minimum and to seek startling optical effects as, for example, in the use of openwork tracery panels in the flying buttresses. The first pier of the nave was pierced at the level of the triforium passage and may have been pierced for an exterior clerestory passage. The designers of west sides of the transept arms had opted for solid piers at the level of the triforium, yet Jehan de Torvoie reverted to the older, more fragile, solution. The flying buttresses of the choir were somewhat flimsy and the upper rim was placed very high in order to join on to the clerestory wall at the level of the upper balustrade. These buttresses were copied by Jehan de Torvoie in the nave. On the other hand, the masters of the nave felt free to break with earlier prototypes in the design of the lateral chapels, with their massive deeply projecting buttresses embodied in the interior of the building, producing a very substantial base for the uprights of the flying buttresses.

Thus, behind the mistakes and disaster of the fourteenth century lay certain factors of a purely artistic nature: the power of the prototype of the Rayonnant upper choir of Troyes Cathedral. Behind the disaster of 1389 there also lay economic and administrative factors. A well-funded workshop would generally attempt to complete a Gothic cathedral in a series of horizontal campaigns of construction: in other words, constructing the entire arcade, then the triforium, the clerestory, and all the vaults and flyers. This approach would allow several different crews to work on different parts of the unfinished structure. However, large amounts of unfinished masonry would be exposed to the weather and extensive thatching and provisional roofs would be necessary to cover the exposed tops of pillars and walls. In the Troyes nave a more conservative approach was adopted: the attempt to complete a single bay at a time, right up to the level of the high vaults and flyers, leaving as much of the old nave as possible. In the mid fourteenth century two bays had been completed in this manner and the foundation of a new nave pier (C

2 in 1372) suggests that a third bay was about to be completed. The disaster of 1389 was not just the result of the design faults of the structure and the use of defective materials; it was also the result of excessive delays during which the unfinished and inadequately supported masonry was drenched by the rain and subject to the damaging effects of frost. These delays obviously reflect the very small size of the workshops and the inadequacy of the fabric fund. They were caused by the profound crisis of the 1350s in the wake of the French defeat at Poitiers.

The form of the nave was affected by the financial problems in another more positive fashion. It has been seen that the lateral chapels were an afterthought of the period around 1270–80—a very profitable afterthought too, since the foundations associated with the altars in these chapels brought thousands of pounds of additional endowment to the chapter.[72] It seems most significant that the very generous donor Henri de la Noue (d. 1325/27) was dean at the time when the additional sources of revenue (anniversaries, etc.) were diverted away from the great chamber and toward the fabric fund. In the principal obituary of the cathedral this dean was remembered directly after certain counts of Champagne and certain bishops.[73] He should be considered as the enlightened administrator who helped the fabric fund survive the difficult years of the early fourteenth century.

Unfortunately, however, this enlightened leadership was not maintained through the later years of the fourteenth century. The *proviseurs* who rendered the account of 1389–90, Pierre d'Arbois and Erart de Vitel, felt free to point the finger of guilt at the unfortunate Jehan de Torvoie. With our wonderful gift of hindsight we may be inclined to assign to the *proviseurs* and to the clergy their own share of the blame. Given the problem of poor maintenance and structural weakness defined by Pierre Faisant in his expertise of 1362, the administrators of the fabric ought to have devoted their meager resources to the upkeep and completion of the nave. Instead, in 1382, they decided to replace the old wooden choir screen with a fashionable stone one, and the seasoned master masons were replaced by two outsiders, Henry de Bruisselles and Henry Soudan. It is, perhaps, significant to note that the *proviseurs* of the fabric at the time (1382–83) were both relatively inexperienced: Jacques Cousin and Thomas Belle had been in office only since 1378. However, the affair of the choir screen must be reserved for the next chapter.

III
Maintenance, Repair, and Embellishment, 1390–1450

FTER THE COLLAPSE OF THE NAVE NO major new work was accomplished toward the completion of the unfinished cathedral for a period of about sixty years.

The reign of Charles V (1364–1380) had seen a false dawn in the fortunes of France.[1] In the aftermath of the treaty of Calais (1360) which ended the first phase of the Hundred Years War, there was a period of comparative peace. Under the able leadership of Bertrand du Guesclin the French were able to make some significant military gains at the expense of the English in Aquitaine. The stability of the monarchy was again jeopardized, however, by the accession of Charles VI (1380–1422), a boy of twelve who was subject to intermittent fits of madness throughout his long reign. His weakness created a vacuum which was conducive to consolidation of power on the part of his over-mighty subjects, particularly the royal uncles, the dukes of Anjou, Berry, and Burgundy. In a wider context, this was the period of the great papal schism, of the Peasants' Revolt in England, and of the challenge to the established church inherent in the doctrines of John Hus.

Internal disintegration was precipitated by the struggle between the Armagnacs, grouped around the house of Orleans, and the Burgundians. The struggle became a blood feud as a result of the murder of the duke of Orléans, in Paris, by the followers of John the Fearless, duke of Burgundy, on November 23, 1407.

Both sides appealed to the English and the Burgundians succeeded in cementing an alliance. In August 1415 Henry V of England crossed to Normandy, and soon afterward (October 25, 1415) gained the overwhelming victory of Agincourt. John the Fearless of Burgundy was able to take advantage of the situation by seizing control of the city of Paris from the Armagnacs in 1418.

The dauphin of France, the future Charles VII, left Paris and continued a successful resistance to the power of Duke John, based upon the cities of Bourges and Poitiers. A most critical event for the city of Troyes was the murder by the Dauphin's men of Duke John of Burgundy during peace negotiations on the bridge of Montereau in 1419. Philip the Good, the new duke of Burgundy, determined to gain revenge, concluded the Treaty of Troyes with Henry V of England, by which Henry was recognized as heir to the French throne, and married the daughter of Charles VI, Catherine (May 20, 1420). The marriage ceremony did not take place in the unfinished cathedral, but in the parish church of Saint-Jean-au-Marché, and was conducted by the archbishop of Sens (June 2, 1420).[2]

Boutiot, the historian of the city of Troyes, records a series of heavy aids and *tailles* imposed upon the city and diocese of Troyes in the early 1400s—taxation which would inevitably reduce the potential revenues of the cathedral fabric.[3] In 1404 an aid of 15,000 pounds was imposed upon the diocese for the repulse of Henry of Lancaster (of which 3,100 pounds were payable by the city); a *taille* of 2,140 pounds was imposed upon the city in 1406; and an aid of 18,000 pounds was demanded from the diocese in 1415 to help finance the resistance against Henry V's invasion. 5,800 pounds of this latter sum were payable by the city.

In the struggle between the Burgundians and the Armagnacs it is no surprise to find that certain groups among the inhabitants of Troyes sympathized with the dukes of Burgundy, the house that had for many years protected the city and provided support of the cathedral.[4] In 1418 John the Fearless set up certain organs of his government in Troyes, including a *parlement* and a mint, and the city remained under Burgundian control for about twelve years. Heavy taxation is recorded during these years; 3,434 pounds in 1423, imposed by the English regent, the duke of Bedford, for the campaigns against Armagnac châteaux in southern Champagne. In January 1424 an attempt to raise 5,470 pounds from Troyes and the surrounding district proved impossible: the collectors reported that many villages had been deserted and they did not dare to go into others.[5] The same situation affected the quests for the fabric of the cathedral, whose revenues fell sharply.

In 1426 Bishop Etienne de Givry died and the new bishop, Jean Léguisé favored the cause of Charles VII. His election was opposed by the Anglo-Burgundians in Troyes. Boutiot, the historian of the city, suggested that in these years a division began to develop in the city between the common people, who favored the Burgundian cause, and certain leading families (including the Molé, the Hennequin, and the Mesgriny) who were loyal to Charles VII.[6] This kind of internal split certainly makes it easier to understand the capitulation of the city to the

45

relatively weak forces of Charles VII and Joan of Arc in 1429, and the reversal of allegiance to the royal house of France. The bishop of Troyes, Jean Léguisé, was instrumental in winning support for Charles VII. In 1429, prior to the entry of the royal forces, he introduced into the city the Dominican brother Richard, who in apocalyptic sermons denounced the rule of the Antichrist and announced the arrival of the Messiah.

No doubt at the initiative of Bishop Jean Léguisé, on July 9, 1430, the consecration of the cathedral took place.[7] The timing of this event had nothing at all to do with the campaigns of construction on the cathedral (obviously the nave still existed in its provisional state) but was intended to celebrate the expulsion of the Anglo-Burgundians from the city and to reaffirm the traditional loyalty of the bishop and chapter of Troyes Cathedral to the royal house of France.

The 1430s and the 1440s saw no significant economic revival in Troyes, despite the cessation of hostilities brought about by the Treaty of Arras, made in 1435 between Philip of Burgundy and Charles VII. In 1436 Paris surrendered to Charles VII and by the 1440s English control was reduced to Normandy and Guienne.

The administrators of the cathedral fabric obviously faced problems in finding funds, both because of the devastation of the countryside and because of the shifting political situation, which would affect patronage. Despite this, revenues continued to trickle in, and significant construction projects were undertaken.

The period opened with a record high receipt for the fabric, totalling 1,398 pounds, 16 sous, and 7 deniers, in the account for 1390–91 (Appendix C). The various sources of income itemized under the nineteen headings of receipt are much the same as those already reviewed in the previous chapter. The largest regular item continued to be quests conducted within the diocese of Troyes, the money being collected in boxes which were opened on the day of the great synod. All the money collected under the nineteen regular items of receipt does not equal the miscellaneous income grouped under the heading *extraordinaire*, which includes substantial donations by the pope, King Charles VI, and the people of the city of Troyes. These were occasional contributions to meet a special emergency: the collapse of the nave. The declining income of the 1390s resulted from the non-continuation of this outside support: in 1391–92 neither the pope nor the king contributed, although the city gave 40 pounds, and the bishop, Pierre d'Arcis, gave 50 pounds. Other contributions from the king are recorded in these years: 100 pounds in 1393–94 and 50 pounds in 1394–95. In the latter year the city of Troyes gave 40 pounds and a former canon (Henrion d'Arcis) gave 90 pounds. With the cessation of major work the annual surpluses of income grew rapidly because the receipts, although relatively small, were not being spent, and were simply being carried over into the following year's account.

This period saw a major new development in the economics of cathedral building in Troyes: institutionalized support on the part of the municipality.[8] In the 1412–13 account the total revenue from the regular sources of income (i.e., everything except money carried over from last year and "extraordinary" money) is very similar to that recorded in 1390–91 (about 550 pounds). This relatively small sum is increased to the grand total of 1,049 pounds as a result of money carried over from last year, miscellaneous income (including 100 pounds from the chapter, earmarked for work on the new crossing tower), and 40 pounds from the *bourgeois, habitans, et clers* of Troyes, whose financial involvement in the tower project had secured them representation among the *proviseurs* or masters of work.

To be sure, municipal support for the construction of the bell tower was not altogether disinterested since the city would expect to gain from such an enterprise. However, it is also expressive of the generally good relations between the clergy and the *bourgeois* of Troyes. The situation arose from the fact that the clergy exercised very little seigneurial power in Troyes: "it was not as chiefs but as fellow-citizens that they [the clergy] behaved."[9] The absorption of Champagne into the kingdom of France and the temporary weakness of the French kings left a power vacuum. It was quite natural to find the bishops of Troyes moving to fill this vacuum. Thus, Henri de Poitiers, Etienne de Givry (1395–1426), Jean Léguisé (1426–1450), and Louis Raguier (1450–1483) all played a leading role in the affairs of the city. Far from attempting to stand in the way of the development of institutions of municipal government, the clergy was actively involved in the development of the *conseil municipal* in the mid fourteenth century, and was heavily represented on this council.

With the devastation of the surrounding countryside and the elimination of an important source of money (the contributions of the faithful of the diocese) for the fabric fund, it was to be expected that the clergy would move to exploit their good relations with the inhabitants of Troyes in order to raise money for construction. In return, the clergy allowed the inhabitants to have a voice in certain key decisions. For example, when the two alternative plans for the choir screen were compared, representatives of the people of Troyes were invited to express their opinion (B, 1382–83, 4). The will of the artisans was actually able to prevail over the will of the clergy when it came to the placing of iron pennants on the pinnacles of the tower (B, 1433–34, 2).

The chapter was also actively involved in the funding of the bell tower, making contributions of 100 pounds in the years 1413–14, 1414–15, and 1415–16. A papal indulgence for the benefit of the work was issued in 1415, but the receipts of the accounts of the following years do not register income from this source.[10] In 1416–17 the chapter reduced its payment to 50 pounds per annum, and in the following year's account no such payment was made. The municipality continued to give 40 pounds annually to the fabric. The account for 1419–20 reveals an interesting situation where the fabric enjoyed gifts both from the duke of Burgundy (20 pounds) and from the king (10 pounds and 10 sous). The very sharp rise in receipts recorded for 1420–21 is explained by a gift of 200 pounds made by the chapter to pay for a new organ. Other gifts from the king and the duke are recorded in the 1420s: 100 pounds from the late Duke John in 1422–23 and 124 pounds, 13 sous, 4 deniers from the king (return on the salt tax) in 1426–27. But on the whole, the years of Anglo-Burgundian domination were unfortunate ones for the fabric. The income from quests carried out in the diocese (normally the largest regular item of receipt) remained very low in these years, falling from a level of over 100 pounds per annum in pre-Agincourt days to as little as 15 pounds in 1422. The receipts from quests in general diminished dramatically: the account for 1416–17 revealed the reason: *pour cause des gens d'armes*.

No significant work was completed in the 1440s and the unspent surplus of the fabric fund, carried over into the following year's receipts, grew ever larger, accounting for the upward trend of the receipts as registered in our chart (Appendix C). By 1448–49 the money carried over from the previous year constituted 77 percent of the "income" for that year. This situation produced total figures for the income side of the account which looked impressive, but which would quickly disappear when building began. Given the weakened state of the fabric fund, it comes as something of a surprise to find that this was the eve of the resumption of major campaigns of construction. As will be seen in the following chapter, this was only possible through the income resulting from a general pardon for the benefit of the fabric, bestowed by Pope Nicholas V.

We must add a last note on the question of the interrelationship between the political balance of power, patronage, and the nature of the workshop in these years. Something of a revolution in the mason's workshop took place in 1382, when the local masons Michelin Hardiot and Jehan Thierry were displaced, and an outsider, Henry de Bruisselles, took over direction of the work on a new choir screen. It is certain that Henry and his brother Phelippot were from the Low Countries, natives of the city of Brussels, and during these years we find many other artisans of Belgian or German origin appearing in the workshop: Jehan de Bruisselles, Michiel de Bruisselles, Hennequin de Bruisselles, Conrot de Strambouc (Strasbourg), Jehan de Couloigne, Hance de Couloigne, Henry de Mont en Allemagne, Girardin de Mont en Allemagne, Henry de Mez, and Gerart de Prague.

This influx of artisans from Germany and the Low Countries may well have resulted from the close links which existed between the bishops of Troyes and the dukes of Burgundy. Bishop Pierre de Villiers (1375–1378) is known to have made his entry into Troyes accompanied by Philip the Bold. Pierre d'Arcis (1378–1395) paid several visits to the Chartreuse de Champmol, Duke Philip's Carthusian foundation near Dijon, where the workshop also had numerous Netherlandish and German artisans, and it is probably this link which first brought Henry de Bruisselles to the city of Troyes.[11] The dedication of the Chartreuse de Champmol was carried out by Pierre d'Arcis in 1388.

Some surprises await us when we turn from the generally dismal economic and political situation to the history of architecture and particularly to the construction of Troyes Cathedral. Important architectural developments were taking place in these years, particularly in the maturing of the "Flamboyant" window based entirely upon a system of curves and countercurves (for example, in the

Lagrange Chapels at Amiens Cathedral).[12] The construction of a cathedral does not necessarily recognize or respect the great events of military history. Thus, in 1415, the year of the disastrous battle of Agincourt, we find the bishop and chapter of Troyes Cathedral meeting with the artisans of the workshop to discuss the grave question as to whether two levels of windows should be built in the crossing tower, or whether a single level would suffice.

The period between 1390 and 1450, then, did not see a total slackening of construction efforts on the unfinished cathedral, and several important projects were accomplished aimed at the consolidation and repair of certain problematic parts of the cathedral, and also at its embellishment. Four major undertakings preoccupied the administrators of the fabric and the workshop during this period. The collapse of 1389 had brought down two of the high vaults of the nave as well as the roof. It was necessary to repair the damage and to close in the upper nave from the weather. This involved the rebuilding of the upper piers and flyers and the construction of a low-level provisional roof and lateral screens to fill the area intended for the triforium and clerestory windows. The interior of the nave, with its low roof and without the great stained glass windows which would be its glory, must have been something of a disappointment to the clergy. Late Gothic taste favored the lavish decorative effects possible only in the form of miniature architecture appropriate for furniture, liturgical equipment, screens, and the like. It is therefore not surprising to find that the clergy looked to enhance the appearance of the interior of their cathedral through the construction of a new choir screen (jubé). A maximum of showy effect could be achieved at a minimum of outlay, and the project allowed the clergy to recruit a new team of masons, immigrants from the Low Countries and Germany, who were able to reassure the clergy that the decoration of the unfinished cathedral was in tune with current taste.

With the interior enlivened with a dazzling new choir screen, the clergy realized to their dismay that the lighting in the area of the transept was inadequate. The great rose window of the north transept area had fallen out immediately after the collapse of the nave in 1389, and the hole it left had been filled in with a provisional wooden screen. It was necessary to replace the tracery of this rose window and to reglaze it with grisaille glass to ensure the adequate lighting of the transept. In the course of this work, major structural problems in the area of the north transept arm were discovered and remedied.

The exterior of the cathedral was also considered in need of a facelift. Although the choir and transept were in their finished state, the west end of the building must have been an odd sight, with the bays of the nave covered under a low-level provisional roof and an additional arch in the north arcade, projecting outside the provisional west wall. To the west of this existed the old west tower, the gros clocher. The clergy considered that the exterior aspect of their cathedral could be enhanced through the construction of a new crossing tower to replace the one that had collapsed in 1365. This new tower was begun in 1410.

49

The passing of time has been cruel to the efforts of our workshops dating from this period. The provisional roof, having been left in place long enough to serve as scaffolding for the Late Gothic vaults of the nave (c. 1490), was then demolished. The choir screen fell victim to the French Revolution in 1792. The unfortunate crossing tower was consumed by fire in 1700. The only remnant of all the outlay of money and effort during this period is the north transept rose, now reinforced with a needle of stone inserted through its middle in the 1460s (Plate 43).

We will now pass in review over each of our four projects: the closing in of the upper nave, the screen, the north transept rose, and the tower.

A simplistic chronology of the upper envelope of the Troyes Cathedral nave allows for only two main building periods: one in the fourteenth century when the two eastern bays were completed and another in the second part of the fifteenth century, when the Late Gothic masters Anthoine Colas and Jehançon Garnache brought all of the upper piers to their full height, installed the clerestory window enclosing arches, constructed the vaults and flyers, and completed the tracery of the triforium and clerestory. This simple division into two basic phases of construction fails to take into account both the highly complex patchwork of campaigns which we can see in the upper nave, and the clear evidence of the texts.

We have seen that an upper nave already existed in the two easternmost bays before the collapse of 1389. A second (provisional) upper nave was erected after that disaster, involving a modification of the upper piers and buttress system already completed, but dislocated as a result of the collapse.

The roof over the eastern bays of the nave of Troyes Cathedral which had been completed in the early fourteenth century had certainly been constructed at its full height prior to the installation of the first high vaults of the central vessel that had collapsed in 1389. Whether two or three bays of the roof had been completed is impossible to say. The new roof, constructed after the collapse by the local carpenter Jehan de Colombe, was covered with slates by Jehan and Colart Neveu, brothers, from the city of Reims.[13] The contract for the covering of the roof (1390) is explicit in stating that it was to extend as far as the pier beside the well (D 3 in the south arcade).[14] Three bays of the nave were thus covered. That this roof was not in its ultimate position, aligned with the roofs of the choir and the transept, is revealed by the clause in the contract which required the roofers to cover over the great arch of the crossing (i.e., the western face of the western crossing arch) which was said to pass over the roof. Such dislocation in the levels of the rooflines of half-completed churches was, of course, a very common phenomenon: a similar situation is still to be seen in the city of Troyes in the roof of the church of Saint-Jean-au-Marché with its sixteenth century choir and transept joining on to the low thirteenth century nave. Saint-Urbain in the same city also had a similar roofline until the completion of the upper nave in the nineteenth century.[15]

50

If we may be certain that the roof constructed in 1390–91 was at a low, provisional level, and that three bays had been covered, the question as to the exact height of this roof cannot be answered from the evidence of the contract of 1390, but rather must be based upon a careful analysis of the masonry of the upper piers at the east end of the nave in order to establish the height to which fourteenth century masonry may be seen to extend.

In the interior of the building, the four capitals of piers C 5, D 5, C 4, and D 4 are clearly fourteenth century in character, belonging to two slightly different periods of construction, C 4 and D 4 being rather dryer in treatment and therefore to be assigned a slightly later date than C 5 and D 5 (Fig. 94, g–j). Above these capitals the vault springers are all fifteenth century, and it is necessary to turn to the exterior of the building for further evidence of fourteenth century campaigns.

This examination of the exterior of the upper central vessel may conveniently be conducted along the two levels of circulation which exist: a passage running along the outside of the triforium and an upper passage level with the sill of the clerestory windows (Figs. 48 & 49).

The outside of the triforium tracery is entirely fifteenth century, and the main piers at this level have a simple rectangular section which is anonymous in terms of dating evidence of a stylistic nature.

One level higher, along the exterior of the clerestory passage, we find a veritable jigsaw puzzle of interlocking building campaigns. The passageway itself is composed of flat rectangular slabs with a chiselled depression to allow the rain water to escape. A clear change in the shape of this depression (from squarish to curvilinear) allows us to assign the slabs of the easternmost bay of the passage on each side to an earlier building campaign (squarish depressions are also used around the transepts) and the remaining four bays on each side to a later building campaign. Since in the easternmost bay of the nave the slabs are actually supported by the tracery of the fifteenth century, it is clear that they have not remained in place from the earliest campaigns on the upper nave, but constitute reused material, reset during the fifteenth-century campaigns of completion.

Above this passage the upper piers of the east end of the central vessel have a rectangular section with attached colonnettes applied to the corners and another colonnette on the outside surface to receive the head of the upper flyer (Figs. 7, 48, 49, 52, 53, 55, 56 & 57). This design is a copy of the type used around the transept (Fig. 63), and there is nothing specifically Late Gothic about it.[16] At the point where the upper flyer abuts the pier this rectangular unit is terminated by a canopy in the form of an ogee arch with inverted curves. The canopy is decorated by clumps of foliage and capped by a *fleuron*. Above the canopy grows a diagonally placed pilaster which ascends to form a diagonal pinnacle at the level at the top of the clerestory wall. The above description applied to two such units on each side of the nave, at bay divisions 5 and 4.

Maintenance, Repair, and Embellishment, 1390–1450

Even a cursory glance reveals that the corresponding units in bay divisions 3 and 2 are thicker in their dimensions (Figs. 7 & 48–51). A completely different plan is used in these western bays, which allows the diagonally placed pinnacle to invade the lower square pier, so that the corners of the diagonal unit can be seen projecting at the mid points of the sides of the lower square (Figs. 7 & 51). These two western units on each side of the nave clearly express the Late Gothic ideas of interpenetration and the inscribed square.

To be sure, all of these piers should be considered as "Late Gothic" (i.e., after 1300), but the four western piers (C 3, D 3, C 2, and D 2) reflect a more fully developed mode of thought, whereas the eastern piers (C 5, D 5, C 4, and D 4) were intended as copies of the earlier work in the choir and transept.

We must now embark upon a closer analysis of the earlier piers in order to date them and establish the height to which the early work extends. The documents reveal that work took place upon the upper piers of the nave at four different periods:

Phase I, c. 1340 up to 1362, completion of the first upper nave bay by Jehan de Torvoie.

Phase II, 1362–70s, after the expertise of Pierre Faisant (1362), rebuilding of the flyers, work perhaps begun by Master Thomas (1365 contract) and continued by Michelin de Jonchery, Michelin Hardiot, and Jehan Thierry.

Phase III, after the collapse of 1389, certain piers were raised again to the level of the provisional nave roof (B, 1390–91, 9).

Phase IV, the completion of the upper nave by Masters Anthoine Colas and Jehançon Garnache, 1470–1500 (see Chapter IV).

Rather than attempting to bury the reader in a lengthy series of archaeological descriptions, we have elected to summarize the descriptive material in an appendix (Appendix D), and, having provided the material necessary to allow readers to reach their own decision, to proceed here to a narrative of what seems to have taken place. The history of repeated builds and rebuilds will be instructive as far as other Gothic cathedrals are concerned: it is sometimes forgotten that such edifices were subject to frequent reworkings and restorations even within the medieval period. Such restoration and rebuildings are not peculiar to the nineteenth century!

The four upper piers at the east end of the nave (C 5, D 5, C 4, and D 4) belong to Phases I, II, and III. In C 5 we see remnants of Phase I in the window jamb mouldings, up to a height of about 2.60m. above the clerestory passage (Figs. 7, 8, & 56). The body of the exterior buttress is not coursed into these mouldings but is placed against them. This suggests a rebuild in Phase II, when the passageways piercing the original upper piers were suppressed. The lower part of the pier leans outward, demonstrating that it must belong to the period before the collapse of the vaults in 1389. In the upper parts of the pier this outward lean has been corrected, suggesting a date in the 1390s, after the collapse, when certain piers were rebuilt. Some of the old window mouldings were reused (on the east side, where three rounded rolls exist); on the west side new mouldings were chiselled (one roll and two concavities).

The corresponding unit on the south side was shaped by a similar set of historical circumstances: lowest courses of the window mouldings from the 1350s, the main body of the pier not coursed into these mouldings (1360s), and the upper parts of the unit rebuilt in the 1390s (Figs. 8 & 57).

The next pier on the north side, C 4, has two phases of construction, the lower parts, with a pronounced outward lean, belonging to some stage of Phase II, before the collapse, and the upper parts to Phase III (Figs. 8 & 52). The matching pier on the south side is all of one piece, and probably belongs to Phase II (Figs. 8 & 53).

The west end of the old provisional roof was supported by our next piers, C 3 and D 3 (Fig. 49). The texts are quite specific in telling us that these piers had been demolished as far as the level of the arcade after the collapse of 1389, and had then been rebuilt (B, 1390–91, 9). The "pier beside the well" mentioned in our text is certainly to be identified as D 3. We may thus attribute the design with the inscribed square to Henry de Bruisselles.

Why was it necessary in the wake of the disaster of 1389 to raise the upper piers back up to support the provisional roof? Why not construct the provisional roof at the level of the triforium sill? It seems probable that a higher level was preferred in order to allow for some lighting in the upper nave and also to bring the piers up to the point where the arch of the flying buttresses could provide some support. The collapse of 1389 affected the vaults and clerestory wall of the cathedral, but the upper piers and flyers were left intact, though dislocated. These were demolished (B, 1389–90, 6) and reassembled with the supporting arches of the flyers left in place, but the tracery panels and the upper rim omitted (Fig. 24). The supposition that such provisional flyers existed allows us to explain two phenomena which otherwise would seem rather odd. First, it is noticeable that whereas the supporting arches of the three eastern flyers join on to the pier in an orderly fashion, the tracery and the upper rim fit most uncomfortably. Second, the Late Gothic master mason who completed the upper nave finished the eastern bays with remarkable speed. It seems probable that he found the supporting arches already in place at 3, 4, and 5 and merely had to add the tracery panels and upper rims. Our reconstruction of the upper nave with its provisional flyers and provisional roof is a novel one, and the complexity of this historical interpretation may offend the tidy-minded reader who looks for bold, simple solutions. Unfortunately, such solutions were not available to the fourteenth-century masons at Troyes. The inside of the provisional roof was not left exposed to the view of the beholder in the nave but was panelled over with a continuous surface, probably in the form of a wooden barrel vault (Fig. 24).[17] If the roof existed at the height which has been suggested, it would follow that a considerable gap would be left between the eaves of the roof and the top of the arcade (Fig. 25). This gap was filled in with provisional screens, called *parois* in the texts. These screens were supported by a

53

framework of heavy posts (which would also help secure the roof), and were plastered and whitewashed (B, 1390–91, 7).

In the absence of the enclosing arches of the clerestory windows and the clerestory wall, it was thought that the great arches of the crossing would exert a thrust toward the west which would threaten to buckle the upper western crossing piers. In order to prevent this, two provisional flying buttresses were built, presumably resting on the triforium sill, abutting the western crossing piers (B, 1390–91, 2). One of these buttresses had existed before the collapse, inside the clerestory window which had been built by Jehan de Torvoie adjacent to the crossing (B, 1389–90, 2); thus it was only necessary to raise it a little higher in 1390–91.

The exact reconstruction of the windows in the lateral screens or *parois* is rendered difficult on account of the ambiguity of the texts. Some of the available area for the windows would have been blocked by the flyers against the crossing and the wall beneath these flyers. The texts make a distinction between windows surrounded by wooden frames and certain stone windows which existed on the south side (B, 1391–92, 2 & 5). It is possible that vestiges of the old glazed triforium survived the 1389 collapse. The windows surrounded by wood are all the same height, and a text for 1391–92 mentions twenty of them, twelve on the north side and eight on the south (fewer on this side because of the existence of the masonry-framed windows [B, 1391–92, 2]). An attempt to divide the number of windows named in the text into the available space suggests that two levels of rectangular windows existed, as reconstructed in Figure 25. We cannot afford to be dogmatic about this reconstruction, however, since there is some ambiguity in the texts concerning the exact number of windows. Thus, we find the blacksmith, Thomas le Chat, making iron fittings for twenty windows, while the glazier, Guiot Brisetour, provided glass for twenty-four windows with wooden frames in the lateral screens, as well as four windows with stone frames (B, 1391–92, 2 & 5).

The provisional wall which closed the west end of the unfinished Gothic nave at bay 3, which must have existed since the beginning of the fourteenth century (B, 1366–67, 10), remained in the same position, and not much work would have been necessary to make the wall fit under the new roof.[18]

The construction of the choir screen takes our narrative back to the period before the collapse of the nave.[19] The commencement of this project in 1381, during the episcopate of Pierre d'Arcis and under the direction of the seasoned master masons of the workshop Michelin Hardiot and Jehan Thierry, seems somewhat akin to Nero's fiddling while Rome burned, since the upper parts of the nave were to collapse only eight years later, and symptoms of structural distress had already been observed in the 1380s. We cannot expect the medieval planners of the cathedral to share our sense of priorities or our hindsight, however.

Michelin Hardiot and Jehan Thierry had directed operations in the cathedral workshop since just after the collapse of the crossing tower in 1365. They, and a third colleague, Michelin de Jonchery, had directed the reconstruction of the nave flyers in the later 1360s, and having thus attempted to secure the stability of the

54

nave, had begun the work of adding the western bays in the construction of a pier (C 2) in the northern arcade of the nave in 1372–73. In the 1380s, however, ideas of completing the western bays were abandoned, due to a renewed anxiety concerning the general stability of the building (B, 1379–80, 2).

The source of the initiative to construct a stone choir screen to replace the wooden one which had existed prior to this date is not recorded. In 1381 Michelin Hardiot and Jehan Thierry produced a drawing (*pourtrait*) of the projected screen, and in July 1381 tracings were made on a flat plaster surface (B, 1381–82, 2 & 3). In the text which records the making of the original drawing, it is said to be in order to show the chapter, no mention being made of the bishop. The contract with Michelin Hardiot and Jehan Thierry to make the choir screen was issued in the name of the dean and chapter in June 1382 (B, 1382–83, 1).

The work on the screen ceased in October 1382 because of a conflict which had arisen over the design. An alternative drawing had been offered by Henry de Bruisselles (B, 1382–83, 4), and at the order of the chapter, the bourgeois and artisans of the city of Troyes were asked to express an opinion as to which of the proposed designs for the screen was superior. It was found that the project of Henry de Bruisselles was the better of the two, and Michelin Hardiot and Jehan Thierry, who had directed the workshop for sixteen years, disappeared from the workshop from this point onwards.

A new contract was made with Henry de Bruisselles, who brought in a partner from Paris, Henry Soudan. The contract stipulates that the partners were each to earn five sous a day, and that they were to work continuously until the screen was finished. The accounts for the following years record that the two masters named in the contract completed the screen by the 1390s, although Soudan's name disappears from the accounts in 1387–88, and Henry de Bruisselles brought in his brother, Phelippot, to help him. In 1392 the work on the screen lapsed because of the absence of Henry de Bruisselles; he was engaged at Auxerre, in work on the cathedral and the church of Saint-Germain. It was decided that henceforth two hundred pounds would be set aside each year for the completion of the screen, and another two hundred pounds for the pavement of the church (B, 1392–93, 1). This is the only instance of advance budgetary planning recorded in the medieval fabric accounts of Troyes Cathedral. In fact, however, although some further work was completed on the pavement, the accounts do not document continuing efforts on the screen. Henry de Bruisselles died in 1398. In that year we find Henry's brother Phelippot in the Troyes workshop, summoned from Brussels to finish some details on the screen.

We know very little about the appearance of the screen.[20] It occupied the space between the eastern piers of the crossing and is thought to have comprised five arched openings. Descriptions mention the existence of medallions with images (presumably sculptured) of the Church Fathers holding scrolls. The latter information is of particular interest, given the links between Troyes and Dijon, where Claus Sluter was erecting his "Moses Fountain" (the Calvary for the cloister

55

of the Carthusian monastery of Champmol). The base of the Calvary features Old Testament prophets with scrolls. In addition to the close relationship with Dijon enjoyed by the bishop of Troyes in this period it is worth noting that Drouet de Dammartin, who visited Troyes Cathedral in 1380, was employed by the dukes at the Chartreuse of Champmol in 1383.[21]

We now come to the third project: consolidation in the area of the north transept, and the installation of the new rose window. The north transept rose had collapsed almost at the same time as the upper nave (B, 1389–90, 5). The transepts were a constant source of structural difficulty in the cathedral of Troyes. The south transept rose had also caused problems (B, 1379–80, 2), and the façade of the south transept arm was in such a poor state of repair by the mid-nineteenth century that it was necessary to rebuild it in its entirety.[22] The north transept façade, in its present state, has a pronounced lean, which had already developed by the fifteenth century, at which time it was deemed necessary to add the two decorative buttresses which flank the portal (constructed in the 1460s by Anthoine Colas).

There were several causes for these difficulties: inadequate foundations and the use of soft local chalk instead of the hard limestone from Tonnerre undoubtedly contributed. Certain design problems inherent in the superstructure of the building may also have been partly responsible. Whereas the lateral thrusts of the high vaults were met by flying buttresses, at the point of the cliff-like transept façade no such support was possible, and the Rayonnant style of the mid-thirteenth century, when the transept façades had been built, favored an exterior flatness which did not allow for heavily protruding buttresses.

After the collapse of the north rose in 1390, the great hole in the façade was filled in with a wooden screen (B, 1390–91, 9). This screen was later reinforced (B, 1396–97, 2). The north transept as a whole was also undergoing certain difficulties: in 1401–2 repairs were made to the gutters to prevent the rain from entering. An expertise took place in the same year, the visiting masters, Jehan Aubelet and Jehan Prevost examining the whole church, but especially certain pillars and "arches on the vaults," later defined as formerets (window arches) which had been damaged by the frost (B, 1402–3, 1). A new master mason, Thomas Michelin, directed the work of repair, and project drawings were made in the tracing chamber to the south of the old west bell tower, the gros clocher (B, 1402–3, 2). Foundations of a pillar were begun, but before the work could advance very far a second expertise was conducted, the visiting master being Jehan de Dijon, master mason of Reims Cathedral. The opinions of Jehan de Dijon on the one hand and Jehan Prevost and Jehan Aubelet on the other were weighed up on the spot, the bishop (Etienne de Givry) and chapter being advised by leading members of the workshop (B, 1402–3, 6). The situation is rather similar to the one which had existed in 1381, when the rival plans of Michelin Hardiot and Jehan Thierry on the one hand and Henry de Bruisselles on the other were compared. In the case of the 1402 expertise no indications are given as to which opinion was favored: it is

56

merely stated that a decision had been made to found the new pillar at the end of the steps, against the pavement.

It is possible to establish the location of the new pillar with some certainty.[23] If the new pillar was at the bottom (or end) of the steps, and if the road is to be taken up in order to found that pillar, then it must have existed beside the only steps which are adjacent to the *Rue de la Cité* on the north side of the cathedral, namely the steps into the north transept. We are given two other vital pieces of information on the pillar in question. It is said to be a pillar which will be *boutant encontre l'autre pillier de l'eglise*, in other words the upright of a flying buttress, and in order to complete it a doorway in the pillar of the church is blocked (B, 1402–3, 4). Before the nineteenth century restoration of the choir there existed immediately to the east of the north transept an upright with a flying arch against an exterior buttress of the north choir aisle (Fig. 33). As can be seen in the pre-restoration lithograph, the head of the flyer met the buttress of the aisle at a point where the latter was pierced by a doorway for the passage around the choir chapels. This doorway would obviously have to be blocked in order to prevent the flyer from pushing it in. When the choir was consolidated in the nineteenth century it was possible to dispense with this support, and the flying element of the buttress was removed, leaving only the upright member, which is still to be seen. There can be no doubt that this unit was the pillar begun in 1401–2.

There is clear evidence that the damage to the formerets repaired in these years was in the north transept. Since it is known that the façade was closed in with only a provisional wooden screen and that rain water was leaking in through the gutters, it is hardly surprising that frost damage had taken place.

At some undocumented date after 1402, but before 1408, the master mason Thomas Michelin installed a new rose window in the north transept façade.[24] It was constructed on a contract basis, Michelin receiving a fixed sum for the project rather than daily pay. Payment of money to him as a result of the contract can be found in the fabric accounts of the years after 1408. Since this rose window is the sole surviving witness of all the building efforts expended between 1390 and 1450, it deserves our special attention (Fig. 43).

In structural terms it is important to note that the rose is not placed underneath or inside the last transverse arch of the high vaults. Instead, it projects a little to the north of this transverse arch, and is in theory, at least, free from any pressure imposed by that arch in its tendency to settle. The rose is inscribed in a square, the top of which constitutes a passageway running in front of the gable of the transept roof. The depth of this passageway gives the extent of the projection of the rose beyond the last transverse arch.

This structural and aesthetic device had been developed in the mid thirteenth century in monuments such as the Sainte-Chapelle in Paris, the chapel of Saint-Germain-en-Laye, and in the aisle windows of Saint-Urbain, Troyes. Thomas

57

Michelin was probably simply responsible for the reconstruction of a rose of the second part of the thirteenth century which had already been of the type described.

The structure of the window enabled Michelin to provide for glazing the entire surface of the square, including the upper corners. The circle of the rose itself is divided into twelve segments, each of which is then subdivided into three. The major divisions of the rose have round-edged tracery bars, and the minor divisions have a sharp-edged section. The head of each of the twelve petals is formed by a two-point arch which encloses a device formed by three interlocking triangles of the type generally called "spherical."[25] The central triangle is designed around an equilateral triangle whose sides are formed by arcs of circles generated from center points on the three apexes of the triangle. The three outer triangles have one concave side (shared with the central unit) and two convex sides which are formed by the continuation of the same arcs which had been used to form the first triangle in the center. The spandrels between the heads of the twelve major units are filled with two mouchettes and one soufflet.

In its general design the rose offers a number of variations on the numbers three and four. The motif of the circle inside the square and the resultant spandrels inevitably produces an emphasis on the number four, but the divisions of the rose itself are organized entirely around groups of three, both in the triplets which occupy each petal and in the three interlocking spherical triangles of the head of each petal. Spherical triangles and squares gained popularity in France in the second half of the thirteenth century, and remained popular throughout the fourteenth century. They provide an interesting link between the design vocabulary of bar tracery at the disposal of masters of the Rayonnant period of the mid thirteenth century, and the forms of the so-called Flamboyant style. In the former period we find geometric forms such as circles, trefoils, or quatrefoils used side by side with pointed arches in such a way as to leave small negative interstices between the positive shapes. The use of interlocking "spherical" forms of the type found in the Troyes rose allows for an interpenetration of forms which reduces the number of negative gaps and in this respect provides a step toward Flamboyant tracery in which soufflets and mouchettes can exist side by side without the presence of negative areas. In geometric tracery of the thirteenth century each shape is produced by arcs of circles generated from inside that shape; whereas in Flamboyant tracery each form (an ogee arch, a soufflet, or a mouchette) is shaped by centers outside as well as inside the unit (Fig. 22). This characteristic is also shared by designs which employ interlocking spherical triangles and squares; for example the concave side of each of the outer triangles in the heads of the petals of the Troyes rose is generated from a center point lying outside the unit. In this respect, too, this phase of Gothic design provides a link with the syntax of forms used in Flamboyant. It is curious to find these tentative steps toward Flamboyant design (also embodied in the mouchettes between the petals of the rose) in a city where the first steps toward Flamboyant had been taken over one hundred years previously in the Saint-Urbain workshop, and where many examples of incipient ogee arches were produced, but then forgotten, or rather not observed, by subsequent generations.

Many possible sources for the use of spherical triangles and squares exist in the vicinity of Troyes. A spherical square constitutes the main element in the great west window of Bourges Cathedral, built with the patronage of the Duke of Berry. It is known that the Troyes workshop had close links with Auxerre in the immediately preceding period (B, 1392–93, 1), and it is therefore of interest to find spherical triangles used as a basis for the design of the north transept rose of the church of Saint-Germain, and also the lower window opening into the cloister bay in front of the north transept façade. On the gable of the south transept of Auxerre Cathedral we find a device consisting of interlocked spherical triangles identical to that used by Thomas Michelin in the petals of the Troyes rose.[26]

The construction of the crossing tower was the last project of this period: one which occupied the dark days of Agincourt, the feud between the Burgundians and the Armagnacs and the Treaty of Troyes.

The gathering of the materials necessary to build the new tower began in November 1410 (B, 1410–11, 1). Oaks from the woods around Ervy-le-Châtel were given by the king of Navarre, and the only expense to be paid by the fabric of the cathedral was for the felling of the trees and their transportation. Wood was also donated by the seigneur of Rimaucourt from his lands around Vendeuvre.

The work on the tower was taken in hand in 1412–13. In this year iron tie rods were installed above the vaults in order to strengthen the upper clerestory walls (B, 1412–13, 1), and two most important steps in the planning of the work were undertaken. In terms of architectural planning, the head carpenter, Jehan de Nantes, was sent to Bourges and to Mehun-sur-Yèvre to look at potential models for the tower (B, 1412–13, 3). Sketches were made of the towers in this area, which were considered to be exceptionally fine. Equally important was the planning of the work in financial and administrative terms. The text transcribed in B, 1412–13, 5 reveals a striking shift toward democratic procedures: a third master of the works was elected, responsible to the people of Troyes, and the bishop assured the people that accurate records of expenses would be kept and made public. The text given under item 6 of the same year describes Jehan de Nantes, the head carpenter, as having been "elected" rather than appointed. The intention of the bishop and chapter was doubtless to ensure the financial commitment of the people of Troyes which would result from the involvement of their elected representative in decisions concerning future expenditure. We find a similar line of thinking behind the general assemblies called in the city of Troyes in the fourteenth century to vote on taxes necessary for municipal defense.[27] Medieval municipal governments generally showed an interest in towers, which served as a symbol for the municipality as well as providing for important practical functions (a lookout in time of war, a place to hang bells, etc.).

It seems clear that at the time work began on the tower a definitive drawing of the elevation had not been made. The drawings mentioned in the 1412–13

59

account (item 2) were only intended for the lower stage, and the junction with the masonry of the vault and upper walls. Thus in 1414–15 we find a debate taking place over a most basic question: should there be two levels of windows in the tower, or a single one? (B, 1414–15, 2). It is of interest to find that such an important decision was reached not as a result of the artistic judgment and technical experience of the master carpenter, but rather in the framework of a general meeting of the artisans. The prudent decision to be content with one level of windows was based upon reasons of economy and the greater security of the work. The tracing out of plans upon a plaster surface, as recorded in the following year, was probably part of the work of planning the level of the windows of the tower (B, 1415–16, 3).

In the following year more traveling was undertaken by the master carpenter to search for models—this time to the city of Paris in order to consult with the master carpenter of the city of Paris and of the duke of Berry on the question of the details of the windows and pinnacles (B, 1416–17, 3 and 4).

By this time the definitive appearance of the tower must have been established.[28] Almost certainly the level of the windows and the upper steeple were octagonal, growing out of a square base. Wooden flying buttresses are mentioned in the texts—perhaps these flyers were used at the point where the octagon was set inside the square, to connect the eight angles of the former to the four corners of the latter. Such a plan would necessitate eight flyers, the number defined in the text given in B, 1416–17, 2.

Jehan de Nantes died in 1418–19, having done his best to secure that the commission of master carpenter would pass to his son-in-law, Perrin Loque (B, 1418–19, 1). Work tended to lapse after his death, to be resumed only in the 1430s. The attachment of the cross and the cock to the top of the steeple, an act which marks the termination of the project, is recorded in the account for 1432–33 (transcribed under item 1 in Appendix B). The text transcribed in Appendix B under the year 1433–34, relating to the iron pennants fitted to the pinnacles of the tower, is of the greatest interest, in that it documents an instance where the artisans of the workshop were able to have their own way in the teeth of opposition from the chapter.

The tower was struck by lighting many times over before the great fire of 1700 in which it was entirely consumed.

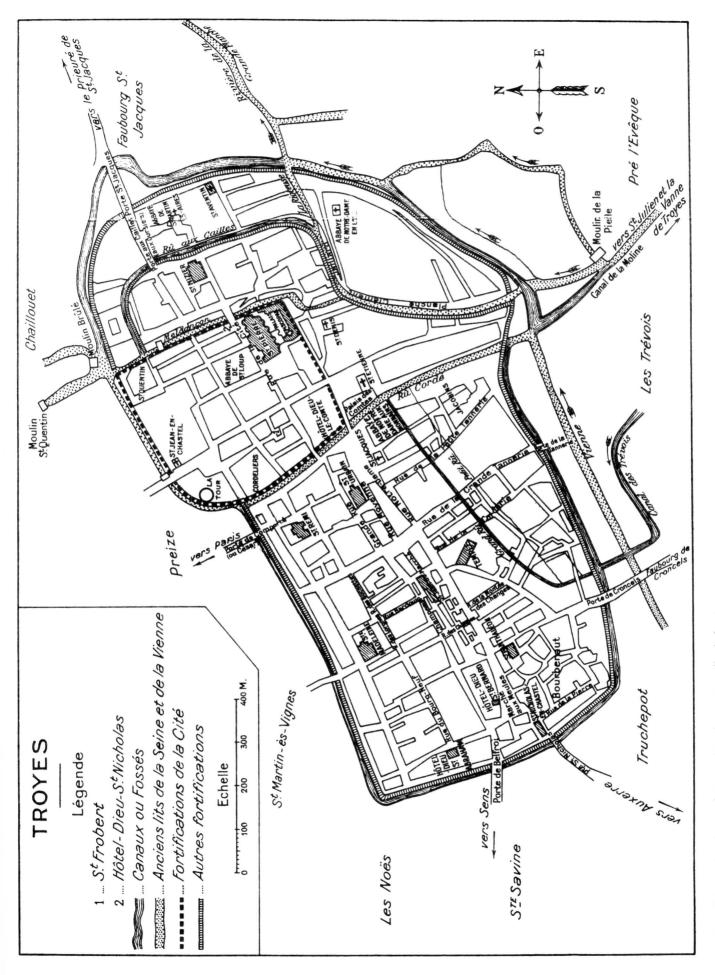

TROYES

Légende

1 ... St Frobert
2 ... Hôtel-Dieu-St Nicholas

〜〜〜 ... Canaux ou Fossés

⋰⋰⋰ ... Anciens lits de la Seine et de la Vienne

▬▬▬ ... Fortifications de la Cité

▰▰▰ ... Autres fortifications

Echelle

0   100   200   300   400 M.

1. Plan of the medieval city of Troyes (E. Chapin, *Les villes de foires*)

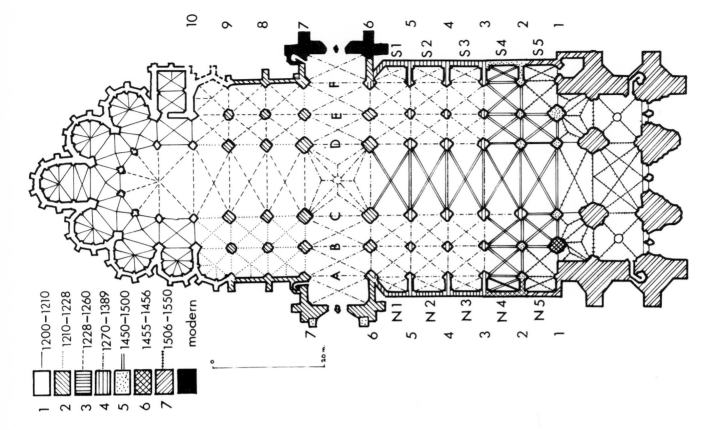

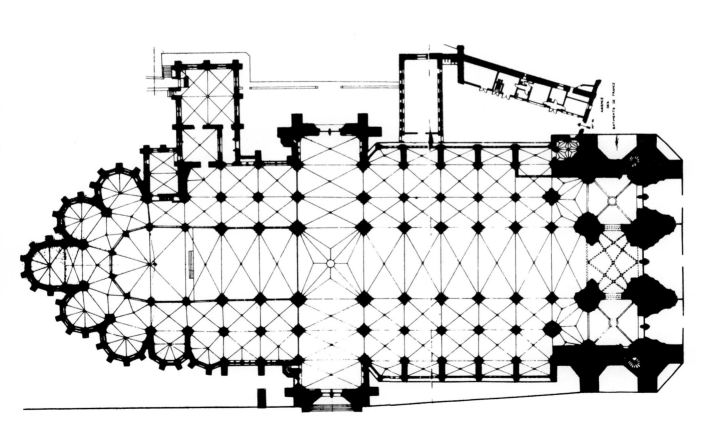

2. Plan of Troyes Cathedral
   a) *Bâtiments de France* plan
   b) Chronology and grid system of reference. Chronology of
      choir after N. Bongartz, *Die frühen Bauteile*

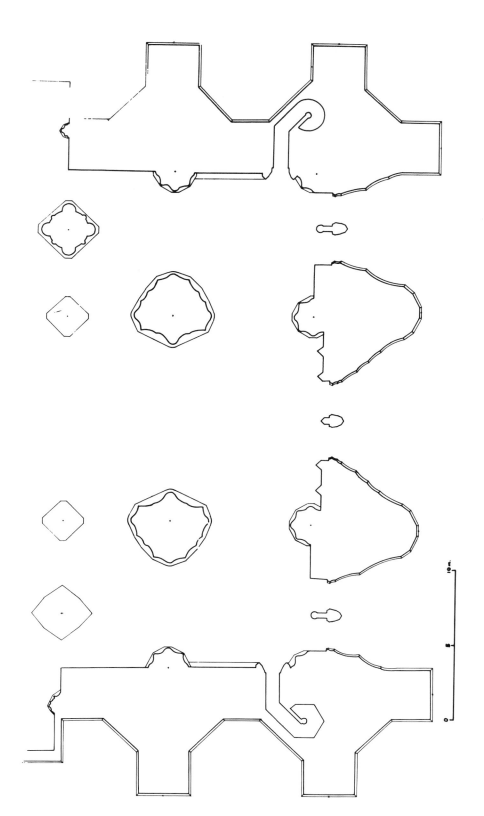

3. Plan of the frontispiece

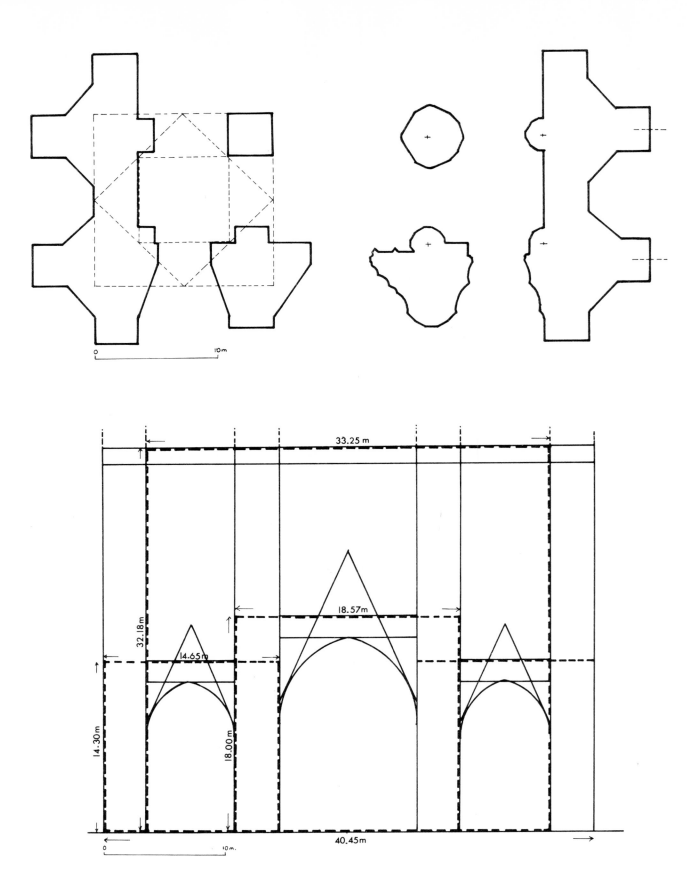

4. Simplified schemes to show the dimensional relationships in the frontispiece
   a) Plan
   b) Elevation

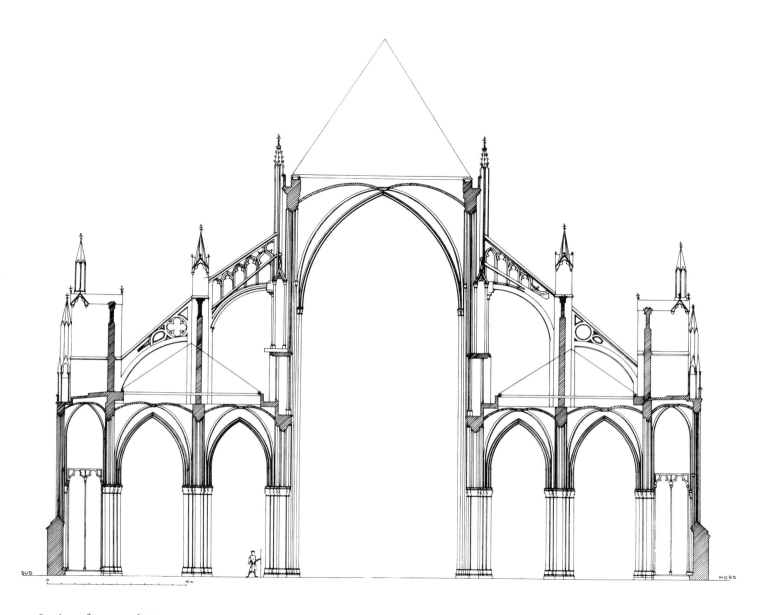

SUD   NORD

5. Section of nave at division 5

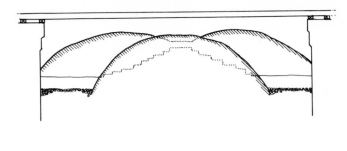

6. Simplified plan and elevation
   of one bay of the vault of
   the central vessel

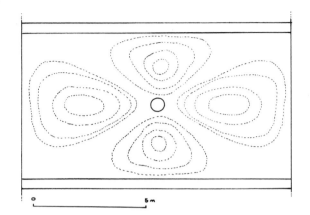

0   5 m

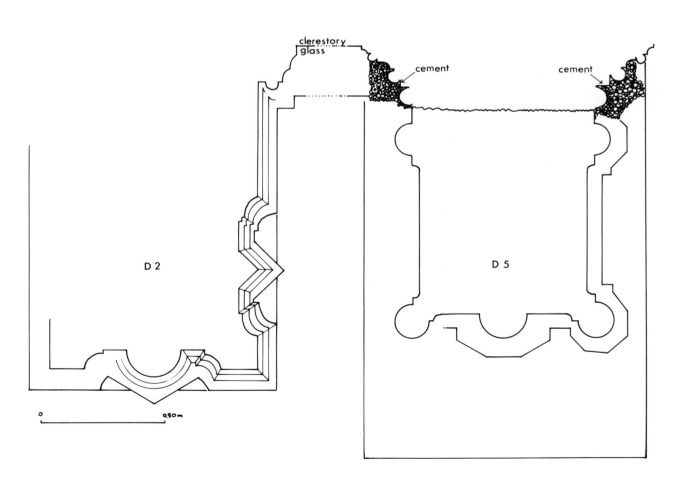

7a. Section of upper nave pier at D 2   7b. Section of upper nave pier at D 5

8. Moulding profiles of the jambs of
the clerestory windows

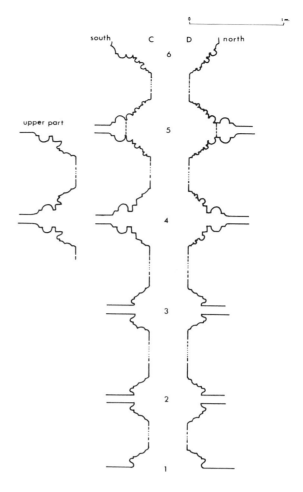

south C   D north

6

upper part

5

4

3

2

1

9. Interior of west towers, section of
attached pier

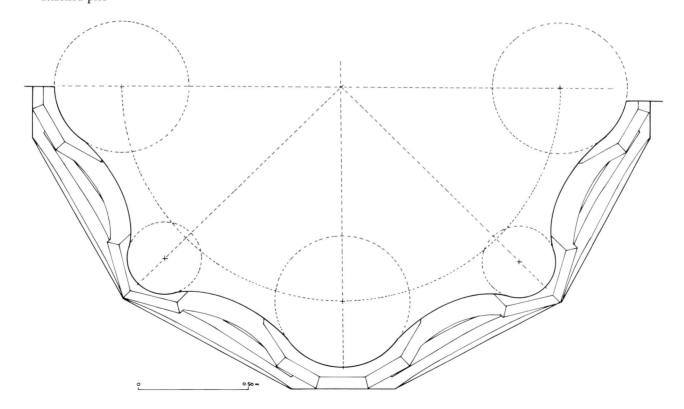

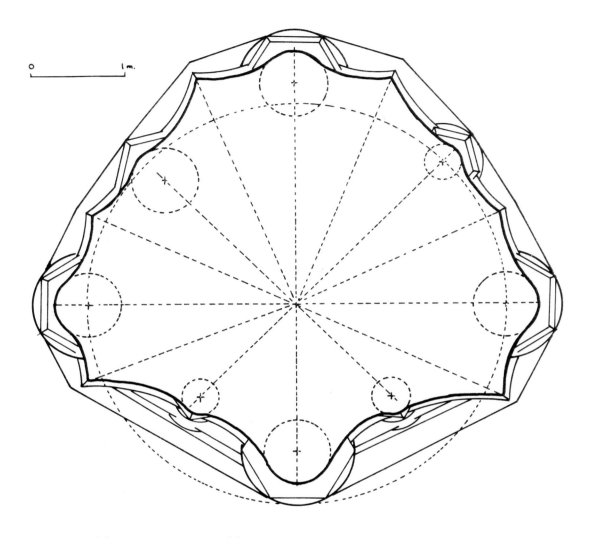

10. Interior of west towers, section of free-
standing pier

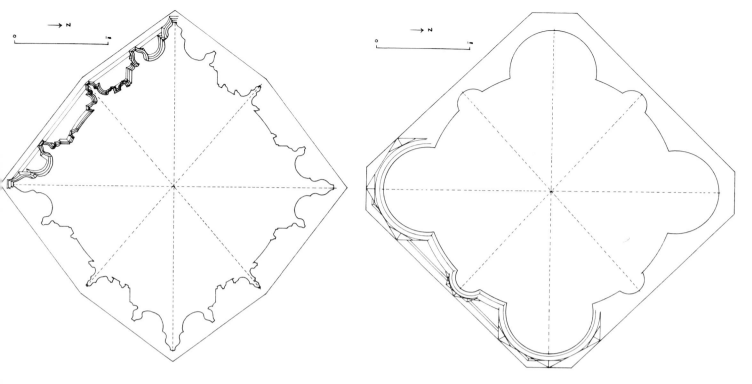

11. Interior of nave, section of pier B 1

12. Interior of nave, section of pier E 1

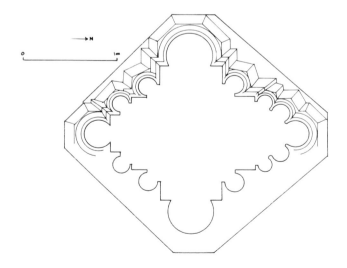

13. Interior of nave, section of pier D 2

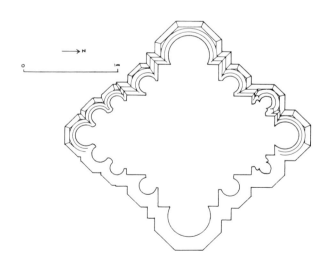

14. Interior of nave, section of pier C 5

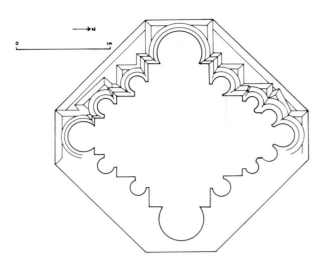

15. Interior of nave, section of pier D 5

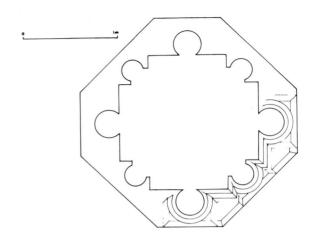

16. Interior of nave, section of pier E 5

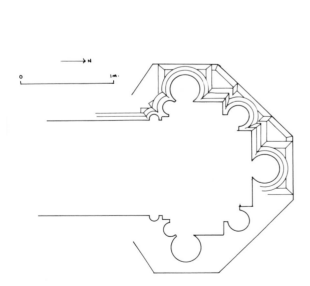

17. Interior of nave, section of pier F 5

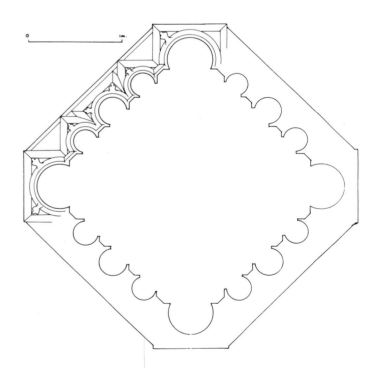

18. Interior of nave, section of pier C 6
(crossing)

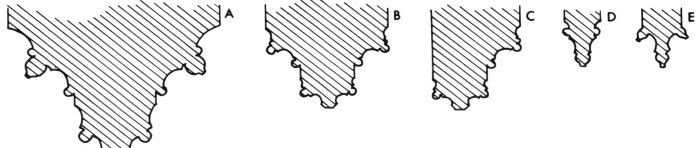

19. Interior of nave, arch and rib profiles
    a) Main arcade, bay 5–6
    b) Aisle, transverse arch, bay 5–6
    c) Lateral chapel, bay 5–6
    d) Diagonal rib, bay 5–6
    e) Diagonal rib, west end of the nave

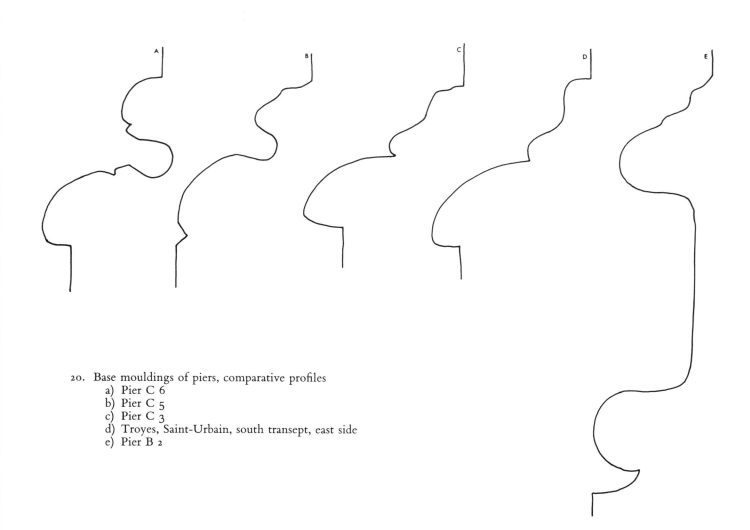

20. Base mouldings of piers, comparative profiles
    a) Pier C 6
    b) Pier C 5
    c) Pier C 3
    d) Troyes, Saint-Urbain, south transept, east side
    e) Pier B 2

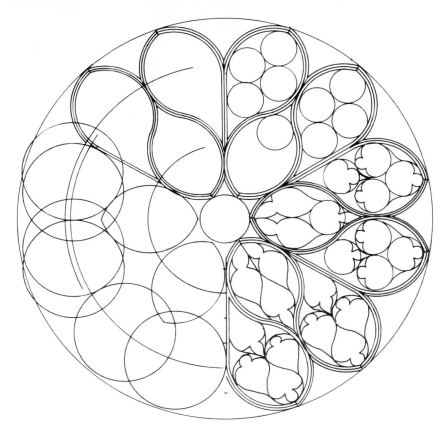

21. Design for a rose window of the type
employed by Martin Chambiges

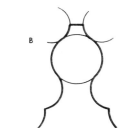

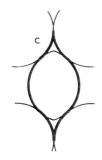

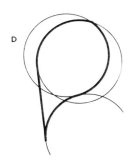

22. Elements of the design vocabulary of Late Gothic
a) Ogee
b) Fillet
c) Soufflet
d) Mouchette
e) Rotated or inscribed squares
f) Inscribed hexagons

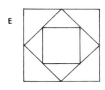

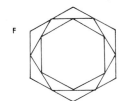

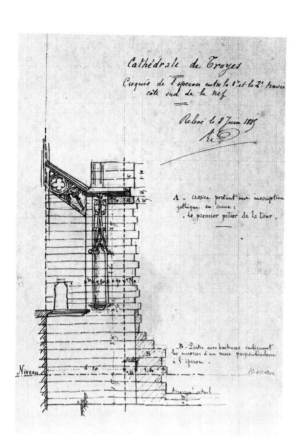

23. Restoration drawing of the spur
at D E 1 by the architect Selmersheim, 1889

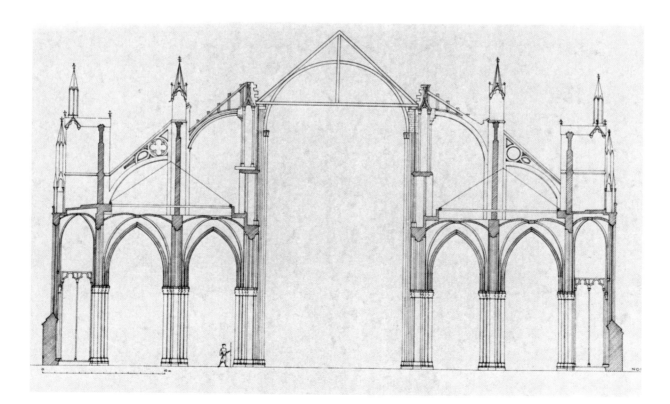

24. The nave in its provisional state, 1390–1450, section

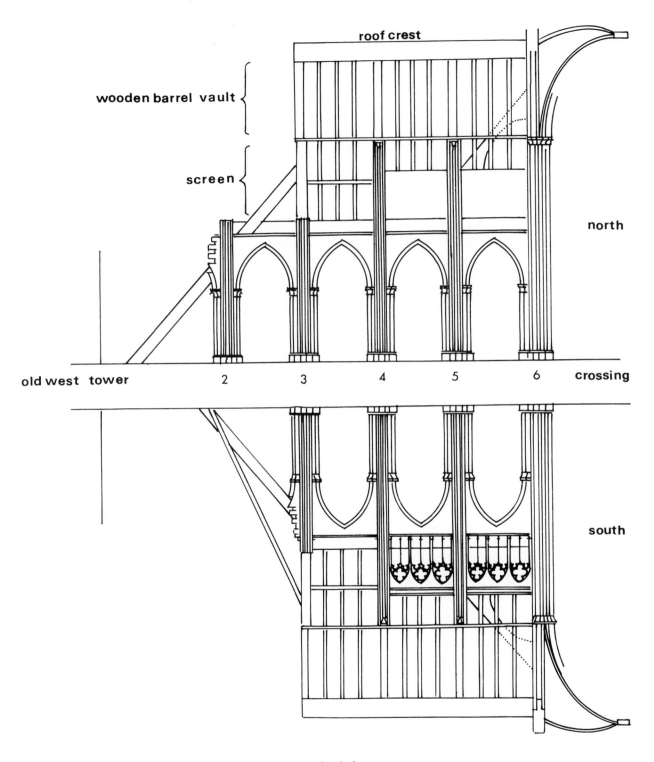

wooden barrel vault

screen

roof crest

north

old west tower

2   3   4   5   6   crossing

south

25. The nave in its provisional state, 1390–1450, longitudinal elevation

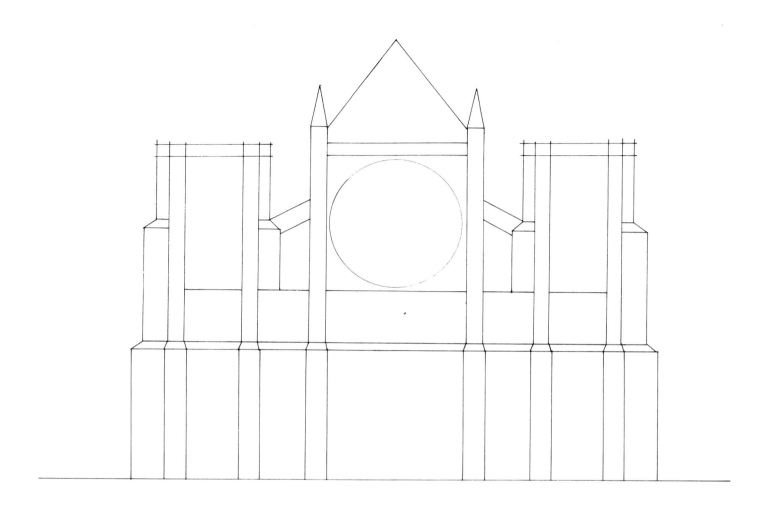

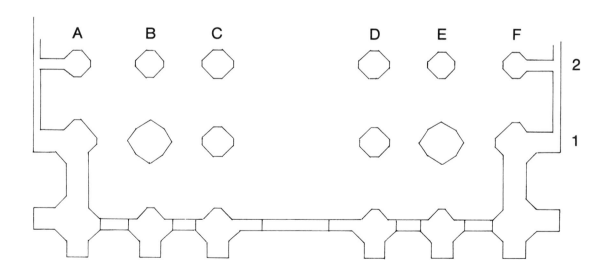

26. Master Bleuet's plan for the west façade

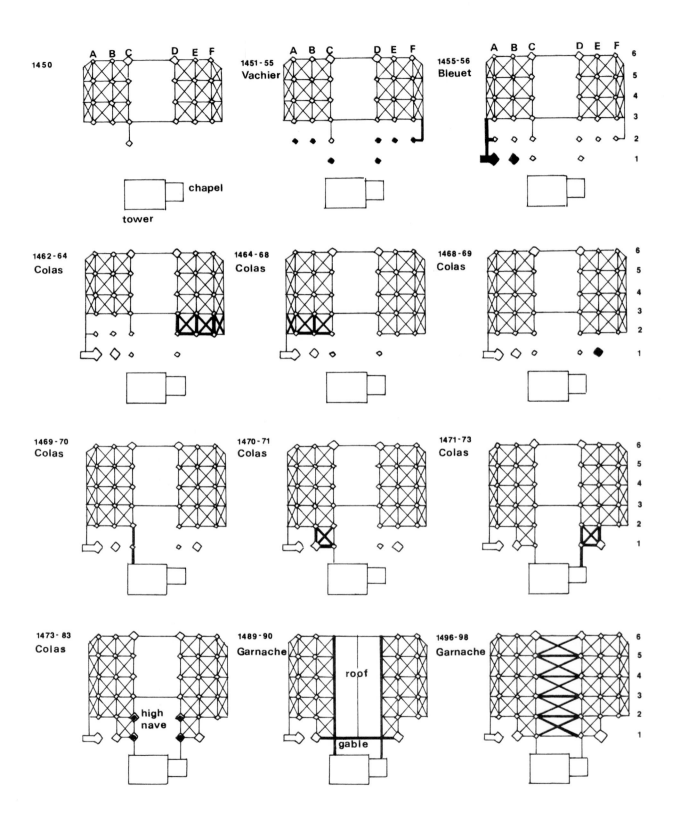

27. Nave, campaigns of construction, 1450–1500

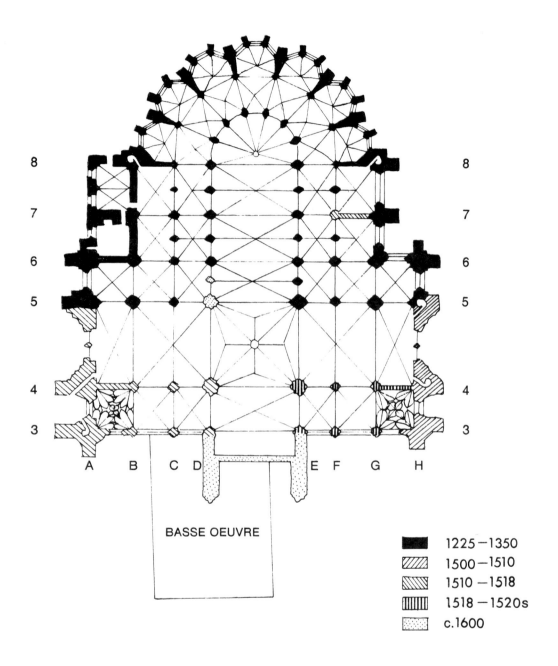

8   8

7   7

6   6

5   5

4   4

3   3

A   B   C D   E   F   G   H

BASSE OEUVRE

■■■   1225–1350
▨   1500–1510
▧   1510–1518
▥   1518–1520s
▦   c.1600

28. Beauvais Cathedral, chronology of the transepts

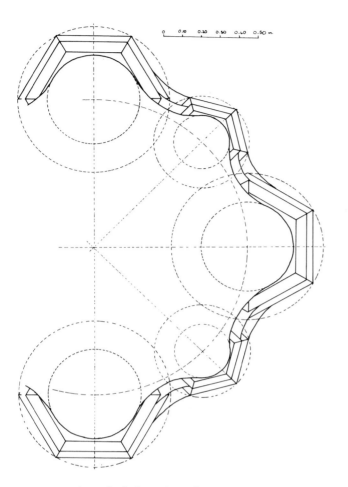

29. Beauvais Cathedral, section of
smaller pier type in transept

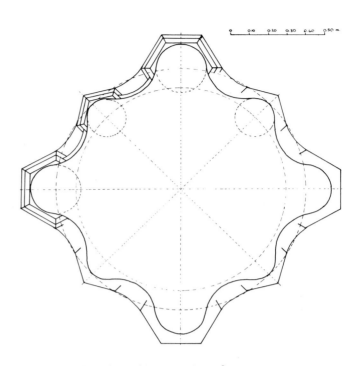

31. Beauvais, Saint-Etienne, section of
pier in main arcade of choir

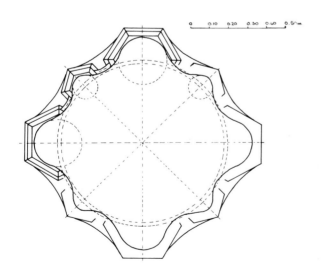

30. Beauvais, Saint-Etienne, section of
pier in choir aisle

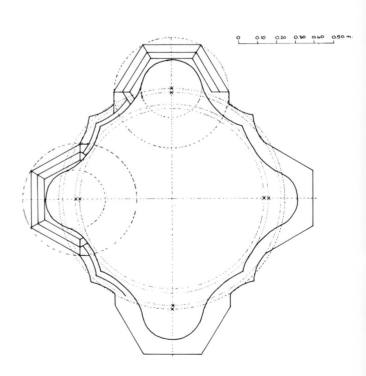

32. Senlis Cathedral, section of sixteenth-century pier in transept

33. Nineteenth-century lithograph of the cathedral, C. Fichot
(photograph by M. Vuillemin)

34. West façade (M. Vuillemin)

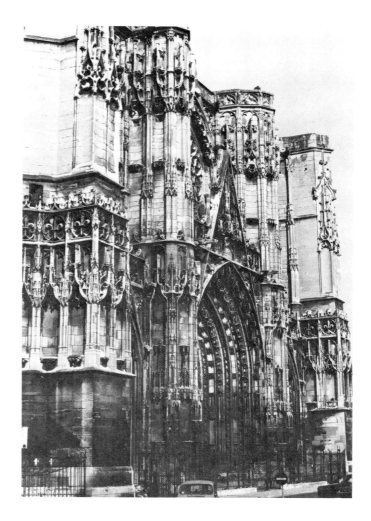

35. West façade, oblique view

36. West façade, center portal, embrasures and jambs

37. Nave, north side, looking east

38. Troyes, Vauluisant Museum, cork model of the cathedral

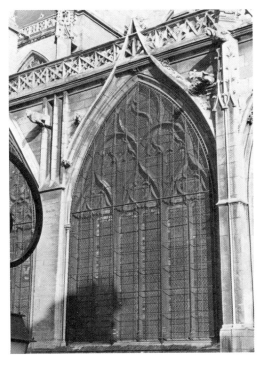

39. Chapel N 4, by Anthoine Colas, c. 1456

40. Nave, south side, tracery of chapel S 4, by Anthoine Colas, c. 1456

41. Nave, north side, three eastern lateral chapels, N 1–3, completed early fourteenth century

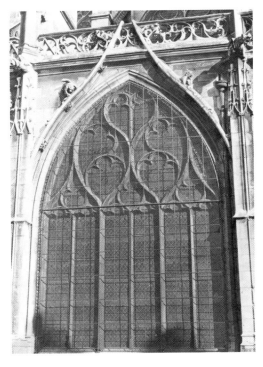

42. Chapel N 5, by the workshop of Chambiges, c. 1521

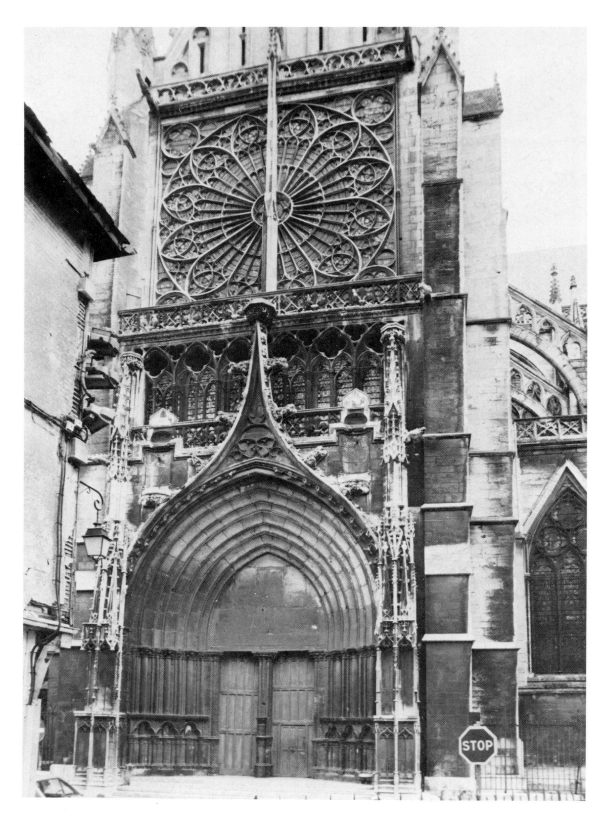

43. North transept façade, begun c. 1210–1220; rose c. 1400; decorative
buttresses and ogee arch by Anthoine Colas, 1462–1463

44. General view of roof of nave and transept, showing flying buttresses

45. General view of upper nave, south side

46. Upper nave, west gable by Jehançon Garnache, 1492

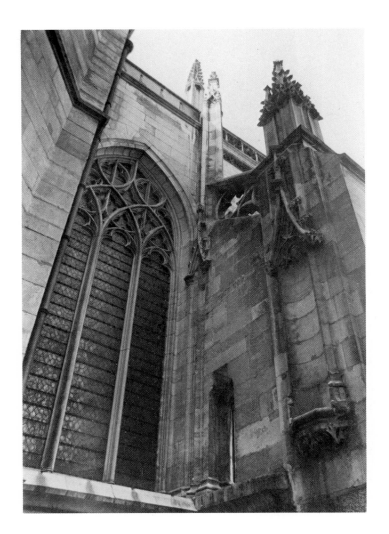

47. Upper nave, south side, spur at D E 1 by Anthoine Colas and Jehançon Garnache, completed 1492, restored by Selmersheim, 1889

48. Upper nave, south side, general view of flyers, looking east

49. Upper nave, north side, view of flyers and clerestory, looking east

50. Upper nave, north side, upper flyer at B C 2 by Jehançon
Garnache, 1492–1493, abutting pier by Anthoine Colas, 1470s

51. Upper nave, south side, upper flyer at D E 2 by Jehançon
Garnache, 1493–1494, abutting pier by Anthoine Colas, 1470s

52. Upper nave, north side, pier C 4
   b) Upper part
   a) Lower part

53. Upper nave, south side, pier D 4
   b) Upper part
   a) Lower part

54. Upper nave, north side, outer upright of flying buttress at A 5, detail of attached pinnacle

55. Upper nave, north side, flying buttress at A B C 5
   b) Upper flyer (*top photo*)
   a) General view

56. Upper nave, north side, pier C 5
    b) Upper part
    a) Lower part

57. Upper nave, south side, pier D 5
    b) Upper part
    a) Lower part

58. Upper nave, south side, flying
buttress at D E F 5
  b) Upper flyer
  a) General view, showing
     change in inclination in
     upper flyer

60. Upper nave, south side, clerestory window at D 1 2 by Jehançon Garnache, 1498–1499, type A

62. Upper nave, south side, clerestory window at D 5 6 by Jehançon Garnache, 1497–1498, type C

59. Upper nave, north side, clerestory window at C 3 4 by Jehançon Garnache, 1499–1500, type A

61. Upper nave, north side, clerestory window at C 2 3 by Jehançon Garnache, 1499–1500, type B

63. Upper transept, west side of north arm, flyer at B 5 6

64. Opposite: Interior, general
view looking east
(M. Vuillemin)

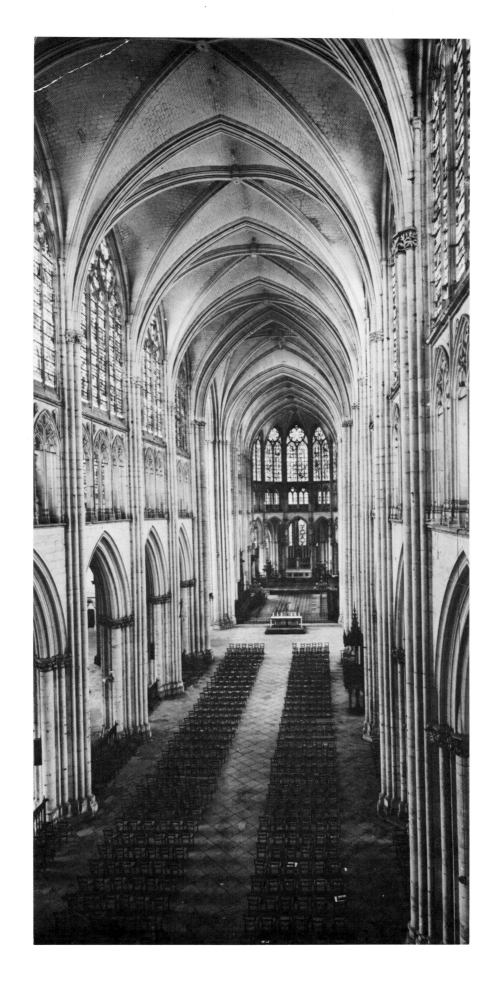

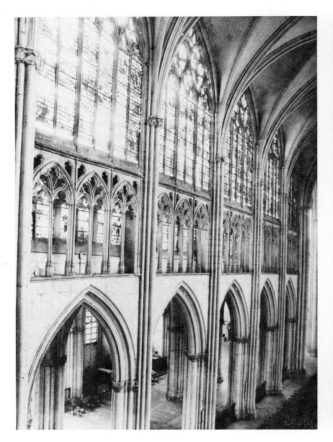 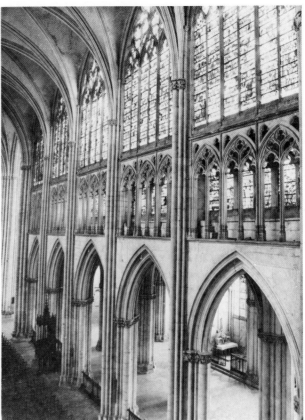

65. Interior nave, north side, looking east   66. Interior nave, south side, looking east

67. Opposite: Interior, eastern bays
of nave; crossing and choir
(Courtauld Institute)

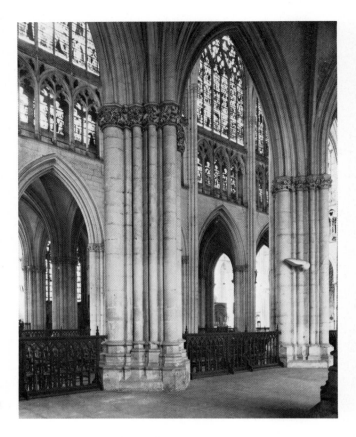

68. Interior, eastern bays of nave seen from south nave aisle (Courtauld Institute)

69. Interior, eastern bays of nave seen from north nave aisle (Courtauld Institute)

70. Interior, eastern bays of nave and west side of south transept (Courtauld Institute)

71. Interior, west side of south transept

72. Interior, east side of north transept

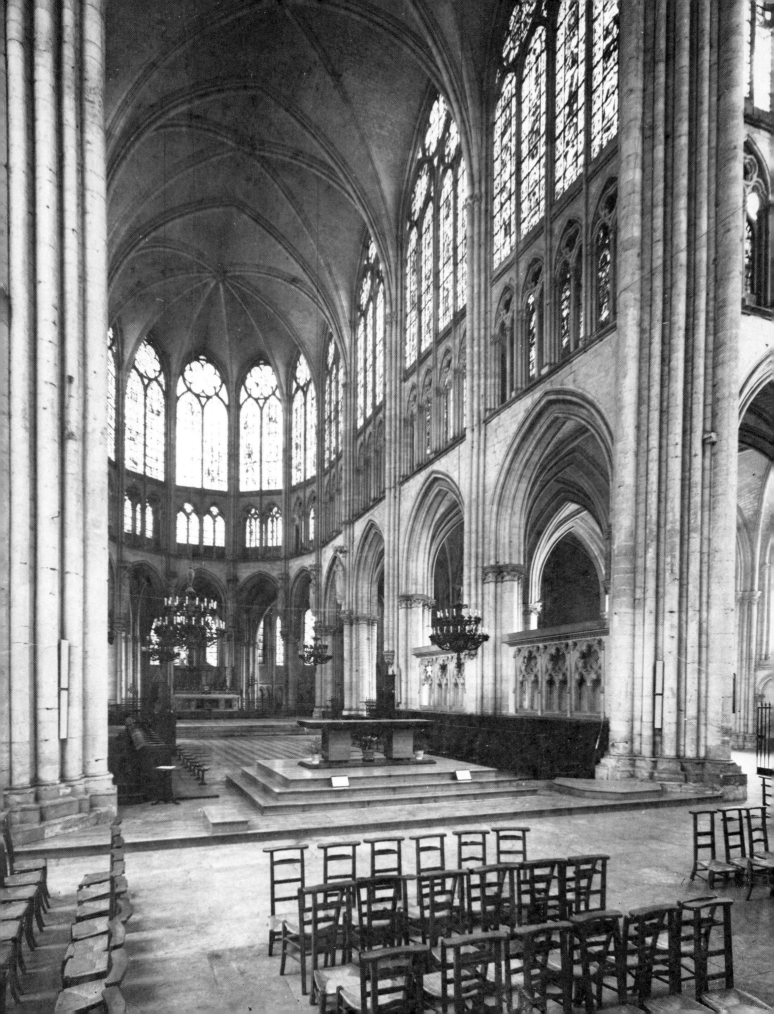

74. Interior, general view of northern
choir aisles looking east (Courtauld Institute)

75. Interior, general view of northern
nave aisles, looking east (Courtauld Institute)

76. Interior west towers, south side, free-standing
pier designed by Pierre Chambiges, 1530s

77. Interior nave, south aisles looking west showing junction with
west façade scheme

78. Interior nave, north aisles, pier
B 1, designed by Master
Bleuet, 1455, and constructed
by Anthoine Colas; capitals
by Colas

80. Interior nave, south aisles, pier E 1, designed and constructed by Anthoine Colas,
after 1468

79. Interior nave, base of pier C 1, designed
and constructed by Jaquet le Vachier,
1452–1453

81. Interior nave, south aisles,
base of pier D 2, designed and
constructed by Jaquet le Vachier, 1452–1453

82. Interior nave, southern
    lateral chapel S 4, south-
    west corner, chapel de-
    signed and constructed by
    Jaquet le Vachier, c. 1452–
    1453

83. Interior nave, northern
    lateral chapel N 2, lower
    wall, early fourteenth
    century

84. Interior nave, south arcade,
    base of pier C 5, c. 1270s,
    by "the Saint-Urbain Mas-
    ter"

85. Left: Interior nave, north aisles, pier C 1, showing capital, arches, and vault by Anthoine Colas, late 1450s to early 1470s

86. Below: Interior nave, south arcade, pier D 1, capital probably begun by itinerant Flemish artist and finished by Anthoine Colas, 1455–1456

87. Left: Interior nave, northern lateral chapel N 4, east end of arch in the chapel mouth, showing corbel added by Anthoine Colas to accommodate inner mouldings of the arch

88. Above: Interior nave, north arcade, capital of pier C 2, 1370s

89. Interior nave, south arcade, capital of
pier D 2, by Anthoine Colas, 1450s

90. Interior nave, south aisles, pier E 2
from the east, pier and capital by Jaquet
le Vachier, early 1450s, vaults by Anthoine Colas, early 1460s

91. Interior nave, south aisles, pier F 2
and chapel wall from the east. Pier,
capital and vault springers by Jaquet le
Vachier, early 1450s, vaults by Anthoine
Colas, early 1460s

92. Interior nave, north aisles, pier and
capital at A 4, early fourteenth century

93. Interior nave, detail of triforium on north side, bay C 1 2 (left)
and C 2 3 (right) by Anthoine Colas and Jehançon Garnache,
1470s to 1490s

94. Interior nave, capitals of high vault of central vessel

a) C 1, by Anthoine Colas, 1470s
c) C 2, by Anthoine Colas, 1470s
e) C 3, by Jehançon Garnache, 1485

b) D 1, by Anthoine Colas, 1470s
d) D 2, by Anthoine Colas, 1470s
f) D 3, by Jaquet le Vachier, 1483–1484

94. Interior nave, capitals of high vault of central vessel

g) C 4, c. 1360s–1370s   h) D 4, c. 1360s
i) C 5, c. 1340s–1350s   j) D 5, c. 1340s–1350s
k) C 6, early fourteenth century

95. Above left: Interior nave, upper
    north side, high capital at C 1 with
    springer placed for diagonal rib by
    Colas but discontinued by Garnache

96. Above right: Interior nave, upper
    south side, high vault springers at D
    4, showing dislocation in window
    mouldings

97. Left: Interior nave, general view
    of the high vaults installed by Je-
    hançon Garnache, 1496–1498

98. Beauvais Cathedral, exterior of south transept façade, lower
parts (to balustrade under the rose) by Martin Chambiges, 1500–
1532, upper parts 1540s–1550s

99. Top left: Beauvais Cathedral, interior of north transept, general view, looking east

100. Top right: Beauvais Cathedral, interior of north transept, base of pier C 4, by Martin Chambiges, soon after 1510

101. Left: Beauvais Cathedral, interior of north transept, chapel vault, soon before 1517

102. Bottom right: Beauvais Cathedral, interior of south transept, chapel vault, c. 1520s

103. Beauvais, Saint-Etienne, interior choir, south elevation

105. Beauvais, Saint-Etienne, interior of sepulchre chapel
to north of choir (present baptismal chapel), detail of
vault

104. Beauvais, Saint-Etienne, interior
choir, north aisles, pier base

106. Melun, Saint-Aspais, exterior of choir, east end, portal
(Arch. phot./S.P.A.D.E.M., Paris/V.A.G.A., New
York, 1986)

107. Paris, Ecole des Beaux Arts, fragment from the Hôtel
le Gendre

108. Paris, Notre-Dame, interior choir, south aisles, pier
base, c. 1300

109. Paris, Saint-Germain l'Auxerrois, interior of west porch, northern bay

110. Paris, SS. Gervais and Protais, interior
choir, general view

111. Paris, Saint-Jacques de la Boucherie,
tower

112. Paris, Saint-Merry, interior nave, west end, pier base

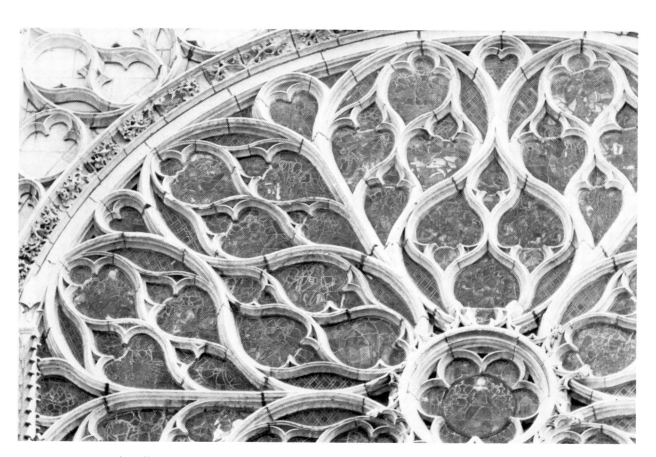

113. Paris, Sainte-Chapelle, exterior west façade, detail of rose window

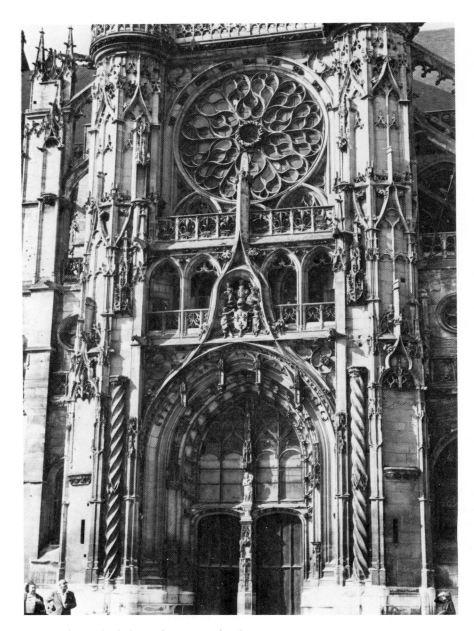

114. Senlis Cathedral, south transept façade

115. Senlis Cathedral, interior south transept, pier base by Pierre Chambiges

116. Sens Cathedral, north transept façade, by Martin Chambiges and
Huges Cuvelier, first decades 16th century

117. Sens Cathedral, south transept façade, begun late 13th century,
completed by Martin Chambiges and Huges Cuvelier, 1489–c. 1500

118. Troyes, Saint-Jean au Marché, north side of choir

119. Troyes, Saint-Urbain, choir, detail of pier base

120. Troyes, Saint-Urbain, choir

IV
The Late Gothic Masters of the Nave, 1450–1502

NGLISH TROOPS HAD BEEN EXPELLED from French soil by the middle of the fifteenth century. Economic recovery was by no means rapid, however, and the reign of Louis XI (1461–1483) saw continuing struggles between the monarch and his over-mighty subjects, crushing taxation, and open warfare.

Despite this, the city of Troyes was steadily regaining its population and economic strength. The bishops of Troyes in this period (Louis Raguier, 1450–1483, and his nephew Jacques Raguier, 1483–1518) enjoyed royal support and patronage. Louis Raguier, who had been a canon of Notre-Dame of Paris, became president of *Cour des Aides* in 1465.[1] During the hostilities between Louis XI and Charles the Rash, Duke of Burgundy (1470–1474), the city of Troyes was, of course, heavily taxed, and it also served as a center for the royal forces. Some inhabitants, unable to meet the demands of taxation, quit the city, but we cannot compare the experience of the 1470s to that of the 1420s or the 1350s and 1360s. By the 1480s the tide of prosperity had turned, and we find the population and wealth growing at a remarkable rate. The city is estimated as having had over 10,000 inhabitants in the thirteenth century, dropping to 6,000 by 1406, then increasing to 12,000 (1474) and 23,083 (1504).[2] Not only was the population growing, but so also were fortunes of the great Troyes families of the late Middle

Ages, families whose patronage is witnessed by many a church window (the Molé, Hennequin, Dorigny, Huyard, Mesgriny, etc.).[3]

Despite the rapid growth of local population and wealth, however, resumption of major campaigns of construction on the cathedral was only possible through external patronage: a general pardon was declared by Pope Nicholas V for all those contributing to the fabric fund (B, 1451, 1452). This pardon, renewed over several terms, provided the major source for the fabric in the two decades after 1450. One quarter of each year's income from this source was given over to the Apostolic Chamber.[4] The total income from this source in the "receipt of the general pardon" for 1451–52 amounted to 876 pounds, a sum which was considerably higher than all of the other items of receipt for this year added together. By 1462–63 income from the general pardon had begun to diminish, standing at less than half of the total receipt of the fabric. The last account in which income from this source is recorded is that for 1470–71, when it provided 37 percent of the total income.

Relations with the papacy were troubled in these years by a series of moves designed to reduce papal control of the French Church. By the Pragmatic Sanction of Bourges (1438) Charles VII had sought to restrict the papal rights of provision, appellate jurisdiction and taxation. Louis XI continued this policy with the support of Bishop Louis Raguier and other leading ecclesiastics of the diocese. At the Gallican council of Orléans (1478) the city of Troyes was well represented.[5]

We also find to our surprise that due to an incredible oversight the portion of the money which should have been paid to the Apostolic Chamber had been left in the upper treasury of the cathedral, from whence it had been stolen (B, 1476–77, 1). Given this kind of laxness on the part of the chapter in making their payments, it is hardly surprising that the general pardon which lapsed in 1470–71 was not renewed by the papacy. The cessation of this source of income had a profound impact upon the construction campaign. Because of lack of funds, the master mason of the workshop was forced to resort to makeshift devices that would cause immense difficulties for the future.[6]

Our analysis of the income of the fabric in 1472–73 reveals the extent of the funding crisis (Appendix C). At the point of time when work was beginning on the upper nave the total receipt was only 482 pounds: this low sum is explained partly by the diminished receipts under all of the regular items (including quests inside the diocese which produced only 96 pounds this year as opposed to sums of well over 100 pounds raised in years such as 1412–13) and partly by the absence of any outside patronage. Under the heading *ordinaire* is recorded a total of 94 pounds: this relatively large sum reflects a growing desire to funnel annual income from rents on houses and land into the fabric fund. The decline in income in these years is accompanied by a decline in the standards of account-keeping.

In 1479–80 a new library was begun at the instigation of the now aging bishop, Louis Raguier, who made a special contribution of 167 pounds to the fabric.[7]

The fabric account for 1482–83 is much more methodical in its presentation and records a considerable amount of work. This revival of initiative may reflect the addition of Jacques Raguier as coadjutor to his aging uncle; it may also reflect the increased financial involvement of Louis Raguier in the fabric, to which he made a contribution of 250 pounds in this year.[8] A considerable amount of money was spent in repairing the provisional roof and lateral screens of the central nave, including the installation of new glass into the windows of the lateral screens. This must indicate that hopes of a rapid completion of the upper nave had lapsed once again.

Through the 1480s income steadily increased, owing above all to the dramatic increase in receipts from rented property, which in some years now supplanted the income from quests inside the diocese as the largest single item of income. Various substantial gifts were also made by individuals in the 1480s: canon Nicholas Tetel (166 pounds in 1484–85), Louis Raguier, the former bishop (574 pounds in 1486–87, 124 pounds in 1487–88, 493 pounds in 1488–89), Jaques Raguier (399 pounds in 1489–90). There is no bishop in the documented history of the cathedral who contributed more to the fabric than Louis Raguier.

Analysis of receipts given for 1491–92 (Appendix C) reveals several important changes. Income from quests inside the diocese has picked up well, and exceeds income from rented property, although this too is at a high level. A new confraternity has been formed in the city, devoted to raising funds for the construction of the cathedral, and the people of Troyes also made a significant contribution directly to the fabric. Despite all this effort the expense still exceeded the income, as it generally did in the 1490s.[9]

In the year 1498–99 five windows were installed in the upper nave (see analysis of receipts in Appendix C). By far the largest item of income for the fabric is now the *recepte ordinaire*, or income from rented property, notably the *logettes*, small houses which had been built by the fabric of the cathedral alongside its northern flank. In the work on the upper nave in this period we sense a certain urgency to get the job finished: one project was often begun before the last one had been completed. This speed was only possible in the financially confident atmosphere of Troyes of the 1490s. The growing resources of the fabric were to lead the bishop and chapter to look beyond the provincial master masons of Troyes for a great architect capable of undertaking the construction of the west façade.[10]

As we turn from the economic and historical background lying behind the Late Gothic campaigns of completion on the nave to the identity of the master masons, we should remind ourselves of some of the problems faced by the clergy and workshop. For a period of more than sixty years, the nave had been maintained in a provisional state, with a low-level roof and lateral screens closing in the sides (Figs. 24 & 25). The effects of high winds upon the considerable expanse of these lateral screens of the upper nave would certainly have led to difficulties, and eventually it seems that the lower windows (triforium level) in the screens were suppressed in favor of a lean-to roof over the inner aisles, leaving a nave interior

The Late Gothic Masters of the Nave, 1450–1502

which would have been dark and aesthetically unsatisfactory (B, 1438–39, 2). At any given point, when expensive repairs became necessary, it is certain that the *proviseurs* of the cathedral fabric must have asked themselves whether they might not be better advised to invest their money into the completion of the building, rather than continuing to maintain roofs and screens which would have to be demolished as soon as the work of completion was undertaken.

In embarking upon new campaigns of construction at a time when no living person could remember the last major new work on the nave (the foundation of pier C 2 in the 1370s), the bishop and chapter obviously faced a problem in finding a master mason able to direct the work. Few major ecclesiastical building projects had been undertaken in the city of Troyes for more than a century, and there was a distinct shortage of local talent. We should not underestimate the problems faced by the master of the cathedral workshop. Where to begin? The initial attempt to construct the nave in the early fourteenth century had envisaged the project in terms of vertical slices: one bay at a time, brought right up to the high vaults, with the adjacent bay brought up to a lower level to provide support. At least two bays had been vaulted before 1389, when they collapsed. Should the work be continued in this fashion? Should the old provisional roof be demolished to make way for the vaults over the eastern bays of the nave? Or would it be better to go on founding new piers and constructing aisle vaults at the west end of the unfinished nave until the entire lower structure was complete, thus tackling the problem more in terms of horizontal levels?

Another major problem to be faced was the stylistic one. The last work on the lower nave was hopelessly out of date in its design. Should the Late Gothic masters of the nave go on reproducing these outdated forms, or should they break the unity of the existing building by continuing the process of invention and innovation that had characterized the development of High Gothic and Rayonnant style? Incidentally, this last problem has given Late Gothic master masons a "bad press" with modern critics whichever solution they have adopted: they are either blasted for being sterile and uninventive, or for having destroyed the unity of the building with new forms which are no longer "valid."[11]

The Late Gothic masters of the nave were conservative in that they respected the general spatial economy of the cathedral, as dictated by the earlier parts of the building. Their distinctive contribution was the use of a more complex type of pier base with greater height and mouldings that flare outward like the bell of a trumpet; of sharpened moulding forms generally termed "fillets";[12] of capitals with foliage wrapped around rather than springing out of the body; and of window tracery whose flowing lines and flickering patterns have given art historians their label for this style: Flamboyant. Although the texts allow us to distinguish the work of four named master masons in this period, three of them worked in the same general spirit, which can be recognized as the fifth of the seven visions embodied in the architecture of Troyes Cathedral. However, one of our four masters (Bleuet, active in 1455–56) was a revolutionary who favored a completely new approach to the design of piers. We therefore assign to Master Bleuet the sixth position in our succession.

The correlation of the written sources with the evidence of the building itself will allow us to gain an extraordinarily precise understanding of the contribution of each of our four masters to the completion of the nave. The sequence of drawings in Figure 27 provides an overview of the situation; we will now proceed to a more detailed look at each master.

Jaquet le Vachier, 1451–1455

The text of the general pardon of 1452 and the account and *manuel* for the fabric in the following year suffice to show that the new work was commenced with the founding of five piers, the first one of which was the pier beside the well, pier D 2 in the south arcade of the nave.[13] No single architect or master mason was named as master of the workshop, but the name of Jaquet le Vachier heads the lists of masons employed by the fabric (B, 1451–52, 6), and it seems significant that Jaquet, and not Jehan Chevallier or any of the other masons, carried the "false templates" ("false" because they were made of paper) for the work on the piers to the quarry (B, 1452–53, 3) and that his name heads the list of masons involved in cutting stone for the base of pier D 2.

The pier in question is a copy of the other piers of the nave arcade: only its base has been modernized (Figs. 13 & 81). The total height of the base has been significantly increased and the mouldings used are of the characteristically tall Flamboyant type with two projecting rounded rims separated by a flat surface. The lower rim of the moulding is a little like the bell of a trumpet. For the first time in Troyes Cathedral we find the hexagon being used in the design of the plinths of the smaller shafts of the pier. Octagons are used for the larger shafts for the transverse arches. The difference between the angles of 135 degrees (for the octagons) and 120 degrees (for the hexagons) produces a variety of planes which might appear to critics of Late Gothic as confused. It is certainly true that the problem of fitting together the different types of polygon has in some cases been too much for Jaquet. In the earliest pier founded (D 2) the octagonal plinths of the larger shafts are not aligned with the main plinth of the pier in a very satisfactory manner, and several other easily noticeable misalignments occur in the placing of the stones.

Nevertheless the base in question has a certain quality of energy and plasticity which makes the bases of the earlier nave piers even seem a little dry and flat beside it. Of particular value is the possibility for defining the less important role of the minor shafts by placing their bases somewhat higher than the bases from the main shaft.

In addition to the five piers mentioned in the text of the general pardon, two other piers may be associated with this campaign and with the work of Jaquet le

65

Vachier: the last two piers of the central vessel of the nave, C 1 and D 1 (Fig. 79). The type of base used is the same, and was certainly designed by Jaquet (B, 1455, 1).

Texts from the period of Jaquet le Vachier also speak of chapels: rubble is purchased for the foundation of the walls of the two chapels "at the ends" (B, 1452–53, *Manuel*, 5). The stylistic evidence allows us to associate one chapel with the work of Jaquet le Vachier with a considerable degree of certainty: the fourth chapel on the south side. The pillar to the west of the opening into the chapel is documented as having been founded in these years (B, 1452–53, 6), and the type of moulding and base used in this pier, and in the other piers of Jaquet, continues around the lower parts of the chapel wall (Fig. 82). Jaquet le Vachier's chapel provided for a bench, like that existing in the older chapels, on top of which sit the bases to receive the shafts which run up into the window mullions, or into the blind panelling attached to the western wall of the chapel. The mouldings are of the same type as those of the piers of Jaquet, and the plinths bear witness to a play on the nature of three different kinds of polygon: the hexagon, the square, and the octagon. In the plinths for the attached shafts for the panelling on the western wall of the chapel and the smaller plinths for the window mullions a hexagon sits directly on top of a square, whereas in the plinths for the larger window mullions the hexagonal upper part of the moulding merges directly into an octagon.

In attempting to define the extent (height) of Jaquet le Vachier's work in the aisle bays and chapel of bay 2–3 on the south side, we are aided by the very firm textual dating of the aisle vaults in these bays to 1462–64, when they were constructed by master Anthoine Colas. Thus we know that Vachier did not remain master of the workshop for long enough to construct the vaults, and we are prompted to look for the signs of the change of identity of the master mason at a point below the springing of the ribs and arches of the vaults. Such evidence exists in the form of a clear break in the springers of the diagonal ribs placed over piers F 2 and E 2 (Figs. 90 & 91). Springers with massive cylindrical bodies have been placed, but Anthoine Colas, the master who built these vaults, has decided to adopt a rib profile of a very conservative type: a central fillet flanked by two rounded rolls in order to join his springers directly on to the stones already placed for the diagonals over piers D 3, E 3, and F 3 in the campaigns around 1300.

This demarkation between the work of Vachier and Colas enables us to attribute four capitals in the southern aisle bays and chapel to the former master's workshop: the small capital in the southwest angle of the chapel at S 4, the matching capital in the adjacent chapel to the west; the capital of the pier dividing the chapels at F 2, and the capital of the pier between the aisles at E 2 (Figs. 90 & 91). The small capital in the chapel S 4 is remarkably conservative, with sprigs of finely chiselled plantagenet (looking rather like luffa sponge) springing directly from the body of the capital. It would be tempting to view this as a reused capital, but the low, simple abacus is clearly fifteenth century in date. The capital of the

66

pier between the chapels (F 2) has rather roughly chiselled, generously proportioned cabbage leaves wrapped around the body of the capital in the approved Late Gothic fashion, accompanied by other types of foliage: a small finely crinkled leaf and a plant bearing fruits like small artichokes (Fig. 91). The capitals of both the aisle pier E 2 and the corner shaft of the last chapel feature the roughly chiselled, rather fleshy leaves of cabbage already described (Fig. 90). The stems of the leaves, which have a squarish section, assume particular importance and in some cases they interlock to give a vigorous linear undulation.

We are left with the impression that Vachier was something of a traditionalist, content to copy and adapt the formulae presented by the existing bays of the nave aisles. His introduction of the hexagon into the vocabulary of pier base design in the Troyes Cathedral workshop is significant, but it must again be emphasized that the hexagonal plinth with trumpet bell mouldings was nothing new in Gothic design, having been used for over two hundred years in more progressive workshops. His capitals (except for the small capital in chapel S 4) have the Late Gothic characteristic of leaves wrapped around the body of the capital rather than springing out from it, but the quality of the sculpture is mediocre. In 1455 an itinerant journeyman was brought in to help carve capitals (B, 1455, 5), and Anthoine Colas, the next master of the workshop engaged in 1456, was hired primarily as a carver of capitals (B, 1456, 7).

The texts indicate that when work had been completed on the piers of the south aisles, it was intended to found the great tower-supporting pier at B 1 (B, 1455, 2). The foundation of the pier B 1 demanded special structural expertise in view of its role as a tower supporting pier, and Vachier was clearly incapable of resolving such a problem. An appeal was therefore made to an outside master, one Bleuet, master mason of Reims Cathedral, who also worked at Notre-Dame-de-l'Epine near Châlons-sur-Marne.[14] After a general trip to visit and inspect west façades, Bleuet devised a plan or *portrait* of the frontispiece for Troyes Cathedral, and introduced a colleague into the workshop at Troyes: Anthoine Colas. Colas' immediate role was as a carver of capitals, but he subsequently took over the role of resident executor of Bleuet's plan for the frontispiece and Jaquet le Vachier, rather than assume a subordinate position, withdrew from the workshop (B, 1455–56).

Master Bleuet, 1455–1456[15]

Master Bleuet's plan for the western frontispiece of Troyes Cathedral was not completed, although we will see that it is possible to reconstruct his intentions. Bleuet formulated the plans for the first parts of the frontispiece to have been erected, namely two tower-supporting piers on the north side (B, 1456, 4 & 9 & 10). One of these piers was subsequently demolished (pier A 1, in 1508–9), but the other pier (B 1) can still be seen today, although the present plan for the frontis-

67

piece does not involve towers in the same location envisaged by Bleuet, and the tower-supporting potential of this pier is now redundant.

Pier B 1 rests upon an eight-sided plinth with a shape resembling a lozenge (Figs. 11 & 78). Its overall dimensions are similar to those of the piers of the transept crossing of the cathedral (Fig. 18). The surface of the pier consists of multiple fillet mouldings. The designer was thinking in terms of a system of continuous mouldings, which allows each fillet of the transverse arches and ribs of the vault to continue down unbroken into the pier. Since the sharp-nosed fillet moulding is the main form used, and the fillet has three times more concave than convex shapes (Fig. 22), the result is highly linear and brittle. A High Gothic pier was designed essentially from the inside. Any kind of round shaft has obviously been formed by a circle with a center point within the mass of that shaft. The concave forms of the fillet mouldings favored by Late Gothic designers, on the other hand, are formed by arcs of circles whose center points lie outside the mass of the masonry, in the surrounding space. This system of design from within and outside the unit lends to Bleuet's pier a general similarity with Flamboyant tracery design, since ogees, soufflets, and mouchettes result from the placing of the point of the compass outside as well as inside the unit. Thus Master Bleuet's pier must be seen in the general context of the Late Gothic search for uniformity in design procedures and uniformity of optical effect. The absence of capitals and the continuation of mouldings directly into ribs and arches have to do with another kind of unity: between the supporting member and the elements being supported.

The form of pier B 1 is significant in another way: being a very thick pier, it was obviously intended to support the corner of a tower. Thus Master Bleuet, in addition to being something of a revolutionary in terms of design, also has the distinction of being the master mason who directed work on the commencement of the western towers.

We also find Master Bleuet's design principles apparent in the lower wall of chapel N 4, where sharp square-nosed fillets are employed rather than rounded colonnettes. These fillets are received on top of base mouldings and plinths which are neither octagonal nor hexagonal, but which simply echo the profile of the fillet itself. The profile of the shaft used in the northwestern angle of the chapel, which receives the diagonal rib of the vault, is of the same type, and it continues on up into the rib unbroken by the presence of a capital.

The significance of the work of Master Bleuet in the sequence of campaigns on the nave is immense. Here for the first time we find an artist who broke the tradition established by his predecessors. He allowed his supporting members (the attached shafts) to assume the same form as the elements which are being supported: in other words he completed the revolution heralded by the "Saint-Urbain master," who had constructed the two piers in the northern nave arcade (C 4 and C 5) and who had transformed rounded shafts into almond-shaped mouldings in response to changes which were affecting the form of the mouldings of transverse

68

arches and ribs. Master Bleuet is the first truly "Late Gothic" master mason of the Troyes Cathedral workshop.

Anthoine Colas, 1456–1483

The founding of the seven piers by Jaquet le Vachier and the commencement of the west frontispiece after the plan of Master Bleuet reveal a situation of financial confidence under the favorable conditions of a substantial annual income from the general pardon. Under Anthoine Colas, however, this income dwindled and disappeared, and progress was slowed by the diversion of attention from the new work in order to consolidate existing parts of the building.

Colas' first work was on the carving of capitals: on the basis of the textual and stylistic evidence we attribute capitals B 2, D 2, and C 1 to this artist (Figs. 85 & 89). Capital D 1 may have been partially cut by Colas (Fig. 86). This master's style is distinguished by a very fine sense of vegetable and animal forms, rendered in a vigorous, plastic manner. His undulating kale leaves with their crinkled edges constitute something of a signature. He favored the use of a chisel with a comb edge, which left the surfaces slightly rough, lending the work a somewhat "painterly" appearance.

From 1462 to 1464 we find Colas engaged in vaulting the two bays over the well: it has been seen that the well exists beside pier D 3, and therefore the bays in question are the two aisle vaults on the south side in Bay 2–3. However, Colas' attention was soon diverted by an urgent structural problem, namely the north transept façade. In order to arrest the rotational movement of this façade Anthoine Colas added two substantial buttresses linked over the portal by an ogee arch (Fig. 43). This is the work on the portal toward Saint-Nicholas mentioned in the account for this year (B, 1462–63, 3).

In order to avoid excessive projection into the road Colas has refrained from placing the buttresses against the existing buttresses of the façade, and instead has placed them directly against the wall. The principle was merely to add sufficient depth of masonry to the lower façade to eliminate the overhang. In a manner which is highly satisfactory to the eye, Colas has unified his buttresses with his consolidation of the rose by means of a continuation of the ogee arch of the portal up into the needle of stone which bisects the rose and helps support the weight of the passage over the rose.

Two stylistic features demand our special attention: the first is the general way in which the masses of masonry are articulated, and the second is the nature of the foliage decoration. A thirteenth century buttress was conceived essentially as a rectangular unit with flat sides and right-angled corners, progressively diminished in projection by weather-mouldings or *glacis* applied to its surfaces. However, the method of articulating the buttresses of the north transept portal is entirely different. In its lowest part each buttress consists of a square pilaster with two

69

tracery panels applied to each of the three exposed faces (Fig. 43). The divisions between these panels are then allowed to continue upward to become the divisions between diagonally placed niches with delicate canopies. The body of the buttress then continues upward as a square turned diagonally to the first square. In the upper parts of the buttress another turn of forty-five degrees is effected, producing a buttress with its sides aligned with the surfaces of the transept façade. The same system of rotated squares is also applied to the articulation of the needle running through the rose.

The principle of the rotated square is, of course, fairly universal in Late Gothic design (Fig. 22) and had already been used in the cathedral workshop in several different contexts.[16] A "premonition" of the idea of inscribed squares coupled with the use of diagonally placed niches can be found in the transept portals of the church of Saint-Urbain, Troyes, from after 1260.

A second noteworthy feature of Colas' style, as embodied in the north transept portal, is his prolific use of foliage decoration, especially the vigorously undulating yet delicately frilly cabbage leaves, which are often rendered with a certain sense of humor, as in the ogee arch over the portal (Fig. 43). Thus we find that two of the leaves springing out of the ogee arch of the portal serve a double function, to embellish the arch and to support the pedestals of the statue niches in the spandrels between the arch and the flanking buttresses; also that cabbage leaves have been liberally sprinkled along the top surface of the ogee, and that they are accompanied by two enormous snails. The quality of the sculpture is remarkable, and the documentation suggests that Colas himself was probably responsible.

While Colas was engaged in the work on the north transept façade his second-in-command, Jaquet de la Bouticle, worked on the vaults of the southern aisles in bay 2–3. In placing the ribs for the two aisle bays in question Colas and Bouticle faced a problem which must have been familiar to Gothic master masons. On the east sides of the bays the springers for the transverse arches and ribs had already been placed at the time of the earlier work on the eastern bays of the nave (c. 1300). The form of the diagonal springer anticipates a rib with a central fillet flanked by two rounded rolls. On the west side, however (with the exception of pier D 2), Jaquet le Vachier had placed springers for the diagonal ribs with a substantial rounded body, into which the mouldings disappear. Colas' diagonals, in continuing the forms determined by the early springers to the east of the bays, meet Jaquet le Vachier's diagonal springers with a considerable amount of dislocation (Figs. 90 & 91). Whereas in the main arcade of the nave in this bay Colas has been obliged for the sake of uniformity to continue the old-fashioned mouldings predetermined by the earlier campaigns, in the transverse arches of the aisles he has felt free to adopt a much more modern profile bristling with fillets and angles between concave surfaces.

The vaults themselves are of the simple quadripartite type, and might strike us as rather dull, although the delicate brightly painted keystones, now defaced, would have added interest. Purchases of earth for centering the vaults are recorded

70

at the time of construction, and the gently rounded concave forms of the severies confirm the notion that whereas the transverse arches and diagonal ribs have been centered over rigid wooden moulds, the severies have been constructed over heaps of earth, humped up to the desired shape on top of platforms on the scaffolding (B, 1463–64, 3). The texts relating to the construction of the nave high vaults confirm that this was the procedure followed.

The window tracery of the fourth chapel on the south side may also be attributed to Anthoine Colas (Fig. 40). In Flamboyant tracery design the formula of three soufflets in a pyramid over three ogee arches is something of a cliché, but Colas had added a touch of novelty in the elegant fleurs-de-lys enclosed in the soufflets. It was certainly a constant hope on the part of the bishop and chapter that royal patronage might be available to meet the costs of construction.

Having completed the vaults of the two aisle bays and chapel on south side, Colas then went on to undertake the same task on the north side during the years 1464–1468, a period for which no documentation exists. We find the now familiar Colas capital over pier B 2 between the north aisles.

Two features distinguish the work on the northern aisle bays and chapel from the matching work on the south. First, in the outer bay of the aisle (A B 2–3) Colas seems to have removed the diagonal springers placed on the east side of the bay (if, indeed, they had been put into position), and he was thus free to impose a much more modern profile on the diagonal ribs, in the form of a central fillet flanked by two flared fillets, rather than the rounded rolls used in the earlier vaults. The keystones of these bays have delicate tracery dominated by powerful sprigs of foliage which emerge from it.

The second major difference relates to the profile of the transverse arch opening into the lateral chapel N 4. In all of the chapels previously constructed this arch had been asymmetric, having an outer order toward the aisle, but no corresponding order toward the chapel (Fig. 19 c). This asymmetry must have offended Colas, who added the extra order toward the chapel, and was forced to provide a resting place for the extra thickness of the arch in the form of a corbel with foliage decoration placed on the west wall of the chapel (Fig. 87). On the east side the extra thickness of the arch is simply squeezed against the diagonal rib.

We may attribute the tracery of the northern chapel (N 4) to Anthoine Colas (B, 1456, 12). It is very similar to the window of the corresponding chapel on the south side, but lacks the fleurs-de-lys (Fig. 39). Colas here, following the plans of Master Bleuet, used concave forms for his window mullions, whereas in the southern chapel he had been forced by Jaquet le Vachier to use rounded mouldings. On the exterior of the chapel we find the use of rotated squares for the pilaster defining the western side, and also the familiar sprinkled kale leaves and snails on the ogee arch over the window.

By the late 1460s Colas is found engaged in work on the foundation of a "great pier on the right side" (B, 1468–69, 1 & 2). Since both piers of the new nave arcade on the right (south) side had been founded by this date, we are left with only one possibility, namely pier E 1, the thickened pier at the west end of the southern aisle, corresponding with the thickened pier on the north side designed by Master Bleuet. Colas' pier consists of a massive cylindrical central core, to which are adossed four very massive shafts for the transverse arches and four smaller ones for the diagonal ribs (Figs. 12 & 80). Since the aisle bays are rectangular rather than square, the diagonal ribs converge with the supporting members at the corners at an angle which is less than forty-five degrees, and this is reflected in the placing of the smaller shafts.

The base mouldings have a monumentality and plasticity to match the great bulk and heavy forms of the pier. Three slightly different mouldings are used, for the body of the pier, for the major shafts, and for the diagonals.

The area of the base mouldings and the plinth of the pier allows for a play upon the nature of the relationship between circles and polygons. The lowest part of the plinth is an irregular octagon, but the hexagon provides the favored form for the individual shafts. The mouldings of the main shafts are duodecagons, which turn into hexagons in their lowest parts. A play upon interlocking hexagons creates a regular twelve-pointed star pattern, the salient angles taking on the monumentality of the ramparts of a Vauban fortress. The smaller shafts have a similar play on duodecagons and interlocking hexagons.

Unlike its counterpart on the north side Colas' pier was designed entirely from center points lying within the body of the pier. It therefore lacks the brittle, linear quality of Master Bleuet's pier, and rather has monumentality and plasticity— although the interlocking polygonal forms used in the plinth create something of a bristling effect. Colas' pier is designed simply to engulf the mouldings of transverse arches and diagonal ribs into its smooth convex surfaces, rather than allowing these mouldings to continue downward to dictate the forms of the surface of the pier. There is something of a paradox in the fact that this artist who was capable of producing such exquisite sculpture favored a pier system which rendered the capital obsolete.

Between 1468 and 1470 Colas completed this great pier at the west end of the southern nave aisles (E 1) and also the upper parts of pier C 1 in the northern arcade (B, 1468–69, 1–4; 1469–70, 2). These piers having been completed, it then became possible to install the two vaults over the inner aisle bays at the west end of the nave in bay 1–2. Here a structural problem arose over the abutment of piers C 1 and D 1 against the western thrust of the very heavy arches of the main arcade. This thrust was capable of causing a newly constructed pier to rotate on its base and to collapse. The problem did not arise with piers B 1 and E 1 since the piers were thicker and the arches lighter. In order to overcome the problem on the north side, a provisional arch of chalk was constructed against the west side of pier C 1, the lower part of the arch resting upon the old bell tower (*gros clocher*) which existed to the west end of the nave (B, 1469–70, 1). This then allowed

72

Colas to install the heavy transverse arches and to vault this bay (B, 1470–71, 1: 1471–72, 2; 1472–73, 1).

The profiles used by Colas for the transverse arches and ribs of this inner aisle bay (B C 1–2) were determined by existing work. The springers for the main arcade arch, transverse arch, and diagonal rib had already been placed over pier C 2 (in the 1370s), and Master Bleuet's great pier B 1 determined the profile of the other two transverse arches of the bay, as well as the diagonal rib. Master Bleuet had intended very massive transverse arches in all four directions over the tower-supporting pier B 1 and thus bequeathed Colas the problem of finding a resting place for these multiple mouldings over pier C 1 in the main arcade. Hence the mess of interpenetrating mouldings seen at this location (Fig. 85).

A similar provisional chalk arch, or flying buttress, against pier D 1 at the west end of the southern nave arcade allowed the matching vault over the inner bay of the south aisle to be constructed (B, 1470–71, 3; 1471–72, 1). This provisional flying buttress rested on top of the chapel to the south of the old west bell tower. The vault over the inner aisle bay was constructed in 1472–73 (B, 1472–73, 2).

This southern aisle vault over bay D E 1–2 was the only one of Colas' eight vaults where that master had complete freedom to choose the forms he desired for transverse arches and diagonal ribs, since he had installed all the springers at all four corners. For the main arcade, he wisely (for the sake of uniformity) chose to follow the same profile as all the other arches to the east, with a combination of rounded rolls and conservative fillets. In the other arches and ribs of the vault the sharp-nosed fillet is predominant.

The inner aisle bays on each side at the west end of the nave provided the abutment necessary for work to continue into the upper parts of the central vessel. We sense a definite reluctance to continue work into the west façade block. Already in 1468–69 Colas had begun to design the units necessary for the upper parts of the nave (B, 1468–69, 3), and in the following year he is found cutting the enclosing arches which will support the top of the triforium and the passage running along the outside of the clerestory windows. Since the upper parts of the three eastern bays had been completed as far as the springers of the clerestory windows, and since further work at the east end was obstructed by the existence of the provisional roof, it comes as no surprise to find work on the upper nave commencing at the west end. The scaffolding erected to facilitate the work is said to be "between two portals," meaning the portals in the old west tower and in the provisional wall closing the Gothic nave at division 3 (B, 1469–70, 7). Between 1469 and 1474 Colas directed work on the completion of the uppermost parts of the four western piers of the central vessel (C 1, C 2, D 1 and D 2), and also began work on the triforium in these bays.

The question has been raised as to whether the nave was built in vertical or in horizontal sections. In founding his seven piers Jaquet le Vachier decided (or was instructed) to adopt the horizontal solution, and Master Bleuet and Anthoine Colas followed his lead. Now that all of the lower parts of the nave had been completed, work could commence on the upper parts, which were also built in a horizontal fashion—that is, completing all of the upper wall at one time, and then all of the flyers and all of the vaults, rather than finishing one bay at a time.

It is fairly easy to isolate the work of Colas in the upper parts of the interior of the western bays at the nave. All four western capitals may be attributed to him (Fig. 94 a–d). The capitals over piers C 2 and D 2 have the vigorous, frilly cabbage leaves which we have come to associate with this master, and the western capitals (of piers C 1 and D 1) have large birds. Although the aisle capitals worked by Colas offer no precedent for the use of a single bird dominating the sculpture area of the capital, yet Colas certainly did favor the use of animal forms (mainly snails) in his capitals; the quality of these western capitals is what one would expect from Colas.

The uniformity of the triforium tracery in all five bays of the nave renders it more difficult to distinguish the work of Colas (Figs. 64–70). In each bay we find three double-lancet units, linked to the clerestory by means of continuous mullions. The individual lancets have simple pointed arches and are surmounted by two mouchettes flanking a soufflet.

We have seen that Colas worked on the enclosing arches and upper passages of the triforium, and it is also possible that he might have worked on the tracery, thus defining the pattern that was to be used throughout the nave. One bay is slightly different from all the others in the nave (bay 1–2 on the north side, Fig. 93). In this case, the two mouchettes over the lancets have a smoothly rounded outline, whereas all of the others have an angular hunchback appearance. It seems possible that this slight difference reveals that this was the first bay begun by Anthoine Colas. The triforium mullion bases in this bay have the "painterly" kind of chiselling that announces the hand of this master.

It is difficult to distinguish Colas' work on the exterior of the upper nave. However, the upper parts of C 2 and D 2 can be attributed to this master (Fig. 49). Here we see square blocks of masonry with a second square turned diagonally and ascending up into the pinnacle. This is a design that had already been used in the adjacent piers to the east, C 3 and D 3, completed in the 1390s by Henry de Bruisselles. In pier C 2 we find the characteristic foliage forms employed by Colas to support the canopy at the level of the head of the flyer. The exterior buttresses of C 1 and D 1, although begun by Colas, were completed only under his successor Jehançon Garnache (Fig. 47).

We may thus summarize the work of Anthoine Colas as follows: under the direction of Bleuet, he completed pier B 1 and chapel N 4; he was responsible for the great pier at the west end of the southern nave aisles (E 1); the reinforcement of the north transept façade; the installation of the six vaults of the aisle and chapel bays at 2–3; the windows of the fourth chapel on each side, and the vaults of the inner bays of the aisles at the west end of the nave. In order to construct the latter he built two flyers resting upon the old bell tower and chapel to the west as a support for piers C 1 and D 1 against the western thrust of the main arcade. He began the upper nave, completing the upper parts of the four western piers and beginning the triforium.

By the mid 1470s the progression of the work had slowed down considerably. The major problem encountered at this stage was that the old provisional roof over the eastern three bays of the nave rested on top of the unfinished upper piers. To complete these upper piers would entail the demolition or modification of this roof to disengage the masonry. This was a major undertaking not even commenced before the death of Colas in 1483.

Jehançon Garnache, 1485–1502

The new master mason was Jehançon Garnache,[17] appointed master of the workshop in 1485 (B, 1485–86, 2). Garnache's name first appeared in the fabric account for 1484–85, directly after the local mason, Jaquet de la Bouticle, had been sent to Reims to seek help in the work of repairing the damaged choir screen (B, 1484–85, 3 & 6). Since Garnache's first project in the cathedral was, indeed, on the screen, it seems highly probable that Garnache, like his predecessors, Bleuet and Colas, had come from Reims. He was to remain in control of the workshop until 1502 when Martin Chambiges' plan for the west façade was accepted by the bishop and chapter, and he remained nominally master mason of the workshop even beyond that, still receiving his annual stipend in lieu of a robe. He died in 1529.

Before discussing the work of Jehançon Garnache, a curious interlude must be mentioned. Between the death of Colas and the appointment of Garnache as master, a brief interregnum existed, during which direction of the workshop was assumed by Jaquet de la Bouticle, who had worked as assistant to Anthoine Colas, and by Jaquet le Vachier (B, 1483–84, 1 & 2). Vachier cut the templates for the repair of the damaged bases of certain nave piers, and then went on to work on the upper parts of certain nave piers which were not as high as the others. This must refer to piers C 3 and D 3 which had carried the west end of the old provisional roof. They also supported the old provisional wall closing in the west end of the three bays of the nave completed around 1300. In order to fix this provisional wall in place, iron hooks must have been set into the masonry of the piers. There is no sign whatever of the holes left by such hooks in the upper parts of C 3 and D 3, and it therefore seems certain that the interior surfaces of the piers had been left incomplete, without the bundle of five shafts ascending to the high capitals and vaults. The existence of these shafts would have rendered it difficult to affix the wood wall to a firm surface. It was now necessary to install these shafts and the high capitals.[18] Vachier started work on the southern pier, D 3 (B, 1483–84, 3). In order to finish these piers it was necessary to free their tops from the tie beams and wall plates of the roof which they had supported. Therefore provisional props were inserted to support the roof—purchase of beams

75

of 31 and 29 feet is recorded for this purpose (B, 1483–84, 5). The high capital of D 3 may be attributed to Vachier (Fig. 94 f). It has leaves wrapped around the body of the pier in the approved Late Gothic fashion, but the chiselling is flat, without much undercutting.

The question arises, of course, as to whether this could be the same Jaquet le Vachier who in the 1450s had begun the campaigns of construction on the nave. This seems probable for two reasons. First, Vachier was hired in 1483 to make templates for the bases of nave piers which had been damaged. The western piers of the nave had been begun by the mason called Jaquet le Vachier thirty years previously, and we might suppose that this was a local man who had been called back to make the templates necessary for the repair. Second, the flatness of the capital, so unlike the work of Anthoine Colas, is not inconsistent with the style of Vachier's capitals in the southern aisle (Figs. 91 & 94 f). Whether or not the same artist was involved, Jaquet le Vachier disappeared from the workshop in the following year, never again to reappear.

Between 1485 and 1500 Jehançon Garnache directed the operations necessary to complete the nave: the construction of the enclosing arches of the clerestory windows and the upper wall; the installation of the roof; the flying buttresses; and the installation of the high vaults and tracery of the clerestory windows. Although these jobs might occasionally overlap, each will be presented as a separate undertaking in order to assist the reader through the rather intricate chronology.

a. *Clerestory window enclosing arches and upper wall.* Jehançon Garnache began his work on the cathedral by completing the upper parts of pier C 3, on the north side (B, 1485–86, 1). The upper part of this pier had been built in the 1390s by Henry de Bruisselles, and Garnache's "completion" of the pier should be understood as referring to the addition of the bundle of five shafts and the high capital. Prior to this, the shafts had only been brought up to the level of the main arcade. The high capital has a sharpness and depth of undercutting which distinguishes it both from the capitals of Vachier and of Colas (Fig. 94 e).

Having completed the upper parts of pier C 3, it was then necessary to modify the provisional roof over the eastern bays of the nave in order to free the tops of the piers, so that they could be continued upward. For each pier it was necessary to cut off the end of the tie beam and wall plate and to improvise support for the shortened ends of the beams. This work is documented between 1485 and 1488 (Appendix B). It was then possible to install the enclosing arches of the clerestory windows. A further problem remained, however: at the west end of the nave it was necessary to improvise provisional supports to prevent piers C 1 and D 1 from being pushed to the west by the thrust of the window arches. Two more provisional chalk flyers were therefore built, the southern one (against pier D 1) resting on the chapel called Dreux, Droyn, Drouin, etc. de la Marche, and the northern one resting on the *gros clocher* (B, 1487–88, 2 & 10). It was then possible to complete all of the clerestory window enclosing arches between 1487 and 1489.

b. *The nave roof and western gable.* In constructing a Gothic cathedral it was the normal practice to install vaults only under the shelter of a roof.[19] The contract for the roof of the nave of Troyes Cathedral was made with Jehan Carbonnier in 1489, directly after the completion of the clerestory wall on top of which the roof would rest (B, 1488–89, 5).

A gable would be necessary for the west end of the roof (Figs. 45 & 46). A problem existed in the coordination of the gable with the western frontispiece, which, of course, did not exist at this date. Garnache obviously experienced some difficulty with the planning of the gable, and at Easter 1489 was sent by the bishop and chapter on a visit to Paris and to Reims in order to study gables, to instruct himself how to construct the gable of the cathedral of Troyes (B, 1488–89, 7).

On returning, he began the gable over the transverse arch at division 1. It is evident that Anthoine Colas, when he constructed the upper parts of the nave piers at this point, had not anticipated that the gable would be placed here. The rather thick transverse arch does not fit on top of the capitals, and it has been necessary to add little colonnettes to receive the extra mouldings on the west side (Figs. 94 a & 95). The northern such colonnette rests on top of a discontinued springer for a diagonal rib, placed for a vault to the west of division 1.

On the exterior at this point (division 1) we find that the solid spurs of masonry constructed by Jehançon Garnache to abut the gable are placed against the piers already constructed by Anthoine Colas (Figs. 23 & 47). These spurs each consist of a solid mass of masonry with a tracery "flying buttress." Each spur continues out from the central vessel to a point roughly corresponding to the thickened piers B 1 and E 1. They were intended to form a brace between the central vessel and towers constructed over the outer bays at the west ends of the aisles. The southern buttress even has an inscription declaring it to be the first pillar of the tower (*premier pillier de la tour*), and the text relating to the purchase of wood to make templates for these spurs refers to them as flying buttresses for the gable as well as for the towers (B, 1491–92, 4).[20]

The gable itself consists of a triangular wall to support the western end of the two faces of the roof (Fig. 46).[21] The thickness of the wall is reduced by means of a relieving arch, and a small rose window with very fluent Flamboyant tracery is set into this thinner wall. A door allows access from the present (nineteenth century) shallow-pitched roof to the west of the gable into the interior of the roof. A great image of St. Michael was set atop the gable (B, 1492–93, 7).

c. *The flying buttresses.* In understanding the chronology of the flying buttresses of the nave, we have to view Jehançon Garnache as one who stood in line of inheritance with a succession of master masons, some named and some unknown, who had worked on the upper nave, including Jehan de Torvoie (completion of the first bay of the nave up to the high vaults), Michelin Hardiot, Michelin de Jonchery, and Jehan Thierry (reconstruction of the faulty flyers in the 1360s), Henry de Bruisselles (adaption of the upper parts of the eastern piers to receive the low provisional roof), and Anthoine Colas. We must not be surprised, therefore, to find a highly complex chronology in the nave flyers (Appendix D).

We saw in Chapter I that the flyers of the nave conform to two basic types (not including the spurs at bay division 1): three upper flyers on each side have vertical tracery panels, mixed with Flamboyant elements in the heads and tails, and one unit on each side (at division 2) is more unified in its use of Flamboyant tracery motifs (Figs. 44, 48–51, 55, 57 & 58). We have advanced the hypothesis that in the fourteenth century campaigns on the nave, flyers had already been built in the eastern three bays of the nave, and that after the collapse of the upper nave in 1389 these units were modified to form provisional supports for the roof. These provisional supports consisted of the entire lower flyers over the outer aisles, and the supporting arches of the upper flyers. It was probably at this time that the slender intermediary strut made its appearance (Fig. 24). Thus, in these three bays, Garnache merely had to complete the tracery of the upper flyers and add the upper rim, and in doing this he was able to reuse masonry from the fourteenth-century flyers which had been dismantled. Only in one bay (at 2) had no flyer ever been constructed, and here Garnache was able to design and construct an entirely new unit.

The documentary evidence reveals that Garnache began his work on the flyers at the west end of the nave, not the east end. First the spurs flanking the gable were built, and then in September 1492 he began work on a flyer on the north side (B, 1492–93, 2 & 3). We can be certain that this flyer was not at the east end of the nave because the texts specifically refer to the construction of the pillars of the buttress, as well as the flying members. The pillars at bay 2 had not yet been built, whereas for all the other flyers pillars already existed at this date. The flyers at the east end of the nave (presumably bay 5) are referred to as existing "between the old pillars" (B, 1494–95, 3). Between September 1492 and August 1493 (about twelve months in all), Garnache and his workshop devised the plans, cut the stones, and installed the pillars and flyers against the "first pillar" on the north side (B, 1492–93, 8—here the texts are specific in defining this as the first flyer), which must refer to the unit at A B C 2. In September 1493 work was transferred to the matching unit on the south side, and ten months of stone cutting and laying followed (until July 1494).

In this month two extremely interesting meetings took place concerning the sequence of the work. On July 25 Jehançon Garnache met with the workers to discuss whether to construct the flying buttresses or the vaults (*les ars boutans ou les voltes*). The word *"ou"* is a little ambiguous as to whether it implies a definite "either-or" choice between the flyers and the vaults. This ambiguity is removed by a text in the chapter deliberation for July 23, 1494, in which the bishop and chapter met to discuss whether it would be better to build the vault of the first bay of the nave or the flyers for the second bay (B, 1494). Indications that the first bay was already being prepared for vaulting can be found in the account for the previous year (B, 1493–94, 2). The first vault would have been over bay 1–2, at the west end of the nave, where the new flyers had been constructed. Some of the scaffolding necessary to center a vault in this bay would have existed already, since a center had already been constructed for the transverse arch under the gable at division 1.

No decision is recorded for the meetings, but the subsequent texts reveal that it must have been decided to finish all of the flying buttresses before beginning any work on the vaults. The inward thrust of the flyers would have been met by the wooden braces in the interior of the nave provided by the scaffolding of the central vessel and the tie beams of the roof.[22]

Whereas work on the two flying buttresses at division 2 is clearly defined in the texts, and we can follow the progress from pillar to flyer, it is impossible to distinguish individual units in the texts referring to work on the other three flying buttresses on each side. Moreover, we find that while construction of the flying buttresses at bay 2 took twelve months for the unit on the north side and ten months for the south side, only thirteen months of work sufficed to complete the southern three units at the east end of the nave, and another thirteen months for the northern three units (August 1494 to September 1495, and September 1495 to October 1496 respectively).

The fact that two flyers, one on each side at division 2, had taken almost as much time to construct as all the other six units of both sides, coupled with the stylistic differences already summarized, suggests quite clearly that whereas the units at bay 2 were designed and built entirely from scratch, substantial amounts of already existing masonry were embodied in the eastern units of 3, 4, and 5.

d. *The high vaults of the nave.* When a cathedral was built in vertical slices we would expect to see an individual bay taken right up to the high vaults (with the adjacent bay completed in its lower parts to provide support) and the installation of the vaults taking place contemporaneously with the construction of the flying buttresses. The sequence of construction of the upper nave of Troyes Cathedral in a horizontal fashion posed a dilemma about whether to finish all of the flyers first and then begin the vaults, or whether to construct both at the same time. In July 1494 it had been decided to abandon the plan to construct each vault simultaneously with its attendant flyers, and instead to complete all of the flyers and then all of the vaults. Thus, while preparations had been begun for vaulting the western bay as early as 1493-94 (B, 1493-94, 2), the actual work of vaulting did not commence until late 1496, and the eastern bay of the nave was the first vaulted.

Given the prolonged and accident ridden campaigns of construction of the nave (over two centuries of work), it comes as something of a relief to see the installation of the five vaults of the central nave taking place without incident in as little as two years. Already in the course of constructing the flyers of the nave, a very important step had been taken in terms of workshop practice. Instead of having the roughly hewn stones brought from the quarries to the cathedral workshop for shaping, a mason was sent to the quarry to chisel stones according to the templates sent to him by Jehançon Garnache, the master mason (B, 1495-96,

1, 2, & 3). This procedure was continued for the high vaults, units where many stones of similar specification would be used, and therefore where mass production techniques were obviously appropriate.

In organizing the construction of a cathedral, the masters of the works had two alternative systems of accounting and paying the artisans: by piecework or by daywork. In the former case a contract defined the units to be constructed in terms of specifications, materials, and pay for the completed unit (regardless of the amount of time taken to construct it), whereas in the latter case a mason would simply be paid for the number of days he had worked, and he would go on working until the unit was finished. A contract might also accompany an agreement to work on a daywork basis, as in the case of the contracts for the choir screen.

The flying buttresses had been built on a daywork basis, but for the vaults the decision was made to adopt a piecework system of organization. Garnache was first offered 50 pounds per vault, a sum subsequently increased to 60 pounds. Since this sum could only have been earned in about 40 weeks by Garnache at his normal daily pay, and since the installation of a vault took a great deal less time than this, the master mason obviously gained by the agreement.[23]

The use of mass production techniques and piecework rather than daywork meant that the accounts no longer recorded the weekly activities of the masons as they cut the stones in the workshop and went about setting them into position. Our chronology for the vaulting of the central nave cannot be as precise as we would like for such an inherently interesting operation. We can assume, however, that while the payment of 60 pounds to Jehançon Garnache need not necessarily have followed directly after the completion of a particular vault, it is unlikely to have been made before its completion.

Work on the high vaults (the easternmost bay) began in November 1496: prior to that month the weekly payments to the masons had specified that work was on the flying buttresses. The first payment to Garnache for the first vault is dated December 1496, and two more contracts recorded in the same account suggest that three vaults had been constructed in the eight-month period between November 1496 and July 1497. This would mean that each unit had taken two to three months to construct. Of course this did not include the cutting of the stone, since this had been carried out at the quarry.

The stereometry of the stone canopy of a rib-vaulted bay is determined by the four arches comprising the sides (two tranverse arches across the nave forming the long sides and two longitudinal arches or formerets forming the short ones), and also by the intersecting arches or ribs running diagonally across the rectangular bay (Figs. 6 & 97). In the case of the nave at Troyes Cathedral we find that very different kinds of arches had been used for the sides of each rectangular bay. The short sides, or clerestory window–enclosing arches, which had already been installed, are simple two-point arches, the two arcs being struck from centers on the opposite capital. The longer sides of each rectangular bay, or transverse arch, across the span of the nave, were installed at the same time as the vault. These transverse arches spring from a lower point than the window arches, but have a wider span and a higher crown. They are struck from center points lying well within the space enclosed by the arch, and therefore have a flattened form. Since the span of the diagonal ribs is even wider still, while their crown (the keystone) is only a little higher than the crowns of the transverse arches (about 0.50m.), they will be even more flattened, approaching the specifications of a round arch.

The geometry of the arches and ribs of the vault was clearly predetermined at the design stage, and was imposed by the use of rigid wooden centering. We find the first mention of centers for the nave vaults in the account for 1493–94 (B, 1493–94, 4). The installation and demolition of each center was also paid for on a contract, piecework basis (at 16 pounds for an installation and removal), and since the payments to Jehan Carbonnier are not dated, we cannot determine with any high degree of accuracy how long the centers were left in position for the mortar to set. One text does reveal that three to four months elapsed between the completion of the first vault of the nave and the removal of the beams and debris of the center (B, 1496–97, 1). The debris must have fallen to the ground in the process of decentering the vault, a little before Easter 1497.

It is of interest to note that in the text cited above the laborer is paid for removing not only the beams (*poutrerie*) of the center, but also the earth. In building the vaults this year large quantities of earth were purchased (242 cartloads are recorded in the account for 1496–97), and in decentering each bay quantities of earth are always removed. The only conceivable use for all this earth would have been to center the severies of the vault bays. The stereometric shape of the severies was a very complex one. The lack of uniformity between the geometry of the arches used on each side of the rectangular bays, coupled with the differing heights for springing points and crowns of arches, produces surfaces that are heavily warped. Moreover it is notable that whereas sections and isometric drawings of Gothic vaults reproduced in the popular literature generally show the ridges of the severies as being straight, the ridges of the Troyes nave vaults are humped up or domed in the middle (Figs. 5 & 6).

Rather than using many flexible planks or laths braced into the desired curves the carpenters have simply constructed a series of platforms (probably of hurdles) on top of which the earth has been heaped and thumped into the desired shape. The semi-shaped stones (*pendans*) of the severies have then been cemented side by side on top of the heaped up earth. This would provide a flexible and inexpensive method for shaping the continuous surfaces of masonry to the irregular curves imposed by the skeleton of ribs and transverse arches. Decentering of the severies would obviously be simple and rapid, if a little messy.

The texts for decentering the woodwork of the centers under the arches suggest that an entire center might sometimes be dismantled for use in the adjacent

The Late Gothic Masters of the Nave, 1450–1502

bay (B, 1496–97, 14). If this were the case then the installation and setting time of a vaulted unit might be as little as three months or so.

The payment for the installation of the two western vaults can be found in the following year's account (B, 1497–98, 6 & 7). The removal of the last center took place in late November 1497 (ibid., 1). Thus the total span of time involved in the installation of the five vaults (including setting time and decentering) was around thirteen months.

e. *The tracery of the clerestory windows*. The last task which the master mason had to undertake for the completion of the nave of Troyes Cathedral was the installation of the tracery into the enclosing arches of the clerestory windows prior to their glazing. The changing forms of window tracery have provided art historians with one of their most useful tests as to the nature of style changes in Gothic, and therefore it seems most appropriate to commence our study of the clerestory windows with an analysis of the tracery forms, and then to continue with a discussion of chronology and problems of construction.

All the clerestory windows have six lancets grouped into pairs, creating three major units which are linked with the corresponding units in the triforium by means of continuous mullions (Plates 45 & 65–66). In the clerestory each of the major units (of two lancets) is topped by an ogee arch, and the upper part of the window is filled with two soufflets which fit between these ogees, and a third soufflet piled on top, occupying the apex of the enclosing arch. The mullions defining the major units have rounded profiles while the smaller mullions have an angular profile resulting from the use of concave forms.

Within this basic pattern three variations exist. On both sides of the nave there is an alternation of types which we style "A" and "B." Type A is found on the north side in bays 1–2, 3–4, and 5–6, and on the south side in bays 1–2 and 3–4 (Figs. 45, 59 & 60). In these windows we find cusped soufflets enclosed inside the ogee arch of each of the major units, while in each of the two large soufflets in the upper part of the window can be seen two generously proportioned mouchettes and a soufflet. The awkward shape of the topmost soufflet is filled by a small central soufflet flanked by two very twisted mouchettes. An interesting difference between the two windows of this type on the south side and the three windows on the north side becomes apparent on closer inspection. In the former (Fig. 60) the two small mouchettes in the topmost soufflet each have their own individual heads, formed of pointed arches, whereas in the three northern windows (Fig. 59) these pointed arches have been omitted, producing a simpler, less fragmented composition.

A second type of tracery design (type B) is found in bays 2–3 and 4–5 on both north and south sides of the nave clerestory (Fig. 61). Two features distinguish the tracery of these four windows from that of the other five. Each type B window has three soufflets in the three major units divided into two mouchettes, producing an S-shaped bar of tracery. This motif had already been used by Anthoine Colas in his chapel windows (chapels N 4 and S 4), which seem to have provided a general source of inspiration for Jehançon Garnache's windows. The two upper soufflets in the type B window are occupied by mouchettes with a much more curvaceous shape than their counterparts in the type A window.

We thus have a carefully restrained alternation of forms with strangely archaic undertones: we think of High Gothic precedents such as the alternation of the pier forms at Chartres Cathedral. A similar stage in the evolution of Flamboyant tracery had been reached in the clerestory of the cathedral at Moulins.[24]

One window at the extreme east end of the south side of the Troyes nave does not conform to either of the types described. We refer the reader to a photograph (Fig. 62) rather than attempting a full description. It can be seen that the details inside the major soufflets are much more complex, each unit retaining a much greater degree of autonomy than in the other windows. This window, which we call type C, would certainly have been considerably more expensive to produce than any of the others.

Flamboyant tracery may be seen as having developed out of thirteenth century "geometric" tracery as a result of the placing side by side of simple shapes like pointed arches, circles, trefoils, and quatrefoils, and the progressive tendency to allow the lines defining these shapes to swing directly from one form to another, causing the small negative interstices of the geometric window to disappear (Fig. 22). A Flamboyant shape such as a mouchette, soufflet, or ogee is formed from arcs of circles generated from center points outside, as well as inside, the unit; it is precisely this characteristic that gives the double-curved swing to Flamboyant tracery. A Late Gothic designer perhaps had a little more freedom than his High Gothic counterpart, although most Flamboyant patterns are produced from a relatively limited vocabulary of forms. The Flamboyant syntax of design sometimes did allow the artist to escape from the tyranny of forms which have been entirely determined by compasses: when we examine the windows of Jehançon Garnache the irregular curvature of some of his shapes leads us to suspect that he might occasionally have relied upon a rather free-wheeling design procedure.

Given the tendency of Late Gothic to move progressively toward interpenetration and streamlining of form, we do not need documentation to tell us that the highly complex window which we have termed type C at the east end of the south side of the nave was the first to have been made; it perhaps represents a trial form. Similarly, it follows that the more complex forms of the windows of type A on the south side are earlier than their counterparts on the north.

A study of the fabric account evidence confirms this conclusion. The first preparation for the installation of clerestory windows is documented in the 1496–97 account, when we find the first payment to the quarry master at Tonnerre, Laurent Germain, for cutting out the stones for the clerestory tracery. Jehançon Garnache measured the first window (defined as being over the *tronc* of the church, or at the east end of the nave) and also the adjacent window, designed the tracery pattern and produced the "false templates" (ie, portable templates made of paper) to send to the quarry for the cutting of the stones (B, 1496–97, 6). In the following year Garnache is found consulting with the glaziers on the design of the window which *monsieur l'advocat* wished to donate to the church (B, 1497–98, 2). The lawyer in question was Guillaume Huyart, *advocat du Roy* in Troyes, who, together with Jehan Huyart, canon, donated the window to the cathedral. In the same year's account is documented a purchase of paper to design the other windows (B, 1497–98, 3). Again, a contract, piecework system was used, Garnache receiving 60 pounds for each of the first two windows and 70 pounds for all of the subsequent ones.

During the period which elapsed between the construction of the enclosing arches of the clerestory windows and the installation of the window tracery the great holes constituted by the windows were filled in with provisional screens. Before beginning the work of installation of the tracery it was necessary to remove the screens, against which quantities of earth and cement had fallen, used in the centering of the vaults. This debris must have littered the platforms of the scaffolding and the passages, and as each window was constructed we find the removal of earth and debris (B, 1497–98, 5).

In the following year Garnache completed the last two windows on the south side and the first three windows on the north side (B, 1498–99, 6). The stained glass was installed with extraordinary speed, using the same scaffolding that had been used in the installation of the tracery. In order to protect the glass that had already been installed, as masons continued their work on the completion of the last windows, sheaves of reeds were purchased to pack against the delicate tracery and glass (B, 1498–99, 1). The text given under item 5 of the same year confirms that the stones for each window were being cut at the quarry rather than in the workshop.

The last two windows on the north side were installed in 1499–1500. The glazing of all the windows followed very soon after the completion of the tracery.[25]

f. *The problem of the western frontispiece.* Jehançon Garnache has been portrayed here as a Late Gothic master who had inherited many problems from the generations of masters who had preceded him in command of the cathedral workshop, the main problems centering around the sequence of operations necessary for the completion of the upper nave, and the commencement of a frontispiece on a site occupied by a west tower which propped up the western bay of the nave. The demolition of this tower could only be attempted after measures had been taken to assure the stability of the western nave, once it had been removed. The inability of Garnache to resolve this problem led to the invitation of a prestigious outside master, Martin Chambiges, to give his advice on the matter, and Chambiges was subsequently appointed master to direct the work on the new towers and portals.

It is of some interest to establish the exact form of the frontispiece which had been intended before the arrival of Martin Chambiges. There were only three possibilities for the plan of a "harmonious" twin-towered façade terminating a five-aisled nave: the towers might exist over the four westernmost aisle bays on

84

each side of the central vessel, thus pulling the two side aisles together under one tower, as at Notre-Dame, Paris; they might exist over the inner aisle bays, directly flanking the central vessel; or they might be placed over the outer aisle bays, leaving a gap between the tower and the central vessel, as in the transept façades of Saint-Denis.

The intentions of the earlier masters of the Troyes nave can, to some extent, be established by noting the disposition of heavy masonry capable of supporting the great weight of a tower. Three such piers had been constructed at the ends of the piers dividing the double side-aisles, the two piers on the north side designed by Master Bleuet in the 1450s and the one on the south by Anthoine Colas between 1468 and 1470. The two piers at the extreme west end of the main arcade, on the other hand (piers C 1 and D 1), are not tower-supporting piers, and this enables us to rule out the possibility that towers had been intended over the inner bays of the aisles. Towers over both aisles together (as at Notre-Dame, Paris) can be ruled out for the same reason.

We are left with the third possibility defined above: a tower over the western outer aisle bay, separated from the central vessel by the space of the inner aisle bay (Fig. 26). The piers necessary to support the inner angles of the east sides of the towers (piers B 1 and E 1) had been built by masters Bleuet and Colas and a second pier (A 1) to support the northeast angle of the north tower had been begun by the same masters. Evidence for the demolition of this pier can be found in the account for 1508–9. The final, most convincing evidence for the existence of a second tower-supporting pier on the north side was the discovery in 1973 of a massive foundation block extending out into the road at a point level with the west wall of the last chapel on the north.[26]

We may thus be certain that the original plan for the frontispiece of Troyes Cathedral involved two towers over the outer aisle bays, separated from the central vessel by flying buttresses, giving a five-segment façade (Fig. 26). The buttresses intended for the east sides of the towers were actually built by Jehançon Garnache, the southern buttress with the inscription declaring it to be "the first pillar of the tower."

One difficulty attending this reconstruction of the first plan for the façade has still not been resolved. In the transept of Saint-Denis and the west façade of Léon Cathedral,[27] where we find the same kind of five-segment façade, the gable of the nave roof is placed level with the outer faces of the towers. At Troyes, Garnache had placed the gable over division 1, which would be level with the east faces of the towers which, had they been completed, would have extended another full bay to the west of division 1. The reasons for this are, of course, given by the continued existence of the old bell tower, which made it impossible to complete the lower parts of the last bay of the nave to bring the central part of the façade forward to match the level of the projected towers. This was precisely why Garnache had experienced difficulty over the placing of the gable, and had under-

The Late Gothic Masters of the Nave, 1450–1502

taken a study trip to Paris and Reims to look at gables. On his return from this trip he placed the gable over division 1, one bay further to the east than anticipated in the plan followed by Master Bleuet and Anthoine Colas.

For the first time in our review of the construction of Troyes Cathedral, we have seen major campaigns of construction by a workshop in which we isolate the identity of the successive master masons. Jaquet le Vachier, a rather conservative master of mediocre ability, began seven piers and the lower parts of chapel S 4, but was unable to maintain his leadership of the workshop because of his inability to carve acceptable capitals or to undertake the great tower-supporting piers of the west façade. The visiting Master Bleuet from Reims and Châlons-sur-Marne was the first truly "Late Gothic" master to lead the cathedral workshop. He introduced a new way of understanding the nature of the pier in its relationship with the arches and ribs which it supports; he devised a plan for the frontispiece and supervised the commencement of pier B 1 and chapel N 4. His companion, Anthoine Colas, was hired to carve capitals, but on the departure of Bleuet, Colas assumed direction of the workshop, completing Bleuet's pier, B 1, then devising a totally different kind of pier for the south tower, at E 1. He then went on to consolidate the north transept façade, which was beginning to slant diagonally, to vault the aisles and chapels in bay 2–3, and to vault the inner aisle bays at 1–2, propping up the westernmost piers of the main arcade by means of provisional flying buttresses. He then extended the four western piers of the nave up to their full height, but died before he could undertake the completion of the upper parts of the eastern piers, or the construction of the clerestory wall. Colas is to be remembered primarily as the sculptor of exquisite capitals. Finally, Jehançon Garnache, brought from Reims in order to repair a broken column in the choir screen, went on to become master of the workshop, completing the upper nave, including the flyers and vaults. On reaching the west end, however, he was unable to begin the foundations, since the way was blocked by the old west bell tower (*gros clocher*) and the adjacent chapel of Dreux de la Marche. These structures could not be demolished, since they provided the platform for a battery of four flying buttresses which supported the westernmost bay of the nave against the tendency of the vaults and transverse arches to push outward. At this point, yet another appeal was made to an outside master to resolve the problem of the plan for the west façade. This time the master invited to Troyes was Martin Chambiges, described in the record of the deliberations of the chapter as *supremus artifex*.

86

V

Martin Chambiges, *Supremus Artifex,* 1502–1532

ETWEEN 1506 AND THE 1550S THE workshop at Troyes completed the most massive project undertaken in the entire three and a half centuries of the construction of the cathedral: the monumental twin-towered western frontispiece (Figs. 35 & 36). This part of the building is always referred to in the contemporary fabric account as the "towers and portals," an expression that seems much more apt than the term "façade," which implies a two-dimensional surface. In the construction of the towers and portals, the cathedral workshop was directed by the most famous master mason of the day—one who is described in the deliberations of the chapter as *supremus artifex* (B, 1502, deliberations of the chapter, 2).[1] Thanks to the infusion of new ideas brought by Master Martin Chambiges, the workshop regained the status that it had not held since the early days of construction on the cathedral: that of a widely recognized trendsetter in Gothic architectural design. This was the seventh, last, and most powerful vision embodied in Troyes Cathedral, and the expression of the final phase of Late Gothic architecture.

When we study the tabulation of gross income and expense in Appendix C we are astonished by the cliff-like escalation peculiar to this period. The rapid growth of receipts is to be understood in relation to the dramatic growth of the city; its population is thought to have doubled between 1474 and 1521. The fabric fund gained enormously from rental property, from the contributions of the faithful of the diocese, and from a new confraternity established in the city for the express purpose of raising money for the completion of the cathedral.

There was a distinct hiatus between the formulation of the new plan for the towers and portals (1502) and the actual beginning of work (1506). This is explained by the need to revert back to the task of consolidating already completed parts of the building (the windows on the east side of both transept arms) and by the need to find a substantial external source of funding. During this hiatus, the unspent surplus of the fabric grew to impressive totals: in 1501–2 about 50 percent of the total sum available for building was money carried over from the previous year (Appendix C). Money collected in the boxes placed in the nave of the cathedral and in association with relics also increased in these years.

Efforts at external fund-raising were directed mainly toward King Louis XII.[2] Royal patronage might be expressed toward a cathedral fabric through the concession of a part of the salt tax or *gabelle*—such a concession had been enjoyed in the immediately preceding period by the fabric of Reims Cathedral (B, 1503–4, 2). At Reims, extensive repairs had been necessary after the fire of 1481, and hopes were also entertained of furthering the work on the towers of the cathedral.[3] Louis XII granted the concession on the salt tax simultaneously to the cathedral of Troyes and to the cathedral of Senlis, which had been badly damaged in the fire of 1504.[4] Revenue from the aid granted by the king was considerable, and on our chart of the income and expenses of the fabric of the cathedral we see the line representing income move rapidly upward (Appendix C).

Although the new confraternity established for the collection of money for the fabric did not survive for many years, the first decades of the sixteenth century brought a consistently high income from quests organized in the diocese, rented property, and collection boxes in the cathedral. When the substantial total derived from these sources was added to the revenue from the king's aid (which, with one brief interruption continued until 1540), a very high level of income resulted. In the account of 1525–26, when work was being completed on the sculptures of the portals, we find that the total income was 7,951 pounds, of which the largest sums were from money carried over from last year (3,638), the king's aid (2,300), and money collected in the diocese of Troyes as a result of quests (1,211).

Three factors lay behind the sharp rise in expenses. The advice and help of Parisian masons (Chambiges and his followers) did not come cheaply. The size of the workshop and the pace of the construction was stepped up. And last, the towers and portals of Troyes Cathedral constitute a new kind of "Super Gothic," being simultaneously massive (requiring huge amounts of material) and highly worked (with a profusion of architectural articulation and decoration). The economic means to support this new "Super Gothic" were provided by the remarkable growth of the city of Troyes[5] combined with the aid from the king.

Whereas the surplus of wealth in the previous period had been consumed by warfare, a considerable part of this wealth was now available for the architectural and artistic development of the city. This development included the establishment of broad, gracious streets, embellished with lavish monuments such as the famous *Belle-Croix*, constructed between 1484 and 1497.[6] The organization of lavish processions and mystery plays for the entries of Charles VIII (1486), Louis XII (1510), and François I (1521) reveals the same interest in extravagant pomp and show.[7] Many of the parish churches of the city and surrounding area were rebuilt in these decades. Since many of them were affected by the stylistic impact of the towers and portals of the cathedral, it would be appropriate to reserve our discussion of them until after an analysis of the work of Martin Chambiges.

By 1501, work on the cathedral was at an impasse. The nave was complete, and it was time to begin the west block of the cathedral. This would involve the demolition of the old west tower, but such a demolition was rendered impossible by the fact that the tower served as a prop for the west end of the nave: four flying buttresses had been built against the old tower and adjacent chapel, two at the level of the aisle vaults, and two at clerestory level.

On June 8, 1502 the chapter of Troyes Cathedral decided to consult leading masons on the question of the construction of the foundations of the west towers which would terminate the prolonged campaigns of construction on the cathedral (B, 1502, deliberations of the chapter, 1). On July 1 it was decided to appeal to the famous Parisian master, Martin Chambiges (B, ibid, 2). Three commissioners were appointed to go to Chambiges, who was at that time directing the work of construction on the south transept of Beauvais Cathedral, and to attempt to persuade him to come to Troyes. Chambiges agreed to come, in return for the payment of twelve golden *escus au soleil* for himself and three for his assistant, Cuvelier, master mason of the workshop of Sens Cathedral (B, ibid, 3).[8] Chambiges spent eight and a half days in the city of Troyes, during which time a trench was dug so that the master could inspect existing foundations (B, 1501–2, 1–8).

The immediate result of Chambiges' visit, as reflected in the fabric account evidence, was a double one. On the one hand, it seems that the master gave directions for the continuation of work, for at Easter 1503 the resident master of the Troyes workshop, Jehançon Garnache, took certain "false templates" made by Martin Chambiges to the quarry at Aulnois (B, 1502–3, 1).[9] On the other hand, an entry in the same fabric account mentions the sending of a parchment plan from Paris to Troyes, with the *portraits* of the towers and portals projected for Troyes Cathedral. In other words Martin Chambiges was proposing an alternative to the plan which had existed in the workshop, and which Masters Bleuet, Anthoine Colas, and Jehançon Garnache had begun to realize (B, 1502–3, 3 & 4).

Work did not immediately commence on the new towers, however. The transept arms of Troyes Cathedral had been a constant source of anxiety on account of their tendency to settle outward (towards the north and south), causing the upper parts to shift diagonally. Between 1503 and 1506 the old geometric tracery of the eastern windows of the transept arms was entirely replaced with Flamboyant tracery, modeled on the windows of the nave (B, 1504–5, 1), and the triforium, which had been blocked, was reopened to the light. The work was carried out by

89

the master mason of the cathedral, Jehançon Garnache, assisted by the local masters Jehan Bailly and Jehan Gailde.

The plans devised by Martin Chambiges had not been forgotten, however, and in the account for 1505–6 an entry refers to the examination of the site and the plan by an outside expert, Michel, master of Saint-Nicholas in Lorraine.

In the following year's account a problematic passage refers to the demonstration of a model of the towers which were projected for the cathedral (B, 1506–7, 1). This text has commonly been interpreted as implying that Jehan Gailde, master mason of the Madeleine, Troyes, was attempting to challenge Martin Chambiges in respect to the latter's commission to construct the cathedral façade.[10] The texts make no reference to the comparing of rival plans (as occurred in the case of the two projects for the choir screen), and it is also possible that the model made by Jehan Gailde was merely to demonstrate in three-dimensional terms the project already formulated by Chambiges.

In October 1506 Martin Chambiges returned to Troyes in order to inspect the site of the foundations of the proposed towers, to visit the quarries, and to compile notes as to how to commence the new work (B, 1506–7, 6). In April 1507 Chambiges returned to show the local masons how to begin work on the foundations, and to issue the templates necessary for cutting the stone to the required size (B, 1506–7, 10–13). Work then continued under the direction of the local master Jehançon Garnache, who retained the stipend and title of master mason, with the occasional help of Jehan Gailde of the Madeleine.

The immediate object of interest at the time when Chambiges first arrived in Troyes had been the construction of the second pier of the north tower at A 1. Thus, we find Jehançon Garnache, Jehan Bailly,[11] and Jehan Gailde visiting a great pier which had been begun on the north side (B, 1501–2, 1), and the trench which was dug during Chambiges' visit to show him the existing foundations was probably at the foot of this pier. The fabric accounts between 1502 and 1509 give several references to a great unfinished pier on this spot: in 1504–5 it was covered over in order to prevent the rain from penetrating into the masonry (B, 1504–5, 2); in 1506–7 the stump was again covered over, and then uncovered and a cartload of thorns was purchased to wind around the pier (like barbed wire) in order to prevent children from climbing up on it (B, 1506–7, 8). The foundations of the north block of the north tower were begun in the same year under the direction of the local masons Jehançon Garnache and Jehan Bailly. Martin Chambiges, who was then directing the work on the foundations of the south transept of Beauvais Cathedral, paid two visits to Troyes, but refused to come a third time (B, 1506–7, 6, 10 & 12).

In the year's work which is recorded in the fabric account dated 1508–9, it became necessary to demolish the existing masonry which had been begun for the north tower belonging to the earlier plan for the west towers (B, 1508–9, 5). The texts reveal that a stretch of wall was also demolished: this would be the lower wall of the western part of chapel N 5. A window and gable were propped up while the chapel wall and window of N 5 were rebuilt: this clearly refers to the window of the adjacent chapel N 4. All this work was necessary in order to effect the junction of the new work with the outer walls of the old nave. It took place partly under the supervision of Martin Chambiges, who had come from Beauvais on January 10, 1509, together with two assistants (B, 1508-9, 2).

This year was a critical one for the Troyes Cathedral workshop and for the subsequent development of ecclesiastical architecture in the area. Until this time Martin Chambiges had directed as an absentee master, and Jehançon Garnache retained his position as resident master, although working under the directions of Martin Chambiges. Garnache's background can hardly have equipped him for work on this new "Super Gothic" and it had been necessary to call upon the master for help and advice at every turn—obviously a source of irritation to Martin Chambiges. In 1509 the workshop was transformed by the infusion of several members of the Chambiges family and workshop, including his son-in-law, Jehan de Damas (also called *de Soissons*), and his son Pierre (B, 1508-9, 8). Very exact specifications were formulated by Martin Chambiges for future purchases of stone (B, 1508-9, 7).[12] The master himself directed the work at the very high wage of forty sous a week regardless of feast days, Garnache and Bailly being retained at five sous a day. Templates were issued by Martin Chambiges for the work on the new north portal (B, 1508-9, 10). In the following year's account Martin Chambiges' son-in-law, Jehan de Damas, appeared at the head of the list of masons in the workshop, a position which he was to retain until his death in 1531 when he was succeeded by Jehan Bailly. Garnache retained his stipend as master mason for several more years, however.

It was necessary to provide for the linking together of the masonry of the lateral block of the north tower with the great aisle pier B 1 by means of a transverse arch, which would, on account of the nature of pier B 1, have to be an arch without capitals, whose mouldings would continue down into the supporting members. Thus, we find the cutting of templates, based on the mouldings of this great interior pier (*pillier parvoie*), intended to facilitate the cutting of the matching mouldings on the interior of the north lateral block at A 1 (B, 1508-9, 11).

In the following year Martin Chambiges paid another visit from Beauvais in order to supervise work on the lateral block of the north tower (B, 1509-10, 1). Work then began on the great buttress to the north of the central portal (B, 1510-11, 3).

In 1511-12 the master paid a brief visit, but left at short notice (B, 1511-12, 2). Pierre Chambiges, Martin's son, was paid to use his influence with his father to persuade him to return again when asked. The master unwillingly spent another ten days in Troyes during the king's visit to that city, and paid a third visit to be present for the commencement of work on the south tower. He took the first opportunity of returning to Beauvais, leaving Troyes four days before expected. It was a five-day ride from Beauvais to Troyes, and the master must have been

Martin Chambiges, *Supremus Artifex*, 1502-1532

heartily sick of the sight of messengers with empty horses intended to convey him back to Troyes.

The year 1512–13 saw the last visit of Martin Chambiges to Troyes (B, 1512–13, 1). Despite the persistent efforts of the chapter and the mediation of the master's wife and son-in-law it proved impossible to pry him away from his work at Beauvais Cathedral, which had now gone as far as the north transept (B, 1514–15, 3). At Troyes, work continued on the lateral wall of the south tower and the buttress to the south of the central portal in the absence of the master. By 1517–18 work on the three portals was almost complete and the carving and installation of the figurative sculpture began (B, 1517–18, 2 etc.).[13]

Between 1518 and 1522 the work of joining the lower parts of the new towers to the western bays of the nave aisles was completed: first the westernmost chapel on the south side and the adjacent aisle bay were vaulted (B, 1520–21, 2) and then the similar work was undertaken on the north side (B, 1521–22, 1). The window tracery of both of these chapels was installed by the Chambiges workshop, and employs round-headed lancets and arches unlike the tightly pointed ogees of the tracery designed by Anthoine Colas in the adjacent chapel (Figs. 39 & 42). On the south side the entire lower wall of the chapel S 5 was built at this time. A piscina set in the lower chapel wall has the vertical pendant cusping characteristic of Chambiges' designs.

The problem which had caused the Troyes chapter to appeal to Martin Chambiges for help in 1502 involved the old bell tower, which had been used as a prop for the west end of the unfinished nave, and which blocked the site of the projected towers and portals. Martin Chambiges' solution to the problem was to design a west block which was deep enough to allow it to be built around the old bell tower, leaving it and its buttresses against the western nave intact. The chapel to the south of the tower was also left intact and propped (for example, B, 1511–12, 11).

By 1530 the masonry of the lateral blocks of the tower and the buttresses flanking the central portal had reached a height above the level of the aisle vaults. The next step to be taken was the foundation of the great interior tower-supporting piers. Thus at this point it became necessary to demolish the old bell tower, and to devise a new way to support the western nave bay. This means of support was achieved by means of extremely long flying buttresses, built between the new masonry of the west towers and piers C 1 and D 1 at the west end of the nave. Such a flyer had already been constructed, but it fell in 1530–31 because of premature decentering. The workman who had been involved in removing the key of the center, Colin Millet, was killed (B, 1530–31, 3). Jehan Bailly was sent to Paris and Beauvais to ask the advice of Martin and Pierre Chambiges on the subject of the foundation of the interior piers of the façade. Martin Chambiges was, at this time, too old to be of practical assistance (he died in 1532), and his son Pierre came to Troyes and directed the construction of wooden props against the nave gable in order to prevent it from settling westward when the support of the old bell tower was removed (B, 1531–32, 2). He was asked for advice on the problem of finding a new master mason to replace the recently deceased Jehan de Damas (B, 1531–32, 4). He remained in Troyes for long enough to issue the templates needed for the cutting of the stone necessary for the interior piers of the façade (B, 1531–32, 3). On his departure, Jehan Bailly assumed direction of the Troyes workshop. Bailly, who died in 1559, can be considered as the last of the "Chambiges men" in control of the Troyes Cathedral workshop.

The intervention of Pierre Chambiges lies behind the rather different forms used in the tower supporting piers of Troyes Cathedral, which, unlike any piers known to have been designed by Martin Chambiges, are asymmetrical and have sharp-edged angles alternating with rounded undulating shafts (Figs. 10 & 76). The same lack of symmetry and use of sharp angles can be seen in Pierre Chambiges' piers in the interior of the transept arms of Senlis Cathedral (Figs. 32 & 115).

The old bell tower having been demolished and the interior piers having been built, it was possible to install the transverse arches under the towers and to continue with the upper parts of the façade.[14] This work, which was directed by Jehan Bailly, was completed without any changes of plan or major difficulties, and the level of the balustrade over the rose was reached by around 1550. At the level of the clock under the north tower (dated by a cartouche to 1554) slight changes were introduced into the vocabulary of forms, and the north tower itself, begun by Gabriel Favereau, has nothing to do with Chambiges' plan.[15] The south tower was never begun.

The general plan for the western frontispiece of Troyes Cathedral comprises two towers and three portals—an ensemble which is familiar to all students of Gothic architecture, and which is sometimes called a "harmonious façade" (Figs. 2, 3, & 34). In the case of this particular building, however, the relationship between the three segments of the west block and the five aisles of the nave can hardly be called "harmonious." The lateral blocks of the towers project into the outer aisles and the plan has generally been considered singularly ill-fitting.

The buttresses flanking the outer segments of the façade are flat-faced in their lowest parts, projecting outward much more deeply than do the complex, polygonal buttresses of the center portal. The mass of these two outer buttresses, as they ascend, is articulated in two different ways. The first way involves the lightening of the mass by piercing niches capped by vigorously curved, three-dimensional canopies. The second way allows the thickness of the buttress to be diminished by placing inside the square section of the lowest part of the buttress a second square, turned at forty-five degrees to the first. Thus, the buttress which had been aligned with the surface of the façade in its lowest parts will turn diagonally with its angle presented toward the beholder. The two means of articulation, niche and rotated square, are skillfully coordinated, as the process of turning the square diagonally is effected by the bipartite division of the lower buttress with its two niches.

93

A strong contrast exists between the bold articulation and depth of the outer buttresses and the more delicate forms of the shallower polygonal buttresses flanking the central portal. The latter have a symmetrical five-sided front face, composed of niches and the pilasters which divide them, but are splayed back in an asymmetric fashion toward the surface of the façade. Toward the central vessel the buttresses are splayed more gently than on their sides toward the lateral segments of the façade. The polygonal nature of the central buttresses and the asymmetric splaying combine to produce a unit with a highly sculptural appearance, as opposed to the flat-sided aspect of the side buttresses. Despite their different appearance, however, the same principles have been applied to both outer and inner buttresses in order to articulate them and diminish them in size. In the side buttresses the application of the system of rotated squares and the use of niches were the means of articulation employed, the former being the dominant element, and providing the vehicle for the latter. In the central buttresses, however, the niches are predominant, and the square pilaster, articulated and diminished by means of the inscribed square, becomes the secondary element, dividing the niches.

The two horizontal levels of the façade are defined by the balustrades and gables capping the three portals, and the continuous balustrade over the level of the rose window. The three straight-sided gables intersected by horizontal balustrades lend a very traditional appearance to the portals, reminding us particularly of works of the mid and late thirteenth century (transepts of Notre-Dame, Paris, Rouen Cathedral, etc.). A closer inspection, however, reveals that these units consist of a highly complex, interwoven calligraphic design which would have only been possible in Late Gothic. The main lines of the composition are provided by the boldly projecting mouldings of the straight gable itself, the two parallel lines of the balustrade, and the outermost order of the portal. Behind these main lines exists a secondary composition consisting of a series of vertical panels formed by mouldings with a lesser degree of projection. In the central portal there are eleven such panels, and in the side portals seven. These vertical mouldings also constitute the vertical mullions of the balustrades, through which they are allowed to continue on up to emerge as spiky projections over the top rim of the gable and balustrade. In a similar fashion they are allowed to continue downward to penetrate the outermost order of the portal, and to protrude as vertical pendant cusping. The gaps between these vertical pendant cusps receive their own trilobed cusping, which is distorted as the angle between the verticals and the voussoir becomes increasingly sharp in the lower parts of the arch. This secondary cusping between the vertical pendants constitutes a sort of free-flowing linkage between the rectilinear elements of the composition, which is repeated in the blind tracery over the spandrels of the portal, where similarly distorted trilobed cusping occurs, and where free-flowing lines are introduced to link the vertical mouldings to the lines of the gable.

Despite the interwoven effect of the lines of the composition of the balustrade and gable, the general effect is two-dimensional and calligraphic. Impinging upon

94

the space of the portals by means of the screen of vertical pendant cusps which almost seem to be dripping downward into the space of the portals, these flat areas of the gables and balustrades provide a foil for the cavernous portals, which open directly inward from the buttresses. We are left with no clear understanding of where the surface of the wall is meant to be, and the areas of the balustrades and gables provide the eye with the only flat surfaces of any considerable expanse in the whole composition.

The voussoirs and the jambs of the portals are articulated by multiple orders of continuous fillet mouldings, some of which carry radiating cusps while others enclose bands of heavily undercut foliage (Fig. 35). Figurative sculpture was confined to a single order in the outer portals, and a double order in the central portal. Such sculpture might also have been contained in the niches which originally existed in the three tympana. These niches disappeared in the Revolution when the tympana were chiselled smooth, presumably to provide flat surfaces upon which revolutionary slogans could be displayed. Statues were also carried by the three trumeaux of the portals: Peter and Paul in the side portals, and Christ in the center.

The planning of the embrasures of the portals is exceedingly complex (Figs. 3 & 36). Multiple fillets, some protruding more heavily than others, are placed at several different angles to the axis of the portal. The lines of some of the most important fillets are then continued downward into the lowest part of the jambs, where they are reflected in the sharp angles which exist between a series of concave scooped out forms.

The screens provided by the gables and balustrades of the portals conceal passageways running in front of the upper segments of the façade. The central segment is occupied by a huge six-petalled Flamboyant rose, each petal consisting of two mouchettes enclosing a soufflet. This basic pattern (Fig. 21) was used by Martin Chambiges for all of his roses (with the exception of the south transept rose at Sens Cathedral which has five petals), although the Troyes rose was made almost twenty years after the death of the master, and does not have the delicate cusping of the Sens roses. The rose is surmounted by a heavily projecting enclosing arch, capped by a gable formed of broken inverted curves. The curves of the gable and the curly candelabra-type cusping of the enclosing arch provide relief from the excessively rectilinear aspect of the gables of the portals.

The upper walls of the side segments of the façade are pierced by ranks of four niches, divided by the familiar square pilaster which turns diagonally as it ascends.

The towers were designed very much to be seen from the side as well as from the front.[16] The forward-facing buttresses at the sides of the façade are linked to the lateral buttress by a diagonal splay (which houses staircase turrets), and by the continuation of the decorative forms across into the side faces of the towers. The area between the two heavily projecting lateral buttresses is bridged by a balustrade and capped by an ogee gable which creates an echo of the gables and balustrades

95

over the portals. The mass of the lateral buttresses is articulated and diminished by means of the same device (rotated squares) as that used on the front of the façade.

Three more points of a more subjective nature may now be made concerning the impact of the façade upon the beholder. It is noticeable that the work is not seen to best advantage from directly in front (Figs. 34 & 35). When one moves to the side, and views the work from an oblique angle, it takes on an extra dimension which is not at first apparent. Thus, it will be seen that whereas the side buttresses project to a much greater degree than the center buttresses, the gable and balustrade over the central portal enclosed between these latter buttresses is pushed out in front of the gables and balustrades of the side portals. Behind the projecting center gable the level of the rose is set back further than the walls bearing the ranks of niches of the side segments of the façade. The effect is of a complex, undulating pattern of relief, totally unlike the flatness of a Rayonnant façade of the mid-thirteenth century. This aspect of rather sculptural, three-dimensional relief is apparent throughout the surface of the façade: in the form of the central buttresses; in the niches; and in the cavernous portals. The concave scoops which constitute the "embrasures" of the portals give the effect that the stone mass has been eaten into by the space around it: that the space of the portals has taken on a positive aspect, and seems to be shaping the masonry.

A second general point relates to the way in which minor forms tend to echo major forms in the design of the façade. Thus, for example, the niches, with their hollowed-out aspect, capped by the intensely linear canopies, echo the forms of the portals, and the articulation of the small pilasters between the niches reflects the inscribed square system applied to the major buttresses flanking the facade. Third, the beholder familiar with the transept façades of Sens and Beauvais Cathedrals, designed by Martin Chambiges in the immediately preceding period, will recognize a certain playfulness in the marshalling of the forms of the buttresses. The polygonal buttresses flanking the central portal are derived from octagonal staircase turrets in a similar position at Sens and at Beauvais. At Troyes Chambiges has retained the form, but has moved the staircase turrets to the more massive outer buttresses.

If the skillful use of articulation on the exterior of the façade is successful in lightening the massive bulk of the masonry employed, in the interior this is a much more difficult task. Three corners of each of the towers rest upon exterior masonry, but the fourth corner is supported upon interior, thickened piers (Figs. 10 and 76). These piers have an asymmetric form, having their mass pushed outward into the lateral segments as much as possible in order to avoid blocking the central vessel, and also to provide support for the towers intended over these side bays. The surface of each of the piers is made up of alternating sharp angles and rounded, undulating shafts which are received upon hexagonal plinths. These massive tower-supporting piers are linked by thick transverse arches to piers attached to the lateral walls of the façade to form the square bays of the towers.

These latter supports have the form of exactly one half of a symmetrical eight-shafted undulating pier (Fig. 9). Each of the undulating shafts (thicker for the transverse arch and thinner for the diagonal) is received on top of a hexagonal plinth, the hexagons of the main shafts presenting their flat sides to the outside of the pier, and the hexagons for the diagonals presenting an angle to the outside.

Diagonally-placed transverse arches and Y-shaped vaults link the lateral walls of the towers, and the interior piers of the façade to the thick piers at the western ends of the aisles (piers B 1 and E 1).

The general effect of the interior of the façade is excessively somber, and the visitor to the cathedral entering through the lateral portals tends to feel oppressed by the sheer bulk of the masonry. The situation is exacerbated by the presence of a heavy neoclassical organ tribune which carries the organ acquired from the abbey of Clairvaux after the Revolution.[17] The tribune not only prevents light from entering through the great west rose, but also conceals the articulation of the inner wall of the façade: delicate tracery work over the portals, and ranks of niches in the upper wall.[18] Another unfortunate aspect of the interior of the façade is the way in which the outer aisles of the nave are partially blocked by the massive lateral walls of the towers (Fig. 77)—although we will see that there was a simple mechanical reason which made this arrangement necessary.

Judgments by earlier writers on the Troyes west façade have for the most part been harsh. A. F. Arnaud, the historian-artist of the monuments of Troyes and the Aube, wrote: "dans cette profusion d'ornemens, les grandes lignes s'echappent et se reproduisent tour à tour; l'oeil se perd, se fatigue. . . ."[19] His judgment on the Late Gothic parts of the nave was also negative.[20] We have seen earlier that the Late Gothic master mason is equally liable to hostile criticism if he went on reproducing the forms of the earlier parts of the building (as one who is over-conservative, without the ability to invent new forms), or if he changed them (as one who has destroyed the symmetry of the building with forms which are somehow no longer "valid"). H. d'Arbois de Jubainville epitomized the negative feelings of many critics toward the façade: "le portail occidental de Troyes n'est qu'une oeuvre médiocre et inachevée du seizième siècle, et sa masse énorme noyée, pour ainsi dire, dans le détail des ornements de goût douteux dont elle est surchargée, n'a rien de l'aspect imposant des monuments analogues construits au douzième siècle et au treizième."[21] L. Pigeotte, the excellent and sensitive historian of the nave and west façade, could only praise "l'imposante masse de son ensemble."[22] Paul Frankl, who contributed so much to our understanding of the nature of Gothic, could find nothing to comment on except the use of inverted curves in the niche canopies.[23] R. Sanfaçon analyzed the work mostly in terms of movement; for example, he commented: "Ces contreforts [centreaux] s'évasent vers l'intérieur et ramènent le regard à la rose, puis au gable principal et au portail central."[24] Similarly, the concept of movement dominates his analysis of the portals, and he presents a discussion of the nature of the different rhythms set up by the succession

Martin Chambiges, *Supremus Artifex*, 1502–1532

of the various kinds of jambs and voussoirs used in the portals. Full and sympathetic descriptions were given by M. Vachon and V. de Courcel.[25] The former described "une façade d'une richesse, d'une élégance exceptionelle . . . un des plus beaux types original du style originaux flamboyant du commencement du XVIe. siècle." Vachon had a chauvinistic axe to grind, however, which at times led him to short-sighted judgments. V. de Courcel, in a careful analysis of the work, praised it as a "façade majestueuse."

Criticisms have been mainly of three kinds: to regret the ill-fitting nature of the west block; to condemn the poor taste of the sculptural decoration; and to berate it as a specimen of a bastard, "in-between" kind of style.

In our narrative of the problems which accompanied the inception of work on the towers and portals owing to the continued existence of the old bell tower, we attempted to show that the greater depth provided by the three-segment plan was absolutely necessary to enable the workshop to construct the exterior walls around the old tower, which could not be demolished until new support for the western nave could be improvised. This additional depth rendered the initial plan for a five-segment west block quite impossible. Far from condemning the use of a three-segment west block to terminate a five-aisled nave, we should admire Chambiges for having found an ingenious solution to a thorny problem!

The sculptural articulation employed by Chambiges (above all the niche and the inscribed square) is entirely at home upon this work whose overall plasticity is such an important feature. Unlike so many Late Gothic master masons, Martin Chambiges did not "turn his building into lace" but rather employed details whose size and vigor were in accord with the scale of the work.

The third type of criticism is harder to tackle: we have to pose the question as to what extent the work can be called "Gothic," and how it relates to High Gothic design. The last years of the fifteenth century saw the growing popularity of Italianate decorative motifs—rinceau, urns, putti, ox skulls, and the like.[26] Very little of this kind of ornament appears in the work of Martin Chambiges. At Troyes the only example of this kind of decoration in the lower parts of the façade is to be seen on the statue pedestals of the portals. In general Martin Chambiges was certainly something of a traditionalist in his vocabulary of decorative forms.

A more pertinent question relates to the extent to which Chambiges' design can be called "Gothic" in its overall planning and design principles. In designing the western termination of Troyes Cathedral, Martin Chambiges was placing himself in line of descent with generations of Gothic masters who had faced the problem of reconciling several potentially conflicting desiderata: to construct an impressive showpiece with towers, yet to avoid blocking the west end of the nave with excessively heavy masonry; to construct lavish portals disposed between the buttresses, and to coordinate the axis of these portals with the interior spaces of the building; to design a façade with integrity in its general proportions, yet to fit this part of the building on to the nave.[27]

In undertaking the planning of a west block with towers, the main problem which the master mason would encounter was the calculation of the proportions of the work in terms of the relationship of mass to void, and the relationship between the size of each of the towers to the gap between them (the central segment of the façade). Our understanding of Gothic design procedures has advanced enormously over the past decades and we no longer see great Gothic masters as spirits who "felt rather than measured," but as rational beings who frequently had recourse to proportional systems designed to relate the dimensions of the part to the size of the whole.[28] Since towers were very often designed around a square plan, simple geometric or arithmetic relationships would have an obvious appeal.

The only part of Chambiges' scheme at Troyes where simple proportional relationships are easily ascertainable is in the lateral faces of the towers (the north wall of the north tower and the south wall of the south tower). The flat-faced buttresses used here measure exactly 3.60m. in their lowest parts. We know that at Beauvais Martin Chambiges used a foot of 0.325m. (the king's foot), and it seems probable that the same unit would have been used at Troyes.[29] The thickness of the buttress is thus eleven feet.

In examining the relationship between the thickness of the buttresses and the width between them in the lateral faces of the towers, the situation remains very straightforward: the latter (7.22m.) is almost exactly twice the former. We thus have a simple relationship of two to one, and in the context of a plan for a square tower we have a traditional Gothic scheme based on the device of the rotated square or quadrature, shown in Figure 4 a.

When we turn to the front faces of the towers we begin to find that the situation is not quite so simple, however. The outer flat-faced buttresses to the north of the north tower and south of the south tower are both around 3.60m. (3.595 for the northern unit), but the complex buttresses flanking the central portal present something of a problem. The front faces of these buttresses have the form of an irregular five-sided polygon. If we measure the thickness of the buttress at the point of transition between the polygon and the embrasures of the portals we find that the thickness of the buttress is 3.72m. or rather more than the lateral buttresses of the towers. Similarly we find that the distance across the side portals (between the buttresses) is rather more than the distance between the lateral buttresses of the towers (7.34m. as opposed to 7.22m). Thus we are dealing with towers which are not quite square, being rather wider in a north-south direction than they are deep, in an east-west direction. The plan for the main towers of Troyes Cathedral does not, therefore, entirely embody the geometric system of quadrature, since this can only operate within a square. Chambiges might have instinctively begun his plan using the quadrature system, and been forced to make slight changes as the construction was taken in hand.

Some vestiges of arithmetic relationships do remain in the plan of the west face of the composition. Thus we find that the dimensions of both the buttresses and the spaces between the buttresses have been increased commensurately. The relationship between the width of one of the central buttresses and the width of the side portal is still very close to one-to-two ($2 \times 3.72 = 7.44$; actual dimension is 7.34m.) and the relationship for the central portal is one-to-three ($3 \times 3.72 = 11.16$; actual dimension is 11.13). Thus we have a central portal which equals the side portal plus the thickness of one buttress. Also we find that a module of somewhere between 3.60 and 3.72m. can be repeated eleven times across the front surface of the façade, fitting into the spaces of the portals and the spaces occupied by the buttresses.

To construct an "ideal plan" like the one reconstructed in our Figure 4 a would have been aesthetically undesirable. The same mass of masonry used in the lateral walls of the towers would not be desirable in the western walls through which the portals are pierced, and which have been thinned somewhat. The thinning of the western wall has caused the interior elements of the façade to be shifted to the west: it is apparent on measuring the façade that the inner piers and attached piers are not on the same axis as the outer buttresses.

Of course, Chambiges, when he sat in his drafting office in Paris to sketch out the *pourtrait* which was sent to Troyes in 1502 or early 1503, had to consider not only the plan of the towers and portals, but also the elevation. It seems certain that he must have been in possession of the main dimensions of the nave, and his problem was to achieve a unit which would fit on to the existing nave, yet have integrity in itself. In thinking about the elevation of a west block with towers, Gothic designers must almost inevitably have been led into thinking in terms of squares. Yet the existence of a rather low nave with double aisles on each side gave a section which would be framed by a rather squat rectangle, measuring 28m. high by 45m. wide. To fit a five-segment design on to such a nave would cause no problems, since this type of façade has an expansive quality (Fig. 26). Such proportions embodied in a three-segment façade would produce an emphasis on width rather than height, which Chambiges clearly wanted to avoid. He has, however, managed to give an elevation which approximates quite closely to a square (Fig. 4 b). He has achieved this by designing a unit which is really a little too narrow for the nave on to which it fits: hence the way in which the lateral walls of the towers crowd into the outer aisles. The proportions of the portals (up to the tops of the balustrades) also approximate to squares, which interlock with the buttresses.

None of the Late Gothic masters of the cathedral, Jaquet le Vachier, Master Bleuet, Anthoine Colas, Jehançon Garnache, or Martin Chambiges, was entirely free to impose his own plan upon the work, regardless of the existing building. In the work of Chambiges, more than that of any of the others, we get a glimpse of an "ideal plan" embodying the concept that a good building is one in which the relationship of the parts to the whole is fixed by some geometric or arithmetic principle. In planning the proportions of the "skeleton" of his plan and elevation,

Chambiges was working in a way which had been followed by three centuries of Gothic master masons. When Master Bleuet was approached to design a west block for Troyes Cathedral half a century earlier, his reaction had been, "go and look at Notre-Dame, Paris, and Reims and Amiens Cathedrals and base your design upon these prototypes." Martin Chambiges, a Parisian, was particularly familiar with Notre-Dame, and his design, which terminates a five-aisled nave with a three-segment west block, owes much to this prototype. The gables and balustrades over the portals similarly owe much to the transepts of Notre-Dame.

It would obviously be foolish to regard Chambiges' design for the west block of Troyes Cathedral as a direct interpretation of thirteenth century prototypes. A survey of the master's earlier work will illustrate his progress toward the evolution of a distinctive personal style.[30]

Martin Chambiges must have been born in the period around 1460, and died in 1532: his working life thus covered the critical fifty-year period (1480s to 1530s) which saw the rapid economic recovery of France and a spate of building to replace churches damaged in the Hundred Years War or to complete major structures which had remained unfinished.

The master's first documented work was at the cathedral of Sens, where between 1489 and 1494 he directed construction of the south transept arm. Although absent after 1494, he continued to supervise the work, directed on the site by his lieutenant, Hughes Cuvelier. Chambiges' experience at Sens was to be of the greatest importance for his future work. The addition of transept arms at Sens Cathedral had begun already in the period around 1300, and involved the demolition of one of the "minor" piers of the continuous alternating arcade and the transformation of the sexpartite vault of the central vessel into a quadripartite crossing vault.[31] The old lateral apsidal chapels were to be suppressed in order to make way for the transept arms. Although the thirteenth century master who began the work must be credited with the master plan behind this transformation, Chambiges was forced to "think big": in other words to apply himself to working on a very large Gothic church, where major structural problems would present themselves. On his arrival in Sens he would have been asked to survey the problem of completing the unfinished transept and propose his own solution: this solution was, no doubt, contained in the *devis de la croisée* mentioned in the fabric account. The work at Sens must have provided Chambiges with the reputation of one who was able to view a great Gothic church in its totality, overcome structural problems, and devise new additions to the building in an appropriate, fashionable style.

The appearance of the new south transept façade at Sens was, to some extent, determined by the fact that the earlier work had gone up to the level of the top of the doorway (Fig. 117). The task of continuing the existing portal embrasures up into the voussoirs was an exceedingly complex one. The irregular series of rounded shafts and sharp mouldings in the jambs are set at a variety of angles to the axis of the portal, and create an overall effect of brittle linearity and perplexing multiplicity. In completing the upper part of this portal Martin Chambiges was forced to respect the general lines of the existing work: although we find one rounded moulding transformed into a sharpened fillet while one fillet is terminated by a pedestal. Chambiges' experience in completing this portal provided him with ideas concerning portal design which he was to develop through the rest of his life. In other words, the multiplicity, complexity, and linearity of the late Rayonnant style lie behind the style of this Late Gothic master.

The most distinctive feature of the upper part of the Sens south transept portal is the sharply linear quality of the mouldings, coupled with an ability to turn stone into molten, plastic forms, which can merge into each other in a disconcerting fashion. Thus, we find the diagonally placed pilasters flanking the portal merging into the surface of the wall, while the outermost moulding of the portal runs on to the surface of the pilaster. Similarly, the radiating cusps framing the tympanum are engulfed by the vertical fillets flanking the portal in such a way as to leave their outlines and tips still visible. The beholder is invited to believe that the *idea* of the cusp is still there, concealed inside the inert mass of masonry.

The vertical panelling of the wall around the upper portal constitutes a brittle screen which interacts with the outermost order of the portal, since the verticals are allowed to penetrate this outer order, and to impinge upon the space of the portal as vertical pendant cusping. Such interaction between rectilinear and curving lines provides a *Leitmotif* in Chambiges' style.[32]

The upper parts of the south transept façade offer us the first two examples of recurrent features of the master's work: the six-petalled Flamboyant rose and the decorated staircase turret (Fig. 117). Each of the petals of the rose comprises a soufflet enclosed by two mouchettes, which nod together. The use of pointed arches at the heads of the soufflets and mouchettes and the delicate interior cusping help produce a lilting, flickering, two-dimensional pattern. The vast sea of glass and tracery of the great central window is enclosed by two octagonal staircase turrets, placed in such a way that the angles of the octagons face outward.

The original designer of the transept façade (c. 1300) had projected flat-faced buttresses, with a shallow projection, and had tucked his staircase turret around to the west of the transept arm. Chambiges, by fusing his buttress with the staircase turret and adding a matching turret on the other side of the façade, created a framing device of considerable plasticity, which provides a certain muscularity totally unlike the delicate two-dimensionality of Rayonnant façades.

In the later north transept at Sens (after 1500) Chambiges was able to develop ideas which had appeared tentatively on the south side (Fig. 116). The north façade is framed by octagonal decorated staircase turrets (with their flat sides outward); the embrasures of the portal, with their multiple fillet mouldings, merge directly with the flanking turrets; an adaptation (with five petals) of the same type of rose is used, and the total depth of the façade is enhanced by the use of very wide passages behind the gable of the portal and in front of the gable of the roof.

Again, this depth and plasticity are combined with intense linearity. The vertical panels above the portal impinge into the space of the portal, and are successfully coordinated with the vertical mullions of the balustrade which intersects the gable of the portal.

Similarly, in the interior of the Sens transept, we see a significant development in the forms used by Chambiges. In the earlier work in the south arm, the attached shafts have an undulating profile, and are received on top of base mouldings which also have a continuous rounded surface. The source for such undulating forms might have lain in thirteenth century prototypes such as the choir of Rodez Cathedral, or, more likely for Chambiges, a Parisian, the undulating shafts framing the entrances of the lateral chapels of the nave of Notre-Dame, Paris. In the later work at Sens in the interior of the north transept arms, however, we see that Martin Chambiges has abandoned the rounded base moulding in favor of a hexagonal form.

On leaving Sens in 1494, Chambiges returned to Paris. Certain scholars have wanted to associate his name with Parisian works undertaken either before or after his stay in Sens (i.e., before 1489 or between 1494 and 1500). Such non-documented attributions have included the west rose of the Sainte-Chapelle, the portal of the convent of the Jacobins, the tower of the now-demolished church of Saint-Jacques-de-la-Boucherie, and the choir of the church of SS. Gervais and Protais (Fig. 110).[33] None of these attributions can be substantiated, however. The rose of the Sainte-Chapelle, reconstructed under Charles VIII, probably in the 1480s, certainly bears a great resemblance to the south transept rose of Sens Cathedral, but the type is a fairly common one in the period around 1500 (Fig. 113). The case of the tower of Saint-Jacques provides us with a useful test (Fig. 111). Many of the motifs employed on the tower resemble the forms developed by Chambiges, especially the niche canopies where verticals intersect curving lines, and the lavish articulation of the buttresses and staircase turret. Indeed, it is tempting to suggest that had the west towers of Troyes Cathedral been completed according to the plans of Martin Chambiges, they would have borne a strong resemblance to the Tour Saint-Jacques. Documentary evidence has demonstrated that the work was completed under the direction of the brothers de Felin, however,[34] and one must conclude that many of the decorative forms used by Martin Chambiges were part of a general "Parisian vocabulary" around 1500.[35]

Between 1499 and 1500 Martin Chambiges was involved in consultations concerning the reconstruction of the collapsed Pont Notre-Dame.[36] The records of the deliberations which accompanied the planning of this project illustrate several important aspects of the master's identity. Firstly, it is clear that he held no title in the city of Paris other than that of "master mason": he was not named as master mason for the king, this post being held by Mathieu de Louans, nor for the *Bureau de la Ville de Paris*. Second, his opinion on structural matters clearly carried weight: he was present at the meetings where the material and form of the bridge and the specifications of the foundations were discussed. Third, these meetings brought

Martin Chambiges into contact with a wide range of other master masons. The lists of masons' names recorded reveal that the masonic fraternity of Paris was numerous and complex: the composition of the groups present at each meeting varied very considerably. Such meetings would obviously provide a forum for the dissemination of new ideas. Thus it is significant to find the de Felin brothers whose names are associated with the Tour Saint-Jacques side by side with Chambiges. Jean de Felin later went on to supervise the construction of the new choir of Saint-Aspais, Melun.[37] A portal in the east wall of the Saint-Aspais choir is so similar to a work of Martin Chambiges that we would attribute it to that master, if clear documentation did not exist to the contrary (Fig. 106). Pierre Tarissel, master mason of Amiens Cathedral, was another colleague of Chambiges in the deliberations. Tarissel was to accompany Chambiges on his first visit to Beauvais, where Chambiges was to be offered the commission of master mason in charge of the construction of the new transept. Amiens Cathedral provides us with two examples of rose windows similar in certain respects to the roses of Martin Chambiges, and a screen in the south transept of Amiens Cathedral has vertical pendant cusping in the "Chambiges style."[38] We conclude that certain decorative motifs were shared by many master masons in the Parisian area and we lack the evidence which would enable us to ascertain the origin of each motif.

When we turn to the question of pier design, however, we find a situation which is radically different. The Sens Cathedral transept has no free-standing piers. It was at Beauvais where Chambiges developed his characteristic pier type. Called to Beauvais in 1500 to examine the site of the new transept of the cathedral, Chambiges was to spend most of the rest of his life in this city, where he died in 1532.[39] Between 1500 and around 1510 Chambiges directed work on the lower part of the south transept façade (up to the balustrade below the great rose window) and from 1510 until shortly after 1518 he transferred work to the north transept façade and the interior piers of the north transept arm (Figs. 28 & 98).[40] Work continued to the interior piers of the south transept (1520s) and the upper parts of the south transept arm (the date 1550 is on the vault). Although no document names Chambiges as the master designer of the new choir of the parish and collegiate church of Saint-Etienne and Saint-Vast, Beauvais, it is highly probable that he directed the commencement of work soon after 1500 (Figs. 30, 31, 103–105). Certain forms such as the undulating pier and the petal vault appear in the church before they are used in the cathedral, suggesting that Chambiges himself was involved.[41]

The piers of the Beauvais Cathedral transept arms and the choir of Saint-Etienne have eight shafts (four large and four small) arranged symmetrically around a central core (Figs 29, 99 and 100). The surface of the pier is an undulating one: it is as if a traditional eight-shafted pier had been cloaked in a heavy, clinging blanket which half reveals, half conceals the geometry of the forms underneath. The function of each shaft is reflected by the placing of the hexagonal plinths: the plinths for the main shafts have a flat side presented toward the outside, whereas

BUILDING TROYES CATHEDRAL

the plinths for the shafts supporting the diagonals have an angle toward the outside. A simple proportional system using inscribed hexagons governs the relationship between the total size of the pier and the dimensions of the two hexagonal plinths.[42] The piers attached to the lateral walls of the towers in Troyes Cathedral constitute one half of a plan such as that employed for the piers of Beauvais Cathedral and the church of Saint-Etienne (Fig. 9).[43]

Chambiges' piers embody a highly "structural" quality: the form of the plinth is designed to reflect the function of the various shafts, and the rounded form of the shafts lends each unit a muscular, plastic quality. If we look to the Parisian background, we find that trends in the capital city were tending in the opposite direction: the forms of the pier were indeed becoming more streamlined, but instead of using rounded shafts to express the function of the pier, Parisian designers were increasingly using angularity. Thus, the sequence of fifteenth-century piers in the church of Saint-Séverin, Paris, demonstrates a movement away from shafts and toward a surface made up of a series of sharp angles which exist between concavities.[44]

Other monuments constructed around 1500 have piers where we see a mannerist play on the relationship between form and function, especially in the "disappearing" bases of SS. Gervais and Protais and Saint-Merry, which grow from the smooth surface of the pier like fungus from a tree (Fig. 112). Piers with an undulating surface can be found in the sixteenth century choir of Saint-Etienne-du-Mont, but the bases lack the "structural" qualities of Chambiges' piers. Thus, Chambiges' ideas concerning pier design stand outside the general trends of Parisian design, and it seems possible that his inspiration came not from contemporary models but from thirteenth century prototypes. The use of the hexagonal plinth became generalized in High Gothic and Rayonnant, and the south choir aisle of Notre-Dame, Paris, offers us an example of a pier with hexagonal plinths linked by concavities much in the manner of Martin Chambiges (Fig. 108).

The Beauvais transepts embody many features familiar to us from Sens Cathedral. The Beauvais south transept is flanked by octagonal decorated staircase turrets (Fig. 98). The portal has multiple fillet mouldings set at a perplexing variety of angles to the axis of the portal. The jambs of the portal are rather more unified with the flanking turrets: this is achieved through the uniformity in height and type in the series of niches extending from the jambs into the flanking turrets. In the Beauvais south transept we find that the gable surmounting the portal now has straight sides rather than the curved sides which were used at Sens. The severely rectilinear pattern made by the intersection of the straight-sided gable and the balustrade is reminiscent of many Rayonnant works. The north transept façade of Beauvais Cathedral provides us with a useful test as to the importance of the decorated staircase turret in the total façade design. Whereas on the south side, Chambiges had demolished the thirteenth-century flat-faced buttress to the east of the transept portal and substituted his own turret, on the north side, this was impossible, owing to a financial crisis brought on by the refusal on the part of the

Martin Chambiges, *Supremus Artifex*, 1502–1532

bishop to contribute his share toward the expenses of the fabric.[45] Thus, in order to avoid expense, the old thirteenth-century flat-faced buttress to the east of the portal was left intact, and Chambiges was forced to construct a matching buttress which was equally plain. In comparison with the rich plasticity of the southern façade, the north transept at Beauvais seems poverty-struck.

An important feature of Martin Chambiges' stylistic vocabulary which appears at Beauvais for the first time is the niche. Not used at Sens, the niche provided Chambiges with an ideal means of voiding his massive walls, much in the same way as Norman and Anglo-Norman designers used the wall passage. Whereas the wall passage ultimately led to a diaphanous effect, the niche and the decorated staircase turret produce an effect which can only be called sculptural. The concavity of the niche itself suggests that the wall has been eaten into from the surrounding space. To cap the niche, Chambiges used a vigorously curving canopy formed of inverted curves, and intersected by a double vertical: the same interaction of straight and curved lines is used over Chambiges' portals.

The final feature of the work at Beauvais which deserves mention is the development of vault forms (Figs. 101–102). In all of Martin Chambiges's documented career, he only supervised the installation of six vaults, having left Sens before the construction of the high vaults, and dying before the construction of the high vaults in Beauvais Cathedral or any of the vaults of Troyes. The six vaults attributable to Martin Chambiges are the units in the aisle to the west of the Beauvais Cathedral transept, four of which are simple quadripartite types and two of which embody elegant curvilinear patterns: those in the chapel to the west of the north transept arm (c. 1515) and in the chapel to the west of the southern arm (c. 1520s). Since there is clear documentary evidence to indicate the northern unit is earlier than the southern one, a comparison between the two will illustrate the direction in which the master's thought was tending as his career progressed. On the north side the vault is a quadripartite type with petals inserted in the spaces existing between the main ribs and the tiercerons. The prototype for this vault is the petal vault in the sepulchre chapel of the church of Saint-Etienne, dated by inscription, 1502 (Fig. 105). In the later vault in the chapel adjacent to the south transept arm of Beauvais Cathedral, we find that the curving lines now cross freely between the main divisions of the vault, to create an overall effect not unlike a modern traffic intersection. Throughout his working life Chambiges remained preoccupied with optical effects, and above all the unification of elements which previously had been separate (the octagonal turret and the staircase, the eight shafts of his pier, etc.).

The work of Martin Chambiges at Beauvais provided the basis for a "Chambiges School" of some importance. If the new choir of Saint-Etienne was not the work of Martin Chambiges himself (we believe it was), then it must be placed at the top of the Chambiges school (Figs. 30, 31, 103–105). The design employed for the plan and elevation at Saint-Etienne offered great advantages in terms of simplicity. The elevation was a soaring two-story type, with ample window space for the display of stained glass, and the plan combined a flat east end, an apsidal termination, and a pseudo-ambulatory.

Features derived from the church and the cathedral in Beauvais appear in several churches in the surrounding area, for example at Gisors, Marissel, Allonne, Compiègne, and Senlis. The most important "copies" of the church of Saint-Etienne may be found in Troyes itself: the churches of Saint-Pantaléon, Saint-Jean-au-Marché, and Saint-Nicholas all embody undulating piers, two-story elevations and variations on the theme of the flat east end, with or without ambulatory.[46] At Senlis Cathedral sixteenth-century work included the reconstruction of the upper parts of the choir and nave which had been devastated in the fire of 1504. Martin Chambiges visited Senlis Cathedral after the fire, and some scholars have suggested that he continued to direct the workshop at Senlis after the fire, but neither the documentary nor the stylistic evidence supports this assumption.[47] The role of Pierre Chambiges in the completion of the transept arms at Senlis is clearly documented, however, and many of the forms of the transept façades and interior piers involve playful adaptations of formulae first conceived by Martin Chambiges.[48] The piers, with their alternation of undulation and sharp angle and their mannered disalignments, constitute a particularly useful document revealing the relationship of the style of father and son (Figs. 32, 114, & 115).

But it is, above all, in the cathedral of Troyes where we see the ideas of Martin Chambiges developed to their full extent. The polygonal turrets flanking the central portal; the undulating piers attached to the lateral walls inside the towers; the characteristic niche; the complexity of the design of portal embrasures and fusion with the flanking buttresses—all these features at Troyes must be seen in the light of prior developments at Sens and Beauvais. At Troyes, however, Chambiges had a considerable degree of freedom to determine the main lines of the new work (at Sens and Beauvais Cathedrals he was limited for obvious reasons). The great bulk of the western block at Troyes allowed Chambiges to exploit to the greatest extent the sculptural qualities inherent in his style.

We are left with the question posed in an earlier part of this section: to what extent is this work "Gothic"? A critic who applies the criteria of High Gothic style will come away disappointed. Our criteria for assessing the work must allow for the fact that Chambiges was to a certain extent the product of his time, and shared many of his most basic ideas with numerous other Late Gothic contemporaneous masters. In certain other aspects, however, he seems to have supplemented his repertoire directly from thirteenth-century sources, as indeed one would expect from a master whose main contribution was the completion of the three great unfinished cathedrals of Sens, Beauvais, and Troyes. Stylistic evolution within the period we call "Gothic" cannot be understood as a single line of development from thirteenth century "classicism" to fifteenth century decadence. Martin Chambiges' style can itself be seen as a kind of orthodoxy which was developed, adapted, and transformed by numerous followers, such as his own son Pierre in the transepts of Senlis Cathedral. At Senlis many of the forms remind us of the

107

work of Martin Chambiges, but a style which had been sharp, severe, and calligraphic became in the hands of Pierre Chambiges softer, more "painterly," favoring the unexpected and picturesque.

The impact of the work of Martin Chambiges upon ecclesiastical architecture in and around Troyes was immense. We have seen that three city churches, Saint-Pantaléon, Saint-Jean-au-Marché, and Saint-Nicholas were all related to the master's design for Saint-Etienne at Beauvais.[49] The master of two of these churches had close links with the cathedral. Jehan Bailly directed the start of work at Saint-Pantaléon after 1508.[50] Work on the parish church was temporarily halted by the great fire of 1524, which devastated much of Troyes. Work was then resumed by Maurice Favereau, who had previously worked under Bailly's direction. At Saint-Jean, construction of a new choir was begun between 1510 and 1520: Jehan Bailly and Jehan Gailde played an important role in the inception of the work, which was continued by Martin de Vaux, son-in-law of Gailde.[51] At Saint-Nicholas construction began after the fire of 1524 under the direction of Gerard Faulchot, son of Colleçon Faulchot, who had worked as an apprentice for Anthoine Colas. Gerard himself had been apprenticed to Jehançon Garnache. Displaced from the cathedral workshop, Garnache worked with Gerard Faulchot on the cloister of the abbey church of Montier-la-Celle, close to Troyes.[52]

The name of Martin Chambiges has been associated by some scholars with the design of the churches of Saint-Jean and Saint-Pantaléon, but these attributions are not confirmed by the written evidence.[53] However, both buildings should be listed at the top of the "Chambiges School," and have many features that are derived directly from the Master's style: steep two story elevations (Fig. 118), undulating piers, and a range of amusing decorative variations. The vaults of Saint-Nicholas are a case in point. Here we see vertical panels intersecting the curving lines of "flying ribs." A composition used by Martin Chambiges in a two-dimensional context (over portals) has here been transformed into the third dimension.

Saint-Jean and Saint-Pantaléon are the most striking examples of a "Chambiges School," elements of which penetrated far into the regions surrounding Troyes. Portals of this "School" appear, for example, at Pont-Sainte-Marie, Arcis-sur-Aube, Saint-André-les-Vergers, Saint-Parres-aux-Tertres, Saint-Phal and Rumilly-les-Vaudes.[54] Undulating piers can be found at Saint-Maure, Auxon, Rumilly-les Vaudes, Chavanges, and Brienne-le-Château, and niches in the Chambiges style appear in scores of rustic churches around Troyes. The strength of the Chambiges School resulted not only from the attractive quality of his design elements (portals, piers, etc.) but also from a network of marriage relationships which secured dependency (Jehan de Damas was son-in-law of Chambiges; Jehan Bailly was son-in-law of Damas, etc.).

Was there a "resistance" to the Chambiges men? Did the local masons resent the intrusion of these highly paid outsiders? Certainly, in the country around Troyes there was a high degree of indifference to the architecture favored by the city folk. This indifference is reflected in the continuing popularity of a church type which might be seen as the antithesis of Saint-Jean-au-Marché. This type, with three vessels the same height (a "hall church") and massive cylindrical piers, can be seen at Sainte-Savine and Saint-André-les-Vergers.

If any mason can be associated with a "resistance" to Chambiges, it is Jehan Gailde, known locally as "Big John."[55] We have seen that this master may have submitted a counter-proposal for the tower and portals of the cathedral. Gailde was master of the workshop of the church of the Madeleine, whose choir offers us another kind of contrast to the type represented by Saint-Jean-au-Marché. At the Madeleine we see a low clerestory and massive cylindrical piers. The most striking aspect of the design is the plan, in which three interlocking hexagons form the east end. We thus have an elision with the space of the eastern chapels and the ambulatory running into each other. Two other city churches followed this plan—Saint-Nizier and Saint-Remi.[56] Some way from Troyes the small church of Brienne-le-Château offers an example of a fusion between the Gailde School and the Chambiges School: at Brienne, the plan features three interlocking hexagons, but the piers are of the undulating type used by Chambiges.[57]

Gailde went on to construct the spectacular choir screen of the Madeleine. This is one of the most striking examples of Flamboyant audacity—an apparently three bay composition in which the supports have been eliminated. This effect is achieved by means of careful stone coursing, lending to the screen the quality of a bridge.

When we compare Gailde's screen with Chambiges' frontispiece of the cathedral, we appreciate the essentially rational quality of the latter work. However, the last laugh was with Gailde. He was buried beneath his fantastic screen, with an epitaph which declared that he expected to meet his maker with no fear of being crushed by the mass of stone above. Chambiges, on the other hand, was buried under the transept crossing of Beauvais Cathedral. When the crossing tower collapsed in 1583, the impact caused the pavement to drop by a foot or more!

We should not blame the architecture of Martin Chambiges for this disaster, however, since the crossing tower at Beauvais had been no part of his plan. Chambiges' works were well-designed and solidly constructed in a style which forms a last statement of the power of Gothic design in the period just before the triumph of Italian taste and ideas. We might conclude by noting that whereas Martin Chambiges was a cathedral man, a Gothic man, his son Pierre was, above all, a builder of châteaux in the modern Italian style.[58]

Martin Chambiges, *Supremus Artifex*, 1502–1532

Conclusion

SKED WHO BUILT TROYES CATHEDRAL, most specialists would probably respond in one of three fashions, or in a combination of all three. The clergy built Troyes Cathedral, in that they provided the incentive, the organization, and part of the funding. The people of the city of Troyes built the cathedral by providing the necessary urban setting and some of the funds. The workshop built Troyes Cathedral in a physical sense, since the masons chiselled the stones and the carpenters cut the timbers. All of these answers contain some elements of truth, but all of them need substantial qualification.

It has been seen that the bishops of Troyes played a minimal role as patrons of the construction. On the other hand, they sometimes became involved in a way which might seem surprising—for example in the discussion that accompanied the making of a decision about the priority of the flying buttresses or the vaults of the nave.

Similarly, the chapter refrained from making a regular annual commitment to the fabric fund. However, it is clear that in the course of the fourteenth century the chapter diverted toward the fabric certain revenues that had previously been received by the cellarer or the great chamber. Similarly, certain individual canons were generous patrons of the fabric.

The most significant way in which the chapter can be said to have built the cathedral was through the succession of *proviseurs*, most of them canons, who oversaw the construction in every way, from the recruitment of masons to the .purchase of materials to the raising of funds. The *proviseurs* are truly the hidden heroes of the prolonged campaigns of construction.

Modern writers have sometimes tended to see Gothic architecture as the expression of the rise of the bourgeois class. In Troyes, however, as in most French cathedral cities, the industrial and mercantile class constructed its parish churches in the suburbs, while the cathedral belonged to the old *castrum*, the core of the medieval city, an area occupied mainly by religious. The fabric accounts reveal that the largest single item of receipt was generally from the faithful of the diocese of Troyes. The municipality provided regular support for the construction only for a very limited period of time when the crossing tower was under construction. The essential contribution of the nonurban population to cathedral construction is often forgotten.

Similarly, the evidence from the fabric accounts has led us to propose several qualifications as far as the use of the word "workshop" is concerned. The expression has been too often used to suggest the existence of a unified group of artisans under the leadership of a powerful master mason. Such unified workshops did, from time to time, exist at Troyes (for example under Martin Chambiges) but the hierarchy of masons was generally characterized by a considerable degree of flexibility. Thus, only the master mason or masons enjoyed a contract with the chapter, the other artisans frequently being hired on an *ad hoc* basis. Master masons were almost always brought in from outside. No organization resembling a guild or trade union can be found among the masons.

In studying the style embodied in the successive campaigns of construction we have paid particular attention to the interaction between the power of existing forms and the personal vision of the master designers. Seven such visions have been detected in the campaigns of construction at Troyes Cathedral between 1200 and 1550. The vision of the first master (hemicycle of the choir) was a distinctly regional one with links to many monuments in the area. A second master brought High Gothic to Troyes in the construction of the straight bays of the choir and lower transept (influence from Chartres and Reims Cathedrals) and a third master who built the upper choir brought Rayonnant. The fourth campaign, involving the beginning of work on the nave and the completion of the upper transept, was a prolonged one, extending from around 1270 to the 1380s. This phase, in which several successive master masons were employed, involved an uneasy dialogue between the forms embodied in the older parts of Troyes Cathedral and forms borrowed particularly from the collegiate church of Saint-Urbain, Troyes, and Notre-Dame of Paris. Progress was slow owing to inadequate funding, the disruptions of the opening phase of the Hundred Years War, and structural failure. The fifth vision belonged to three successive master masons, Jaquet le Vachier, Anthoine Colas, and Jehançon Garnache, who completed the nave in the half century between 1450 and 1500. Although the contribution of each of these three masters can be distinguished, the spirit was the same; this is particularly true of Anthoine Colas and Jehançon Garnache, who both came from Reims. Thus, in the clerestory windows, constructed in the 1490s, Garnache used tracery forms derived from the chapel windows built by Colas in the 1470s. In 1455–56 a new style was brought to Troyes by Master Bleuet, who began work on the west façade scheme. This is our sixth vision, and it involved an interior articulated with bristling fillet mouldings continuing from pier to arch and rib without the intervention of a capital. A conflict is inherent between our fifth and sixth visions since Anthoine Colas favored the use of a completely different type of pier with smooth surfaces into which the mouldings of the ribs and arches disappear. Finally, the seventh phase in Troyes Cathedral is the new "Super Gothic" of Martin Chambiges. While this master was dependent upon Rayonnant prototypes for the forms he employed in his piers, portals, and decorative motifs, the sculptural handling of the great masses of masonry disposed by this master lends his work an appearance quite different from earlier monuments.

A consideration of the structural aspects of the construction of the cathedral leads us to question certain traditional assumptions. We have been led to see thirteenth century architecture as the supreme realization of Gothic. However, in structural terms, it is certainly correct to see the Late Gothic parts of Troyes Cathedral as the best constructed. The foundations of the nave and west façade have proved to be adequate (unlike those of the choir) and little settlement has taken place at foundation level. Masons such as Anthoine Colas and Jehançon Garnache wisely refrained from piercing the upper piers with passageways at triforium and clerestory levels and introduced important modifications to the type of flying buttress used. The western frontispiece of Martin Chambiges is particularly solidly constructed.

To do battle with the traditional assumptions concerning the decadent quality of Late Gothic would be like tilting at windmills. We have attempted to demonstrate the factors which lay behind some of the key decisions of an artistic nature, for example in the planning of the western frontispiece. Ultimately, however, one's positive or negative reaction to the Late Gothic parts of Troyes Cathedral will be a matter of personal taste. The study of the building of Troyes Cathedral has certainly revealed the extraordinary power of the vocabulary of architectural forms that we call Gothic to flourish for a period of more than three centuries, and yet to undergo a series of vital transformations.

The last decades of Gothic architecture in Troyes (1500–1530s) were among the most productive in the history of the city and the surrounding area. The triumph of Italianate forms in architecture was not the result of the inherent decadence of Late Gothic, but may be understood rather in terms of the iconography of taste and the growing importance of construction projects of a secular type (houses, châteaux, etc.). Late Gothic went out not with a whimper, but a bang. The western frontispiece of Troyes Cathedral is the best expression of this truly magnificent demise.

Appendix A
Handlist of Fabric Accounts

1294	Bibliothèque Nationale lat. 9111.	1373–74	Bibl. Nat. lat. 9113.
1294–95	ditto.		
1295–96	ditto.	1377–78	Bibl. Nat. lat. 9113.
1296–97	ditto.	1378–79	ditto.
1297–98	ditto.	1379–80	Arch. Aube G 1559.
1298–99	ditto.	1379–80	Arch. Aube G 1560.
1299–1300	ditto.	1380–81	Bibl. Nat. lat. 9112.
1300–1	ditto.	1381–82	ditto.
		1382–83	ditto.
1333–34	Bibl. Nat. nouv. acq. lat. 1949 (formerly Phillipps Collection code 8569, vol. 2).	1382–83	Arch. Aube G 1559.
		1383–84	Bibl. Nat. lat. 9112.
		1384–85	ditto.
1334–35	ditto.		
1335–36	ditto.	1386–87	Bibl. Nat. lat. 9111.
1336–37	ditto.	1386–87	Arch. Aube G 1559.
1337–38	ditto.	1387	Bibl. Nat. lat. 9111.
1338–39	ditto.	1387–88	ditto.
1339–40	Bibl. Nat. nouv. acq. lat. 1950 (formerly Phillipps 8569, vol. 3).	1387–88	Arch. Aube G 1559.
		1388–89	Bibl. Nat. lat. 9111.
1366–67	Arch. Aube G 1559.	1389–90	ditto.
1367–68	ditto.	1390–91	ditto.
		1391–92	ditto.
1372–73	Bibl. Nat. lat. 9112.	1392–93	ditto.
1373	ditto.	1393–94	ditto.

Note: a particular manuscript may include another copy of an account or manual for a given year. The presence of such copies is not recorded in the above list.

1394–95	ditto.		
1395–96	ditto.		
1396–97	ditto.		
1397–98	ditto.		
1398–99	ditto.		
1401–2	British Museum add. 15803.		
1402–3	ditto.		
1407–8	Trinity College Dublin.		
1409–10	Brit. Mus. add. 15803.		
1409–10	Arch. Aube G 1559.		
1410–11	Brit. Mus. add. 37676.		
1410–11	Arch. Aube G 1559.		
1411–12	Arch. Aube G 1560.		
1412–13	Brit. Mus. add. 15811.		
1412–13	Arch. Aube G 1561.		
1413–14	ditto.		
1414–15	ditto.		
1415–16	ditto.		
1416–17	ditto.		
1417–18	ditto.		
1418–19	ditto.		
1419–20	ditto.		
1420–21	ditto.		
1421–22	ditto.		
1422–23	ditto.		
1423–24	Arch. Aube G 1562.		
1425–26	Arch. Aube G 1562.		
1426–27	ditto.		
1427–28	ditto.		
1428–29	ditto.		
1431–32	Arch. Aube G 1562.		
1432–33	ditto.		
1432–33	Bibl. Nat. nouv. acq. fr. 21233 (formerly Phillipps 9726).		
1433–34	Arch. Aube G 1562.		
1438–39	Arch. Aube G 1562.		
1439–40	ditto.		
1440–41	ditto.		
1441–42	ditto.		
1442–43	ditto.		
1443–44	Arch. Aube G 1563.		
1444–45	ditto.		
1445–46	ditto.		
1446–47	ditto.		

1447–48	ditto.		
1448–49	ditto.		
1449–50	ditto.		
1450–51	ditto.		
1451–52	ditto.		
1452–53	Arch. Aube G 1572.	(*manuel*)	
1452–53	Arch. Aube G 4417.		
1453–54	ditto.	(*compte* and *manuel*)	
1455	Arch. Aube G 4417.	(*manuel*)	
1454–55	ditto.	(*manuel*)	
1456	ditto.	(*manuel*)	
1457–58	ditto.	(*manuel*)	
1460	Arch. Aube G 4417.	(*estat*)	
1460–61	ditto.	(*estat* and *compte*)	
1462–63	Arch. Aube G 1564.		
1463–64	ditto.		
1468–69	Arch. Aube G 1565.		
1468–69	Arch. Aube G 1566.		
1469–70	Arch. Aube G 1565.		
1469–70	Arch. Aube G 1566.		
1470–71	Arch. Aube G 1565.		
1470–71	Arch. Aube G 1566.		
1471–72	Arch. Aube G 1565.		
1471–72	Arch. Aube G 1566.		
1472–73	Arch. Aube G 1565.		
1472–73	Arch. Aube G 1566.		
1472–73	Arch. Aube G 1572.	(*manuel*)	
1473–74	Arch. Aube G 1566.		
1473–74	Arch. Aube G 1572.	(*manuel*)	
1474–75	ditto.	(*manuel*)	
1475–76	Arch. Aube G 1567.		
1476–77	ditto.		
1476–77	Arch. Aube G 1572.	(*manuel*)	
1477–78	Arch. Aube G 1567.		
1478–79	ditto.		
1479–80	ditto.		
1480–81	ditto.		
1482–83	Arch. Aube G 1568.		
1483–84	ditto.		
1484–85	ditto.		
1485–86	ditto.		
1486–87	ditto.		
1487–88	ditto.		
1488–89	Arch. Aube G 1569.		
1489–90	ditto.		

BUILDING TROYES CATHEDRAL

1491–92	Arch. Aube G 1569.			1522–23	ditto.	
1492–93	ditto.			1523–24	ditto.	
1493–94	ditto.			1524–25	Arch. Aube G 1590.	
1494–95	ditto.			1525–26	ditto.	
1495–96	Arch. Aube G 1570.			1526–27	Arch. Aube G 1591.	
1496–97	ditto.			1527–28	ditto.	
1496–97	Arch. Aube G 1572.	(manuel)				
1497–98	Arch. Aube G 1571.			1530–31	Arch. Aube G 1592.	
1498–99	ditto.			1531–32	ditto.	
1499–1500	ditto.			1532–33	Arch. Aube G 1593.	
1499–1500	Arch. Aube G 1572.	(manuel)		1533–34	Arch. Aube G 1594.	
1500–1	Arch. Aube G 1571.			1534–35	ditto.	
1500–1	Arch. Aube G 1572	(manuel)		1535–36	Arch. Aube G 1595.	
1501–2	Arch. Aube G 1573.			1536–37	ditto.	
1502–3	Arch. Aube G 1574.			1537–38	Arch. Aube G 1596.	
1503–4	ditto.			1538–39	ditto.	
1504–5	Arch. Aube G 1575.					
1504–5	Arch. Aube G 1576.			1540–41	Arch. Aube G 1597.	
1505–6	ditto.			1541–42	ditto.	
1506–7	Arch. Aube G 1577.			1542–43	ditto.	
1507–8	ditto.			1543–44	Arch. Aube G 1598.	
1508–9	Arch. Aube G 1578.			1544–45	ditto.	
1509–10	Arch. Aube G 1579.			1545–46	Arch. Aube G 1599.	
1509–10	Arch. Aube G 1580.			1546–47	ditto.	
1510–11	ditto.			1547–48	Arch. Aube G 1600.	
1511–12	Arch. Aube G 1581.			1548–49	ditto.	
1512–13	Arch. Aube G 1582.					
1513–14	Arch. Aube G 1583.					
1514–15	Arch. Aube G 1584.					

Records of Chapter Deliberations

1361–74	Arch. Aube G 1273.
1360–1404	Arch. Aube G 1274.
1420–48	Arch. Aube G 1275.
1459–81	Arch. Aube G 1276.
1477–84	Arch. Aube G 1277.
1484–93	Arch. Aube G 1278.
1493–1503	Arch. Aube G 1279.

1516–17	Arch. Aube G 1585.
1517–18	Arch. Aube G 1586.
1518–19	Arch. Aube G 1587.
1519–20	Arch. Aube G 1588.
1520–21	ditto.
1521–22	Arch. Aube G 1589.

Appendix A. Handlist of Fabric Accounts

Appendix B

Selected Texts Relating to the Construction of the Nave and Western Frontispiece of Troyes Cathedral

Notes

1. The original texts contain many words that have been abbreviated or contracted. Thus, *pour* is often rendered as po, *pillier* as pillr, and so on. These abbreviations were intended to save time in writing out the account, and to save space. In most cases the abbreviated words have been completed in the transcriptions.

2. In the case of certain very commonly recurring words the original has been transcribed verbatim:

aud.	audit(e)
d.	denarii, deniers, unit of money, twelve in each sou
dessusd.	dessusdit(e)
l.	livre, pound, containing 20 sous
lad. led.	ladite, ledit
me.	maître
messrs	messieurs, usually the clergy of the chapter
par.	parisis, referring to the units of money used in the Paris region
s.	solidi, sous, unit of money containing 12 deniers
t.	tournois: originally referring to currency minted in Tours; later designating a type of royal currency based upon the model of coins from Tours.

3. Where appropriate, an acute accent has been added over the final "e" (for example in past participles, *taillé*). Punctuation has been added.

4. Figures are all in Roman numerals in the original texts. They have been transcribed as Arabic numerals.

5. It should be remembered that the following texts are extracts. Thus, the original manuscript contains multiple entries recording the prices paid for materials, the salaries paid to artisans, etc. Here, however, it has only been possible to select a limited number of entries relating to the identity of the artisans, the definition of the work in hand, etc.

6. Spellings of a particular word or proper noun may vary considerably, thus, *tailler/taillier/taller*, *Bally/Bailly*, etc. Every effort has been made to preserve these variations in the transcribed texts. Proper names are transcribed in their archaic form.

Appendix B. Selected Texts Relating to Construction

1294 Fabric Account (henceforth F.A.) Bibl. nat., lat. 9111.
206 rº. Pro 500 de *pendanz* de croya septimana post Ascensionem Domini 25s.

1. For 500 chalk vault stones, the week after the Ascension of Our Lord, 25s.

206 vº. Item Symoni fabro pro introitu taschie sue ad retinendas campanas 15s.

2. Item, to Simon the smith for the beginning of his work on securing the bells, 15s.

206 vº. Magistro Henrico, magistro fabrice, pro expensis suis in perreria . . . 50s.

3. To Master Henricus, master of the fabric, for his expenses in the quarry . . . 50s.

1294–95 F.A., Bibl. nat., lat. 9111.
208 rº. . . . pro merreno et latis pro voltis 18s. . . . pro merreno empto *pour les aleors* 23s. 6d. . . . et pro sex trappannis pro voltis 3s.

1. For timber and for lath for the vaults 18s. . . . For timber purchased for the scaffolding, 23s. 6d . . . and for 6 planks for the vaults, 3s.

208 rº. . . . et pro 500 de plumbo pro conductis pilariorum supra voltas solidandis 4 l. 10s. . . .

2. . . . and for 500 [sic] of lead for reinforcing the conduits of the pillars above the vaults, £4 10s. . . .

208 rº. Pro duabus voltis mundandis et dealbandis et duabus clavibus voltarum de novo pingendis 12s. 4d.

3. For cleaning and whitewashing 2 vaults and for painting 2 keystones for the first time, 12s. 4d.

208 vº. Pro plastro empto ad voltas reparandas 55s. 8d.

4. For plaster purchased for repairing the vaults, 55s. 8d.

1295–96 F.A., Bibl. nat., lat. 9111.
210 rº. Septimana sancti Nicolai, Garnoti fabro pro duobus *estriers* ad magnam campanam 6s.

1. In the week of Saint Nicholas, to Garno the smith for 2 stirrups for the great bell, 6s.

210 rº. Septimana ante festum sancti Thome pro clavis 18d. et dealbatori et pictori voltarum et pro coloribus 26s.

2. In the week before the feast of Saint Thomas, for nails, 18d., and for whitewashing and painting the vaults and for colors, 26s.

1296–97 F.A., Bibl. nat., lat. 9111.
211 vº. . . . pro merreno empto pro rota ingenii 6s. 2d.

1. For the purchase of timber for the wheel of the [lifting] engine, 6s. 2d.

211 vº. . . . pro merreno empto pro campanili 30s.

2. For the purchase of timber for the bell tower, 30s.

1297–98 F.A., Bibl. nat., lat. 9111.

Note: no topographical indications.

1298–99 F.A., Bibl. nat., lat. 9111.

Same.

1299–1300 F.A., Bibl. nat., lat. 9111.
218 v⁰. . . . pro quadam belleria ad campanam
15d. pro grossa corda ad ingenium facienda 12 l.
18s.

1. . . . for a certain ring for the bell, 15d. For
thick rope for making the [lifting] engine £12
18s.

1300–1 F.A., Bibl. nat., lat. 9111.

Note: no topographical indications.

1301–33: *lacuna*.

1333–34 F.A., Bibl. nat., nouv. acq. lat. 1949.
3 r⁰. . . . dicto Blanchart, coopertori, et sociis
suis, ad recooperiendum in navi ecclesie 30s. 10d.

1. . . . to the said Blanchart, roofer, and to his
companions, for roofing in the nave of the
church, 30s. 10d.

3 r⁰. Pro veste magistri Jacobi, lathomi, tam pro
panno quam pro forratura 63s. 6d.

2. For the robe of Master Jacobus, mason, both
for the cloth and for the fur, 63s. 6d. *Note*:
Jacobus would receive an annual payment for a
robe in recognition of his position as master
of the workshop.

1334–35 F.A., Bibl. nat., nouv. acq. lat. 1949.
5 r⁰. Dicta die pro reparendo batallium parve
campane 18d.

1. On the said day, for the repair of the clapper
of the small bell, 18d.

5 v⁰. Dicta die pro alnis et clavis pro faciendo
formas per magistrum Jacobum 14s. 8d.

2. On the said day for alders [wood] and nails for
making frames [centers] by Master Jacobus, 14s.
8d.

1335–36 F.A., Bibl. nat., nouv. acq. lat. 1949.
8 r⁰. Die sabbati dicto pro 12 alnis ad faciendam
secundam formam per magistrum Jacobum 7s.

1. On the said Sabbath day, for 12 alders for
making the second frame [center] by Master Jacobus, 7s.

8 v⁰. Pro Guillelmio, carpentario, pro uno die
cum famulo suo qui operavit in campanillo 3s.

2. For Guillelmus, carpenter, for one day with
his apprentice who worked in the bell tower, 3s.

8 v⁰. Dicta die pro 3 operariis qui accitaverunt
marrenum in navi ecclesie 8s.

3. On the said day, for 3 laborers who fetched
the timber into the nave of the church, 8s.

8 v⁰. In crastino Omnium Sanctorum magistro
Hugoni et magistro Petro, carpentariis, qui visitaverunt rameuram 20s.

4. On the day after All Saints, to Master Hugo
and to Master Petrus, carpenters, who visited the
roof, 20s.

1336–37 F.A., Bibl. nat., nouv. acq. lat. 1949.
11 v⁰. Dicta die tradidi Jacomardo fabro pro
batallio succursu et pro batallio magne campane
nove et pro pluribus aliis ferraturis 7 l.

1. On the said day I gave to Jacomardus the
smith for fixing the clapper, and for the clapper
of the great new bell and for several other pieces
of iron work, £7.

11 v⁰. Dicta die Guillelmo, carpentario, cum 2
sociis qui operaverunt in voltis novis 21s.

2. On the said day, to Guillelmus, the carpenter,
together with 2 companions, who worked in
the new vaults, 21s.

119

11 vᵒ. Dicta die pro marreno empto pro dictis voltis 17s. 8d.

12 vᵒ. Expense pro fattura ingenii incepti ante festum beatorum Petri et Pauli apostolorum.

13 rᵒ. Item Guillelmo, carpentario, pro faciendo unum ingenium parvum pro descendendo magnam campanam . . . 7s. 8d.

13 vᵒ. Dicta die pro marreno empto . . . et cordis ad levandum dictam campanam 10s. 6d.

1337–38 F.A., Bibl. nat., nouv. acq. lat. 1949.

1338–39 F.A., Bibl. nat., nouv. acq. lat. 1949.

1339–40 F.A., Bibl. nat., nouv. acq. lat. 1950.

1340–66: *lacuna.*

1362 Deliberations of the Chapter [henceforth D.C.], Archives de l'Aube, G 1273. 6 vᵒ-7 rᵒ, d'Arbois, Documents, XI. C'est la cedule de la visitacion de l'eglise de Troyes, faite par maistre Pierre Faisant, maçon, l'an 1362, le samedi aprés feste Saint Martin d'yver.

Premierement, il est assavoir que en toutes les naues des basses vostes sont a recimenter, c'est assavoir de celles d'entour le cuer de la dicte eglise.

Item en plusieurs lieux des entablemens qui sont endroit les gargoles sont a refaire et a remestre sus.

Item il faut faire 1 arc boutant endroit la chappelle mons. l'evesque par devers la court, qui mouvera dessus l'enchappement, et convient que il voise tant haut sus la queue darriere comme jusques a l'amortissement de la premiere fillole, et ne faut en cellui que 1 seul arc boutant.

3. On the said day for purchasing timber for the said vaults, 17s. 8d.

4. Expense for making an engine, begun before the feast of Saints Peter and Paul, apostles.

5. Item, to Guillelmus, the carpenter, for making a little engine for lowering down the great bell . . . 7s. 8d.

6. On the said day, for the purchase of timber . . . and for cords for lifting the said bell, 10s. 6d.

Note: no topographical indications.

Same.

Same.

This is the record [lit. receipt] of the visitation made by Master Pierre Faisant, mason, to the church of Troyes, in the year 1362, on the Saturday after the feast of Saint Martin in the winter [Nov. 12].

1. First, it is to be known that all the gutters of the low vaults are to be repointed, that is those [the gutters] around the choir of the said church.

2. Item, in several places the entablatures [balustrades] which are by the gargoyles are to be redone and re-erected.

3. Item, it is necessary to make 1 flying buttress by the chapel of my lord the bishop toward the court [south side of the choir] which will spring above the gutter and it is necessary that it [the flyer] should go as high above the rear tail as up to the base of the first pinnacle, and this only involves 1 single flying buttress.
Note: this probably refers to the construction of a new flyer springing above the gutter of the choir chapels at E 9 and butting against the upright at E 8. The unit was demolished in the nineteenth century.

Item encor semble au dit maistre qui a resgardé la nouvelle euvre maistre Jehan de Torvoye, et li semble que il n'y ait nul deffaut, fors tant que les ars bouterez sont mis trop haut, et est assavoir dou haut arc bouteret, et li semble que il reconvient mettre jus le dit ouvraige jusques a la hauture des filloles que meuvent des angles, et est pour sauver entout et partout la maçonnerie, et coustera bien ce a refaire et mettre a point de son mestier pour 250 florins.

Item encor autre chose que li ars bouterez neuf par devers la maison le grant arcediacre que il y a deffaut, et le monstrera ce mestiers est, car ou cas que li ouvraiges est empliz de plastre et de mortier n'est mie suffissans ouvraiges, dit par son serement que li ouvraiges n'en est point moins fors, ne n'en vault point pis, combien qu'il en soit plus laiz.

Item li semble que les pillers des avans pis des hautes voies sont desmorcelez et descimantel[e]z, et coule l'eaue contre val les murs.

Item en plusieurs lieux, c'est assavoir és jonctures des alees, l'eaue coule tout parmi les murs, et y faut mettre remede.

Item ou quatre naues dou clochier il y faut mettre remede, c'est assavoir es jonctures parsus les ars bouterez, et y a molt grant deffaut et y convient mettre remede.

Et est touz vostres li diz maistres pour estre vostres propres ouvriers se mestier est.

Acta fuerunt hec anno 62, die sabbati post yemale beati Martini, presentibus magistro Aymerico Helie, Guillelmo Cochardi, Perrino Cellario, Jehanconno de Troancio et pluribus aliis.

4. Item, further, it seems to the said master who has looked at the new work of Master Jehan de Torvoie, and it seems to him that there is no fault except that the flying buttresses are placed too high, that is to say the upper flying buttress, and it seems to him that it is necessary to demolish the said work to the height of the pinnacles which rise from the angles, and [he] is for saving the [old] masonry completely throughout, and to do this and to put things right according to his profession will easily cost 250 florins.

5. Item, further, another thing, that there is a problem with the new flying buttress toward the house of the great archdeacon [north side of choir], and he will show it, if need be, for if the work is augmented with plaster and cement, it is not at all adequate. [He] says on his oath that although it might be uglier, it would not be any less strong or less worthy on that account. *Note*: this probably refers to a flyer springing from B 9 against B 8, matching the unit discussed in clause 3 above. This was an openwork flyer, and the plaster and cement would be used to strengthen the unit through the blocking of the open panels. Faisant does not approve of this makeshift solution.

6. Item, it seems that the pillars of the balustrade of the high gutters [of the clerestory wall] are fragmented and without cement, and the [rain] water is running down the walls.

7. Item, in several places, that is to say in the joints in the passageways, the [rain] water is running down through the walls, and this must be remedied.

8. Item, the four gutters of the bell tower need to be fixed, that is at the joints above the flying buttresses, and there is a major defect and it should be remedied.

9. And the said masters are at your disposal to be your own workers, if necessary.

Enacted this year, 1362 etc.

Appendix B. Selected Texts Relating to Construction

1365 D.C., Arch. Aube, G 1273, d'Arbois, Documents, XII.

21 r⁰. Le samedi 12e jour de juillet l'an 1365 en nostre chapitre presens et capitulans mons. le dean, l'arcediacre de Saincte Margerie, l'arcediacre d'Arceix, maistre Hemart Hemart [sic] de Saint Oulph, maistre Renaust de Laingres, mess. Estienne Gillebert, mess. Guillaume de Crené, mess. Pierre d'Arbois le jeune et mess. Jacques Cousin, entre maistre Thomas, masson de l'euvre de l'eglise de Troies et maistre de la dicte euvre, et les diz dean et chapitre, accordé et traictié est seur le salaire des journees que le dit maistre Thomas ouvrera en la besoinge de la dicte euvre en la maniere qui s'ensuit: c'est assavoir que le dit maistre Thomas gaignera pour chascun jour ouvrant que il sera en la dicte besoigne dés le jour de huy jusques au jour de la Saint Remy prochain venant 3 gros et demi, et dés le dit jour de la Saint Remy jusques au jour de Pasques prochain ensuignant pour chascun jour ouvrant qu'il ouvrera en la dicte besoigne il gaingnera 3 gros tournois; et de illec en avant, pour tant comme il ouvrera en la dite besoingne sera paiez chascun jour par les condicions et manieres que dit est; et ce dit accort et traictié [lesdiz maistres Thomas-*added*] parmi ce que la maison qui touz jours li a esté baillee de la dite euvre tant comme il a esté maistre masson de la dite euvre enssemble sa robe que il doit avoir chascun an, a juré aus sains Euvangiles de Dieu tenir et avoir fermé et establé tant comme il sera en la dite euvre avecques ce que bien et lealment et diligenment ouvrera et se occupera en la dite euvre et que autre euvre senz la licence des diz dean et chapitre il ne pranra en la ville de Troies ne autre part. [Signed] Ita est.

Ce jour Michelin de Donchery, Michelins Hardioz et Jehans Thierriz, maçons et ouvriers de taillie en la dite euvre, ont promis et accordé de ouvrer en la dite euvre dés le jour d'uy jusques audit jour de la Saint Remy pour 3s. 6d. pour jour que il[s] y ouvreront, et d'illec jusques audit jour de Pasques, pour 2 gros tornois ; et ainssin de illec en autre chascun an aux diz termes par les formes et manieres que dit est tant comme il plaira a chapitre.

On Saturday the 12th day of July in the year 1365 in our chapter in the presence and with the agreement of my lord the dean, the archdeacon of Sainte Margerie, the archdeacon of Arcis, Master Hemart de Saint Oulph, Master Renaust de Langres my lord Etienne Gillebert, my lord Guillaume de Creney, my lord Pierre d'Arbois the younger and my lord Jacques Cousin an agreement and a contract were made between Master Thomas, mason of the work of the church of Troyes and master of the said work, and the said dean and chapter on the salary for the days which the said Master Thomas shall work in the service of the said fabric in the manner that follows: that is to say that the said Master Thomas shall earn for each working day that he shall be in the said service from today until the next day of Saint Remi 3½ *gros* and from the day of Saint Remi until the following Easter for each working day in the said work he shall earn 3 *gros tournois*. And thus, from then onward, as long as he shall work in the said service, he shall be paid each day according to the conditions and in the manner that are defined. And this agreement and contract includes the house that has always been provided by the said fabric as long as he has been master mason of the said fabric together with his robe that he should have each year. He has sworn on God's Holy Gospels to abide by, and that he has agreed and established, that as long as he shall be in the said work he shall work and occupy himself loyally and diligently in the said work and that he will not take on other work without the permission of the said dean and chapter whether in the city of Troyes or elsewhere. [Signed] So be it.

This day Michelin de Jonchery, Michelin Hardiot, and Jehan Thierry, masons and carvers in the said work, have promised and agreed to work in the said work from today to the day of Saint Remi for 3s. 6d. for each day that they shall work, and from then until the day of Easter for 2 *gros tournois* and thus in each year at the said terms by the form and manner that have been said for as long as it is pleasing to the chapter.

1365 Arch. Aube, G 2592, charter of King
Charles V, August 31, d'Arbois, Documents,
XIII.

. . . cum nuper, videlicet die Mercurii ante festum
Assumptionis beate Marie virginis ultimo preteri-
tum, insurgente a casu quodam turbine seu vento
horibili et validissimo campanile ecclesie cathed-
ralis Sancti Petri ville nostre Trecensis . . . ex
impetu et impulsione violentis et validissimi venti
seu turbinis supradicti ruptum et precipitatum
ceciderit supra dictam ecclesiam. . . .

Since the bell tower of our cathedral church of
Saint Peter in our city of Troyes . . . has recently
(that is on the Wednesday before the feast of
the Assumption of the blessed Mary the Virgin
[August 13]) been broken and cast down through
a whirlwind or terrible and most powerful wind
that rose up by some chance, and through the
impulse and force of the above-mentioned violent
and most powerful wind or whirlwind [it] has
fallen upon the said church. . . .
Note: the charter allowed the dean and chapter to
acquire rents worth 200 pounds without having
to pay the usual tax on the transaction.

1366 D.C., Arch. Aube, G 1273. d'Arbois, Documents, XIV.

35 rº. Anno domini 1366, die veneris post festum
beati Luce evvangeliste, constituti Michelinus de
Joncheriaco, Johannes Thierrici et Michelinus
Hardieti, lathomi, Trecis commorantes, locaverunt se et se et suas operas locavisse recognoverunt
venerabilibus et discretis viris, dominis decano et
capitulo Trecensi conducentibus et retinentibus
dictos lathomos et operas eorundem pro operando
ad opus fabrice dicte ecclesie et pro ipsa fabrica
exnunc quamdiu placuerit dominis decano et
capitulo predictis absque eo quod dicti lathomi
possint aliud operagium accipere, ita tamen quod,
si dicti domini decanus et capitulum opus dicte
fabrice cessari voluerint, ipsi per unum mensem
ante cessationem hujusmodi eisdem lathomis
significare debebunt ac tenebunt; promiseruntque
dicti lathomi in opere dicte fabrice continuare
et operagia sua bene et fideliter facere et con-
struere, sub pena restaurationis omnium dampno-
rum missionem et interesse dictorum decani et
capituli, quas et que incurrere contigerit per
defectum et culpam dictorum lathomorum, quas
et que reddenda et restituenda se obligaverunt; et
hoc pro ac mediantibus 4 solidis turonensium,
monete nunc currentis, cuilibet dictorum lathomorum pro qualibet dieta tam in yeme quam
in estate ac 40 solidis anno quolibet ad Resurrec-
tionem Domini cuilibet eorum pro curialitate
reddendis et solvendis; obligantes se etc. Actum
in curia, presentibus magistro Jo. Gueraudi, Dro.
de Marchia, Guillelmo de Creneyo, Gauffrido
Gebennensi et P. Flamingi testibus. [signed] G.
de Vaudis. Ita est.

In the year of Our Lord 1366, on Thursday after
the feast of Saint Luke, Evangelist, Michelin de
Jonchery, Jehan Thierry, and Michelin Hardiot,
masons, dwelling in Troyes, came to an agreement and contracted and recognized that they
and their laborers had contracted with the venerable and discreet persons, my lords the dean and
chapter of Troyes, hiring and retaining the said
masons and their laborers to work for the fabric
of the said church from now as long as it is
pleasing to my lords the aforementioned dean
and chapter. The said masons are precluded from
accepting any other work; however, if the said
lords, the dean and chapter wish to cease the
work of the said fabric they should give notice to
these masons one month before the stoppage.
The said masons promise to continue in the work
of the said fabric and to make and construct its
works well and faithfully, under pain of making
good all losses and expenses and interest of the
said dean and chapter which, through the negligence and fault of the said masons may be incurred, which they have obligated themselves to
give back and restore. And this for 4 *solidi* of
Tours in current money to each of the said masons for each day in winter and in summer and
40 *solidi* each year at Easter time to be rendered
and paid as a gratuity. Enacted in chapter etc.

1366–67 F.A., Arch. Aube, G 1559.

7 v°. Pro 25 lapidibus nuncupatis *quartiers*, emptis 3ª die octobris ... pro quodam parvo arcu faciendo existente retro magnum arcum ex parte Thesauri dicte ecclesie 58s. 4d.

7 v°. Pro uno mill. de *pendens* ad reparandas votas cappellarum que delacerate fuerant per corrupcionem magni campanilis, empto per lathomos ecclesie a Jacobo lathomo 4 l. 10s.

10 r°. Septimana in qua fuit festum Decollationis beati Johannis Baptist. tailliendo et perficiendo magnum arcum et parvum a parte chori. ...

11 r°. Septimana in qua fuit festum Omnium Sanctorum, in qua inceperunt tailliare pro faciendo grossum pilerium et magnum arcum in alia parte versus grenarios ecclesie.

13 v°. Septimana in qua fuit festum beati Martini estivalis, in qua inceperunt situare in dicto grosso pilerio et magno arcu versus dictos grenarios ecclesie.

14 v°. Pro quodam magno conducto marreni de 40 pedibus de longo, posito in grosso campanile, per quem discurrunt aque navis ecclesie 60s.

15 r°. Septimana in qua fuit festum beati Petri ad vincula in qua dicti operarii cooperuerunt supra capellam beate Helene que fuerat delacerata per lathomos ecclesie ad faciendum *les allours*.

15 r°. Septimana in qua fuit festum Decollationis beati Johannis Bapt., in qua situaverunt duas dictarum chanlatarum, unam supra primam capellam a parte curie, et aliam supra capellam domini Jacobi de Noa a parte pavimenti.

15 v°. Septimana in qua fuit festum beati Luce evvangeliste, in qua cimentaverunt *chanlatas** ecclesie et cooperuerunt supra capellam beati Michaelis et in pluribus aliis partibus dicte ecclesie.

1. For 25 stones called *quartiers* purchased on October 3 ... for making a certain little arch behind the big arch on the side of the treasury [south side of choir], 58s. 4d.

2. For 1,000 vault stones to repair the vaults of the chapels that were broken by the fall of the great bell tower, purchased by the masons of the church from Master Jacobus the mason, £4 10s.

3. In the week of the feast of the decapitation of Saint John Baptist, for cutting and finishing the great arch and the small one on the side of the choir. ...

4. In the week of the feast of All Saints in which cutting was begun to make the big pillar and the great arch on the other side toward the store chamber of the church.

5. In the week of the feast of Saint Martin in the summer in which they began to place [stones] in the said big pillar and great arch toward the said store chamber of the church.

6. For a certain great wooden conduit 40 feet long, placed in the big [west] bell tower by which the water of the nave [roof] runs away, 60s.

7. In the week of the feast of Saint Peter in Chains in which the said workers roofed over the chapel of Saint Helen which was damaged by the masons of the church in making the scaffolding.

8. In the week of the decapitation of Saint John Baptist in which they placed two of the said timbers for the eaves one over the first chapel on the side of the [bishop's] court, the other over the chapel of lord Jacobus de Noa on the side of the road [N 3].

9. In the week of the feast of Saint Luke, Evangelist, in which they cemented the timbers for the eaves of the church and roofed over the chapel of Saint Michael [N 1] and in many other parts of the church.

*A *chanlate* was a wooden beam behind the gutter. Since gutters themselves were often wooden, the word was sometimes applied to the gutter itself.

124

18 rᵒ. Pro curialitate facta lathomis ecclesie, qui retinuerunt parietam existent. in arcu supra puteum ecclesie 4a. die Augusti 2s.

1367–68 F.A., Arch. Aube, G 1559.
30 rᵒ. Expense pro lathomis et eorum famulis situando et perficiendo grossum pilerium a parte curie episcopalis versus granarios ecclesie.

32 rᵒ. Septimana in qua fuit festum beate Lucie virginis, in qua inceperunt taillare pro alio arcu et parvo pillerio.

34 vᵒ. Septimana in qua fuit festum beati Dyonisii, in qua situaverunt duas *chanlatas* supra capellam beati Lazari versus grenarios ecclesie.

34 vᵒ. Septimana in qua fuit festum beatorum Symonis et Jude apostolorum, in qua cooperuerunt tecta delacerata pro faccione grossi pilerii novi et alatorum ejusdem.

1368–72: *lacuna*.

1372–73 F.A., Bibl. nat., lat. 9112.
28 vᵒ. Et sciendum est quod dicti lathomi, scilicet Michelinus de Joncheri, Johannes Thierrici et Michelinus Hardioti se affirmaverunt et locaverunt dictis dominis meis de capitulo, modo et forma qui sequit., videlicet quod quislibet dictorum lathomorum qualibet die lucrabit a prima die martii usque ad primam diem novembris 3s., et ad primam diem novembris usque ad dictam primam diem martii 2s. 6d.

30 vᵒ. Macelino, carpentario, pro agusando *les estoz* positos in fundamento novi pilerii . . . 21s.

47 rᵒ. Et sciendum quod predictum marrenum totum est positum in fundamento novi pillerii. . . .

47 vᵒ. Pro curialitate facta lathomis ecclesie ad assedendum primum lapidem novi pillerii per ordinatonem capituli. . . .

10. As a gratuity paid to the masons of the church who secured the screen existing in the arch above the well of the church [at division 3], on the 4th day of August, 2s.

1. Expense for masons and their apprentices to put in place and to finish the big pillar on the side toward the bishop's court near the store chambers of the church.

2. In the week of the feast of Saint Lucy, Virgin, in which they began to cut for the other arch and the small pillar.

3. In the week of the feast of Saint Denis in which they placed two timbers for eaves over the chapel of Saint Lazare [S 3] toward the store chamber of the church.

4. In the week of the feast of Saints Simon and Jude, Apostles, in which they worked on the roofs damaged through the work on the big new pillar and its scaffolding.

1. And it is to be known that the said masons, that is Michelin de Jonchery, Jehan Thierry, and Michelin Hardiot, confirm and contract with my said lords of the chapter according to the mode and form that follows: that is that from the first day of March to the first day of November each of the said masons shall earn 3s. and from the first day of November to the said first day of March 2s. 6d.

2. To Macelinus, carpenter, for sharpening the stays placed in the foundations of the new pillar . . . 21s.

3. And it is to be known that the aforementioned timber has all been placed in the foundation of the new pillar. *Note*: wooden stays to keep the earth back.

4. For a gratuity paid to the masons of the church at the laying of the first stone of the new pillar, by order of the chapter. . . .

Appendix B. Selected Texts Relating to Construction

1373–74 F.A., Bibl. nat., lat. 9113.
14 r⁰. Pro curialitate facta lathomis qui visitaverunt ecclesiam de precepto dominorum meorum . . . 10s.

1. For a gratuity paid to the masons who visited the church on the orders of my lords . . . 10s.

1374–77: *lacuna.*

1375–76 F.A., now lost, extracts transcribed by Gadan.
A Michelin de Ioncheri, masson, en la sepmaine de l'Assumption Notre Dame, pour asseoir les bancs en forme premiere devers le pavement a la partye devers la ville, pour un jour 3s. 9d.

1. To Michelin de Jonchery, mason, in the week of the Assumption of Our Lady, to place the *bancs* [misreading?] in the first window toward the street facing the city for one day, 3s. 9d.
Note: one of the clerestory windows on the west side of the north transept is being prepared for glazing.

A Iehan Thierri, masson, en la sepmaine de S. Michiel, pour apparillier le grand oiteau devers le pavement, et mettre les ronds, bariaux et autres fers, pour 4 jours 4s. 9d. valent 15s.

2. To Jehan Thierry in the week of Saint Michael, for fixing the big window toward the road and placing roundels, bars and other irons for 4 days at 4s. 9d. makes 15s.
Note: probably the north transept rose.

Despence pour les verrieres neuves. A maistre Guillaume Brisetout [sic], verrier, pour verrer a tierce forme [sic] de la croisee devers le pavement a la partie devers la ville, en laquelle sont 269 piez de verre blanc, et couste chacun pié 4s. Et le pié d'ymaginé couste 12d. plus dou blanc lequel plus de lad. forme Guillaume Gauterel a paié valent les 269 piez a 4s. pour pié 53 l. 16s.

3. Expense for new windows. To Master Guillaume Brisetout [misreading for Brisetour], glazier, to glaze the third window of the crossing toward the road on the side toward the city, in which there are 269 feet of white glass, and each foot costs 4 sous. And the foot of glass with figurative work costs 12d. more than the white. . . .

Audit maistre Guillaume Brisetout, pour verrer le grand oiteau de ladite croisee devers le pavement, ouquel sont 686 piez de verre blanc qui valent a 4s. 137 l. 3s. Et pour le verre ymaginé 68 piez qui valent plus dou blanc pour pié 12d. valent en tout somme 140 l. 12s.

4. To the said Master Guillaume Brisetout for glazing the great window of the said crossing toward the road, in which there are 686 feet of white glass which are worth at 4s. [the foot] £137 3s. And for the glass with figurative work, 68 feet, which is worth 12d. more than the white per foot for the total sum, £140 12s.

1377–78 F.A., Bibl. nat., lat. 9113.

Note: Large-scale work has ceased.

1378–79 F.A., Bibl. nat., lat. 9113.

Same.

1379–80 F.A., Arch. Aube, G 1559.
52 r⁰. A Richart le Sarrurier pour 33 pois 9 l. de fer ouvré tant en ront comme en barriaux, montans et verges pour la forme de la verriere du milieu de la rameure par devers chapitre au costé par devers le revestiere, en laquelle est la Resur-

1. To Richard the locksmith for 33 *pois* 9 pounds of wrought iron in roundels, bars, posts, and rods for the frame of a window in the middle of the roof toward the chapter on the side toward the vestry where the Resurrection of Our Lord is

reccion Nostre Sire, avec 16 barriaux pesans 8 pois et demi qui estoient des garnison[s] des autres verrieres precedantes pour chascun pois 25s. valent les 33 pois 9 livres 41 l. 13s. 4d.

55 r⁰. Pour faire viseter la massonerie de la roë par devers la court l'official et toute l'eglise tant en haut comme en bas le 26e jour de janvier par Droet de Dampmartin, masson, demorant a Paris . . . 4 l.

1380–81 F.A., Bibl. nat., lat. 9112.
11 r⁰. Pour blanchir la roë et le pignon par devers chapitre par marché fait en tasche . . . 31s. 3d.

14 v⁰. Pour verrer la roë par devers la court l'official, en la quelle a 680 pies de verre, et les basses verrieres audessoubz de la dite roë, es quelles il a 260 piez de verre, ansin monte la somme du verre tant de la roë, comme des dites basses verrieres 940 piez de verre, qui vallent a 3s. 9d. pour chacun pié 176 l. 5s. 0d.

1381–82 F.A. Bibl. nat., lat 9112.
57 v⁰. Pour nettoier et blanchir les ymaiges dou portau d'entre, refaire le dyadime de l'imaige de Dieu, la main destre, la teste de l'aigle, une des clez et les 2 piez, et croistre les clez dou buef et mettre le dit portau en premier estat, qui fut par marchié fait en tache a Denisot le pointre et a Droin de Mante, pour leur paine et salaire present messr. Pierre Darbois 4 l. 2s. 6d.

58 r⁰. Pour faire le pourtrait dou jubé en une pel de parchemin par Michelin et Jehan Tierri pour monstrer a messrs., pour ce 5s.

58 r⁰. Pour faire une aire en la ramure de costé le gros clochier pour faire les portrais dou jubé, en la 2e. sepmaine de juillet 20s.
Pour 20 tumeleres de terre pour faire la dite aire 16s. 8d.

located, with 16 bars weighing 8½ *pois* which were taken from other previous windows in the store, for each *pois* at 25s. the 33 *pois* 9 pounds [makes] £41 13s. 4d.

2. For a visit on January 26 to the masonry of the rose window toward the official court [south transept] and the entire church, both upper and lower parts by Droet de Dammartin, mason, dwelling in Paris . . . £4.

1. To whitewash the rose window and the gable on the side toward the chapter by contract for piece work . . . [i.e., at a fixed price, as opposed to payment by the day] 31s. 3d.

2. To glaze the rose window toward the official court in which there are 680 feet of glass, and the low windows [triforium] beneath the said rose, in which there are 260 feet of glass, and so the total glass both for the rose and for the low windows is 940 feet of glass which is worth 3s. 9d. for each foot, £176, 5s. 0d.

1. To clean and whitewash the images of the entrance portal, to remake the diadem of the image of God, the right hand, the eagle's head, one of the nails and the two feet and to enlarge the nails of the ox and to put the portal back into its original condition, by contract for piece-work made with Denisot the pointer and Droin de Mantes, for their work and salary [paid] in the presence of Pierre d'Arbois £4 2s. 6d.

2. To make the portrait of the choir screen in a sheet of parchment by Michelin and Jehan Thierry in order to show to my lords, for this 5s.

3. To make a [drawing] surface in the roof beside the big [western] bell tower in order to make the portraits of the choir screen in the 2nd week of July, 20s. For 20 carts of earth to make the said surface 16s. 8d. *Note*: the drawing surface was over the vault of the chapel to the south of the old west bell tower. The earth was necessary in order to fill the pockets of the vault to make a flat surface.

Appendix B. Selected Texts Relating to Construction

62 v⁰. Autre despense faicte pour rapparillier la rameure de la dite eglise en la quelle la fouldre chey, le 9e jour de juillet.

63 v⁰. Pour marchander a Rainz par messr. Jehan de Saint Bernart a Jehan Lescaillon, cuvreur d'escaille, demorant a Rainz, pour venir a Troyes pour recouvrir la dite rameure, li quelz devoit gaignier par marchié fait a lui, pour chascun jour qu'il ouvreroit 7s. par. et son vallet 2s. par. pour le vin dou marchié . . . 7s. 6d.

64 v⁰. Pour courtoisie faite a frere Guillelme le Provincial, de l'ordre des freres meneurs, qui fut a estandre le feu de la dite rameure dou commandement de messrs., fait en chappitre le mercredi 15e jour d'octobre, baillié pour ce 4 l.

1382–83 F.A., Bibl. nat., lat. 9112.
76 r⁰. Autre despense pour massonnerie, c'estassavoir pour le jubé. L'an 1382 le 6e jour de juing, marchanderent messrs. dean et chapitre de l'eglise de Troyes a Michelin et Jehan Thierry, maçons, de faire ung jubé de pierre en la dite eglise, c'estassavoir que les diz maçons ouvreront oudit jubé continuelment jusques il soit assouvis, senz ouvrer autrepart se n'est dou consentement de mesdiz Signeurs parmi ce que le dit Michelin aura pour chascun jour ouvrant tant en yver comme en esté pour despens et pour salaire 4s. 2d. Et Jehan Thierri pour chascun jour ouvrant 3s. 9d. Et ont promis et juré les diz maçons d'ouvrer ou dit ouvraige bien et diligenment et lealement.

76 r⁰. Item le 14e jour d'avril l'an 1383 les dessusdiz Michelin, Jehan Thierry et Jaquot de Pouant, maçons, vendirent 11 pierres renduez, traictés a la perriere par de la Tonneurre . . . c'estassavoir une de 4 pies de long a main et de 3 piez et demi de large et de 2 piez et demi a main d'espez. Item deux autres pierres chascune de 4 piez a main de long et 3 piez a main de large et de deux piez et demi d'espez. Item quatre autres pierres chascune de long d'un moole baillé au dessusdiz par Henry de Bruiselles, maçon, et de 2 piez et demi d'espez. Item 4 autres pierres chascune de long doudit moole, et de 2 piez et ung quart d'espez. Item une autre pierre de 5 piez a main de long, de 4 piez de large et de pié et demi d'espez . . . 12 l. 2s. 6d.

4. Other expense made for fixing the roof of the said church, struck by lightning on July 9.

5. For a contract made at Reims by my lord Jehan de Saint Bernard with Jehan Lescaillon, slater dwelling in Reims, to come to Troyes to re-cover the said roof, who, by the contract made with him, should earn 7s. of Paris for each day he works, and his apprentice 2s. of Paris, for the wine for the contract . . . 7s. 6d.

6. For a gratuity paid to brother Guillaume le Provincial of the order of minor friars, who extinguished the fire in the said roof, paid at the order of my lords, done in chapter on Wednesday October 15, paid for this £4.

1. Other expense for masonry, that is to say for the choir screen. In the year 1382, on June 6, my lords the dean and chapter of the church of Troyes made a contract with Michelin and Jehan Thierry, masons, to make a stone choir screen in the said church. The said masons shall work on the said screen continuously until it is finished without working anywhere else except with the consent of my lords, and the said Michelin shall have for each working day in winter and in summer for his expenses and salary 4s. 2d. And Jehan Thierry [shall have] for each working day 3s. 9d. And the said masons have promised and sworn to labor well and diligently in the said work.

2. Item, on April 14, 1383, the above-mentioned Michelin, Jehan Thierry, and Jaquot de Pouan, masons, sold 11 stones, extracted and cut at the quarry of Tonnerre . . . that is one [stone] of 4 feet long [measured] by hand and 3½ feet wide and 2½ feet thick by hand. Item, 2 other stones each of 4 feet by hand in length and 3 feet by hand in width and 2½ feet thick. Item, 4 other stones, the length of each according to a template supplied to the above-mentioned [masons] by Henry de Bruisselles, mason, and 2½ feet thick. Item, 4 other stones each the length of the said template and 2¼ feet thick. Item, another stone 5 feet by hand in length, 4 feet wide and 1½ feet thick . . . £12 2s. 6d.

78 r⁰. A maistre Girart de Han, tailleurs d'y-
maiges, pour faire l'ymaige de Saint Pol par le
commandement de monsr. le dean, monsr. le
chantre et messr. Pierre Darbois, baillié 6 l. A
Droyn de Mante, tailleur d'ymaiges, pour l'y-
maige de saint Pierre fait par led. Droyn par le
commendement de messr. Jacque Cousin et
messr. Guillaume de Creney, baillié 100s.

78 r⁰. Autre despense pour le ledit jubé faite
depuis le 27ᵉ jour d'octobre que Michelin et Jehan
Thierry, maçons, cesserent ledit ouvraige.
Primo pour ung pourtrait fait en parchemin pour
ledit jubé par Henry de Bruisselles, maçon, dou
commendement de messrs. pour monstrer aux
bourgois et aux ouvriers de la ville encontre ung
autre pourtrait fait par Michelin le maçon, au
quel pourtrait fait par ledit Henry les diz bourgois
et ouvriers se sont tenu pour estre le meilleur,
pour ce paié audit Henry dou commendement de
messigneurs 20s.

78 r⁰. Pour faire venir de Paris Henry Soudan,
maçon, a la requeste doudit Henry de Bruisselles
a Troyes pour marchander doudit jubé, et luy
retourner a Paris, pour ses despenses baillié par le
commendement de messigneurs 30s.

78 v⁰. C'est le marchié que messigneurs dean et
chapitre de l'eglise de Troyes ont fait a Henry
Soudan, maçon, demorant a Paris en la Rue de
Joy d'entre l'ostel au Gros Tournois prez de
l'ostel maistre Jehan des Marelz, et a Henry de
Bruisselles, maçon, le 28ᵉ jour d'octobre l'an
1382, pour faire ung jubé en la dite eglise par la
maniere qu'il est pourtrait et gictié en une pel de
parchemin de la main doudit Henry de Bruisselles. Primo les diz maçons doivent ouvrer oudit
jubé continuelment yver et esté sens ouvrer autre
part, par quelque maniere que ce soit, se n'est
dou congié et licence de mesdissigneurs, jusques
il soit parfais et assouvis de tout ouvraige de
maçonnerie senz les ymaiges les quelles messrs.
feront faire a leur plaisir et a leur propres coux et
despens, parmi ung mouton d'or que ung chascun
des diz deux maçons aura pour chascune sepmaine
de tout l'an a commencier au jour qu'il entreront
oudit ouvraige, soient festes ou autres jours ouvrans. Et ou cas que lesdiz maçons on l'un d'eux
cessera d'ouvrer a ung des jours ouvrans, soit

3. To Master Girart de Ham, carver of images [or
statues] for making the statue of Saint Paul on
the order of my lord the dean, my lord the
chanter and my lord Pierre d'Arbois, paid £6. To
Droyn de Mantes, carver of statues, for the
statue of saint Peter made by the said Droyn at
the order of my lord Jacques Cousin and my lord
Guillaume de Creney, paid 100s.

4. Other expense for the said choir screen incurred since October 27 when Michelin and
Jehan Thierry stopped work. First, for a portrait
for the said choir screen made on parchment
by Henry de Bruisselles, mason, on the orders of
my lords to show to the bourgeois and to the
laborers of the city side by side with another
portrait made by Michelin, the mason. The said
bourgeois and laborers held that the portrait of
Henry de Bruisselles was the better, paid for this
to the said Henry at the orders of my lords 20s.

5. To fetch Henry Soudan, mason, from Paris to
Troyes on the request of the said Henry de
Bruisselles in order to contract for the said choir
screen, and for him to return to Paris, paid for
his expenses at the order of my lords 30s.

6. This is the contract that my lords the dean
and chapter of the church of Troyes have made
with Henry Soudan, mason, dwelling in Paris in
the Rue de Joy between the Hôtel au Gros
Tournois next to the Hôtel of Master Jehan des
Marelz, and with Henry de Bruisselles, mason,
on October 28, 1382, to make a choir screen
in the said church according to the manner in
which it is portrayed and sketched in a sheet of
parchment in the hand of Henry de Bruisselles.
First, the said masons should work on the said
choir screen continuously winter and summer
without working anywhere else at all except
with the leave and permission of my said lords
until it [the choir screen] is finished and complete
in all masonry work without the statues which
my lords will have done at their pleasure and at
their own cost and expense. Each of the masons
shall have one *mouton d'or* [25s.] for each week
for the entire year, regardless of feast days or
working days, starting from the day when they
enter into the said work. And in the case that the

Appendix B. Selected Texts Relating to Construction

de sa volenté, par maladie ou autrement, il luy sera rabatu et descompté pour chascun jour 5s. t. pour 5e. partie d'un mouton d'or. Item ont promis les diz maçons de continuer ledit ouvraige dés la Nativité Nostre Dame en septembre jusques a Pasques, dés le soloil levant jusques au soloil couchant senz partir de la loige que pour disner compentement une fois pour jour. Item durant ledit ouvraige le maistre de l'oeuvre de la dite eglise leur fera finance de charbon pour chauffer en la loige quant il sera necessaire. Et dés Pasques jusques a la dite Nativité Nostre Dame les diz maçons continueront ledit ouvraige dés ung petit aprés le soloil levant par la maniere que dit est, jusques a heure qu'il peussent avoir soupe a heure de soloil couchant. Et ou cas qu'il plaira a messrs. d'anvoier les diz maçons ou l'un d'eulx a la perriere pour traire de la pierre pour ledit ouvraige doudit jubé, il y yra, parmi gaignant chascun ung mouton pour sepmaine comme dit est avec 10s. t. chascun pour ses despens pour chascun sepmaine. Item ont promis les diz maçons de donner bonne caucion a messigneurs jusques a 400 frans, de faire bon ouvaige et loyal selons le pourtrait dessusdit, audit d'ouvriers et de gens coignoissans en ce et de continuer ledit ouvraige bien et loyalment comme dit est dessus et de ce se doivent obliger chascun pour le tout. Et parmi ce messrs. leur doivent faire lire qu'il[s] ne les debouteront point doudit ouvraige, se n'est par leur coulpe et deffaut. Et avec ce baillent d'avantaige durant ledit ouvraige mesdissrs. une maison a Troyes souffisante pour leur demorance. Et de toutes les convenances desdiz maçons tenir et accomplire sont obligé soubz le seel dou chastellet de Paris iusques a 400 frans ledit Henri Soudan, tant pour luy, comme pour Henry de Bruisselles, et Marguerite, jadis femme de feu Jehan de Huy, demorant a Paris au coing de la Rue des Billettes par devers la Rue de la Verrerye, mere de la femme doudit Henry Soudan, comme plesge principale, renderesse et paieresse, se deffaute avoit oudit ouvraige.

1383–84 F.A., Bibl. nat., lat. 9112.
105 r⁰. Pour faire 4 pieces sur les 4 colombes devant extraictés par Henry de Bruisselles et par Henry Soudan, maçons, par nuit, par 2 yvers, par eulx et leurs gens . . . 32 l.

said masons or one of them shall stop working on a working day, whether of his choice or through sickness or otherwise, 5s. *tournois* or one fifth of a *mouton d'or* shall be deducted for each day. Item, the said masons have promised to continue the said work from the Nativity of Our Lady in September until Easter from sunrise to sunset, only leaving the lodge duly once per day to dine. Item, during the said work the master of the works of the said church shall reimburse them for the coal to heat the lodge when necessary. And from Easter to the Nativity of Our Lady the said masons shall continue the said work from a little after sunrise according to the fashion that has been stated, until the time when they might have soup at sunset. And if it should please my lords to send the said masons or one of them to the quarry to cut stone for the said work on the choir screen, he shall go, each earning one *mouton d'or* per week as has been stated with 10s. *tournois* each per week for his expenses. Item, the said masons have promised to give up to 400 francs good caution [money] to my lords, that they will work well and faithfully according to the above-mentioned portrait [shown] to the said laborers and knowledgeable persons and to continue the work well and faithfully as stated above, and in this each person obliges himself for all. And in this my lords should have it read to them [i.e., they cannot read themselves] that they shall not expel them from the said work unless through their own fault and negligence. And in this [the chapter] shall also provide a house adequate for them to live in for the duration of the work. And the masons are obliged to hold to and to accomplish all these clauses under the seal of the Châtellet in Paris [with a penalty clause] as much as 400 francs, the said Henry Soudan, as well as for him as for Henry de Bruisselles, and Marguerite, former wife of the late Jehan de Huy, living in Paris at the corner of the Rue des Billettes, toward the Rue de Verrerye, mother of the wife of the said Henry Soudan as main pledge, guarantor and payer, should there be any fault in the work.

1. To make 4 pieces of the 4 columns previously cut out by Henry de Bruisselles and by Henry Soudan, masons, over two winters at night, by them and by their men . . . £32.

105 rº. Pour remettre ung post et ung lien de-soubz ung des grans trez de la rameure de la nef de l'eglise, qui estoyent brisié en la 3e sepmaine de mars.

1384–85 F.A., Bibl. nat., lat. 9112.
129 rº. Despense pour matieres pour faire les fondemens dou dit jubé.

1385–86: *lacuna.*

1386–87 F.A., Bibl. nat., lat. 9111.

1387–88 F.A., Bibl. nat., lat. 9111.
37 vº. A Jehan Raoulin, ouvrier de bras, qui servi ledit Jehan de Rameru, en faisent l'arc boutant de croye qui boute contre la croisee pour 4 jours pour jour 20d. sont 6s. 8d.

1388–89 F.A., Bibl. nat., lat. 9111.
66 rº. A Fierabraz pour 4 jours a faire les alours pour refaire l'osteau de la grant roë par devers le pavement 3s 4d. par jour, 13s. 4d.

68 vº. A Guiot Brisetour pour faire un ymage de Dieu en l'oo, et son siege, tout de couleurs, par devers le pavement, contenant environ 24 piez et demi, au fuer de cinq solz le pié font 6 l. 2s. 6d.

1389–90 F.A., Bibl. nat., lat. 9111.
87 vº. Ab ista septimana citra fuerunt operarii in opere navis ecclesie, excepto uno, scilicet Hane-quino.

88 vº. Despens pour charpentiers. La sepmaine de la Conception Nostre Dame. A Fierabraz pour estaier un pillier de croye qui est dedans la forme que jadiz fist et dreça feu maistre Jehan de Tor-voye, lequel pillier a esté gelez et cheoit, se il n'y eust pourveu, par 2 jours 6s. 8d.

2. To put a post and a tie beneath one of the great beams of the roof of the nave of the church, which was broken, in the 3rd week of March.

1. Expense for materials to make the foundations of the said choir screen.

Note: work continues on the choir screen.

1. To Jehan Raoulin, laborer, who helped the said Jehan de Rameru in building the chalk flyer that butts against the crossing for 4 days at 20d. per day is 6s. 8d.

1. To Fierabras [carpenter] for 4 days to make the scaffolding to remake the window of the great rose toward the road [north transept rose] at 3s. 4d. per day makes 13s. 4d.

2. To Guiot Brisetour for making an image of God and His throne, all in colors, in the rose window toward the road [north transept], con-taining about 24½ feet at the price of 5s. per foot makes £6 2s. 6d.

1. From this week [2nd week in June] onward the laborers were in the work of the nave of the church, except for one, that is Hennequin. *Note:* until this point the masons were involved with the work on the choir screen.

2. Expense for carpenters. The week of the Con-ception of Our Lady [3 weeks before Christmas, 1389]. To Fierabras for propping up a chalk pillar [or buttress] that is inside the window formerly built and erected by the late Jehan de Torvoie: the pillar has been frozen [i.e., damaged by frost] and would fall if not prevented, for 2 days 6s. 8d. *Note:* the word *forme* can mean the framework or center for building an arch of a window, or it can mean the arch or window itself, see earlier, 1375–76.

131

88 vᵒ. Despens pour couvreurs. La sepmaine de la Conception Nostre Dame A Girart le couvreur pour son salaire de descouvrir et recouvrir les tois qui sont dessoubz le grant pillier que jadis fist feu maistre Jehan de Torvoie, le quel il a convenu estayer, pour ce que le pillier de croye qui est dedans cheoit pour la gelee . . . 16s. 8d.

3. Expense for roofers. The week of the Conception of Our Lady, To Girart the roofer for his salary for having uncovered and covered again the roofs which are below the great pillar formerly built by the late Master Jehan de Torvoie. It has been necessary to prop [this pillar] because the chalk pillar [buttress] which is inside [the window] would fall because of the frost . . . 16s. 8d. *Note*: the great pillar probably flanked the clerestory window which had been propped up through the insertion of the buttress mentioned in item 2 above.

89 rᵒ. Autre despense de charpentiers, couvreurs et autres ouvriers faite depuis le jour de Noel 1389, que la nef de l'eglise chut par la choiste d'une grant forme qui estoit dessus la dite nef.

4. Other expense for the carpenters, roofers, and other laborers incurred since Christmas 1389 when the nave of the church fell because of the fall of a great window which was over the said nave.

89 vᵒ. La sepmaine de la Circoncision Nostresr. que l'oo chut.

5. The week of the Circumcision of Our Lord when the rose window [of the north transept] fell.

90 rᵒ. Au Jay, maçon, et a ses compaignons pour marchié fait a eux en tasche par messr. Pierre Darbois, Henry de Bruisselles et moy du commandement de messrs. d'abatre un grant pillier de pierre sur lequel estoit le nid de la cygoinne 14 l. t.

6. To Jay, mason, and to his companions, for a contract for piece work with them made by my lords Pierre d'Arbois, Henry de Bruisselles, and myself, on the orders of my lords, to demolish a great stone pillar upon which was the stork's nest, £14 t.

90 rᵒ. La sepmaine de saint Anthoine. . . . A Girart Daubeterre pour couvrir sur les chapelles par 3 jours. 10 s.
A Felisot Jaque pour abatre et descendre les pierres pour 3 jours 7s. 6d.

7. The week of Saint Anthony. To Girart d'Aubeterre to roof over the chapels for 3 days, 10s. To Felisot Jaque to demolish and lower down the stones for 3 days, 7s. 6d.

95 rᵒ. A Perinot Calon du Meiz Robert pour 8 chevrons achatez de luy pour faire les alours des maçons autour des pilliers 15s.

8. To Perinot Calon du Mez Robert for 8 rafters purchased from him in order to make the masons' scaffolding around the pillars, 15s.

95 vᵒ. A Perot de Fromgnicourt pour une tronche de tramble achetee de luy pour faire trappens a faire mooles pour la maçonnerie de pilliers . . . 21s. 3d.

9. To Perot de Fromgnicourt for a piece of aspen purchased from him to make planks to make templates for the masonry of the pillars . . . 21s. 3d.

1390 Arch. Aube, G 2592, d'Arbois, Documents, XX.
. . . Jehans Nepveu, dit Lescaillon, demourant a Rains, et Colart Lescaillon son frere, demourant a Troyes, . . . recognurent . . . avoir marchandé a

Jehan Nepveu, called the slater, living in Reims, and his brother Colart, living in Troyes . . . recognized that they have entered into contract

venerables et discretes personnes dean et chappistre de l'eglise de Troyes de covrir la ramee de leur eglise dés les grans pilliers de la grant croissiee jusques au pillier qui est de costé le puis, ledit pillier comprins dedans ladicte couverture tout franchement et un pié oultre, ensemble la vossure dou grant art de la ditte croissié, laquelle passe d'une part et d'autre la ditte ramee audessus. . . .

1390–91 F.A., Bibl. nat., lat. 9111.
109 v⁰. Despense pour les journees des maçons qui font le jubé.

115 v⁰. Autres journees de maçons et ouvriers de braz qui ont bouchees certainnes fenestres estans soubz la ramee et haucié les 2 ars boutans qui boutent contre la volte du clocher de la croisee et soubzmurer les paroiz d'icelle.

123 r⁰. . . . pour 7 grans pieces de merrien d'un pié a main de face au graille bout achatees de luy par Jehan Colombe et Fierabraz pour faire les posts des paroiz qui portent la ramee 70s.

124 v⁰. A Jehan et Colart diz les Escaillons, freres, pour covrir d'escaille la ramee nueve dés les grans pilliers jusques au puis, le gros pillier franc et un pié oultre, et doivent livrer l'escaille, le clo et mettre en euvre par marché fait en tasche avec eulx par messrs. 350 l. t.

126 v⁰. Despens pour faire la grant paroiz qui clost l'eglise et les heles d'une part et d'autre.

127 r⁰. . . . et de blanchir en la nef ung des ars et pillier de la dite nef. . . .

127 v⁰. Despens pour plastrer et faire de plastre les paroiz de la dite ramee.

128 v⁰. Achat de chamberil pour chambrilier la ramee et ouvriers pour le mettre.

with venerable and discreet persons the dean and chapter of the church of Troyes to cover the roof of their church from the great pillars of the great crossing as far as the pillar which is beside the well [D 3] including the said pillar completely inside the said roof and one foot beyond, together with the voussoir of the great arch of the crossing which passes from one side to the other above the roof. . . .

1. Expense for the days of the masons who are making the choir screen.

2. Other days of the masons and laborers who have blocked certain windows existing under the roof and have heightened the 2 flying buttresses that lean against the vault of the bell tower of the crossing and have walled in under the screens.

3. . . . for 7 great pieces of timber the width of a hand at the thin end purchased from him by Jehan Colombe and Fierabras to make the posts of the screens which carry the roof, 70s.

4. To the brothers, Jehan and Colart, called the Slaters, for covering the new roof with slate, from the great pillars to the well [including] the great pillar and 1 foot beyond, and they should supply the slate and nails and put them to use, by contract for piecework [made] with my lords £350 t.

5. Expense for making the great screen that closes in the church and the aisles on one side and the other.

6. . . . and to whitewash in the nave one of the arches and one pillar of the said nave. . . . *Note:* pier C 2 and the arch of the main arcade to the east had been left exposed outside the provisional wall at division 3.

7. Expense to plaster and have plastered the screens of the said roof.

8. Purchase of panels for panelling [the inside of] the said roof and workers to install it.

129 rº. Despens pour forge. A Thomas le Chat pour 127 aggrappes de fer pesans 127 livres, livrees par luy et mises és pierres du grant pillier par devers la court l'official, qui a esté levez jusques au haut de la ramee; et pour 98 aggrappes mises en l'autre pillier qui a esté levez de maçonnerie a l'opposite par devers le pavement, pesans 98 l. Item pour 118 aggrappes mises ou pillier par devers le puis, le quel a esté abatuz jusques a la vossure de l'ars et depuis refait et assavoir les dites aggrappes mises pesans 118 l. Item pour 8 bandes de fer mises és bechaux et entrez de la dite ramee, pesans 37 l. Item pour 4 bandes de fer et les clos pesans 18 l. mises és travers qui tiennent les trappans dont le grant oo par devers le pavement est bouché, qui font en tout 398 l. fer . . . 19 l. 2s. 6d.

131 rº. . . . pour cuire le plastre a mettre les aggrappes és pilliers que les maçons ont levez pour porter la ramee. . . .

1391–92 F.A., Bibl. nat., lat. 9111.
148 vº. A Jehan Fierabraz pour 3 jours a faire les alours pour mettre le chambril 10s.

152 vº. A Thomas le Chat, fevre, pour forger et faire les barreaux de fer et les verges des verrierez mises en 20 fenestres toutes pareilles de haut et large, les quelles sont en la ramee neuve, c'est assavoir 12 és paroiz devers le pavement et 8 en l'autre pan par devers la court l'evesque, dont les barreaux et verges d'une chascune d'icelles 20 fenestres pesent 23 l.; pour ce icy pour les dites 20 fenestres 460 l. fer. Pour 3 tirans de fer mis és fenestres de maçonnerie qui sont ou pan devers la court l'evesque, 6 barres loquetees et 46 verges mises és dites fenestres verreez senz les paillettez qui seront comptees cy aprés, pour tout 137 l. fer. Item pour 6 autres fenestres d'une moison dont les 4 sont oudit pan devers la court l'evesque et les autres deux ou pignon 78 l de fer.

153 vº. Façon de verrieres. A Guiot Brisetour, verrier, au quel a esté marchandé de mettre en oeuvre certain verre tant blanc comme de coulours qui estoit en diverses pieces en la plomberie

9. Expense for iron work. To Thomas le Chat for 127 iron hooks weighing 127 pounds, supplied by him and placed in the stones of the great pillar toward the official court, which has been raised up to the height of the roof, and for 98 hooks weighing 98 pounds placed in the other pillar on the opposite [north] side toward the road, which has been raised up in masonry. Item, for 118 hooks placed in the pillar beside the well [D 3] which has been demolished to the voussoirs of the arches and then re-made, the said hooks weighing 118 pounds. Item, for 8 iron bands placed in the *bechaux* and ties of the roof, weighing 37 pounds. Item, for 4 iron bands and nails weighing 18 pounds placed in the cross beams holding the planks which fill the great rose window toward the road [north transept], which makes in all 398 pounds of iron . . . £19 2s. 6d.

10. To heat plaster to set the hooks in the pillars which the masons have heightened to carry the roof. . . .

1. To Jehan Fierabras for 3 days to make the scaffolding to install the panelling [inside the nave roof] 10s.

2. To Thomas le Chat, smith, to forge and make iron bars and rods for the glass placed in 20 windows all of the same height and width, which are in the new roof, that is to say 12 in the screen toward the road and 8 in the other bay toward the bishop's court; in each of these 20 windows the rods and the bars weigh 23 pounds, for this for the said 20 windows 460 pounds of iron. For 3 iron ties placed in the masonry windows which are in the bay toward the bishop's court, six bars with latches and 46 rods placed in the said glazed windows without the solder grains which will be reckoned afterwards, in all 137 pounds of iron. Item, for 6 other windows of a size, of which 4 are in the said bay toward the bishop's court and the 2 others are in the gable, 78 pounds of iron.

3. Making of windows. To Guiot Brisetour, glazier, with whom a contract has been made to install certain glass, both white and colored, in various pieces in the plumbery and some of it

tant de cellui du grant O cheu comme d'autre
et en faire verrieres pour mettre en la ramee
nueve, parmi ce qu'il aura 1 gros tournois du pié
et l'en li livrera soldure du quel il a livré 8
verrieres contenans 162 piez en septembre 1391
qui valent audit fuer 13 l. 10s.

153 v⁰. Audit Guiot qui le jeudi aprés la Toussaint
1391, 9ᵉ jour de novembre, a livrees 18 verrieres
mesurees en la presence mess. Pierre Darbois
et d'autres, contenans 300 piez de verre, tout de
sien, dont les 16 sont és deux grans paroiz de
la dite ramee et les deux ou pignon devant . . . au
fuer de 3s. 9d. pour pié valent 56 l. 5s. t.

153 v⁰. A lui pour 4 verrieres blanches a bouillons
mises és formes de pierre au pris que dessus
contenent 66 piez font 12 l. 7s. 6d.

154 r⁰. A Jehanin et Gautherin de Vitel, huchiers,
pour entailler les colombes de bois des formes ou
les verrieres sont assises en la dite ramee afin de
y mettre les barreaux et verges de fer pour mettre
et asseoir les dites verrieres . . . 26s. 8d.

1392–93 F.A., Bibl. nat. lat. 9111.
168 r⁰. Et est assavoir que par le temps dessusdit
maistre Henry de Bruisselles a esté a Auceurre ou
il avoit certains ouvraiges pour l'eglise d'Aucerre
et celle de Saint Germain, auquel lieu il avoit ia
menez les autres ouvriers de la loge, et encor y
mena ledit Guerart. Et par ainsin cessa l'ouvraige
dudit jubé par long temps. Pendant lequel fu
advisé qu'il seroit bon de faire marchié en tasche
audit maistre Henry de assouvir ledit jubé. Et
pour ce en la presence de monsr. l'evesque et en
son hostel, presens messrs. ou la plus grant partie
d'iceulx fu advisié combien l'euvre povoit valoir
et avoit a despendre an pour autre. Et finallement
fu conclut de mettre chacun an oudit jubé 200
l., ou pavement 200 l., et le demorant seroit pour
secourir aux autres charges de la dite euvre. Et
que venu le dit maistre Henry l'en parleroit a lui
sur le fait dessusdit. Et en oultre fu ordonné
que messieur Pierre Darbois et Erart de Vitel
avec li parleroient aux maçons pour savoir ou l'en

from the great rose that fell [north transept rose],
as well as other glass, and to make windows of
it to place in the new roof, and for this he shall
have 1 *gros tournois* per foot, and he will be
supplied the solder, of which he has delivered 8
windows containing 162 feet in September 1391,
which totals at the said rate £13 10s.

4. To the said Guiot, who on Thursday after All
Saints, 1391, the 9th day of November, has
delivered 18 windows, measured in the presence
of my lord Pierre d'Arbois and others, containing
300 feet of glass, all of it his [i.e., not from the
stockpile] of which 16 [windows] are in the great
screen of the said roof and 2 are in the west
gable . . . at the price of 3s. 9d. per foot totals
£56 5s. t.

5. To him for 4 windows of white glass with
bull's eyes, placed in the stone windows at the
[same] price as above, containing 66 feet makes
£12 7s. 6d.

6. To Jehanin and Gautherin de Vitel, joiners,
for cutting the wooden columns of the window
frames where the panes are set in the said roof in
order to install the iron bars and rods to install
and to set the said panes. . . . 26s. 8d.

1. And it is to be known that during the above-
mentioned period Master Henry de Bruisselles
has been in Auxerre where he had certain work
for Auxerre Cathedral and the church of Saint-
Germain, to which place he had already taken
the other laborers of the lodge, and he took
the said Guerart there too. And thus the work on the
choir screen ceased for a long time. During
which time it was recommended that it would be
good to make a contract for piecework with the
said Henry to finish the choir screen. Therefore,
in the presence of my lord the bishop, and in
his palace, in the presence of my lords [the
chapter], or most of them, advice was taken on
how much the fabric [fund] was worth and had
to spend from one year to the next. And finally it
was decided to spend 200 pounds each year for
the said screen, 200 [pounds] for the pavement,
and the rest would be to meet the other expenses
of the said work. And that when Master Henry

Appendix B. Selected Texts Relating to Construction

pourroit trouver bon pavement pour paver l'e-
glise, et marchenderoient si povoient bonnement.

1393–94 F.A., Bibl. nat., lat. 9111.
186 r⁰. Et premierement pour le pavement de
ladite eglise. A Henry de Bruisselles, Felisot
Iaque, Jaquot Mignart, Jehan Gilot et Jehan de
Fontainnes, maçons, auxquelx a esté marchandé
le 10e jour de janvier 1392 de paver l'eglise de
Troyes de pavement bon et souffisant de la perriere de Lisignes ... 266 l.

187 r⁰. Audit Fierabraz pour retenir la dite paroiz
comme dit est, et pour abatre une attendue de
merrien qui estoit suz le pillier nuef qui est
dehors la dite parois, le quel merrien par force du
vent trambloit et estoit en peril d'abatre partie
de la ramee ... 20s.

1394–95 F.A., Bibl. nat., lat. 9111.

1395–96 F.A., Bibl. nat., lat. 9111.
230 v⁰. A maistre Henry de Bruisselles, Felisot
Iaque, Jaquot Mignart, Jehan Gilot et Jehan
de Fontainnes, maçons, auxquelx a esté marchandé de paver l'eglise et livrer la toise de 8
piez de toutes esquarrures assise pour 70s. t. si
comme plus a plain est contenu ou compte prece-
dant, les quelx en ceste annee en ont livrees
assises 31 toises et demie par devers le biau portail
... 110 l. 5s.

230 v⁰. Autres maçons pour retenir le pillier de
dessoubz le biau portail.

1396–97 F.A., Bibl. nat., lat. 9111.
242 r⁰. Et premierement pour maçons pour tailler
les degrez devant le beau portail.

243 r⁰. Et est assavoir que pour ce que la dite
cloison n'estoit mie sehurement asseuree pour les
grans vens, et auxi l'entablement de pierre qui
est sur le dit O s'avaloit et estoit en peril de
cheoir, par le commendement de messr. Pierre

came back, they should discuss the above matter
with him. And further, it was determined that
Pierre d'Arbois and Erart de Vitel [*proviseurs*]
should talk to masons to find out where to find
good pavement [stone] to pave the church, and to
make a contract, if they could get a good one.

1. And first, for the pavement of the said church.
To Henry de Bruisselles, Felisot Iaque, Jaquot
Mignart, Jehan Gilot, and Jehan de Fontainnes,
masons, with whom it has been contracted on
January 10, 1392, to pave the church of Troyes
with good and adequate pavement from the
quarry of Lisignes ... £266.

2. To the said Fierabras to secure the said screen,
as has been said, and to demolish a wooden lean-
to which was above the new pillar which is
outside the screen [C 2], which piece of timber
was being shaken by the force of the wind and
was threatening to knock down a part of the roof
... 20s.

Note: nothing of importance. Henry de Bruisselles
continues work on the choir screen.

1. To Master Henry de Bruisselles, Felisot Iaque,
Jaquot Mignart, Jehan Gilot, and Jehan de Fontainnes, masons, with whom a contract has been
made to pave the church and to supply [paving
stone] at the fathom of 8 feet, for all slabs set for
70s. t. as is more fully contained in the preceding
account, who in this year have delivered 31½
fathoms toward the Beautiful Portal [north transept portal] ... £110 5s.

2. Other masons for retaining the pillar below
the Beautiful Portal.

1. And first for masons to cut the steps in front
of the Beautiful Portal.

2. And it is to be known that because the said
partition [in the north transept rose] is not at all
adequately secured on account of the great winds,
and also [because] the stone entablature above
the said rose was coming down and was in danger

Darbois, maistre Henry, les charpentiers et le grant chamberier monterent amont pour adviser quelle retenue l'en y pourroit faire, et fu par eux advisé qu'il estoit de nécessité d'avoir 8 grans pieces de merrien, chascune d'environ de 38 a 40 piez de long et d'un pié a sole de fourniture, les quelles seroient mises dedens et de hors a bonnes clefs de bois sur postes qui porteroient sur l'alee des basses verrieres. . . .

245 r⁰. Audit Estienne Audigier pour mettre tables de plonc tout autour de l'arc de la grant croisee contre lequel la nouvelle ramee est assise, pour ce que l'yaue entroit entre le dit arc et la couverture d'escaille et cheoit sur le chanberil . . . 33s. 4d.

247 v⁰. A Pieret, l'ymagineur, pour la façon du Coronnement qui est ou jubé, le quel il a taillé a Saint Loup par accort fait avec lui par messr. Pierre Darbois, Bougin et Vitel, 7 l. 10s. Pour les despens du maistre maçon, de Fierabraz et des autres compaignons qui aiderent a admener dudit Saint Loup jusques en l'eglise la pierre ou est le dit Coronnement, et l'aiderent a monter iusques ou lieu ou elle est assise . . . 8s. 4d.

1397–98 F.A., Bibl. nat., lat. 9111.

1398–99 F.A., Bibl. nat., lat. 9111.

1399–1401: *lacuna.*

1401–2 F.A., Brit. Mus., Add. 15803.
113 v⁰. A Felisot le couvreur pour plomber en la croisee par devers le pavement par devers l'ostel Richard le Sarrurier, pour ce que és allees y pleuvoit que les jointures de l'entablement estoient toutes vuydes de cyment et y fut par 3 jours, 10s.

116 r⁰. Autre despense faite du commendement de messrs. pour aler a Paris et autrepart querir maçons et autres ouvriers pour visiter l'eglise. Et premierement pour les despens de messr. Jehan Gaillart qui par mesdiz seigneurs fu envoiez a Paris pour parler a maistre Remond, maistre des euvres du Roy, et savoir a lui se il pourroit venir

of falling, on the orders of my lord Pierre d'Arbois, Master Henry, the carpenters and the great chamberlain climbed aloft to advise as to how to retain it, and their advice was that it was necessary to have 8 great pieces of timber, each of about 38 to 40 feet long and one foot across, which would be placed inside and outside with good wooden pegs on top of posts which would sit on the passageway of the low windows [the triforium]. . . .

3. To the said Etienne Audigier for placing lead sheets all around the arch of the great crossing against which the new roof is set because the [rain] water was coming in between the said arch and the slate roof and was falling on the panelling [of the wooden barrel vault] . . . 33s. 4d.

4. To Pieret the image-maker [sculptor] for making the Coronation which is on the choir screen, which he carved at Saint-Loup according to the agreement made with him by my lord Pierre d'Arbois, Bougin and Vitel, £7 10s. For the expenses of the master mason, of Fierabras and the other workers who helped bring the stone in which is [carved] the Coronation from Saint-Loup to the church, and helped raise it to the place where it is set . . . 8s. 4d.

Note: no significant new work.

Note: Henry de Bruisselles is now dead.

1. To Felisot the roofer for lead work in the crossing toward the road by the house of Richard the locksmith because the passageways there were leaking because the joints of the entablature were quite empty of cement, and he was at it for 3 days, 10s.

2. Other expense made at the orders of my lords to go to Paris and elsewhere to seek masons and other workers to visit the church. And first, for the expenses of my lord Jehan Gaillart who was sent by my said lords to Paris to talk with Master Remond, master of the king's works, and to find out from him if he could come here to

Appendix B. Selected Texts Relating to Construction

pardeça pour visiter l'eglise. Le quel s'excusa en la presence de monsr. d'Auceurre et bailla audit messr. Jehan Gaillart, maistre Jehan Aubelet et maistre Jehan Prevost, son neveu, pour ycelle visite . . . Les dessusdiz maistre Jehan Aubelet, son nepveu et un leur varlet a trois chevaux arriverent a Troyes le jeudi aprés la saint Andry audit an environ prime; et incontinent il se mistrent a visiter l'eglise en hault et embas en la presence de monsr. l'evesque, appellez avec eulx Thomas Michelin, Colin Guignon, Jehanin Gilot, maçons, Jehan de Nantes et Remond, charpentiers, et les autres ouvriers de l'eglise qui touz jours furent avec les dessusdiz Aubelet et Prevost. Et fist ledit maistre Jehan Aubelet escripre la visitacion et devisa de certains pilliers et ars a faire sur les voltes et autrepart, la quelle fut vehue et lehue en plain chapitre. . . .

116 v⁰. Autre despense faite du commendement de messrs. pour l'achat de 18 grans pieces de merrien achatees pour faire estaies et autres choses necessaires en l'eglise.

1402–3 F.A., Brit. Mus., Add. 15803.
134 v⁰. Premierement pour les journees des maçons et autres ouvriers a tailler et refaire les ars de pierre dure sur les voltes appellez ars formerez qui estoient de croye et tous esgelez.

139 v⁰. A Thomas Michelin, au quel a esté marchandé, present monsr. l'evesque, a entrepranre la cusançon de faire le giet des pilliers que l'en a avisé de faire pour la sehurté de l'eglise, et doit gaignier chacun jour 4s. t. . . . A Guillaume le Cur (?) de Nogent, pour faire tout a nuef de plastre le pourtrait sur la chapelle Dreue de la Marche pour y tracier le pilier que l'en veult faire 12s. 6d.

140 v⁰. La sepmaine de Sainte Mastie, commencant le 6e. de may, pour estaier le pillier, pour ce que l'en vouloit furger le fondement dudit pillier.

visit the church. [Master Remond] excused himself in the presence of my lord [the bishop] of Auxerre and offered to the said lord Jehan Gaillart [the services of] Master Jehan Aubelet and Master Jehan Prevost, his nephew, for the said visit. . . . The above-mentioned Master Jehan Aubelet, his nephew, and one of their apprentices arrived in Troyes on 3 horses the Thursday after Saint Andrew in the said year, around dawn, and immediately they set about visiting the church from top to bottom in the company of my lord the bishop, [and] summoned with them [were] Thomas Michelin, Colin Guignon, Jehanin Gilot, masons, Jehan de Nantes and Remond, carpenters, and the other laborers of the church who were with the above-mentioned Aubelet and Prevost all the time. And the said Master Jehan Aubelet had the visitation written down and he made notes [or sketches] concerning certain pillars and arches to be done on the vaults and elsewhere, which was seen and read in full chapter. . . .

3. Other expense made at the commandment of my lords for the purchase of 18 great pieces of timber purchased to make props and other things necessary in the church.

1. First, for the days of masons and other workers to cut and re-make the arches of hard stone on the vaults called *formerets* [wall arches] which had been of chalk and were damaged by the frost.

2. To Thomas Michelin with whom a contract has been made in the presence of my lord the bishop to undertake the care of the project of the pillars which it has been recommended should be made for the safety of the church and he should earn 4s. t. each day. . . . To Guillaume le Cur of Nogent for making a new portrait in plaster on [top of the vault of] the chapel [of] Dreux de la Marche in order to trace out the pillar which was to be made, 12s. 6d. *Note*: the area above the vault of the chapel to the south of the west bell tower served as the masons' drafting office.

3. The week of Saint Mastida beginning on May 6 for propping the pillar because they wanted to dig the foundation of the said pillar.

141 r⁰. A Thomas Michelin pour boucher et murer un huis qui estoit oudit pillier et y fu 2 jours 8s.

156 v⁰. A maistre Jehan de Diion, maistre maçon de l'eglise de Reins, lequel vint a Troyes du commandement de messrs. pour visiter l'eglise, et vint a Troyes la sepmaine de l'Assumpcion Nostre Dame, le quel visita la dite eglise et ordonna plusieurs choses a faire qui furent mises par escript et vehues par monsr. l'evesque et messrs. et demora pour 6 jours entiers, au quelx furent donnez par mesdiz seigneurs 6 escus font 6 l. 15s.

157 r⁰. Pour les despens faiz cheux Jaquinot Clivet par Thomas Michelin, Jehan Gilot, Colin Guignon, Colerne, Jehan Doce, maçons, maistre Jehan Colombe, Jehan de Nantes, Nicolas Matan, Remond, charpentiers, et plusieurs autres illec assemblez et mandez pour avoir advis avec monsr. l'evesque et messrs. assemblez sur le lieu du fondement du pillier assez tost aprés le depart dudit maistre Jehan de Diion pour savoir la quelle opinion seroit tenue, ou celle de maistre Jehan Aubelet, ou celle dudit maistre Jehan; et pour mieulx eulx adviser leur furent les opinions des deux maistres exposees, les quelx cy dessus nommez, tout veu et consideré, determinerent a pramre le fondement dudit pillier suz le bout des degrez et qu'il seroit boutant encontre l'autre pillier de l'eglise, et ainsin fut conclut. Pour quoy fut demandé congié a monsr. le bailli. au procureur du Roy et aux voyeurs de la ville qu'il souffrissent a furger dessoubz le pavement. . . .

1403–7: *lacuna.*

1407–8 F.A., Trinity College, Dublin, MS. 1775–9, Iq 8 II a.
La sepmaine commencent le 12e. jour de septembre. . . . A Jehan de Nantes et ses compaignons, et estoient 5, qui osterent la cintre de l'arc du pillier neuf devers le pavement. . . .

Despense pour ouvraiges. Et premierement pour rechaussier de pierre les murs autour de l'eglise, c'estassavoir dés le pillier qui est delez l'uis de Saint Linart jusques a l'uisserie du jardin monsr. l'evesque . . .

4. To Thomas Michelin for blocking and walling up a doorway which was in the said pillar and he was at it for 2 days, 8s.

5. To Master Jehan de Dijon, master mason of the church at Reims, who came to Troyes on the orders of my lords to visit the church, and he came to Troyes the week of the Assumption of Our Lady. [Master Jehan] visited the said church and ordered that several things should be done, which were put in writing and were seen by my lords the bishop and my lords [the chapter] and he stayed for 6 complete days, to whom was given by my said lords 6 *escus* making £6 15s.

6. For the expenses incurred in the house of Jaquinot Clivet by Thomas Michelin, Jehan Gilot, Colin Guignon, Colerne, Jehan Doce, masons, Master Jehan Colombe, Jehan de Nantes, Nicolas Matan, Remond, carpenters, and several others assembled there and asked for their advice with my lord the bishop and my lords [the chapter] assembled at the place of the foundation of the pillar soon after the departure of the said Master Jehan de Dijon to know which opinion should be held, either that of Master Jehan Aubelet or that of the said Master Jehan [de Dijon]. And to advise them better, the opinions of the two masters were exposed. The above-named, having seen and considered everything, determined to make the foundation of the said pillar at the bottom of the steps and that it should butt against the other pillar of the church and so it was concluded. For which [reason] permission was sought from my lord the bailiff, from the king's procurer and from the *voyeurs* of the city to dig beneath the road. . . .

1. The week beginning on September 12. . . . To Jehan de Nantes and his companions, and there were 5 of them, who removed the center from the arch of the new pillar toward the road. . . .

2. Expense for work. And first to underpin with stone the walls around the church, that is from the pillar which is beyond the door of [the chapel of] Saint Leonard as far as the door of the garden of my lord the bishop . . .

Appendix B. Selected Texts Relating to Construction

1408 Arch. Aube, G 2593, charter, d'Arbois, Documents, XXI.

Saichent tuit, que par devant Guillaume Belin et Nicolas Cochart, clerc jurez et establiz ad ce faire a Troies de par le roy nostre sire, fu present en sa personne Guiot Brisetour, verrier, demorant a Troies si comme il disoit, et recognut avoir traictié et marchandé a et avec venerables et discretes personnes les doyen et chappitre de l'eglise de Troies de voirrer tout a neuf de bon voirre tout blanc ung grant osteau que l'en fait tout de neuf en ladicte eglise, ouquel osteau seront faiz les quatres evvangelistres en quatre rons qui seront oudit osteau, avec huit escuçons qui seront en huit autres rons en telles armes que par lesdiz venerables lui seront dictes et declarees.

Let it be known to all that Guiot Brisetour, glazier, dwelling in Troyes, so he said, was present in person before Guillaume Belin and Nicolas Cochart, sworn clerk and established to do this in Troyes by the king our lord, and he recognized that he had agreed and contracted with venerable and discreet persons the dean and chapter of the church of Troyes to glaze anew with good white glass a great window which is newly made in the said church; in the said window the four evangelists in four roundels shall be made with eight shields which shall be in eight other roundels with [heraldic] arms that shall be told and declared to him by the said venerable [persons of the chapter]. *Note*: the contract allowed Guiot 3s. 4d. for each foot of glass.

1409–10 F.A., Arch. Aube, G 1559.

125 rº. . . . pour l'ostiau nuef et asseoir, soder et encramponner les cleres voyes dessus led. ostiau et la viz qui [est decoste—deleted] et pillier qui sont au deux costes et tant pour massonnerie comme forge et autres matieres ad ce necessaires.

1. For setting, soldering, and clamping in the new window and the balustrade over the said window and the staircase which [is beside—deleted] and pillar on either side, both for masonry and for forge and other necessary materials.

126 rº. Despense pour recouvrir d'escaille et later ce qui estoit a faire ou pignon dessus l'osteau nuef. . . .

2. Expense for covering with slates and lath where necessary on the gable above the new window . . .

1410–11 F.A., Arch. Aube, G 1559.

163 rº. Despense pour le fait du grant clochier, commencee le 21e. jour de novembre 1410.

1. Expense because of the great tower begun on November 21, 1410.

Et premierement pour le bois de Hervy. Pour ung present de 8 pintes de vin fait par l'ordenance des messrs. au chancellier, tresorier, secretaire et plusieurs autres conseilliers du Roy de Navarre, qui estoient en l'ostel Jehan Poignant le 21e. jour de novembre, lequel jour icelui seigneur donna a l'eglise 40 chasnes de son bois d'Ervy pour led. clocher la pinte 15d. valent 10s.

And first for timber from Ervy. For a present of 8 pints of wine made at the orders of my lords to the chancellor, treasurer, secretary, and several other counsellors of the king of Navarre who was in the house of Jehan Poignant on November 21, on which day the said lord gave to the church 40 oak trees from his forest in Ervy for the said bell tower, at 15d. a pint makes 10s.

1411–12 F.A., Arch. Aube, G 1560.

21 rº. Despense pour le fait du grant clochier. Et premierement pour l'amenaige du bois de Hervy.

1. Expense because of the great bell tower. And first for the carting of wood from Ervy.

24 rº. Ci aprés s'en suivent aucuns payemens fais par moy du commandement de messrs. a maistre Thomas le maçon sur les 100 l. qui par eux li estoient dehuez a cause du darrenier traictié fait avecques lui par mesdis seigneurs.

2. Hereafter follow several payments made by me at the order of my lords to Master Thomas the mason on the £100 they owe him because of the last contract [made] with him by my lords. *Note*: this payment is probably connected with Michelin's work on the north transept rose.

1412–13 F.A., Arch. Aube, G 1561.

19 rº. Despense pour achever de mettre et asseoir les barreaux de fer dessubz les vostes de l'eglise en la sepmaine aprés la Magdelene. Et premiers a hoster 2 posteaux des tremiez de la maistre voste de la croissee . . .

34 vº. Audit Jehan de Nantes pour l jour de ly, son genre, maistre Thomas Michelin, Remon Pienne et Nicolas Ladvocat en l'ostel de monsr. l'evesque le jeudi avant les Brandons a pourtraire la façon en gros de l'assiete dou clochier 21s. 8d.

35 vº. Pour l voyaige fait par led. Nantes et maistre Thomas Michelin, maçon, a Bourges et a Meun sur Yevre, pour veoir les clochiers des eglises desd. lieux, qu'on disoit moult bons, les quelx partirent a fere led. voyaige le jeudi 17e. jour d'aoust, et demorerent jusques au venredi au soir, 25e. jour doud. mois. 13 l. 17s. 1d.

35 vº. Pour papier de grant forme et parchemin par eulx pour ce pour gicter et pourtraire les clochiers desd. lieux, 5s.

37 rº. A savoir que le lundi 13e. jour de mars 1412, lendemain des Brandons fu commencé de charpenter et taillier le clochier de l'eglise de Troyes, pour le quel fere a esté plusieurs fois faite assemblee en la sale du Roy nostre sire, en chap-itre, en l'ostel de monsr. l'evesque, et tousjours les clers, bourgeois et habitans de Troyes presens qui, d'un commun consentement ont conclu de fere led. clochier aprés plusieurs atercacions et en la dite sale ont esleu avec les maistres de l'euvre dessusd. maistre Michau de Loches, et fait jurer et asseerementer sur ce par mond. sr. monsr. l'evesque, presens toux, le quel a accepté la charge de savoir depar les habitans et raporter devers eulx, quant requis en sera, comment l'argent des aides et suffraiges qu'ilz ont toux promis d'y fere sera despensé, et de chascun dimenche estre present a escripre les journees des ouvriers.

1. Expense for finishing the work of placing and setting the iron bars above the vaults of the church in the week after [the feast of the] Magdalene. And first for removing two posts from the severies of the master vault of the crossing. . . .

2. To the said Jehan de Nantes for himself, his son-in-law, Master Thomas Michelin, Remon Pienne, and Nicolas Ladvocat for 1 day in my lord the bishop's palace on the Thursday before *Brandons* [first Sunday in Lent] to draw out the form of the base of the tower in general terms, 21s. 8d.

3. For a trip made by the said Nantes and Master Thomas Michelin, mason, to Bourges and to Méhun-sur-Yèvre to see the bell towers of the churches of those places which are said to be very fine. The above-mentioned left on the said trip on Thursday August 17 and stayed there until Friday the 25th day of the same month in the evening, £13 17s. 1d.

4. For large format paper and parchment for them for sketching and portraying the bell towers of the said places, 5s.

5. It should be known that on Monday March 13, 1412, the day after *Brandons* [first Sunday in Lent] the carpentry work and cutting of the bell tower of the church at Troyes was begun, for which reason several meetings have taken place in the chamber of our lord the king, in the chapter, in the bishop's palace with the clergy, bourgeois and inhabitants of Troyes always present, who, with common accord, after several discussions, have agreed to make the said bell tower and in the said room have elected Master Michau de Loches together with the above-mentioned masters of the works. They have had my lord the bishop swear and give his word in the presence of everyone. [Michau de Loches] has accepted the charge of letting the inhabitants [of Troyes] know, and reporting to them when required, how the money from the aids and subsidies which they have all promised to make shall be spent, and to be present each Sunday to write down the days of the laborers. . . .

Appendix B. Selected Texts Relating to Construction

37 rᵒ. A maistre Jehan de Nantes, charpentier, maistre esleu a conduire led. ouvraige par toux les dessusdis, pour 6 journees de ly, qui doit avoir 5 s. pour jour durant led. ouvraige. . . .

1413–14 F.A., Arch. Aube, G 1561.
69 rᵒ. Despense pour le clochier.

1414–15 F.A., Arch. Aube, G 1561
101 vᵒ. A Symon Jehanine, soyeur dou long pour 5 jours ly et son compaignon a soyer trapens pour fere moolez a moler les grans posteaux de l'assise doud. clochier a 5s. 10d. pour jour valent 29s. 2d.

108 vᵒ. Pour avoir donné a digner a toux les ouvriers charpentiers de Troyes le lendemain de Pasques flories, qui furent assemblé par l'ordonnance de messrs. pour conseiller l'eglise sur la façon dou clochier, pour ce que aucuns vouloyent que on y feist 2 paires de fenestraiges et double tonnette, et les autres ne le vouloyent pas, pour quoy furent iceulx ouvriers assemblé, et fu par eulx conclu tant pour la seurté de l'ouvraige comme pour eschoir despense que on n'y feroit que une tonnette et que une paire de fenestraiges pour ce 25s.

1415 Indulgence, Arch. Aube, G 2593, d'Arbois, Documents, XXV.

1415–16 F.A., Arch. Aube, G 1561.
131 rᵒ. Despense pour rapareillier l'osteau devers chapitre que le vent avoit empiré et abatu 2 formes des verrieres dicelly, et pour avoir arresté led. osteau par liens de fer a la piece de merrien qui de long temps estoit derriere icelluy osteau. . . .

139 rᵒ. A maistre Jehan de Nantes pour 6 jours de ly és bois de l'Eschange a escarier les posteaux pour les fenestraiges doudit clochier 30s.

140 vᵒ. En la sepmaine commencent le lundi 6e. jour de juillet A maistre Thomas Michelin, maçon, pour 3 jours de Pierre, son valet, a cuyre et batre plastre et faire l'aire de la chambre a poutraire pour ce 10s.

6. To Master Jehan de Nantes, carpenter, elected master by all the above-mentioned people to conduct the said work, who should have 5s. each day during the said work, for 6 days. . . .

1. Expense for the bell tower.

1. To Symon Jehanine, a ripsaw operator, for 5 days, him and his journeyman, to saw planks to make templates to form the great posts of the base of the tower at 5s. 10d. per day makes 29s. 2d.

2. For having given dinner to all the carpenters of Troyes who were assembled the day after Palm Sunday on the orders of my lords to advise the church on the making of the bell tower, because some people wanted there to be 2 pairs of windows and a double drum and others did not want this, for which reason the laborers were assembled, and it was decided by them that for reasons of safety and in order to avoid expense there should be a single drum and one pair of windows, for this, 25s.

Note: Issued by Cardinal Alamannus, granting 40 days of remission to those who contributed to the fabric.

1. Expense for repairing the window toward the chapter which the wind had damaged, and knocked down 2 frames of the glass of the said [window] and for having secured the said window with iron ties to the piece of timber which for a long time was behind the said window. . . .

2. To Master Jehan de Nantes for his 6 days in the wood of Echange to square the posts for the windows of the said bell tower, 30s.

3. In the week beginning on Monday July 6. To Master Thomas Michelin, mason, for 3 days of Pierre, his apprentice, to heat and mix plaster and to make the [drawing] surface in the tracing chamber, for this, 10s.

1416–17 F.A., Arch. Aube, G 1561.
166 r⁰. A Colin Noot pour 2 trapens de noyer a fere moolez pour moler les posteaux des fenestraiges achetes par led. Nantes, 2s. 11d.

166 v⁰. . . . pour avoir cerchié . . . 8 courbes longues pour les ars boutans doud. clochier. . . .

167 r⁰.-v⁰. Pour 1 voyaige a Paris par moy, J. Blanche, qui fuy envoyes par messrs. et avec moy fu led. maistre Jehan de Nantes, maistre de l'ouvraige doud. clochier, envoyes par monsr. l'evesque et par messrs. de l'eglise et autres de la ville pour avoir collacion avec maistre Jehan Guerart, maistre des euvres de mons. de Berry et de la ville de Paris et autres ouvriers doud. Paris sur la façon des fenestraiges, pignacles et clerez voyes doud. clochier, et ainsy pour adviser les diversités des façons des clochiers de la dite ville de Paris, 6 l. 12s. 6d.

167 v⁰. Led. maistre Jehan Guerarrt monstra aud. maistre Jehan de Nantes plusieurs [façons—deleted] pourtrais et sy pourtrahy present icelly Nantes plusieurs formes touchans led. ouvraige, 35s.

1417–18 F.A., Arch. Aube, G 1561.

1418–19 F.A., Arch. Aube, G 1561.
223 r⁰. Despense pour l'ouvraige de charpenterie pour le clochier nuef, faite par l'ordonnance de messrs. aprés le trespassement de feu maistre Jehan de Nantes, maistre charpentier, qui led. clochier a fait jusques a parfaire les fenestraiges, pignaclez et les clerezvoyez d'icelly clochier. Et depuis le trespassement d'icelly de Nantes, le quel trespassa le 16e. jour de juin l'an 1418, led. ouvraige a esté conduit par Perrin Loque, charpentier, genre d'icelly feu de Nantes, lequel avoit esté continuement avec icelly feu Nantes a pourtraire et faire les giez et devises qui sur le fait doud. ouvraige ont esté fais tant par led. feu de Nantes comme par autres ouvriers a ce cognoissans, au quel Perrin Loque led. feu de Nantes avoit singulierement devisé et fait entendre son entencion sur ce et baillié la forme par escript pour la necessité de lever led. clochier avec toux les pourtrais par ly et autres ouvriers fais sur la

1. To Colin Noot for 2 walnut planks to make templates to form the posts of the windows purchased by the said Nantes, 2s. 11d.

2. . . . for having sought . . . 8 long curved [pieces of wood] for the flying buttresses of the said bell tower. . . .

3. For a trip to Paris [undertaken] by me, J. Blanche [*proviseur*], who was sent by my lords, and with me was the said Master Jehan de Nantes, master of the work on the said bell tower, sent by my lord the bishop and my lords of the church and others in the city to confer with Master Jehan Guerart, master of the works of my lord [the duke] of Berry and of the city of Paris on the making of the windows, pinnacles, and balustrades of the said bell tower, and also for giving advice on the variety of forms of the bell towers of the said city of Paris. £6 12s. 6d.

4. The said Master Jehan Guerart showed to the said Jehan de Nantes several [ways—deleted] portraits and drew several forms connected with the said work in the presence of the said Nantes, 35s.

Note: work continues on the bell tower.

1. Expense for the carpentry work for the new bell tower made on the orders of my lords after the death of the late Master Jehan de Nantes, master carpenter, who has made the said bell tower as far as the completion of the windows, pinnacles, and balustrades of the said bell tower. And since the death of the said de Nantes who died on June 16, 1418, the said work has been directed by Perrin Loque, carpenter, son-in-law of the late de Nantes, who had been continuously with the said late de Nantes to make the portraits, projects, and notes which had been made on the said work both by the late de Nantes and also by other knowledgeable workers. And the late de Nantes had made specific notes and had explained his intention on this to the said Perrin Loque, and had left the plan in writing on the need to raise the said bell tower, together with all the portraits made by him and other workers

Appendix B. Selected Texts Relating to Construction

forme, giet et devise d'icelly clochier, ouquel estoyent a faire 6 formes des fenestraiges, ensemble les pignacles et toutes les clerez voyes dessubz la terrasse, qui sont lyees avec les ars boutans doud. clochier en la maniere qui s'ensuit.

on the form, project, and plan of this bell tower, in which 6 frames for the windows were to be done, together with the pinnacles and all the balustrades above the terrace which are linked with the flying buttresses of the said bell tower in the following manner.

1419–20 F.A., Arch. Aube, G 1561.

Note: work continues on the bell tower.

1420–21 F.A., Arch. Aube, G 1561.

Note: work on the bell tower has lapsed.

1421–22 F.A., Arch. Aube, G. 1561.
303 vº. Despense pour lever les 2 engins qu'avoit fais feu maistre Jehan de Nantes, charpentier, pour lever le merrien du clochier par ly charpenté, affin que lesd. engins ne fussent empirez et perduz par deffault d'estre assemblez.

1. Expense for raising up the 2 engines which the late Jehan de Nantes, carpenter, had made in order to hoist up the timber of the bell tower that he had cut, so that the said engines should not be spoiled and lost because they are not assembled.

1422–27 F.A., Arch. Aube, G 1561–62.

Note: no important work.

1427–28 F.A., Arch. Aube, G 1562.
70 vº. Despense faite pour monter et asseoir la plate forme et les premiers posteaux du clochier neuf, atayer la tonnette du viez clochier et demolir la vielle plate forme d'icelly, qui estoit pourrye et gastee en plusieurs lieux, et abatre les posteaux dud. viez clochier jusques aux premieres moysez dud. viez clochier et icelles moyses retenir sur atayes. . . .

1. Expense made to raise up and set the platform and the first posts of the new bell tower, to prop up the drum of the old bell tower [the *gros clocher*], and to demolish the old platform of this [tower] which was rotten and spoiled in several places and to demolish the posts of the old tower as far as the ties of the said old tower and for propping up the said ties. . . .

1428–29 F.A., Arch. Aube, G 1562.
94 rº. Despense pour lever la plate forme et les premiers posteaux avec les croisees du clochier nuef, commensee en l'annee precedante et non parfaite et de retenir la couverture pour seulement passer le temps d'yvers.

1. Expense for raising up the platform and the first posts with the crossings of the new tower, begun in the previous year, but not complete and for securing the roof just in order to get through the winter.

1429–31: *lacuna.*

1431–32 F.A., Arch. Aube, G 1562.
113 vº. . . . pour couvrir d'escaille autour de la tonnette dud. clochier. . . .

1. . . . for covering around the drum of the bell tower with slates. . . .

1432–33 F.A., Arch. Aube, G 1562.
133 vº. Despense pour le clochier nuef, pour dorer la crois, le batin et la huesse, faire et dorer le coq et lez monter et asseoir sur led. clochier et plusieurs autres choses pour icelly clochier. . . .

1. Expense for the new bell tower, for gilding the cross, the rod, and the peak [lit. boot], for making and gilding the cock and for mounting and setting them in place atop the said bell tower and for other things for the said bell tower. . . .

1433–34 F.A., Arch. Aube, G 1562.

158 v⁰. Despense pour le clochier nuef a later et couvrir d'escaille l'esguille dudit clochier.

1. Expense for the new bell tower, to lath and cover the steeple of the said bell tower with slates.

165 v⁰. A Jaquinot Ladvocat, sarrurier, pour 2 banieres de fer faites par le conseil des ouvriers pour mettre sur les ars boutans dud. clochier, lesquelles messrs. n'ont pas volu y estre mises tant pour la grant charge comme pour le peril de vent, pour ce 35s.

2. To Jaquinot Ladvocat, locksmith, for 2 iron banners made at the recommendation of the workers to place on the flying buttresses of the said bell tower. My lords had not wanted them to be placed partly because of the great weight and because of the danger of [high] wind, for this, 35s.

166 r⁰. Despense faite ou viez clochier a abatre l'esguille et y restablir 1 bechaut portant 4 arestiers avec les sablieres et autres choses a ce necessaires. . . .

3. Expense made on the old tower to demolish the steeple and to reconstruct 1 *bechaut* [peaked roof ?] carrying 4 corner rafters with the wall plates and other necessary items. . . .

1434–38: *lacuna.*

1438–39 F.A., Arch. Aube, G 1562.

191 v⁰. A Felisot Clement pour six journees qu'il a besongné a netoyer et vuidier les gargoles et rebouchier plusieurs pertuiz és basses vostes et en autres lieux en l'eglise et pour mettre en euvre 150 livres de plomb sur les alees devers la maison ou souloit demourer Villemor. . . .

1. To Felisot Clement for 6 days which he has worked to clean and empty the gargoyles and to fill in several holes in the low vaults and elsewhere in the church and for putting 150 pounds of lead into use on the passageways toward the house where Villemor used to live. . . .

196 r⁰. En la seconde sepmaine d'aoust. A Jehanin Loriot pour deux jours a mettre lad. chanlate en l'appendiz qui a esté fait entre la basse ramee et les basses vostes, pour ce 6s. 8d.

2. In the second week of August. To Jehanin Loriot for 2 days to put the said eaves in the lean-to roof which has been made between the low roof [of the nave] and the aisle vaults, for this 6s. 8d.

200 v⁰. A Gilet du Pont pour deux jours a palleçonner, torcher les fenestrages de dessoubz l'appendiz que on a fait contre la paroiz de la basse ramee devers le pavé, dont on a osté les verrieres pour ce 6s. 8d.

3. To Gilet du Pont for 2 days to close in and daub with cob the windows under the lean-to roof that has been made against the screen of the low roof, from which the windows have been removed, for this, 6s. 8d.

Accounts for 1439 to 1451 are preserved in Arch. Aube, G. 1562–63, but they record no significant work.

1451 Indulgence, Arch. Aube, G 2593, d'Arbois, Documents, XXVII.

Cum itaque, sicut ex insinuatione carissimi in Xristo filii, Caroli, Francorum regis illustris ac venerabilis fratris nostri, Ludovici, episcopi Tre-

Since therefore, as we have learned from the report of our dearest son in Christ, Charles, illustrious king of the French, and of our venerable

Appendix B. Selected Texts Relating to Construction

censis, necnon dilectorum filiorum decani et capituli ecclesie Trecensis accepimus, ecclesia Trecenis ... miraculose erecta seu constructa, et exinde magnifice et sumptuose saltim usque ad illius navim continuata et completa fuerit; tamen causantibus guerris, que partes Francie diutius afflixerunt, navis hujusmodi, defitientibus ad id necessariis, incompleta remansit, ad cujus perfectionem seu complementum fabrice ac etiam decani et capituli hujusmodi (quorum prebende fructus, redditus et proventus adeo tenues et exiles existunt, quod ex illis singulis dicte ecclesie canonicis cedentibus, ipsi singuli canonici non valent decenter sustinari) proprie non suppetunt facultates, sed pia fidelium devotionis suffragia plerumque censentur ad hoc accommoda et etiam opportuna. ...

1452 Indulgence, Arch. Aube, G 2593, d'Arbois Documents, XXVIII.
Nos igitur, attendentes, quod vos licet pro complemento dicte navis diligentiam adhibueritis, et fundamenta quinque piliariorum non sine magnis expensis fieri feceritis. ...

1451–52 Arch. Aube, G. 1563.
223 vº. C'est l'estat et recepte du pardon general de l'eglise de Troies, qui a commancié ceste annee. ...

227 rº. Autre despense faicte par moy depuis le premier pardon general, qui a esté ceste annee le jour de Quasimodo l'an 1452 pour faire les preparacions des matierez touchant la perriere de l'eglise, qui est empres Bar sur Seinne, audessus de Bourgoignons, appellee la perriere d'Aigremont, qui fut donnee a ceste eglise par le conte Milon, jadis conte de Bar sur Seinne, lad. perriere visitee par deux maçons en presence de messire Nicole Tetel, chanoine de ceste eglise, et de moy; et pour la conduite des ouvrages cy aprés declarez, qui ont esté deliberez a faire en chappitre, presens monsr. l'evesque, monsr. le lieutenant, l'advocad et procureur de Roy nostresire en grant nombre

brother Louis [Raguier], bishop of Troyes, and also of our dear sons the dean and chapter of the church of Troyes, the church of Troyes, ... miraculously erected and constructed was then continued and completed magnificently and sumptuously at least as far as the nave. However, because of the wars that afflicted parts of France for a long time, the nave, in the absence of necessary [funds], has thus remained unfinished. The products of the prebends of the dean and chapter rendered and received until now are small and weak; although individual canons of the said church have yielded [money] from their prebends, these individual canons cannot decently support [the fabric]. The dean and chapter thus do not have the means to finish and to complete the fabric, but the pious alms of the faithful are generally sufficient and appropriate to achieve this. ... *Note*: Pope Nicholas V granted a full indulgence to all those who visited the church during Lent and made a contribution to the fabric. One quarter of the funds raised to be used for the repair of churches in Rome.

1. Hoping, therefore, that you will apply diligence to the completion of the said nave, and you cannot have the foundations of five pillars made without great expense. ...

1. This is the state and receipt of the general pardon of the church of Troyes which began this year.

2. Other expense incurred by me since the first general pardon which this year was on *Quasimodo* [first Sunday after Easter] 1452 to prepare the materials concerning the quarry of the church which is near Bar-sur-Seine above Bourguignons, called the quarry of Aigremont, which was given to this church by the Count Milon, formerly count of Bar-sur-Seine. This quarry was visited by two masons in the presence of my lord Nicole Tetel, canon of this church, and by myself. [Expenses also] for the conduct of the work declared hereafter, which has been discussed in chapter in the presence of my lord the bishop, my lord the lieutenant, the lawyer and procurer

de messrs. du conseil, bourgoys et habitans de ceste ville, et fut deliberé de en commancier de faire ung gros pillier du costé devers le puis.

227 r⁰. . . . pour faire deux cros de costé les pilliers pour savoir se les fondemens des pilliers estoient de croye et ont trouvé que environ 4 piez a mont c'est roche et le remenant en bas c'est grosse croye pour ce 20s.

232 v⁰. A Jaquet, Jehan Chevallier, Jehanin Fajot, maçons, pour avoir ouvert de maçonnerye a faire le fondement dud. pillier au reix des terres par la maniere que dit est sans pilotiz chacun 6 jours a 4s. 2d. pour jour valent 75s. t.

233 v⁰. Pour commancier a faire les deux cros des pilliers d'emprés le gros pillier d'un costé et d'autre.

234 r⁰. A Jaquet le maçon pour 3 jours de luy et son varlet qu'ilz ont ouvert [sic] en la 2e. semaine dudit moys a faire le quarré dudit gros pillier pour chacun jour deulx deux 6s. 8d. valent 20s.

235 v⁰. A Michau, varlet de Jaquet le Vachier, maçon, 4 jours et Denis, son varlet, 3 jours, a assemillier le gros [pillier—deleted] maaillon a 2s. 11d. pour jour valent 20s. 5d.

1452–53 Manuel, Arch. Aube, G 1572.
1 r⁰. Manuel de la despense faite pour le commencement du pillier qu'il sera fait de costé le puis par devers l'antree de l'eglise. . . .

8 r⁰. Pour commancier a faire les deux cros des pilliers d'empres les gros pilliers d'un costé et d'autre.

11 v⁰. Pour 2 mains de papier de grant volume de mauvais papier a coler pour faire les faulx moles pour les pierres de la perriere d'Aigremont. . . . A Jaquet le maçon pour porter lesd. faulx moles a Aigremont pour ses despens, 3s. 4d.

of our lord the king and great number of my lords of the counsel, bourgeois and inhabitants of this city, and it was decided to begin to make a big pillar on the side toward the well. *Note:* the first pier to be built was D 2 in the south arcade. C 2 had been built in 1372.

3. To make 2 holes beside the pillars to know if the foundations were of chalk, and it was found that around 4 feet down it is [hard] rock and that the rest deep down is large [pieces of] chalk, for this, 20s.

4. To Jaquet, Jehan Chevallier, Jehanin Fajot, masons, for having worked in masonry to make the foundations of the said pillar at the level of the earth in the manner that has been said, without [wooden] piles for each of them six days 4s. 2d. per day makes 75s. t.

5. To begin to make two holes for the pillars beside the big pillar on one side and the other. *Note:* probably the aisle piers, B 2 and E 2.

6. To Jaquet the mason for 3 of his days and 3 days of his apprentice working in the second week of the same month to make the square [foundation] of the said great pillar for each day of the two of them, 6s. 8d., makes 20s.

7. To Michau, apprentice of Jaquet le Vachier, mason, for 4 days, and Denis, his apprentice, 3 days to cut the great [pillar—deleted] rubble at 2s. 11d. per day makes 20s. 5d.

1. Manual of the expense made for the beginning of the pillar which will be made beside the well at the entrance into the church [D 2]. . . .

2. To begin to make the two holes of the pillars beside the great pillars on one side and the other [B 2 and E 2].

3. For 2 hands of large format paper of poor quality to stick [together] to make false templates for the stones of the quarry of Aigremont. . . . To Jaquet the mason for carrying the said false templates* to Aigremont for his expenses, 3s. 4d.

*Note: a template was a pattern generally made of wood, and was used to fix the shape of a particular moulding or tracery form. A false template was the same pattern cut out of paper so that it could be carried more easily. At the quarry, such a false template could easily be rendered into a rigid wooden template.

Appendix B. Selected Texts Relating to Construction

12 rº. . . . pour avoir servi les maçons pour achever le crot d'emprés le puis et ouvré ou crot d'emprés le gros pillier du costé du clochier, lequel crot a esté fait 26 piez en parfont, et le samedi ensuivant fut espuisié et maçonné sans pilotis, maiz l'eaue ne fut pas prinse, pour lesd. 20 hommes chascun 5 jours a 2s. 6d. pour jour valent 12 l. 10s.

13 rº. . . . pour lesd. 18 hommes, tous manouvriers, chascun 5 jours pour avoir servi les maçons ou crot d'emprés le pillier qui est devant le gros clochier et pour en commencier a descouvrir au bout devant en la perriere du Pont Humbert pour tirer du maillon pour faire les fondemens des chappelles des deux bous d'un costé et d'aultre a 2s. 6d. pour jour valent 11 l. 5s.

20 vº. . . . pour lesd. 4 hommes manouvriers, qui ont ouvré chascun 5 jours a faire le crot pour faire le fondement du pilier qui fait la chappelle par devers les greniers a 2s. 6d. pour jour valent 50s.

24 rº. A Jehan Michel, hucher, pour 6 jours de lui et de son aprentis le jour d'eulx de 5s. pour faire les mosles des pilliers portant basses soubzbasses et pié droit pour ce 30s.

24 rº. Jaquet le Vachat, maçon, pour 6 jours a estre avec led. Michel tant pour trasser et compasser lesd. mosles, qui sont des trapens de popelin dessusd. comme pour barrer et clorre la barre ou les maçons ouvre[n]t le jour 4s. 2d. valent 25s.

24 vº. En la sepmaine commencent le lundi 20e. jour de novembre que l'en commença a taillier les basses et souzbasses desd. pilliers. A Jaquet le Vachat, maçon, et son varlet, chascun 5 jours le jour d'eulx deux 6s. 8d. valent 33s. 4d.

1452–53 F.A., Arch. Aube, G 4417.

1452–53 Estat du pardon general, Arch. Aube, G 4417.
45 vº. Pour ung voyage fait par Laurent Herault et Jacquet le maçon pour aler veoir a Notre

4. . . . for having helped the masons finish the hole beside the well [D 2] and having worked on the hole beside the big pillar at the side of the [west] bell tower [Pier C 1?], which hole has been dug 26 feet deep and on the following Saturday it was drained and masonry work was done without piles, but the water was not fully drained for the said 20 men, each one 5 days at 2s. 6d. per day makes £12 10s.

5. . . . for the said 18 men, all laborers, each of them for 5 days to help the masons in the hole near the pillar in front of the big [west] tower, and for beginning to uncover [the banks of stone] in the front end of the quarry of Pont Humbert in order to get rubble for making the foundations of the chapels at the two ends on one side and the other [chapels N 4 and S 4] at 2s. 6d. per day makes £11 5s.

6. . . . for the said 4 laborers, each of whom has worked for 5 days to make the hole for the foundations of the pillar which forms the chapel toward the store chamber [chapel S 4] at 2s. 6d. per day makes 50s.

7. To Jehan Michel, joiner, for 6 of his days and 6 of his apprentice at 5s. a day to make the templates for the pillars carrying bases, lower bases, and plinths for this, 30s.

8. Jaquet le Vachat [Vachier], mason, for 6 days he has been with the said Michel, both for tracing and compassing the said templates which are [made of] poplar mentioned above, as well as for closing in the place where the masons work, at 4s. 2d. a day, makes 25s.

9. In the week beginning on Monday November 20 when work began on cutting the bases and lower bases of the said pillars. To Jaquet le Vachat [Vachier], mason, and his apprentice, each for 5 days at 6s. 8d. for their day makes 33s. 4d.

Note: no details on the work.

1. For a trip made by Laurent Herault and Jaquet the mason to go to Notre-Dame de l'Epine to see

BUILDING TROYES CATHEDRAL

Dame de L'Espine ung angin a deux roes en fasson d'un col de grue pour monter les pierres et l'ont pourtrait en pappier pour en faire ung pour led. voyage avec la loyage d'un cheval 35s.

1453–54 F.A., Arch Aube, G. 4417.

1454–55: Manuel, Arch. Aube, G 4417.

1455 Manuel, Arch. Aube, G 4417.
137 r⁰. C'est le manuel fait par moy Jehan Cheuriat, chanoine et maistre de l'euvre de l'eglise de Troyes des ouvrages et matieres de maçonnerie pour commancier a fonder les deux gros pilliers devers le gros clocher d'une part et d'autre part devers la chappelle Droin. . . . A Jaquet le Vachat 5 jours a 4s. 2d. pour jour valent 20s. 10d.

139 r⁰. En la sepmaine commancent le lundi 5e. jour de may pour tailler pierres pour les soubzbasses du gros pillier que l'en fera devant le gros clocher et pour descouvrir en la perriere de l'eglise au Pont Humbert.

161 r⁰. En la sepmaine commancent le lundi 13c. jour d'octobre pour maçonner de pié droit le gros pillier devers la chappelle Drouyn et oster lesd. terres. A Jaquet le Vachier pour 5 jours a 4s. 2d. pour jour valent 20s. 10d.

161 v⁰. En la sepmaine commancent le lundi 20e. jour d'octobre pour achever led. pillier jusques au chappitiau, oster lesd. terres et pour matieres.

166 r⁰. A ung compaignon de Brucelles qui avoit marchandé de taillier ung chapiteau dud. pillier a 6 l. t., lequel n'a fait dud. ouvrage que pour 40s. et s'en est alé, pour ce 40s.

168 r⁰. En la sepmaine commancent le lundi 15e. jour de mars. Pour les despens de Bleuet, maistre maçon de Rains, pour avoir son advis par quelle maniere en poursuivrat pour faire les tours devant l'eglise 27s. 6d. Lequel a bailliee response a messrs. qu'il seroit bon de visiter plusieurs eglises comme Rains, Amiens et Nostre Dame de Paris et se la fait il donroit son advis. Somme par soy 27s. 6d.

---

an engine with 2 wheels in the form of a crane with a neck to hoist stones, and [they] made a portrait of it on paper in order to make one of them, for the said trip with the hiring of a horse, 35s.

Note: no details on the work.

Same.

1. This is the manual [preliminary fabric account] made by me, Jehan Cheuriat, canon and master of the work of the church of Troyes of the works and masonry materials to begin to found 2 big pillars toward the big [west] bell tower, on one side and the other, toward the chapel of Droin [Dreux de la Marche]. . . . [piers C 1 and D 1] To Jaquet le Vachat [Vachier], 5 days at 4s. 2d. per day totals 20s. 10d.

2. In the week beginning on Monday May 5, for cutting stones for the lower bases of the big pillar that is to be made in front of the big [west] bell tower, and for uncovering [stone] in the quarry of the church at Pont Humbert.

3. In the week beginning on Monday October 13 for setting the stones of the plinth of the great pillar toward the chapel of Drouyn [Dreux de la Marche; pillar D 1] and for removing the said earth. To Jaquet le Vachier for 5 days at 4s. 2d. per day totals 20s. 10d.

4. In the week beginning on Monday October 20 for finishing the said pillar up to the capital; [for] taking away earth and for materials.

5. To a journeyman from Brussels who had made a contract to cut a capital for the said pillar at £6 t. who did the said work for only 40s. and left, for this, 40s.

6. In the week beginning on Monday March 15. For the expenses of Bleuet, master mason of Reims, to have his advice as to how to proceed in order to make the towers at the front of the church, 27s. 6d. Who has sent an answer to my lords that it would be good to visit several churches, such as Reims, Amiens, and Notre-Dame of Paris, and he would give his advice based upon this. Total, 27s. 6d.

Appendix B. Selected Texts Relating to Construction

1456 Manuel, Arch. Aube, G 4417.

196 r°. C'est le manuel fait par moy, Jehan Cheuriat, chanoine et maistre de l'euvre de l'eglise de Troyes des ouvrages et matieres de maçonerie qui se feront a fonder la 2e. chapelle neufve devers le pavement royal et ung pilier devant le gros clochier aprés le 5e. pardon general qui fut le 4e. jour d'avril 1456 a Quasimodo. . . . A Jaquet le Vachier, maçon, pour taillier pierres 5 jours, le jour 4s. 2d. valent 20s. 10d.

197 r°. Pour la despense faite pour aler visiter par l'ordonnance de messrs. et mener avec moy messr. Nicole Tetel, maistre Bleuet, maistre masson de l'eglise de Rains, maistre Pierre Trubert et Jaquet pour visiter les tours de Rains, d'Amiens et de Nostre Dame de Paris pour 12 jours oudit voiage tant pour nous et nos chevaux 13 l. 12s. 6d. Aud. me. Pierre Trubert pour son salaire dud. voiage 70s. Aud. me. Bleuet pour son salaire d'avoir fait led. voyage et pour avoir pourtrait les tours et le portail en deux parchemins au retour dud. voyage en ceste ville par l'espace de 11 jours 11 l.

201 r°. A Nicolas Lombart pour ses despens pour aler querir a Nostre Dame de l'Espine Bleuet, maistre maçon de l'eglise de Rains, par l'ordonnance de messrs. pour mettre conclusion ou se commenceroit la tour du costé du pavement, pour ce 15s.

201 r°. . . . lesdiz 3 manouvriés pour avoir ouvert chacun 5 jours a commencier a faire le crot du gros pillier qui portera ung pan de la tour du costé devers le gros clochier. . . .

201 v°. A Bleuet, maistre maçon de Rains, pour son salaire d'estre venu au mandement de messrs. pour mettre conclusion ou se commenceroient les tours que l'en fera 55s.

201 v°. Et nota que la tour qui sera devers le pavement se commensera au premier gros pillier que l'en fera de costé le gros clochier et aura en la nef de l'eglise en chacun costé 5 chapelles avec la voste de la tour et sera lad. nef de 6 haultes vostes.

1. This is the manual [preliminary fabric account] made by me, Jehan Cheuriat, canon and master of the work of the church at Troyes of the works and masonry materials for the foundation of the second new chapel [N 5] toward the royal road, and one pillar [B 1] in front of the big [west] bell tower after the 5th general pardon which took place on April 4, 1456 on *Quasimodo* [the first Sunday after Easter]. . . . To Jaquet le Vachier, mason, for cutting stones for 5 days at 4s. 2d. per day totals 20s. 10d.

2. For the expense made to go and visit the towers of Reims, Amiens, and Notre-Dame of Paris, at the orders of my lords, taking with me my lord Nicole Tetel, Master Bleuet, master mason of the church of Reims, Master Pierre Trubert, and Jaquet for 12 days on the said trip both for us and for our horses, £13 12s. 6d. To the said Master Pierre Trubert for his salary on the said trip, 70s. To the said Master Bleuet for his salary for having made the trip and for having depicted the towers and portal on 2 [sheets of] parchment on his return from the said trip to this city, for the period of 11 days, £11.

3. To Nicolas Lombart for his expense for going to Notre-Dame de l'Epine to seek Bleuet, master mason of the church of Reims, at the orders of my lords, to settle the question as to where to begin the tower toward the road, for this, 15s.

4. . . . [to] the said 3 laborers for each having worked 5 days to begin to make the hole for the big pillar which shall carry a bay of the tower toward the big [west] tower. . . .

5. To Bleuet, master mason of Reims, for his salary for having come at the orders of my lords to settle the question as to where to begin the towers that are to be made, 55s.

6. And it is to be noted that the tower that shall be toward the road shall start at the first great pillar that shall be made at the side of the big [west] bell tower, and there shall be 5 chapels on each side of the nave, and with the vault of the tower there shall be 6 high vaults in the said nave.

206 vº. En la sepmaine commancent le lundi 9e.
jour d'aoust. . . . Pour les despens de Bleuet,
maistre maçon de l'eglise de Rains, lequel amena
ung compaignon ouvrier de taille pour faire les
deux chapiteaux des deux pilliers devers le gros
clochier pour lui et son cheval 3 jours 10s. Aud.
compaignon, nommé Anthoine, par marché fait a
luy present messr. Nicole Tetel et Jaquet le
maçon pour faire lesd. deux chapiteaux 20 l. t. et
20s. pour unes paires de chausses, pour ce 21 l.

209 vº. En la sepmaine commancent le lundi 11e,
jour de octobre pour taillier le chapiteau du gros
pillier de costé la chapelle Drouyn, lequel chapp-
piteau a esté commencie par ung compaignon
passant. A Anthoine Coulas, maçon, pour 6 jours
a 4s. 7d. pour jour valent 27s. 6d.

210 rº. En la sepmaine commancent le lundi
premier jour de novembre, pour taillier comme
dessus. A Anthoine pour 4 jours le jour a 4s. 7d.
valent 18s. 4d. A Bleuet, maistre maçon de l'eglise
de Rains, lequel a vacqué en ceste ville 12 jours
pour pourtraire les mosles pour faire les gros
pilliers qui porteront la tour par devers le gros
clochier et les gros ars doubleaus pour son salaire
68s. 9d. Pour les despens de lui et de son cheval
40s. A Thassin le huchier pour avoir aidié a faire
lesd. mosles 20s. Pour bois et cole.

210 vº. En la sepmaine commancent le lundi 22e.
jour de novembre pour commancier a taillier les
basses et soubzbasses du gros pillier qu'il [sic]
portera la tour du costé du gros clochier. Aud.
Anthoine pour 4 jours a 4s. 2d. pour jour valent
16 8d.

214 rº. En la sepmaine commancent le lundi 4e.
jour d'avril pour dressier le grant angin vers le
gros pillier d'emprés le gros clochier pour asseoir
les chapiteaux. . . .

214 vº. En la sepmaine commancent le lundi 18e.
jour d'avril pour faire les mosles de . . . trapens
pour faire une forme de verriere en chapelle
neufve par devers le pavement.

7. In the week beginning on Monday August 9.
. . . For the expenses of Bleuet, master mason
of the church of Reims, who brought a companion stone carver to make the 2 capitals of the 2
pillars toward the big [west] bell tower, for him
and his horse, 3 days, 10s. To the said companion,
named Anthoine, by contract made with him in
the presence of my lord Nicole Tetel and Jaquet
the mason, for making the said 2 capitals £20 t.
and 20s. for a pair of breeches [or boots], for this,
£21.

8. In the week beginning on Monday October 11
for cutting the capital of the big pillar [D 1] on
the side toward the chapel Drouyn [Dreux de la
Marche] which had been begun by an itinerant
journeyman. To Anthoine Colas, mason, for
6 days at 4s. 7d. per day, totals 27s. 6d.

9. In the week beginning on Monday November
1 for cutting as above. To Anthoine for 4 days
at 4s. 7d. per day totals 18s. 4d. To Bleuet, master
mason of the church of Reims, who has spent 12
days in this city to draw the templates for making
the big pillars that shall carry the tower on the
side toward the big [west] bell tower, and the big
transverse arches, for his salary 68s. 9d. For his
expenses and those of his horse 40s. To Thassin
the joiner for having helped in making the said
templates 20s. For wood and glue.

10. In the week starting on Monday November
22 for beginning to cut the bases and lower bases
of the big pillar that shall carry the tower on
the side of the big [west] bell tower. To the said
Anthoine for 4 days at 4s. 2d. per day totals
16s. 8d.

11. In the week beinning on Monday April 4 for
setting up the great engine toward the big pillar
[C 1] near the big [west] tower for setting the
capitals. . . .

12. In the week beginning on Monday April 18
for making templates of . . . planks to make a
window frame in the new chapel toward the
road.

Appendix B. Selected Texts Relating to Construction

215 r⁰. En la sepmaine commancent le lundi 25e. jour d'avril qui fut le lendemain de Quasimodo 1457 que le pardon general de l'eglise de Troyes ne c'est pas tenu pour la suspencion que a faite nostre saint pere le Pape Kaliste pour l'occasion du Grand Turc et n'a esté ledit pardon que 5 ans. . . .

1457–58 Manuel, Arch. Aube. G 4417.

1458–60: *lacuna.*

1460–61 F.A., Arch. Aube, G 4417.
263 r⁰. Despense pour maconnerye faicte en la sepmaine commancent le lundi 11e. jour d'aoust a taillier pierres pour couvrir le chappitiau du pillier emprés le puis.

264 v⁰. En la sepmaine commancent le lundi 10e. jour dudit mois a taillier les charges du chappitiau du pillier d'emprés celui dessusd. du costé par devers le clochier.

266 v⁰. En la sepmaine commancent le lundi 16e. jour dud. mois a mettre les charges sur led. pillier et sur l'autre pillier d'emprés le puis, a couvrir et taillier.

267 r⁰. En la sepmaine commancent le lundi 23e. jour dud. mois a mettre les charges sur led. pillier, commancier a faire les alours pour faire le cintre de l'arc desdis pilliers.

269 v⁰. A Anthoine Coulas, maçon de l'eglise auquel a esté accordé par messrs. et le maistre de l'euvre precedent . . . chacun an a Noel pour une robbe 4 l. t.

1462–63 F.A., Arch. Aube, G 1564.
28 r⁰. A Anthoine Colas, maçon de l'eglise, et maistre des maçons d'icelle et de l'ouvraige, qui doit avoir chascun jour ouvrier qui besoingera pour lad. eglise 4s. 2d. t. avec chascun an au terme de Noel 4 l. t. pour le drap d'une robe et la maison qui tient emprés la maison de lad. eglise, apellé l'ostel des trois visaiges en la rue en alant a la tour. Pour cinq jours a maçonner les

13. In the week beginning on Monday April 25, which was the day after *Quasimodo* 1457 [Sunday after Easter] when the general pardon of the church of Troyes was no longer in effect because of the suspension made by our Holy Father Pope Calixtus on the occasion of the Great Turk, and the said pardon has only been [in effect] for 5 years. . . .

Note: no indications as to the nature of work.

1. Expense for masonry made in the week beginning on Monday August 11 to cut stones to place over the capital of the pillar [D 2] near the well.

2. In the week beginning on Monday the 10th day of the said month to cut the charges [the stones above the capital] of the capital of the pillar next to the one toward the bell tower [C 2].

3. In the week beginning on Monday the 16th day of the said month to place the charges on the said pillar and on the other pillar near the well, for covering and for cutting.

4. In the week beginning on Monday the 23rd day of the said month, to place the charges on the said pillar and to begin to make the scaffolding for making the center for the arch of the said pillars.

5. To Anthoine Colas, mason of the church, to whom has been granted by my lords and by the previous master of the works . . . each year at Christmas for a robe £4. t.

1. To Anthoine Colas, mason of the church and master of the masons of this [church] and of the work, who should have each working day he works for the said church 4s. 2d. t. with each year £4 t. at Christmas time for the cloth for a robe and the house that he holds near the house of the church called the House of the Three Faces in the road toward the tower. For 5 days to

deux arcs d'emprés le puis du travers de lad. eglise, a tailler des oisives pour faire les vostes à 4s. 2d. per jour pour ce 20s. 1od.

set stones for the 2 arches near the well across the church, to cut ribs for making vaults at 4s. 2d. per day, for this, 20s. 1od. *Note*: this refers to the vaults of the south aisle of the nave at 2–3.

29 v°. A Jehan du Monstier, maçon, pour faire une aire de plastre en la chappelle et emprés faicte neufve devers la rue pour faire une chambre aux traiz pour les maçons a 3s. 9d. pour jour pour ce 7s. 6d.

2. To Jehan du Monstier, mason, for making a plaster [tracing] surface in and around the chapel [N 4] that has been newly made by the road for making a drawing chamber for the masons, at 3s. 9d. per day, for this, 7s. 6d.

30 v°. Aud. Anthoine pour 4 jours a commancer a tailler pour le portail devers le pavé de Saint Nicolas aud. pris de 4s. 2d. pour jour pour ce 16s. 8d.

3. To the said Anthoine for 4 days to begin to cut for the portal toward the road of Saint-Nicolas at the said price of 4s. 2d. per day, for this, 16s. 8d.

31 r°. Aud. Anthoine pour 5 jours en continuant l'ouvraige dud. portail et du pied droit du gros pillier d'emprés le gros cloichier. . . .

4. To the said Anthoine for 5 days continuing the said work on the said portal and on the plinth of the big pillar [B 1] near the big [west] tower. . . .

1463–64 F.A., Arch. Aube, G 1564.
168 r°. Pour 4 jours a continuer a tailler pour le biau portail dessus le pavé a 4s. 2d. pour jour pour ce 16s. 8d.

1. For 4 days to continue to cut for the Beautiful Portal [north transept] above the road, at 4s. 2d. per day, for this, 16s. 8d.

169 v°. Aud. Jaquet [de la Bouticle] pour cinq [jours a] commancier a eschaffauder pour faire une voste emprés le puis et pour commancier lad. voste a 3s. 4d. pour jour pour ce 16s. 8d.

2. To the said Jaquet [de la Bouticle] for 5 days to begin to build scaffolding for making a vault near the well [D E F 2–3] and for beginning the said vault at 3s. 4d. per day, for this, 16s. 8d.

174 r°. A Pierre Guiot pour 42 voitures de terre et sablon pour les deux vostes darrenierement faictes a 1od. t. la voiture, 35s.

3. To Pierre Guiot for 42 carts of earth and sand for the 2 vaults just done, at 1od. t. the cart, 35s.

182 v°. Aud. Anthoine pour deux jours a commancier pour fonder le fondement dud. portail au pris de 4s. 2d. pour jour pour ce 8s. 4d.

4. To the said Anthoine for 2 days to begin to lay the foundations of the said portal at the price of 4s. 2d. per day, for this, 8s. 4d.

1464–68: *lacuna.*

1468–69 F.A., Arch. Aube, G 1565.
26 r°. Despense pour chaulx pour maçonner et fonder un pillier.

1. Expense for lime to set stones and found a pillar.

27 r°. A me. Anthoine Colas, maçon, pour 1 jour a tailler pour le gros pillier du costé destre a 4s. 2d. pour jour pour ce 4s. 2d.

2. To Master Anthoine Colas, mason, for 1 day to cut for the big pillar on the right side [E 1] at 4s. 2d. per day, for this, 4s. 2d.

Appendix B. Selected Texts Relating to Construction

31 rº. Aud. me. Anthoine pour 5 jours a commancer faire les mooles et tailler pour le hault
pillier de la nef au pris dessusd. pour ce 20s. 10d.

32 vº. Aud. me. Anthoine pour 6 jours a commancer escharffauder pour maçonner les charges
du gros pillier devers le pavé. . . .

1469–70 F.A., Arch. Aube, G 1565.
97 vº. Despense pour pierre de croye . . . pour
faire ung arc de croye contre le gros clochier ou
sont les grosses cloches. . . .

98 rº. Despense pour chaulx amenee ceste annee
pour continuer les ouvrages de maçonnerie et
assouyr de fonder le pilier commancey l'an prece-
dant.

101 rº. Aud. maistre Anthoine pour 5 jours a
continuer maçonner oudit gros pillier au pris
dessusd. 10s. 10d.

106 rº. Aud. me. Anthoine pour 4 jours a continuer taillier les arcs des premieres aleez au pris de
4s. 2d. pour jour pour ce 16s. 8d.

107 rº. Aud. me. Anthoine pour 6 jours a taillier
les archetz de la premiere alee d'entre les hault[z]
pilliers de la nef au pris dessusd. pour ce 25s.

111 vº. Aud. me. Anthoine pour 5 jours a continuer et a lever les escharfaulx de la grande nef au
pris dessusd. pour ce 20s. 10d.

126 rº. A Jehan Fremault, charpentier, varlet de
me. Laurent Herault, pour 4 jours a faire des
escharffaulx entre deux portaulx pour maçonner
et haulcier les pilliers neufz a 3s. 4d. pour jour
pour ce 13s. 8d.

131 vº. A Jehanin du Bechot pour 4 jours a
chevronner, later et couvrir ung arc de croye fait
de nouvel contre le gros pillier neuf devant la
loge aux maçons attenant du gros clochier. . . .

3. To the said Master Anthoine for 5 days to
begin to make the templates and to cut for the
high pillar of the nave at the above-mentioned
price, for this, 20s. 10d.

4. To the said Master Anthoine for 6 days to
begin to make scaffolding to lay the stones of the
charges of the big pillar toward the road. . . .

1. Expense for chalk stone . . . for making a chalk
arch against the big [west] tower where the big
bells are [hung]. . . .

2. Expense for lime brought this year to continue
the masonry work and to finish the foundation
of the pillar begun last year.

3. To the said Master Anthoine for 5 days to
continue to lay stone on the said big pillar at the
above-mentioned price, 10s. 10d.

4. To the said Master Anthoine for 4 days to
continue to cut the arches of the first passageways
[triforium] at the price of 4s. 2d. per day, for
this 16s. 8d.

5. To the said Master Anthoine for 6 days to cut
the little arches of the first passageway between
the high pillars of the nave at the above-mentioned price for this, 25s.

6. To the said Master Anthoine for 5 days to
continue to raise up the scaffolding of the great
nave at the above-mentioned price, for this 20s.
10d.

7. To Jehan Fremault, carpenter, apprentice of
Master Laurent Herault, for 4 days to make
scaffolding between 2 portals for laying stones
and heightening the new pillars at 3s. 4d. per
day, for this 13s. 8d. *Note*: this refers to the area
between the portal in the provisional wall at
division 3, and the old west tower: piers C 1, C
2, D 1, and D 2.

8. To Jehanin du Bechot for 4 days to place
rafters and lath and to roof a chalk arch recently
made between the big new pillar in front of
the masons' lodge against the big [west] bell
tower. . . .

138 r⁰. Audit Perrin pour avoir troys autres agrappes pour tenir led. pillier contre les vostes et troys chevilles de fer, pesant tout ensemble 16 l. de fer la livre 7d. pour ce 9s. 4d.

1470–71 F.A., Arch. Aube, G 1565.
176 v⁰. A me. Anthoine Colas, maçon de ceste eglise, a continuer taillier pour l'arc doubliau devant l'uys de la loge aux maçons a 4s. 2d. pour jour pource pour 4 jours 16s. 8d.

179 v⁰. Aud. me. Anthoine pour 6 jours a ma-çonner és arcs devant la loge des maçons au pris dessusd. pource 25s.

184 v⁰. Aud. me. Anthoine pour 6 jours a taillier pour l'arc d'emprés la chappelle Droyn au pris dessud. pource 25s.

185 v⁰. Aud. me. Anthoine pour 6 jours a con-tinuer taillier des oysives pour faire une voste au pris dessusd. pource 25s.

191 r⁰. Despense pour la charpenterie faicte de nouvel devant le gros clochier pour faire une voste nouvelle emprés led. gros clochier.

1471–72 F.A., Arch. Aube, G 1565.
241 r⁰. . . . pour faire ung arc de croye attenant de la chapelle Droyn. . . .

246 v⁰. A maistre Anthoine Colas, maçon de l'eglise, pour deux jours a couvrir les deux arcs doubliaulx et le gros pillier faictz derrenierement de trappens, latez et de cloz a 4s. 2d. pour jour pource 8s. 4d.

246 v⁰. Aud. me. Anthoine pour 3 jours a com-mancier a taillier pour haulcier le pillier hault de la nef prés du puis d'icelle nef au pris dessusd. pour ce 12s. 6d.

251 v⁰. A maistre Anthoine pour 6 jours a com-mancier maçonner sur ung pillier et a taillier le chappitiau dud. pillier au pris dessusd. pour ce 25s.

9. To the said Perrin for having 3 other hooks for holding the said pillar against the vaults and 3 iron pegs weighing all together 16 pounds of iron at 7d. per pound makes 9s. 4d.

1. To Master Anthoine Colas, mason of this church, to continue to cut for the transverse arch in front of the door of the masons' lodge at 4s. 2d. per day for this for 4 days makes 16s. 8d.

2. To the said Master Anthoine for 6 days to lay stones in the arches in front of the masons' lodge at the above-mentioned price, for this, 25s. [west end of north nave aisles].

3. To the said Master Anthoine for 6 days to cut for the arch near the chapel of Droyn [Dreux de la Marche] at the above-mentioned price, [west end of the south nave aisles], for this, 25s.

4. To the said Master Anthoine for 6 days to continue to cut ribs for making a vault at the above-mentioned price, for this, 25s.

5. Expense for new carpentry in front of the big [west] bell tower to make a new vault near the big bell tower.

1. . . . to make a chalk arch against the chapel of Droyn [Dreux]. . . .

2. To Master Anthoine Colas, mason of the church, for 2 days to cover over the 2 transverse arches and the big pillar just made with planks and lath and with nails at 4s. 2d. per day, for this 8s. 4d.

3. To the said Master Anthoine for 3 days to begin to cut [stones] to heighten the high pillar of the nave near the well of the same nave [pier D 2] at the above mentioned price, for this, 12s. 6d.

4. To Master Anthoine for 6 days to begin to lay stones on a pillar and to cut the capital of the said pillar, etc. *Note*: probably one of the high capitals at the west end of the nave.

Appendix B. Selected Texts Relating to Construction

253 vº. Aud. me. Anthoine pour ung jour avec les charpentiers a faire ung cintre pour faire une voste, 4s. 2d.

256 rº. Aud. me. Laurent Herault . . . a faire les eschaffaulx des maçons, monter l'engin dessus et faire la roë neufve, ensemble les bras d'icelle, et pour commancier a taillier et lever ung toit et un appendiz contre la chapelle Droyn pour faire une voste dessoubz led. tour. . . .

1472–73 F.A., Arch. Aube, G 1565.
306 vº. A maistre Anthoine Colas, maçon de l'eglise, a commancer a escharfauder pour mettre le cintre, et pour faire une voste devant l'uys de l'ouvroir desd. maçons et dessoubz le gros clochier pour 4 jours au pris de 4s. 2d. pour jour pource 16s. 8d.

306 vº. Aud. me. Anthoine pour 5 jours a commancier mettre la clef et des oysives de ladicte voste au pris dessusd. pour ce 20s. 10d.

311 vº. Aud. me. Anthoine pour 3 jours a commancier une voote et a taillier en la loge au pris dessusd. pour ce 12s. 6d.

312 rº. A Jehan Girart pour 30 voictures de terre pour maçonner la premiere voote a 10d. la voicture pour ce 25s.

312 rº. Aud. Jaquet pour 6 jours a faire la seconde voote. . . .

312 vº. Aud. Jehan Girart pour 24 voictures de terre pour la seconde voote au pris dessusd. pour ce 20s.

313 vº. Aud. Jaquet pour 2 jours a commancier a monter ung pillier emprés la chapelle Droyn pource 5s. 10d.

1473–74 F.A., Arch. Aube, G 1566.
307 rº. A maistre Anthoine Colas, maçon de l'eglise, pour deux jours a taillier pour les aleez d'ung pillier d'emprés la chappelle Droyn au pris de 4s. 2d. pour jour pource 8s. 4d.

5. To the said Master Anthoine for 1 day with the carpenters to make a center for making a vault, 4s. 2d.

6. To the said Master Laurent Herault . . . to make scaffolding for the masons, to mount an engine on [the scaffolding] and to make a new wheel together with the arms of [the wheel] and to begin to cut and raise a roof and a lean-to against the chapel of Droyn [Dreux] to make a vault under the said tower. . . .

1. To Master Anthoine Colas, mason of the church, to begin to make scaffolding for placing the center and for making a vault in front of the door of the workshop of the said masons and below the big [west] tower, 4 days at 4s. 2d. per day makes 16s. 8d.

2. To the said Master Anthoine for 5 days to begin to place the key and the ribs of the said vault at the above-mentioned price, for this, 20s. 10d.

3. To the said Master Anthoine for 3 days to begin a vault and to cut in the lodge at the above-mentioned price, for this, 12s. 6d.

4. To Jehan Girart for 30 carts of earth for laying the stones of the first vault at 10d. per cart, for this, 25s.

5. To the said Jaquet for 6 days to make the 2nd vault. . . .

6. To Jehan Girart for 24 carts of earth for the 2nd vault at the above mentioned price, for this, 20s.

7. To the said Jaquet for 2 days to begin to raise up a pillar near the chapel of Droyn [Dreux], for this, 5s. 10d. [pier D 1].

1. To Master Anthoine Colas, mason of the church, for 2 days to cut [stone] for the passageways of a pillar near the chapel of Dreux [triforium level of D 1] at the price of 4s. 2d. per day, for this, 8s. 4d.

310 rº. Audit me. Anthoine pour 5 jours a continuer et tailler le chappitiau d'ung pillier au pris dessusd. pour ce 20s. 10d.

314 rº. Aud. Jehan le Fevre pour 5 jours a maçonner et haulcier le pillier d'emprés la chapelle Droyn au pris dessusd. de 2s. 11d. pour jour pource 14s. 7d.

314 vº. Aud. me. Anthoine pour 5 jours a haulcier et maçonner le pillier de devant le gros clochier au pris dessusd. de 4s. 2d. pour jour pource 20s. 10d.

1474–75 Manuel, Arch. Aube, G 1572.
132 rº. A Jaquet de la Bouticle pour 6 jours a commancier haucier et maçonner ou hault pilyer de la nef d'emprés le gros clochier et emploier plusieurs pierres tailleez au pris dessusd. pour ce 17s. 6d.

1475–76 F.A., Arch. Aube, G 1567.
30 vº. Aud. Colin . . . pour ung jour a mettre et cheviller des trappens sur le gros pillier emprés le gros clochier a 2s. 6d. pour jour 10s.

1476–77 F.A., Arch. Aube, G 1567.
80 rº. A notre saint pere le pape Sixte et a la Chambre apostolique, ausquelx estoit deu des indulgences de l'eglise pour les trois darrenieres annees, c'estassavoir pour les annees 1469, 1470 et 1471, la somme de trois cens quatre vins neuf livres 3 solz 11d., et le ters d'ung denier, comme par les instrumens appiert, laquelle somme a falu paier a monsr. Bertholomi, evesque de Nice, comme par le mandat de nostred. saint pere Sixte appert, et laquelle a esté paie[e] entierement, comme par les quictances appert; et pource que led. argent a esté longs temps en depost ou Tresor hault de l'eglise pour ce que nus ne le venoit querir ne demander en a esté pris et desrobé oudit Tresor par messire Laurent de la Hupperoye, vicaire de lad. eglise, par la coulpe et faulte de messire Nicole Mergey, marreglier, presbytre de lad. eglise, qui a mal gardeez les clefz dud. Tresor, la somme de 230 livres 6s. t. . . .

86 rº. A Pierre Hardouyn, maçon de Roucelot, pour 4 jours a massonner et haulcier l'arcboutant de croye qui est contre la chappelle Drouyn a 2s. 11d. pour jour 11s. 8d.

2. To the said Master Anthoine for 5 days to continue and to cut the capital of a pillar at the above-mentioned price, for this, 20s. 10d.

3. To the said Jehan le Fevre for 5 days to lay stones and to heighten the pillar near the chapel of Dreux [D 1] at the above-mentioned price of 2s. 11d. per day, for this, 14s. 7d.

4. To the said Master Anthoine for 5 days to heighten and to lay stones of the pillar in front of the big [west] bell tower [C 1] at the above-mentioned price of 4s. 2d. per day, for this, 20s. 10d.

1. To Jaquet de la Bouticle for 6 days to begin to heighten and to lay stones on the high pillar of the nave near the big [west] bell tower, and to use several cut stones [pillar C 1] at the above-mentioned price, for this, 17s. 6d.

1. To the said Colin . . . for a day to place and to peg some planks on the big pillar near the big [west] tower at 2s. 6d. per day, 10s.

1. To our Holy Father the Pope Sixtus and to the Apostolic Chamber to whom was due from the indulgences of the church for the last 3 years, that is for the years 1469, 1470 and 1471 the sum of £389 3s. 11⅓d. as appears in the instruments, which [sum of money] should have been paid to Bertholomi, Bishop of Nice, by mandate of our father Sixtus, and which [money] has been entirely paid, as appears in the quittances. And because the money has been deposited for a long time in the upper treasury of the church since no one came to search or to ask for it, it has been taken and stolen by my lord Laurent de la Hupperoye, vicar of the said church, through the fault of my lord Nicole Mergey, warden and priest of the said church, who did not guard the keys of the said treasury properly, the sum of £230 6s. t. . . .

2. To Pierre Hardouyn, mason from Roucelot, for 4 days to lay stones and heighten the chalk flying buttress which is against the chapel of Dreux at 2s. 11d. per day, 11s. 8d.

Appendix B. Selected Texts Relating to Construction

86 vº. A Jehan Carbonnier, charpentier, pour 5 jours a commancier mettre une poultre garnie de lyens a branche en la nef emprés la chappelle Droym de la Marche et pour avaler aucunes poultres et l'angin qui pourrissoient oud. lieu, dont avoient esté escharfaudé les maçons a lever et haulcier les 4 pilliers d'entre les deux portaulx d'emprés led. chapelle Droyn a 2s. 11d. pour jour pour ce 14s. 7d.

1477-78 F.A., Arch. Aube, G 1567.

1478-79 F.A., Arch. Aube, G 1567.

1479-80 F.A., Arch. Aube, G 1567.

1480-81 F.A., Arch. Aube, G 1567.

1481-82: *lacuna.*

1482-83 F.A., Arch. Aube, G 1568.
46 rº. A maistre Anthoine Colas, maçon, . . . pour avoir refait et reparé la formette neufve d'une verrine de l'une des chapelles neufves pour ce a luy paié pour chacune journee 4s. 2d. t. valent 8s. 4d. t.

49 rº. . . . a recouvrir les renvers des basses allees d'aissy et pour avoir mis des chanlattes entre les pilliers neufz. . . .

59 vº. Aud. Valeton, Symon Felix et Pierre Vatat pour avoir esté chascun par deux jours en lad. sepmaine a plomer dessoubz les verrines du costé de droit vent pour ce que, quant y pleuvoit, le vent boutoit l'eaue dedans l'eglise. . . .

75 rº. Despense de charpanterie pour faire le comble de la ramee neufve de la nef de lad. eglise faicte entre la nef de lad. eglise et la chapelle Drouyn.

81 rº. Despense pour torcher et blanchir lad. nef. . . . de torcher, rancontrer et blanchir tant du costé des appandis devers la chapelle Droyn que des appandis devers la rue du costé du gros cloché affin que le vent n'entre par dessoubz les tois de lad. nef. . . .

3. To Jehan Carbonnier, carpenter, for 5 days to begin to place a beam with branched ties in the nave near the chapel of Dreux de la Marche and for lowering down several beams and the engine which were rotting in the said place, where scaffolding had been erected by the masons to raise up and heighten the 4 pillars between 2 portals near to the said chapel of Dreux [pillars C 1, C 2, D 1 and D 2] at 2s. 11d. per day, for this, 14s. 7d.

Note: no significant work.

Same.

Note: construction of a new library.

Same.

1. To Master Anthoine Colas, mason . . . for having re-made and repaired the new frame of a window in one of the new chapels [N 4 or S 4]. for this, paid to him for each day 4s. 2d. t. makes 8s. 4d. t.

2. To re-cover the reverse side of the lower passageways [triforium] with shingles and for having placed eaves boards between the new pillars. . . .

3. To the said Valeton, Simon Felix, and Pierre Vatat for each having been 2 days in the said week to undertake lead work below the windows on the windward side because when it rains the wind blows water into the church. . . .

4. Expense for carpentry work to make the top of the new roof of the nave of the church made between the nave of the said church and the chapel of Dreux.

5. Expense for daubing with cob [mud] and for whitewashing the said nave. . . . to daub with cob, smooth and whitewash both on the side toward the lean-to toward the chapel of Dreux and the lean-to toward the road by the big [west] bell tower to stop the wind from entering below the roof of the said nave. . . .

81 v°. Pour douze planches pour mettre entre les pilliers et les posteaux de la nef en hault pour tenir les pallesons. . . .

87 v°. Despense pour les verrines de lad. nef. A Girard le Noquat, verrier, pour avoir fait toutes les verrines des deux costés du hault de lad. nef neufve, esquelz y a 490 piedz de verre a luy baillé comme a esté marchandé par messrs. aud. verrier de chacun pied 2s. 6d. t. qui valent en somme 61 l. 10s. t.

1483–84 F.A., Arch. Aube, G 1568.
125 v°. Audit Jaquet de la Bouticle pour avoir esté par 5 jours en lad. sepmaine a escaire et tailler les grosses pierres de Tonnerre pour les embassemens des gros pilliers de la nef neuve, lesquelz estoient tous gallés et pourris de la pluye et des terres d'autour a 3s. 4d. t. pour jour valent 16s. 8d. t.

126 r°. A Jaquet le Vachier, maçon, pour avoir esté par cinq jours en lad. sepmaine a tailler les mosles et patrons desd. pilliers et a tailler lesd. embassemens pour ce paié pour chacun jour 3s. 4d. t. valent 16s. 8d. t.

128 r°. Audit Jaquet le Vachier, maçon, pour avoir esté par quatre jours et demi en lad. sepmaine a commancer de tailler les pierres des deux pilliers de la ramee neufve, qui ne sont pas si haut que les autres pour ce paié pour chacun jour 4s. 2d. t. valent 18s. 9d.

131 r°. Despense de charpanterie pour faire l'eschafault pour montter le pillier devers l'ostel monsr. l'evesque, ou estoit la paroir que on a rompue en la nef neufve.

131 v°. Pour avoir estaier [estaié] pour soutenir la vielle ramee a l'endroit du pillier que on hausse. A Jehan Carbonnier, charpentier, . . . a mettre deux grans estais faisant arboutant, l'une de 31 pied de long, et l'autre de 29, pour soutenir lad. ramee, pour ce que faloit desimer et abattre les posteaulx et paroir qui soutiennent lad. ramee pour faire l'eschafaut des maçons pour lever led. pillier. . . .

6. For 12 planks for placing between the pillars and the posts of the upper nave [the posts of the lateral screens] to hold the screens. . . .

7. Expense for the windows of the said nave. To Girard le Noquat, glazier, for having made all the windows on both sides of the new upper nave, in which there are 490 feet of glass, paid to him according to the contract made with the said glazier by my lords, 2s. 6d. for each foot, which makes in total £6 10s. t.

1. To the said Jaquet de la Bouticle for having been 5 days in the said week to square and cut the big stones from Tonnerre for the plinths of the big pillars of the new nave, which were all spoiled and rotten from the rain and from the earth [heaped up] around, at 3s. 4d. t. per day makes 16s. 8d. t.

2. To Jaquet le Vachier, mason, for having been 5 days in the said week to cut the templates and patterns and to cut the said plinths for this paid 3s. 4d. t. each day makes 16s. 8d. t.

3. To the said Jaquet le Vachier, mason, for having been 4½ days in the said week to begin to cut the stones of the 2 pillars of the new roof which are not as high as the others [piers C 3 and D 3, which had supported the end of the old provisional roof] for this paid 4s. 2d. t. for each day, makes 18s. 9d.

4. Expense for carpentry work to make the scaffolding to heighten the pillar toward the bishop's palace [D 3] by the screen that has been demolished in the new nave.

5. For having put props to support the old roof of the nave at the place where the pillar is being heightened. To Jehan Carbonnier, carpenter, . . . to put 2 great props forming a flying buttress, one 31 feet long and the other 29 feet, to support the said roof because it was necessary to pull down and demolish the posts and screen that supported the said roof in order to make the scaffolding for the masons to heighten the said pillar. . . .

Appendix B. Selected Texts Relating to Construction

138 vº. Aud. Valeton pour avoir esté par cinq jours en lad. sepmaine a mettre deux chanlattes sur ung gros pillier neuf devers la rue, ou est le fondement de la tour. . . .

141 vº. Aud. Valeton pour avoir esté par cinq jours en lad. sepmaine a continuer de couvrir esd. appendis et avoir mis une chanlatte sur la chapelle neufve de saint Loÿs et avoir mis une grosse chanlatte a deux eaues entre le gros cloché et les deux gros pilliers neufz que sont commencés pour faire la tour. . . .

1484–85 F.A., Arch. Aube, G 1568.
180 vº. Despense de maçonnerie pour achever le pillier de la ramee commencé par mon predecesseur.

186 rº. A Pierre Robin pour 5 journees de lui tant a [le] servir led. torcheur comme pour avoir abatu une cloison de trapens qui fermoit la neufve chappelle devers le pavement. . . .

190 rº. Despense pour refaire l'ung des pilliers du jubé qui porte l'image de monsr. saint Savinian, et premiers pour matieres a faire les estaymens.

190 rº. Aultres despense pour les journees des ouvriers qui ont fait led. pillier en la premiere sepmaine de juillet, 1485. A Jehan Garnace, maistre maçon de l'eglise, pour six journees de lui a commencer de faire lesd. trois murailles a l'environ dud. pillier pour soustenir le jubé a 3s. 9d. le jour valent 22s. 6d.

200 rº. A Girard le Noquat, verrier, auquel a esté marchandé par messrs. de faire les verrieres de l'eglise, et doit avoir de chascun pied de verre ouvré 5s 1od. et pour avoir fait toute la verriere qui est en la formette estant en la chappelle de nouvel faicte du costé du pavement 61 l. 16s. 8d.

202 rº. A Jaquet de la Bouticle, maçon, pour ses despens et salaire d'avoir esté a Rains querir me. Denis Aubert, maçon, pour viseter le pillier du jubé payé 2os.

6. To the said Valeton for having spent 5 days in the said week to put 2 eaves boards on a big new pillar [A 1] toward the road where the foundation of the tower is. . . .

7. To the said Valeton for having been 5 days in the said week to continue to roof the said lean-to and for having put an eaves board over the new chapel of Saint Louis and for having put a big eaves board [gutter] with two channels between the big [west] bell tower and the 2 new big pillars which have been begun to make the tower [piers A 1 and B 1]. . . .

1. Expense for masonry to finish the pillar of the roof [D 3] begun by my predecessor.

2. To Pierre Robin for 5 of his days both to help the said plasterer and to have demolished a screen made of planks which closed in the new chapel [N 4] toward the road. . . .

3. Expense for re-making one of the pillars of the choir screen which carries the statue of my lord Saint Savinien, and first for materials to make the props.

4. Other expense for the days of the workers who have made the said pillar in the first week of July 1485. To Jehan Garnace [sic], master mason of the church for 6 of his days to begin to make the said three little walls around the said pillar in order to support the choir screen at 3s. 9d. the day makes 22s. 6d.

5. To Girard le Noquat, glazier, with whom a contract has been made by my lords to make the windows of the church and he should have for each foot of glass used 5s. 1od. and for having made all the glass in the window in the new chapel [N 4] toward the road £61 16s. 8d.

6. To Jaquet de la Bouticle, mason, for his expenses and salary for having gone to Reims to seek Denis Aubert, mason, to visit the pillar of the choir screen, paid 2os.

1485–86 F.A., Arch. Aube, G 1568.

229 v°. Despense pour maçonnerie pour la nefz de l'eglise. Et premiers pour commencer de achever le pillier de lad. nef du costé de la rue, lequel pillier n'estoit que jusques aux basses voltes des chappelles et portoit la grant cloison qui fermoit l'eglise au droit de l'aultre pillier, qui est de l'aultre costé devers l'ostel episcopal, qu'on a darrenierement haulcé et levé.

229 v°. En la sepmaine commencent le lundi jour de saint Jehan Decolace fut retenu Jehançon Garnache pour me. maçon de l'eglise.

229 v°. Aud. Jehançon pour 5 jours de lui a commencer de tailler pour led. pillier et faire les traitz pour lever le mosle a faire les ars des verrieres a 3s. 9d. valent 18s. 9d.

230 r°-v°. Aud. Jehançon Garnache . . . pour faire cuire du plastre pour faire une aire sur la volte de la chappelle Droin pour faire les traiz de toute la massonnerie qu'il fauldra pour les pilliers de lad. nef a 3s. 9d. le jour valent 18s. 9d.

233 r°. Aud. Jehançon pour six jours a continuer de tailler et lever led. pillier et pour commencer de descombrer et faire les eschaffaux autour de l'aultre pillier attenant d'icelluy a 4s. 2d. le jour valent 25s.

234 v°. Aud. Jehançon pour 5 jornees a continuer de tailler led. 3e. pillier a 4s. 2d. le jour valent 20s. 10d.

241 r°. Ausd. Emery et Nicolas pour 11 jornees d'eulx deux a faire led. angin et pour avoir descombré les parois qui estoient autour du pillier qu'on a levé en lad. nef et pour avoir mis ung grant posteau avec une semelle et ung lian a l'encontre dud. pillier, lequel posteau porte la ramee d'ung des costés dud. pillier a 3s. 4d. valent 36s. 8d.

1486–87 F.A., Arch. Aube, G 1568.

281 v°. Despense pour la maçonnerie faicte a l'eglise. Et premiers pour achever le 3e. pillier de la nef du costel de la rue, qui estoit commencé de l'annee precedante.

1. Expense for masonry for the nave of the church. And first for beginning to complete the pillar of the said nave toward the road [C 3], which pillar was only completed up to the low vaults of the chapels [i.e., aisles] and carried the great screen that closed the church opposite the other pillar which is on the other side toward the bishop's palace, which [pillar] has been recently heightened and raised.

2. In the week beginning on Monday the day of Saint John's beheading, Jehançon Garnache was retained as master mason of the church.

3. To the said Jehançon for 5 of his days to begin to cut [stone] for the said pillar and for making the drawings for raising the form work to make the arches of the [clerestory] windows at 3s. 9d. makes 18s. 9d.

4. To the said Jehançon Garnache . . . to have plaster heated to make a [drawing] surface on the vault of the chapel of Dreux to make the drawings of all of the masonry necessary for the pillars of the said nave at 3s. 9d. the day makes 18s. 9d.

5. To the said Jehançon for 6 days to continue to cut and to heighten the said pillar [C 3] and to begin to disengage and make scaffolding around the pillar next to it [C 4] at 4s. 2d. the day makes 25s.

6. To the said Jehançon for 5 days to continue to cut for the said 3rd pillar [C 5] at 4s. 2d. the day makes 20s. 10d.

7. To the said Emery and Nicolas for 11 days of the two of them to make the said engine and for having taken down the screens which were around the pillar[C 3] which has been heightened in the said nave and for having put a great post with a footing and a tie against the pillar, which post carries the roof alongside the said pillar at 3s. 4d. makes 36s. 8d.

1. Expense for the masonry work done at the church. And first to finish the 3rd pillar of the nave toward the road, which had been begun the year before.

282 r⁰. A Claude Bourgois, mannouvrier, pour deux jornees de lui a esbatre une partie d'ung grant arboutant de croye qui est contre le gros pillier qui soustient le clocher du costel du pavement affin de prendre les mesures pour tailler une partie dud. pillier, qui n'est pas achevé a 2s. 1d. valent 4s. 2d.

283 r⁰. Aud. Jehançon pour cinq jornees a continuer de taillier et de lever pour led. pillier et pour avoir fait le mosle d'une partie du gros pillier qui soustient le clocher, qui n'est pas ancor achevez devers la rue a 4s. 2d. valent 20s. 10d.

284 r⁰. Aud. Jehançon pour 3 jornees a achever de lever led. pillier et commencé de tailler de l'autre costel pour ce 11s. 3d.

284 v⁰. Aud. Jehançon pour six jornees de lui a continuer de taillier pour led. pillier du costel episcopal a 3s. 9d. valent 22s. 6d.

285 v⁰. Aud. Jehançon pour six journees de lui a commencer de taillier pour les deux pilliers actenans dud. premier pillier a 3s. 9d. valent 22s. 6d.

287 r⁰. Aud. Jehançon pour 4 jornees de lui a continuer de tallier et lever lesd. pilliers et pour commencer de taillier les deux aultres pilliers dud. costel episcopal a 4s. 2d.

288 v⁰. Audit Jehançon Garnache pour cinq jornees de lui a continuer de lever et taillier lesd. deux darreniers pilliers a 4s. 2s. valent 20s. 10d.

290 v⁰. . . . a coper deux chevrons de lad. ramee et avoir mis des estaiz au bout desd. chevrons pour les soustenir. . . .

291 r⁰. . . . et ainssin copper par dessoubz les sablieres au droit du pillier de lad. grant volte du costel de la rue affin que les maçons puissent prendre les mesures pour achever ledit pillier, qui n'est pas de la haulteur des aultres.

2. To Claude Bourgois, laborer, for 2 of his days to demolish part of a great chalk flying buttress which is against the big pillar supporting the bell tower [of the crossing] on the side toward the road in order to take measurements to cut a part of the said pillar that is not yet finished at 2s. 1d. makes 4s. 2d. *Note*: this is the chalk flyer built against the crossing at the time of the 1389 collapse.

3. To the said Jehançon for 5 days to continue to cut and to raise [stones] for the said pillar and for having made the template for a part of the big unfinished pillar [C 6] supporting the bell tower [of the crossing] on the side of the road at 4s. 2d. makes 20s. 10d.

4. To the said Jehançon for 3 days to finish raising the said pillar [C 6] and having begun to cut for the other [south] side, for this, 11s. 3d.

5. To the said Jehançon for 6 of his days to continue to cut for the said pillar on the bishop's [south] side at 3s. 9d. makes 22s. 6d.

6. To the said Jehançon for 6 of his days to begin to cut for the 2 pillars next to the said first pillar at 3s. 9d. makes 22s. 6d.

7. To the said Jehançon for 4 of his days to continue to cut for and heighten the said pillars and to begin to cut for the 2 other pillars on the bishop's [south] side at 4s. 2d.

8. To the said Jehançon Garnache for 5 of his days to continue to raise and cut the said 2 last pillars at 4s. 2d. makes 20s. 10d.

9. . . . to cut 2 rafters of the said roof and for having placed props under the rafters to support them. . . .

10. . . . and also to cut underneath the wall plates in front of the pillar [C 6] of the said great vault on the side toward the road so that the masons could take the measurements necessary to complete the said pillar, which is not as high as the others.

1487-88 F.A., Arch. Aube, G 1568.

341 r°. A Jehançon Garnache, me. maçon de l'eglise, pour cinq journees de luy a avoir maçonne et achevé de lever le gros pillier de la ramee du costé de l'ostel episcopal jusques aux ars boutans; et pour avoir commancé de taillier les vossois des ars, esquelx se mettent les formettez des verrieres a 4s. 2d. le jour valent 20s. 10d.

341 v°. A Jehan Babelin de Bellé pour trois cens trois quarterons et demi de quarreaux deschargez en l'eglise pour faire l'arboutant qui se prant sur la chapelle Droyn tout du long du gros pillier afin que l'arc ne se puisse ouvrir payé au pris de 16s. 8d. le cent valent 64s. 7d.

341 v°. Aud. Jehançon Garnache pour 4 jornees de luy a continuer de taillier lesd. voissures, et ausy commancé de maçonner et lever led. arboutant, qui est de croye, contre led. gros pillier a 4s. 2d. le jour valent 16s. 8d.

343 r°. Aud. Jehançon pour cinq journeez a continuer de taillier lesd. quarreaux et les pilliers d'entre les voissures, et pour avoir achevé le premier arc desd. verrieres sur le bout du cloistre a 4s. 2d. valent 20s. 10d.

345 v°. . . . a achever de maçonner et lever led. second arc jusques aux entablemens. . . .

346 r°. Aud. Jehançon pour six journees de luy a taillier une gargole et commancer de taillier les armes de mons. l'ancian pour les mettre en ladite muraille et ancor continuer de taillier des vossures a 3s. 9d. valent 22s. 6d.

348 v°. . . . a avoir fait deux cintres tous neufz pour soustenir les deux arcs du millieu dud. costé episcopal. . . .

348 v°. A Jehan Carbonnier . . . pour avoir coppé 4 chevrons de lad. ramee et mis des estayez faisans colummes dessoubz lesd. chevrons. . . .

1. To Jehançon Garnache, master mason of the church, for 5 of his days to have set stones and finished raising the great pillar of the roof on the side of the bishop's palace up to the flying buttresses, and for having begun to cut the voussoirs of the arches where the frames of the [clerestory] windows will be placed at 4s. 2d. the day makes 20s. 10d.

2. To Jehan Babelin de Bellé for 303½ *quarterons* of *quarreaux* [stones] unloaded in the church for making the flying buttress which rests on the chapel of Dreux all the length of the big pillar so that the arch cannot open, paid at the price of 16s. 8d. for the hundred makes 64s. 7d.

3. To the said Jehançon Garnache for 4 of his days to continue to cut the said voussoirs and also for beginning to lay stone and raise the said flying buttress which is [made] of chalk against the said big pillar [D 1] at 4s. 2d. the day makes 16s. 8d.

4. To the said Jehançon for 5 days to continue to cut the said *quarreaux* [stones] and the pillars between the voussoirs and for having finished the first arch of the said [clerestory] windows at the cloister end [east end of the south side] at 4s. 2d. makes 20s. 10d.

5. . . . to finish laying stones and raising the said second arch up to the entablature. . . .

6. To the said Jehançon for 6 of his days to cut a gargoyle and begin to cut the arms of my lord the former [bishop, Louis Raguier] in order to set them in the said wall and to go on cutting the voussoirs at 3s. 9d. makes 22s. 6d.

7. . . . for having made 2 completely new centers to support the 2 middle arches on the bishop's side. . . .

8. To Jehan Carbonnier . . . for having cut 4 rafters of the said roof and placed stays in the form of columns below the said rafters. . . .

Appendix B. Selected Texts Relating to Construction

350 v⁰. . . . et pour avoir mis ung grant posteau debout qui porte le tref qui est contre la volte dud. clocher a cause qu'il a falu coper led. tref, qui portoit sur le gros pillier, affin de le povoir lever. . . .

350 v⁰. Aud. Jehançon pour six jornees a continuer de taillier et lever le darrenier pillier et arc dud. costé episcopal, et pour commancer de faire ung arc boutant de croye en l'aultre costé, et est fondé sur les fondemens du gros clocher affin de commancer de faire les ars a 4s. 2d. valent 25s.

353 r⁰. A Jehan Carbonnier . . . pour avoir mis des contrefixes entre les pilliers dud. costé de la rue affin que ne se puissent ouvrir. . . .

1488–89 F.A., Arch. Aube, G 1569.
31 r⁰. A Jehançon Garnache, maistre maçon, pour quatre journees de luy a continuer de tailler et lever les deux premiers ars prés du gros clocher du costé de la rue en lad. ramee a 4s. 2d. le jour valent 16s. 8d.

31 v⁰. Audit Jehançon pour 6 journees de luy a continuer de tailler pour commancer les aultres trois arcz dud. costé de la rue. . . .

36 v⁰. Audit Jehançon pour six journees de luy a commancer de tailler les clerevaux qui se assierront sur lad. muraille a 3s. 9d., 22s. 6d.

56 r⁰. S'ensuit les receptes et mises faictes par moy, Nicole Coiffart, chanoine, doyen et me. de la fabrique de l'eglise de Troyes, pour faire la ramee de la nef de lad. eglise, commancee au mois de mars avant Pasques 1488.

63 r⁰. A Jehan Carbonnier, charpentier, auquel a esté marchandé de faire lad. ramee de son mestier de charpenterie et livrer tout ce qu'il faudra pour ce faire selon la divise sur ce faicte et cy la doit enverner [?] avec la vielle qui soustient le grant

9. . . . and for having placed a great vertical post to carry the beam which is against the vaults of the said [crossing] tower because it was necessary to cut the said beam which was being carried by the big pillar in order that [the pillar] could be raised. . . .

10. To the said Jehançon for 6 days to continue to cut and raise the last pillar and arch on the said bishop's [south] side and for beginning to make a flying buttress of chalk on the other [north] side, and it is founded on the base of the big [west] bell tower in order to begin to make the arches, etc. *Note*: this is a provisional flyer springing from the old west tower and leaning against the pier at C 1 to prevent it from being pushed outward by the arch of the clerestory window.

11. To Jehan Carbonnier . . . for having placed retaining ties between the pillars on the said side of the road to prevent them from opening. . . .

1. To Jehançon Garnache, master mason, for 4 of his days to continue to cut and raise the 2 first [clerestory] arches near the big [west] bell tower on the side of the road [north] in the said roof at 4s. 2d. the day makes 16s. 8d.

2. To the said Jehançon for 6 of his days to continue to cut in order to begin the other 3 [clerestory] arches on the said side of the road. . . .

3. To the said Jehançon for 6 of his days to begin to cut the balustrades which will be set on the said [clerestory] wall at 3s. 9d., 22s. 6d.

4. There follow the receipts and expenses made by me, Nicole Coiffart, canon, dean, and master of the fabric of the church at Troyes, to make the roof of the nave of the said church, begun in the month of March before Easter 1488.

5. To Jehan Carbonnier, carpenter, with whom a contract has been made to make the said roof according to his profession of carpentry and to deliver everything necessary for this according to the plan made on this, and [the roof] should

clocher et ancor faire deux fenestres flameiches
ou il luy sera divisé; et esbatre la vielle ramee qui
fault oster au profit de l'eglise et quant il en sera
requis, comme tout est contenu ou marché surce
fait, present monsr. de Troyes et plusieurs aultres,
et pour tout, quant il aura fait, doit avoir la
somme de neuf cens cinquante livres tournois,
dont on luy a rabatu 12 l. jusques ad ce qu'il ait
abatu les trefz et paroix de la vielle ramee, qu'on
ne peut abatre jusques ad ce qu'on ait volté,
pour ce cy payé 938 l. t.

adjoin [?] with the old [roof] which supports the
great [crossing] tower and further, he should
made 2 dormer windows where it is indicated
and knock down the old roof which should be
removed for the profit of the church when
required, as is laid out in the contract made concerning this in the presence of my lord [the
bishop] of Troyes and several others, and for this,
when it is done, he should have the sum of
£950 *tournois* of which £12 has been kept back
until he has demolished the beams and screens of
the old roof, which cannot be demolished until
the vaults have been built, for this paid £938 t.

64 vº. Aud. Jehan le Valeton, couvreur, pour
avoir houldré le cintre qui est dessoubz l'ardoub-
leau du pignon de lad. nef qui fait cloture de
lad. nef et demoura jusques ad ce qu'on face les
tours et les porteaux et est houldré d'aissy et
de latez a ardoise.

6. To the said Jehan le Valeton, roofer, for
having covered over the center which is under
the transverse arch of the gable of the said nave
which closes in the nave, and which shall remain
until the towers and portals shall be done and
[the center] is covered with shingles, and lath for
slates.

65 vº. A Jehançon Garnache, me. maçon, pour sa
despense faicte ou voyage fait par luy a Paris et
a Reins es feries de Pasques par l'ordonnance
de monsr. de Troyes a visiter les pignons des
eglises, affin de soy regler a faire le pignon de
lad. ramee et autres ouvrages qui sont a faire en
l'eglise, payé 70s.

7. To Jehançon Garnache, master mason, for his
expense made at the feast of Easter, on a trip
undertaken on the orders of my lord [the bishop]
of Troyes to Paris and to Reims to visit gables
of churches in order to instruct himself how to
make the gable of the said roof and other jobs to
be done in the church, paid 70s.

1489–90 F.A., Arch. Aube, G 1569.
110 rº. A Jehançon Garnache, maistre maçon de
l'eglise, pour 4 journees de luy a continuer de
tailler les clerevaux et les pilliers pour asseoir sur
la muraille de la ramee . . . a 4s. 2d. le jour valent
16s. 8d.

1. To Jehançon Garnache, master mason of the
church for 4 of his days to continue to cut the
balustrades and the pillars for setting on the wall
of the roof [i.e., the clerestory wall] . . . at 4s.
2d. the day makes 16s. 8d.

111 vº. Aud. Jehançon pour trois jours et demi de
luy a continuer de tailler lesd. pilliers et clere-
vaulx et commancer de tailler les formettez des
basses verrieres de la nef dedans et dehors aud.
pris valent 14s. 7d.

2. To the said Jehançon for 3½ of his days to
continue to cut the said pillars and balustrades
and begin to cut the frames of the low windows
[triforium] of the nave, inside and outside, at
the said price makes 14s. 7d.

112 vº. Pour ung C. de plastre pour faire l'aire de
lad. chambrette de l'eglise pour faire les traictz
desd. formettez et du pignon de garnison, neant.

3. For 100 [sic] of plaster to make the [drawing]
surface in the small chamber of the church for
making the drawings of the said windows and of
the gable, from the stores, nothing.

Appendix B. Selected Texts Relating to Construction

114 rº. A Nicolas Ludot pour avoir colé du papier de grant volume et y en a dix grans pieces pour faire les mosles de l'osteau qu'on fait ou pignon de lad. nef par marché fait payé 11s. 8d.

114 vº. Audit Jehançon Garnache pour . . . commancer de tailler pour le pignon de lad. nef aud. pris de 3s. 9d. valent 15s.

115 vº. A Huguenin Viremignot et Pierre Guiot, manouvriers, pour 2 journees a porter les pierres de la muraille qu'on despece sur les basses vooltez prés du darrenier pillier de lad. ramee pour y faire ung arc boutant massy a 2s. 1d. valent 4s. 2d.

116 rº. Audit Jehançon pour 4 jornees a continuer de tailler pour lesd. formettez et pignon et pour oster la muraille qui estoit du costé de la rue contre le gros pillier qui soustient le grant clocher affin d'en faire ung arc boutant contre le darrenier pillier de la ramee devers le gros clocher aud. pris valent 15s.

122 rº. A Jehan le Valeton . . . pour avoir . . . mis ung chanleton d'environ 20 piez darriere ung arc boutant qui est sur la chapelle Saint Ladre a 2s. 6d. pour jour valent 22s. 6d.

1490–91: *lacuna.*

1491–92 F.A., Arch. Aube, G 1569.
155 rº. A Jehançon Garnache, me. maçon de l'eglise pour quatre jornees de luy a continuer de tailler, lever et maçonner le gros pillier qui est devers la rue pour faire l'arboutant du pignon de la nef qui estoit commancé a 4s. 2d. pour jour valent 16s. 8d.

159 rº. Aud. Jehançon pour cinq jornees a continuer de tailler et maçonner et lever led. pillier avec l'arboutant a 4s. 2d. valent 20s. 10d.

159 vº. En la 2e. sepmaine de may. . . . Aud. Jehançon pour cinq jours a continuer de tailler, lever et maçonner led. pignon aud. priz de 4s. 2d. valent 20s. 10d.

4. To Nicolas Ludot for having glued large format paper including 10 big pieces to make the templates of the window that is being made in the gable of the said nave through contract made, paid, 11s. 8d.

5. To the said Jehançon Garnache for . . . beginning to cut for the gable of the said nave at the said price of 3s. 9d. makes 15s.

6. To Huguenin Viremignot and Pierre Guiot, laborers, for 2 days to carry the stones of the little wall that is being demolished on the low vaults near the last pillar of the said roof in order to make a massive flying buttress at 2s. 1d. makes 4s. 2d.

7. To the said Jehançon for 4 days to continue to cut for the said windows and for the gable and to remove the little wall which was on the side toward the road against the big pillar that supports the great [crossing] tower in order to make a flying buttress against the last pillar of the roof toward the big [west] bell tower at the said price makes 15s.

8. To Jehan le Valeton . . . for having . . . put a gutter of about 20 feet long behind a flying buttress which is above the chapel of Saint Ladre [N 3] at 2s. 6d. per day makes 22s. 6d.

1. To Jehançon Garnache, master mason of the church, for 4 of his days to continue to cut, raise, and lay stones for the big pillar which is toward the road [C 1] in order to make the flying buttress of the gable that was already begun at 4s. 2d. per day makes 16s. 8d.

2. To the said Jehançon for 5 days to continue to cut and lay stones and raise the said pillar with the flying buttress at 4s. 2d. makes 20s. 10d.

3. In the 2nd week of May. . . . To the said Jehançon for 5 days to continue to cut, raise, and lay stones for the said gable at the said price of 4s. 2d. makes 20s. 10d.

162 r°. A Jehan Labbé de Lusigny pour 13 trapens de noyez chacun 9 piez de long achetez par Jehançon pour faire les mosles des gros pilliers qui feront arboutants tant du pignon comme des tours payé le derrenier jour de mars 40s.

1492–93 F.A., Arch. Aube, G 1569.
205 r°. Audit Jehançon pour trois jornees et demye pour avoir achevé ledit pignon et mis l'osteau dudit pignon audit pris valent 14s. 7d.

205 r°. En la premiere sepmaine de septembre. . . . Audit Jehançon pour quatre jornees de luy a continuer de faire les mosles pour faire les ars boutans et commance[r] de tailler des quarreaux pour lesd. arboutans de lad. nef a 4s. 2d. valent 16s. 8d.

210 v°. En la 3e. sepmaine dud. mars. Audit Jehançon pour six jornees de luy a continuer de tailler lesd. pilliers et arboutans et pour commance[r] de lever et maçonner le pillier de l'arboutant du costé de la rue aud. pris de 4s. 2d. valent 25s. t.

211 v°. En la 2e. sepmaine de may. . . . Aud. Jehançon pour 4 jornees de luy a avoir achevé le premier pillier dud. arboutant et a continuer de tailler l'autre pillier aud. pris de 16s. 8d.

212 r°. Aud. Jehançon a continuer de tailler le 2e. pillier et maçonnez sur les ars qui sont autour dud. pillier aud. pris valent 25s.

213 r°. Audit Jehançon pour cinq jornees et demie a achever de tailler le premier arboutant et faire les mosles de l'autre arboutant pour les tailler aud. pris de 4s. 2d. valent 22s. 10d.

214 r°. Autre despense pour le saint Michel mis sur le pignon de ladite nef. Et pour l'escu de France mis sur ledit pignon.

215 v°. Charpentage fait en la 3e. sepmaine de juing pour les cintres du premier arboutant du costé de la rue. A Jehan Carbonnier . . . a faire deux cintres en l'arboutans qui est ou premier pillier du costel devers la rue. . . .

4. To Jehan l'Abbé de Lusigny for 13 walnut planks, each 9 feet long, purchased by Jehançon to make the templates for the big pillars which shall make flying buttresses both for the gable as well as for the towers paid on the last day of March, 40s.

1. To the said Jehançon for 3½ days to have finished the said gable and placed the window of the said gable at the said price makes 14s. 7d.

2. In the first week of September . . . To the said Jehançon for 4 of his days to continue to make the templates to make the flying buttresses and begin to cut the *quarreaux* for the said flying buttresses of the said nave at 4s. 2d. makes 16s. 8d.

3. In the 3rd week of the said March. To the said Jehançon for 6 of his days to continue to cut the said pillars and flying buttresses and to begin to raise and lay stones on the pillar of the flying buttress toward the road [A 2] at the said price of 4s. 2d. makes 25s. t.

4. In the 2nd week of May. . . . To the said Jehançon for 4 of his days to have finished the first pillar of the said flying buttress [A 2] and to continue to cut the other pillar [B 2] at the said price of 16s. 8d.

5. To the said Jehançon to continue to cut the 2nd pillar and to lay stones on the arches around the pillar at the said price makes 25s.

6. To the said Jehançon for 5½ days to finish cutting the first flying buttress and to make the templates for cutting the other flying buttresses at the said price of 4s. 2d. makes 22s. 10d.

7. Other expense for the Saint Michael placed on the gable of the said nave. And for the shield of France placed on the said gable.

8. Carpentry work done in the 3rd week of June for the centers of the first flying buttress on the side of the road. To Jehan Carbonnier . . . to make 2 centers in the flying buttress [A B C 2] which is at the first pillar toward the road. . . .

Appendix B. Selected Texts Relating to Construction

1493–94 F.A., Arch. Aube, G 1569.
266 v°.-267 r°. En la premiere sepmaine de septembre. A Jehançon pour six jornees de luy a achever et de lever et maçonner lesd. arboutans, et pour commancer de tailler pour les pillier de l'autre costel devers l'ostel de l'evesché a 4s. 2d. vallent 25s. t.

270 v°. Et est assavoir que ce jour des Brandons je envoye ledit Denis a la perriere de Tanlay pour essemeler des pierres pour l'arc doubleau et les ogives et doubleaux et la clef de la premiere volte. . . .

272 r°. Aud. Jehançon Garnache pour six jornees de lui a continuer lesd. pilliers et arboutans et commancer de lever et maçonner sur led. pillier pour faire lesd. arboutans a 4s. 2d., 25s. t.

275 r°. Despense pour faire les cintres de la premiere volte de la nef de l'eglise.

1494–95 F.A., Arch. Aube, G 1569.
375 r°. En la seconde sepmaine commancant le cinquiesme jour de may 1494. A Jehançon Garnache, maistre maçon de ceste eglise pour trois journees pour avoir continuer de tailler et maçonner ou premier pillier et arc boutant du costé de la maison de reverend pere en Dieu, monsr. de Troyes pour chacun jour 4s. 2d. tournois valent 12s. 6d. t.

380 r°. A Jehançon Garnache pour 4 jours pour avoir tailler et maçonner oud. pillier et arc boutant, et aussin pour avoir commancer de tailler l'aultre arc boutant ensuivante du costé de la maison episcopal, pour chacun jour quatre solz deux deniers t. valent 16s. 8d. t.

398 v°. Et est a savoir que l'arc boutant d'entre les viez pilliers du costé de l'ostel de monsr. de Troyes prés du grant clocher a esté achevé en ceste dite sepmaine.

402 r°. Le 25e. jour de juillet, l'an 1494, baillé a Jehançon Garnache, maçon, pour le vin des ouvriers que led. Jehançon assembla pour avoir leur oppinion de faire les ars boutant ou les voltes la somme 5s. t.

1. In the first week of September. To Jehançon for 6 of his days to complete and to raise and to lay the stones of the said flying buttress and to begin to cut for the pillars on the other side [E 2, F 2] toward the bishop's court at 4s. 2d. makes 25s. t.

2. And it should be known that this day of *Brandons* [first Sunday in Lent] I sent the said Denis to the quarry at Tanlay to cut the stones of the transverse arch and the ribs and arch and keystone of the first vault. . . .

3. To the said Jehançon Garnache for 6 of his days to continue the said pillars and flying buttresses and begin to raise and lay stones on the said pillar to make the said flying buttresses at 4s. 2d., 25s. t.

4. Expense for making the centers of the first vault of the nave of the church [C D 1–2].

1. In the second week, beginning on May 5, 1494. To Jehançon Garnache, master mason of this church, for 3 days for having continued to cut and lay stones on the first pillar and flying buttress on the side toward the house of reverend father in God, my lord [the bishop] of Troyes, for each day 4s. 2d. *tournois*, makes 12s. 6d. t.

2. To Jehançon Garnache for 4 days to have cut and laid stones on the said pillar and flying buttress, and also to have begun to cut the other flying buttress adjacent on the bishop's side [D E F 3] at 4s. 2d. t. for each day makes 16s. 8d. t.

3. And it should be known that the flying buttress between the old pillars on the side of my lord the bishop of Troyes near the great [crossing] tower has been finished this week.

4. On July 25, 1494, paid to Jehançon Garnache, mason, for the wine of the laborers assembled by the said Jehançon to have their opinion as to whether to make the flying buttresses or the vaults, total, 5s. t.

425 rº. Charpentage fait en la derreniere sepmaine de may pour faire deux cintres és pilliers
du costé de monsr. l'evesque. Et premiers. A
Jehan Carbonnier et ses varlez pour 15 jours a
faire led. cintre et lever pour l'arc boutant de
dessus les basses voltes de lad. eglise aux viez
pilliers prés du cueur du costé de monsieur l'evesque et avoir abatue la charpenterie de dessus
lesd. basses voltes de costé desd. viez pilliers pour
chacune journee 3s. 2d. t. valent lesd. journees
50s. t.

1494 Deliberations of the Chapter, Arch. Aube,
          G 1279.
39 rº. Mercurii vicesima tercia julii. Item ordi-
naverunt quod loquatur domino episcopo et certis
burgensibus et operariis cognoscentibus, ad sciendum quod melius est, facere voltam primam navis
ecclesie, aut facere arcus pro secunda volta.

1495–96 F.A., Arch. Aube, G 1570.
36 vº. Autre despense pour journees et ouvraiges
d'ouvriers pour essemiller les pierres en la perriere
de Tanlay. A Denis Michel, lequel fut envoyé
aud. Tanlay le dimenche 20e. jour de septembre
l'an de ce present compte pour aller essemillier
des doubleaux, couvertures, admortissemans et
clerevoix pour les arcs boutans du costé du pavé
ay baillé pour sa despense 35s. t.

38 vº. A Jehançon Garnache pour ung voyage
faict par luy a Tonnerre le 27e. jour de septembre
oudit an, pour aller monstrer aud. Denis Michel
et a Martin des Molins les traicts des admortisse-
mens et aultres pierres qui convient avoir pour les
arcs boutans, auquel voyage il a esté trois jours
. . . 12s. 11d. t.

39 vº. Pour ung voyage faict par Jehançon Garnache en la 4e. sepmaine du moys de juing a lad.
perriere pour trasser les cleresvoix contre les
bans de lad. perriere et monstrer aud. Colleçon la
façon d'esboscher lesd. cleresvoix avec trois
pierres qui viennent de dessus les pignacles pour
adjoindre ausd. clerevoix et aussi la maniere de
desboscher les augyves et doubleaux pour les
voltes et aller par les villages qui ont accoustumé
de charrier la pierre pour les faire venir incontin-
ant pour lesd. arcs bouttans, 16s. 8d. t.

5. Carpentry work done in the last week of May
to make 2 centers for the pillars on the side of
my lord the bishop. And first, to Jehan Carbonnier and his apprentices for 15 days to make
and raise the said center for the flying buttress
above the low vaults of the said church at the
old pillars near the choir on the side toward my
lord the bishop [D E F 5] and for having demolished the woodwork above the low vaults
towards the said old pillars for each day 3s. 2d. t.,
the said days make 50s. t.

6. Wednesday July 23 [1494]. Item, it was ordered
that consultations should take place with my
lord the bishop and with certain knowledgeable
bourgeois and laborers to know which is better:
to make the first vault of the nave of the church
[C D 1–2] or to make the arch [flyer] for the
second vault [i.e., at division 3].

1. Other expense for the days and the work of
laborers to cut stones in the quarry of Tanlay. To
Denis Michel, who was sent to the said Tanlay
on Saturday September 20 in the year of this
present account to go and cut the arches, covers
[i.e., upper rims], springers, and open work for
the flying buttresses toward the road, [I] have
given [him] for his expense, 35s. t.

2. To Jehançon Garnache for a trip he made to
Tonnerre on September 27 in the said year to go
and show Denis Michel and Martin des Molins
the plans of the springers and the other stones
which are necessary for the flying buttresses, on
which trip he spent 3 days . . . 12s. 11d. t.

3. For a trip made by Jehançon Garnache in the
4th week of the month of June to the said quarry
to trace the open work [i.e., the tracery panels of
the flyers] against the banks of the said quarry
and to show to the said Colleçon the way to cut
out the said open work with 3 stones which
will come above the pinnacles to join on to the
said open work and also the manner of cutting
out the ribs and transverse arches for the vaults
and to go through the villages which generally
cart stone in order to bring the stone for the said
flying buttresses without delay, 16s. 8d. t.

Appendix B. Selected Texts Relating to Construction

53 v⁰. A Jehançon Garnache, maistre maçon de l'eglise, pour quatre journees de luy a continuer de tailler et lever les arcs boutans des voltes du costé de monsr. l'evesque a 4s. 2d. pour jour valent 16s. 8d. t.

54 r⁰. Aud. Jehançon Garnache pour quatre journees de luy a continuer de tailler, maçonner les arcs boutans de la croisee dud. costé a 4s. 2d. pour jour valent 16s. 8d. t.

56 r⁰. Aud. Jehançon Garnache pour cinq journees de luy a continuer et parfaire lesd. arcs boutans du costé dud. monsieur l'evesque et commance[r] la taille des arcs boutans du costé devers la grant rue a 4s. 2d. pour jour valent 20s. 10d. t.

1496–97 F.A., Arch. Aube, G 1570.
209 r⁰. A Colleçon Faulchot pour avoir osté toute la terre et poutrerie qui estoit en la nef a cause de la premiere volte, 20d. t.

209 v⁰. A Jehan du Bois pour avoir osté la terre de dessoubz la seconde volte aprés que les eschaffaulx et le cintre ont estés ostés, 2s. 6d. t.

210 v⁰. A Gillot de Lessart pour avoir nettoyé les chanlettes dessus les basses chapelles qui estoient pleine de terre que les maçons y avoient faict cheoir en faisant les voltes, pource cy payé 20s. t.

230 v⁰. A Jehançon Garnache pour quatre journees a continuer la taille et maçonnerie des ars bouttans devers le pavé a 4s. 2d. t. pour jour valent 16s. 8d. t.

234 v⁰. Le darrenier jour d'octobre payé aud. Jehançon pour parachever l'assiete des clerevoix devers le pavé pour la journee 4s. 2d. t.

235 r⁰. Audit Jehançon Garnache et Colas Savetier pour chacun unze journees qu'ilz ont esté a prandre les mesures de deux bees de verrieres, c'estassavoir de celle de dessus le tronc et celle d'aprés, trasse[r] tous les remplissages desd. deux verrieres, et faire tous les faulx mosles pour porter

4. To Jehançon Garnache, master mason of the church, for 4 of his days to continue to cut and raise the flying buttresses of the vaults on the side of my lord the bishop at 4s. 2d. per day makes 16s. 8d. t.

5. To the said Jehançon Garnache for 4 of his days to continue to cut and lay the stones of the flying buttresses of the crossing on the said side at 4s. 2d. per day makes 16s. 8d. t.

6. To the said Jehançon Garnache for 5 of his days to continue and to finish the said flying buttresses on the side of the said lord bishop and begin to cut the flying buttresses on the side toward the great road at 4s. 2d. per day makes 20s. 10d. t.

1. To Colleçon Faulchot for having removed all the earth and beams which were in the nave because of the first vault [April, 1497] 20d. t.

2. To Jehan du Bois for having removed the earth below the second vault after the removal of the scaffolding and the center, 2s. 6d. t.

3. To Gillot de Lessart for having cleaned the gutters above the low chapels which were full of earth that the masons had dropped as they made the vaults, for this, 20s. t.

4. To Jehançon Garnache for 4 days to continue to cut and lay stones of the flying buttresses toward the road at 4s. 2d. t. per day makes 16s. 8d. t.

5. The last day of October, paid to the said Jehançon to finish setting the openwork toward the road. 4s. 2d. t. for the day. *Note*: this openwork might be the tracery panels of a flying buttress or, more likely, the decorative balustrade on the clerestory wall.

6. To the said Jehançon Garnache and Colas Savetier for each of them 11 days that they spent to take the measurements of 2 bays of the [clerestory] windows, that is to say the one above the [collecting] box and the one afterward, to draw out the tracery of the said 2 windows and to

a la perriere de Tonnerre pour sur yceulx esboscher lesd. pierres desd. verrieres aud. Jehançon
pour sa part 45s. 10d. t.

236 r⁰. Aultre despense pour maçonnerie. A
Jehançon Garnache, maçon, auquel messieurs de
ceste eglise ont marchandé de faire la premiere
volte de la nef, celle de dessus le tronc, de toutes
façons quelx conques en luy livrant toutes matieres, passé en chapitre le 3e. jour de decembrie
l'an de ce present compte a la somme de cinquante livres tourn. pour ce cy payé a luy a
plusieurs foiz comme appert par ses quittances
lad. somme de 50 l. t.

236 r⁰. Item aud. Jehançon auquel messrs. ordon-
nerent bailler oultre lad. somme de cinquante l.
t. pour la façon d'icelle volte, la somme de dix l.
t., comme appert par le double du registre de
chapitre faict le 3e. jour d'avril aprés Pasques l'an
de ce present compte pource cy 10 l. t.

236 r⁰. Aud. Jehançon pour la façon de la 2e.
volte ensuivante auquel messieurs ont ordonné
payer la somme de soixante livres t. laquelle
somme je luy ay payee comme appert par ses
quittances pour ce cy 60 l. t.

236 r⁰. Aud. Jehançon pour la façon de la troisme. volte d'icelle nef auquel messieurs ont
ordonné payer comme dessus la somme de soixante l. t., laquelle somme je luy ay payee comme
appert par ses quittances. . . .

237 r⁰. Despense pour terre a maçonner.

238 r⁰. Despense faicte pour charpenterie. En la
2e. sepmaine d'aoust. A Jehan Carbonnier et trois
de ses varles pour 19 journees et demie qu'ilz
ont esté a tailler et lever quatre cintres pour les
arcs bouctans devers la rue a 3s. 4d. t. pour jour
valent 65s. t.

240 r⁰. Aud Carbonnier au quel messieurs ont
marchandé de abatre le cintre de la premiere
volte, le redresser, copper et abatre les deux trefz
de la 2e. volte, arrester les deux parois des deux
formettes d'une part et d'aultre, dresser led. cintre
pour la 2e. volte bien et devrement et anssi que
le maistre maçon de demandrera . . . 16 l. t.

make all the false templates to take to the quarry
in Tonnerre in order to cut out the stones of
the said windows on the said [templates], to the
said Jehançon for his part, 45s. 10d. t.

7. Other expense for masonry. To Jehançon
Garnache, mason, with whom my lords of this
church have contracted to make the first vault of
the nave, the one over the [collecting] box in
all respects, supplying him with all the materials,
passed in chapter on December 3 of the year of
this account at the sum of £50 *tournois* for this,
paid to him on several occasions, as appears in his
quittances the said sum of £50 t.

8. Item, to the said Jehançon to whom my lords
ordered to be paid in addition to the said sum
of £50 t. for the making of the said vault the
sum of £10 t. as appears in the copy of the
register of the chapter, made on April 3 after
Easter, the year of this account, for this £10 t.

9. To the said Jehançon for making the second
vault adjacent, to whom my lords have ordered
to be paid the sum of £60 t. which sum I have
paid him as appears in his quittances, for this
£60 t.

10. To the said Jehançon for the making of the
3rd vault of the said nave to whom my lords
have ordered to be paid as above the sum of £60
t., which sum I have paid him as appears in his
quittances. . . .

11. Expense for masoning earth.

12. Expense made for carpentry. In the second
week of August. To Jehan Carbonnier and 3 of
his apprentices for 19½ days to cut and raise 4
centers for the flying buttresses toward the road
at 3s. 4d. t. per day makes 65s. t.

13. To the said Carbonnier with whom my lords
have contracted to demolish the center of the
first vault, re-erect it, cut and take down the 2 tie
beams of the second vault, secure the 2 screens
of the 2 windows on one side and the other, put
up the said center for the 2nd vault well and
properly and as the master mason shall require
. . . £16 t.

Appendix B. Selected Texts Relating to Construction

240 rº. Aud. Carbonnier pour abatre et redresser led. cintre pour la 3e. volte et faire les choses dessusd., payé 16 l. t.

240 vº. Item aud. Carbonnier payé sur la façon du cintre de la quatriesme volte la somme de 10 l. t.

1497–98 F.A., Arch. Aube, G 1571.
35 rº. A Jehan du Boys, manouvrier, pour dix journees qu'il a esté avec les charpentiers ce pendant que on devaloit le cintre de la darreniere volte . . . a 2s. 1d. pour jour valent 20s. 10d.

35 vº. A Jehançon Garnache, Colas Savetier et aux deux verriers ausquelx j'ay baillé cinq solz t. pour boire ensemble pource qu'ilz ont esté longe temps a regarder les traictz des formettes pour sur iceulx prandre leurs mesures de la verriere que monsr. l'advocat vouloit faire faire, et fut le jour de la Circumcision, pour ce cy 5 s. t.

35 vº. A Nicolas Ludot, papetier, pour quatre douzaines de feuilles de papier collé a la grande et a la petite marges pour faire des mosles pour les formettes, pour ce cy payé en janvier 15s. t.

36 vº. A Nicolas Savetier, maçon, pour avoir esté a Tonnerre par cinq jours pour porter a Colleçon Faulchot aulcuns faulx mosles et luy monstrer la maniere d'eschemiller les pierres sur lesd. faulx mosles et fut en la troisme. sepmaine d'avril a 4s. 2d. pour jour valent 20s. 9d. t.

36 vº. A Pierre Prevost, manouvrier, pour avoir esté par deux jours a oster les terres de la 2e. formette et les pierres . . . A Denis Michel pour avoir esté par lesd. deux jours avec led. Prevost pour descramponner et avaller les pierres de lad. 2e. formette a cause que ce n'est pas du marché de Jehançon payé 6s. 8d.

57 vº. Despense pour maçonnerie. A Jehançon Garnache, maistre maçon de ceste eglise, pour la façon de la quatriesme volte de la nef de l'eglise au quel messrs. ont ordonné payer la somme de 60 l. t.

14. To the said Carbonnier for demolishing and re-erecting the said center for the 3rd vault and for doing the above-mentioned things, paid £16 t.

15. Item, to the said Carbonnier for making the center of the 4th vault, paid the sum of £10 t.

1. To Jehan du Bois, laborer, for 10 days that he has spent with the carpenters while the center of the last vault was being taken down at 2s. 1d. per day makes 20s. 10d.

2. To Jehançon Garnache, Colas Savetier, and to 2 glaziers to whom I have paid 5s. t. to drink together because they have been a long time in looking at the drawings of the windows in order to take from [the drawings] the measurements for the window that my lord the lawyer wished to have made, and it was the day of the Circumcision, for this 5s. t.

3. To Nicolas Ludot, paper-maker, for 4 dozen sheets of paper glued together with wide and narrow margins to make the templates of the windows, for this, paid in January, 15s. t.

4. To Nicolas Savetier, mason, for having been to Tonnerre for 5 days to carry certain false templates to Colleçon Faulchot to show him the manner of cutting out the stones on the said false templates, and it was the 3rd week of April at 4s. 2d. per day makes 20s. 9d. t.

5. To Pierre Prevost, laborer, for having spent 2 days to remove the earth and stones from the 2nd window. . . . To Denis Michel for having been with the said Prevost for 2 days to undo and lower down the stones of the second window since this was not part of Jehançon's contract, paid, 6s. 8d.

6. Expense for masonry. To Jehançon Garnache, master mason of this church, for making the 4th vault of the nave of the church, to whom my lords have ordered to be paid the sum of £60 t.

57 v°. Item aud. Jehançon pour la façon de la cinquiesme et darreniere volte d'icelle nef auquel ont pareillement mesdissrs. ordonné payer la somme de 60 l. t.

58 r°. Aud. Jehançon Garnache auquel messrs. ont convenu pour le parachevement de la formette commancee sur le tronc et de faire et dresser celle d'aprés ensuivant a la somme de six vingts livres tourn. pour lesd. deux formettes. Et pour les trois aultres ensuivants, soixante et dix livres t. pour chacune.

58 v°. Despense pour les destrapes qu'il a convenu faire en l'eglise a cause des parois qui estoyent es lieux ou il convenoit asseoir les formettes. Et premiers. A Jehan du Bois, manouvrier, pour deux journees a oster les terres de la premiere formette devers monsr. l'evesque en la 3e. sepmaine de mars a 2s. 1d. pour jour valent 4s. 2d.

60 r°. Aud. Carbonnier pour avoir arresté la grant parois du hault pignon pour ce quelle pendoit devers l'eglise et y a convenu mettre une longue piece de bois du travers de lad. parois avec plusieurs gros crampons de fer attachez a l'arc doubleau dud. pignon qu'il a convenu faire avant que abbattre le cintre de lad. darreniere volte . . . 60s. t.

1498–99 F.A., Arch. Aube, G 1571.
187 v°. A ung nommé Cayel de Pont Saincte Marie pour ung cent et demy de gerbes de roseaulx pour boucher les bees des verrieres, payé 15s. t.

189 r°. A messire Jaques Robelin, organiste de Sainct Estienne, pour avoir faict pourtraire une verriere estant en l'eglise des Carmes d'Orleans, lequel l'a fait tirer par ung verrier, dont il dict avoir payé 6s. 6d. t. . . .

189 v°.–190 r°. A Jehançon pour cinq journees a ruer jus ung grant pan de mur qui estoit sur la premiere formette devers le pavé, et y avoit plusieurs pierres de Tonnerre qu'il a convenu devaler a la roe, et avoir refaict l'entablement de

7. Item, to the said Jehançon for making the 5th and last vault of the said nave to whom my lords have similarly ordered paid the sum of £60 t.

8. To the said Jehançon with whom my lords have agreed for the completion of the window begun over the [collecting] box and to make and erect the next one at the sum of £120 t. for the said 2 windows. And for the 3 following [windows] £70 t. each.

9. Expense for demolition work necessary in the church because of the screens which were in the places where it was necessary to set the windows. And first. To Jehan du Bois, laborer, for 2 days to remove the earth from the first window toward my lord the bishop in the 3rd week of March at 2s. 1d. per day makes 4s. 2d.

10. To the said Carbonnier for having secured the great screen of the high gable because it was leaning toward the church and it was necessary to place a long piece of wood across the said screen with several big iron clamps attached to the transverse arch of the said gable. It has been necessary to do this before demolishing the center of the last vault 60s. t.

1. To someone called Cayel de Pont-Sainte-Marie for 150 sheaves of reeds to block up the bays of the windows, paid, 15s. t. *Note*: to protect the glass.

2. To my lord Jaques Robelin, organist of Saint-Etienne, for having had a window in the Carmelite church in Orleans depicted, which he had drawn by a glazier, to whom he says he paid 6s. 6d. t. . . .

3. To Jehançon for 5 days to demolish a great bay of stone wall which was in the first window toward the road and there were several stones of Tonnerre in it which had to be lowered down with the wheel and for having re-made the

Appendix B. Selected Texts Relating to Construction

lad. formette qui estoit fort dommaigé pour ce payé en may, 16s. 8d. t.

190 r⁰. A Jehan Verrat et Balthazar, verriers, ausquelz a esté deu par le fin de la verriere monsieur l'Advocat 40s. t. a eulx payé au moys de juing 40s. t.

216 v⁰. Despense pour eschemillage. A Colleçon Faulchot auquel a esté marchandé de eschemiller toute la pierre qu'il convient avoir pour les cinq formettes du costé du pavé selon les faulx mosles a luy donnez par Jehançon le maistre maçon, parmy ce qu'il en doit avoir pour chacune formette la somme de 12 l. 10s. t. qui valent ensamble lesd. cinq formettes soizante deux livres dix solz t.

217 r⁰. A Jehançon Garnache . . . pour la 4e. formette par devers monsr. l'evesque . . . pour la façon de la cinqme. formette dud. costé . . . pour la façon de la premiere formette du costé du pavé qui est le sixme. . . . pour la façon de la 7e. formette par devers led. pavé . . . pour la 8e. formette par devers led. pavé. . . .

1499–1500 F.A., Arch. Aube, G 1571.
326 v⁰. A Jehançon Garnache pour la façon de la neufme. et dixme. formette. . . .

329 r⁰. Despense pour couverture. A Ancelet la Cane pour six journees qu'il a esté en la darreniere sepmaine d'aoust, que on a commancé a descouvrir toutes les cropes des chappelles devers monsr. l'evesque pour disposer la charpenterie pour bailler jour aux verrieres nouvellement faictes, et aussi bailler le cours des eaues, par quoy a convenu lever toutes les chanlattes et y en mettre des nouvelles a 3s. 4d. t. valent 20s. t.

1500–1 F.A., Arch. Aube, G 1571.
496 v⁰. A Jehan Carbonnier pour quatre journees a mettre une grant piece de bois au travers du pignon devers le grant clocher pour tenir la paroy dud. pignon laquelle estoit hors de sa place et en danger de tumber, pour ce payé 12s. 4d. t.

entablature of the said window which was seriously damaged, for this paid in May, 16s. 8d. t. *Note*: this wall inside the eastern clerestory window on the north side must constitute the remains of a flying buttress against the west side of the crossing.

4. To Jehan Verrat and Balthazar, glaziers, to whom was due from the completion of the window [of] my lord the lawyer 40s. t. paid in the month of June 40s. t.

5. Expense for stone cutting. To Colleçon Faulchot with whom a contract has been made to cut all the stone necessary for the 5 windows on the side toward the road according to the false templates given him by Jehançon, the master mason, and he should have £12 10s. t. for each window, which totals for the said 5 windows £62 10s. t.

6. To Jehançon Garnache . . . for the 4th window toward my lord the bishop . . . for the making of the 5th window on the same side . . . for the making of the 1st window toward the road which is the 6th . . . for the making of the 7th window toward the said road . . . for the 8th window toward the said road. . . .

1. To Jehançon Garnache for making the 9th and 10th window. . . .

2. Expense for roofing. To Ancelet la Cane for 6 days he spent in the last week of August when work began on demolishing all the roofs of the chapels towards my lord the bishop to arrange the woodwork to provide light to the newly made windows [of the triforium] and to provide passage for the [rain] water, for which reason it has been necessary to lift [out] all the gutters and to put in new ones at 3s. 4d. t. makes 20s. t.

1. To Jehan Carbonnier for 4 days to put a big piece of wood across the gable toward the great bell tower [of the crossing] in order to secure the screen in the said gable which was dislodged and in danger of falling, for this paid 12s. 4d. t. *Note*: this refers to one of the transept gables.

1502 Deliberations of the Chapter, Arch. Aube, G 1279.

365 v⁰. Mercurii octava die predicti mensis junii. Ista die domini proposuerunt consulere peritos artifices et lathomos super constructione fundamentorum turrium navis [huius] ecclesie.

369 v⁰. Veneris prima die mensis Julii. . . . Insuper domini proposuerunt consilium habere peritissimorum artificum lathomorum nonnullorumque burgencium et mercatorum huius civitatis Trecensis super constructione et fundatione turrium navis huius ecclesie, committentes dominos Huyart sen., Nicolaum Solacii, de Venlay, de Veluz-Guichart et alios dominos in hoc negotio interesse volentes. . . . Ad quam domini fuerunt opinionis quod evocetur quidam supremus artifex magister Martinus Chambiche, Parisius commorans.

375 r⁰. Mercurii 17a. predictis mensis Augusti. . . . Deinde commiserunt dominos de Veluz, Solacii et de Venlay ad concordandum cum magistro Martino Chambiche, lathomo ecclesie Belvacensis, de suo veagio et consilio dato dominis pro perfectione hujus ecclesie et turrium navis ipsius. Qui concordaverunt ad duodecim scuta auri *au souleil* gallice et tria scuta *au souleil* data suo famulo, scilicet magistro lathomo ecclesie Senonensis, nuncupato H [passage lost] et solvit eciam magister fabrice huius ecclesie omnes expensas oris per ipsos in hac civitate factas, de quibus faciet expensam in suo compoto.

1501–2 F.A., Arch. Aube, G 1573.

39 r⁰. A Jehançon Garnache, Grant Jehan et Jehan Bailly, maçons, lesquelx par l'ordonnance de messrs. vindrent visiter l'eglise, c'estassavoir le gros pillier commancer par devers le pavey pour avoir leurs advis et savoir quelle provision de pierre et de quelle sorte on la devoit faire venir pour commancer lad. maçonnerie leur ay baillé pour aller soupper ensamble le 6me. jour de juillet de l'an present 10s. t.

1. On Wednesday the 8th day of the aforementioned month of June. On this day my lords proposed to consult with skilled artisans and masons on the construction of the foundations of the towers of the nave of this church.

2. On Friday the first day of the month of July. . . . Then my lords proposed to have the advice of several very skilled artisans, masons, and bourgeois and merchants of this city of Troyes on the construction and foundation of the towers of this church, charging my lords Huyart the elder, Nicolas Solacium, de Venlay, de Veluz, Guichart, and other lords with the affair. . . . Upon which, my lords were of the opinion that a certain leading artist should be summoned, Master Martin Chambiche dwelling in Paris. *Note:* the *proviseurs* at Troyes generally favored the form *Cambiche*. At Beauvais, however, the name is more often rendered *Chambiges*, and this is the form the master used himself in a signed charter.

3. Wednesday 17th of the said month of August. . . . Then they commissioned my lords de Veluz, Solacium, and de Venlay to negotiate with Master Martin Chambiges, mason of the church of Beauvais regarding his trip [to Troyes] and the advice he gave to my lords on the completion of this church and its towers. Who [i.e., Chambiges] agreed at the price of 12 *scuta au soleil* of Gaul and 3 *scuta au soleil* for his apprentice, that is the master mason of the church at Sens, named H__, and the master of the fabric of this church paid all the expenses for food incurred by these [Chambiges and his apprentice] in this city, which he will enter as an expense in his account.

1. To Jehançon Garnache, Grand Jehan, and Jehan Bailly, masons, who at the orders of my lords came to visit the church, that is the great pillar [A 1] begun toward the road in order to have their advice and to know what provision of stone and what sort should be fetched to begin the said masonry given to them to go and dine together on the 6th day of July this year, 10s. t.

Appendix B. Selected Texts Relating to Construction

40 vº. Despense pour la venue de maistre Martin Cambiche, maistre maçon de Beauvaiz, Huguet Hamelier, maistre maçon de Sens.

40 vº. Aud. maistre Martin pour dixneuf journees qu'il a occupees a venir dud. Beauvaix, sejourner par huit jours et demy en ceste ville et la reste pour retourner aud. Beauvaix pour ses peinnes et voyages . . . au mois d'aoust luy fut baillé . . . 12 escus au soulel de 22 l. t.

40 vº. A Huguet Hamelier, son serviteur, pour le temps qu'il a esté avecques led. maistre Martin son maistre par l'advis de mesd. srs. et led. maistre Martin luy baillé trois escus d'or a la couronne de 105s. t.

40 vº. A Jehançon Garnache pour cinq journees ouvrans qu'il a esté a accompaigner led. maistre Martin a 4s. 2d. t. pour jour valent 20s. 10d. t.

41 rº. Item aud. maistre Martin pour une bource que je envoyee a sa femme achettee par monsr. Jaquoti. . . . 14s. t.

41 rº. Audit Henrion Sonnet pour certaine despense faicte au soir en sa maison par lesd. maçons, Jehançon, autres maçons et charpentiers de la ville comprins, le jour que led. maistre Martin fist son rapport en chapitre, et pour tout le temps qu'il a esté logé chez led. Henrion pour ce payé 20s. 8d. t.

41 rº. A Jehan du Bois et ung autre manouvrier pour chacun une journee a faire une fosse contre la loge des maçons pour veoir par led. maistre Martin les fondemens de l'ancienne maçonnerie a 2s. 6d. t. valent 5s. t.

1502–3 F.A., Arch. Aube, G 1574.
41 vº. A Jehançon Garnache, maçon, pour ung voyage fait par l'ordonnance de messrs. a Aulnay pour porter les faulx mosles faiz par maistre Martin Cambiche, maistre maçon de Beauvaix, pource qui est a faire et commancer la maçonnerie . . . la somme de 22s. t.

2. Expense for the arrival of Master Martin Chambiges, master mason of Beauvais, Huguet Hamelier, master mason of Sens. *Note*: the master mason of Sens was actually called Cuvelier.

3. To the said Master Martin for 19 days he spent to come from the said Beauvais, stay for 8½ days in this town and the rest to return to Beauvais, for his trouble and travel . . . in the month of August, paid to him . . . 12 *escus au soleil*, £22 t.

4. To Huguet Hamelier, his servant, for the time that he was with the said Master Martin, his master, on the advice of my lords and of the said Master Martin paid to him 3 gold *escus d'or a la couronne* of 105s. t.

5. To Jehançon Garnache for 5 working days that he spent accompanying the said Master Martin at 4s. 2d. t. for each day totals 20s. 10d. t.

6. Item, to the said Master Martin for a purse, purchased by my lord Jaquoti, that I sent to his [i.e., Martin's] wife . . . 14s. t.

7. To the said Henrion Sonnet for a certain expense made in the evening in his house by the said masons, Jehançon, and the other masons and carpenters of the town included, the day that the said Master Martin made his report in chapter and for all the days that he has been lodged in the said Henrion's house, for this paid 20s. 8d. t.

8. To Jehan du Bois and another laborer each of them for 1 day to make a trench against the masons' lodge to show the said Master Martin the foundations of the old masonry at 2s. 6d. t. makes 5s. t.

1. To Jehançon Garnache, mason, for a trip made at the orders of my lords to Aulnois to carry the false templates made by Martin Chambiges, master mason of Beauvais for the work which is to be done and to begin the masonry . . . the sum of 22s. t.

42 rº. A Jehan Bailly et Jehançon Garnache, maçons, Jehan Carbonnier, Jehan de Grey, Jehan de Dijon, charpentiers, et Ancelet La Canne, couvreur, pour avoir visité les six formettes de la croisee pource que messrs. avoient ordonné que le bas d'icelle seroit mys a jour pour le verrer comme le cueur et la nef, a quoy faire ilz furent toute la matinee . . . baillé 10s. t.

2. To Jehan Bailly and Jehançon Garnache, masons, Jehan Carbonnier, Jehan de Grey, Jehan de Dijon, carpenters, and Ancelet la Canne, roofer, for having visited the 6 windows of the crossing because my lords had ordained that the lower part of the windows should be opened to the light to glaze it like the choir and the nave, and they spent all morning at it . . . paid, 10s. t.

43 rº. A ung nommé Jaques le Fuzelier, messager de ceste ville, pour avoir apporté de Paris jusques en ceste ville les pourtraiz des tours et portaulx de ceste eglise faiz par maistre Martin Cambiche et envoyez par mons. maistre Jaques Guichart, pour ce payé 10s. t.

3. To someone called Jaques le Fuzelier, messenger of this town, to have carried from Paris to this town the portraits of the towers and portals of this church made by Master Martin Chambiges and sent by my lord Master Jaques Guichart, for this paid, £10 t.

43 rº. Aud. maistre Martin pour avoir faiz lesd. pourtraiz [blank].

4. To Master Martin for having made the said portraits. . . . [blank].

1503–4 F.A., Arch. Aube, G 1574.
332 rº. A Jehançon et Grant Jehan, massons, pour avoir prins les mesures des tables et meneaulx qui convient és formettes dessus l'autel saint Anthoinne pour envoyer a Aulnoy pour boire ensemble, payé 5s.

1. To Jehançon and Grand Jehan, masons, for having taken the measurements of the slabs and mullions necessary for the windows above the altar of Saint Anthony [east side of the transept arms] to send [the measurements] to Aulnois, 5s., to drink together.

334 rº. A monsr. maistre Pierre Jacoti pour avoir esté en court par l'ordonnance de messrs. dés le 8e. jour d'avril aprés Pasques mil cinq cens et quatre jusques au [blank] jour de mars ensuivent par devers monsr. l'evesque et monsr. le gouverneur pour sçavoir se par leur moyen on pourroit obtenir du Roy ce que ceulx de Rains prennent sur les greniers a sel de France, au quel je baillé par plusieurs fois, comme appert par sa cedulle, tant en or comme en argent, la somme de 141 l. 5s. t.

2. To my lord Master Pierre Jacoti for having been to court on the orders of my lords from April 8 after Easter 1504 until the [blank] day of the following March to ascertain from my lord the bishop and my lord the governor whether through their mediation it would be possible to obtain from the king what the [clergy] at Reims are taking from the salt tax of France, to whom I have paid on several occasions as appears on his account, both in gold and in silver the sum of £141 5s. t.

1504–5 F.A., Arch. Aube, G 1576.
47 rº. A Jehançon Garnache, maçon, auquel a esté marchandé par messieurs en leur chapitre . . . de faire tout a neuf le remplaige d'en hault des six formettes . . . de la façon et selon les trects des formettes qu'il a darrenierement faictes en la nef de ceste eglise . . . qui font en somme toute 324 l. t.

1. To Jehançon Garnache, mason, with whom a contract has been made by my lords in their chapter to make entirely anew the upper tracery of the 6 [clerestory] windows . . . in the manner and according to the forms of the windows that he has just made in the nave of this church . . . which makes in total sum £324 t.

57 rº. Item avoir recouvert . . . sur le gros pillier de la tour attenant du pavey.

2. Item, for having covered over the great pillar of the tower against the road [A 1].

Appendix B. Selected Texts Relating to Construction

1505–6 F.A., Arch. Aube, G 1576.
173 r⁰. A ung nommé maistre Michel, maistre maçon de Saint Nicolas en Loraine, et ung autre maistre maçon du duc de Loraine, pour avoir visité la place ou il convient faire les tours ou commencer la nouvelle maçonnerie, avoir veu la plate forme et les articles faictz par maistre Martin, maçon de Beauvaix, avoir visiter l'oteau devers le chapitre, lequel ilz trouverent bon . . . le cinqme. jour de juing . . . 20s. t.

1506–7 F.A., Arch. Aube, G 1577.
36 v⁰. A Grand Jehan le maçon, Jehançon Garnache, Jehan Bailly, aussi maçons, Jehan Carbonnier et Jehan de Dijon, charpentiers, ausquelz led. Grant Jehan monstra en chapitre le jour saincte Croix en septembre une plate forme qu'il avoit faicte des deux tours qu'on veult faire en lad. eglise . . . pour aller desjuner ensemble . . . 5s. t.

37 r⁰. Audit Grand Jehan Gayde, maçon, pour avoir faict lad. plateforme et pourtraict desd. tours par luy monstré et exbibé, comme dit est . . . 7 l. t.

49 v⁰. Despense pour couverture. . . . Et avoir relatté et recouvert partie du gros pillier emprés lequel convient besongner pour les fondemens de la grosse tour qu'on veult faire prés du pavé. . . .

49 v⁰. . . . a descouvrir, deslater et entasser la tuille et abbatre le viel bois qui estoit sur le gros pillier et sur ung pan de mur qui est joignant de la maison du sonneur. . . .

57 r⁰. Despense pour faire les fondemens de l'une des deux tours que messrs. de l'eglise de Troyes ont intention de faire faire en ladicte eglise de Troyes, c'est assavoir pour celle de devers la rue.

57 r⁰. A maistre Martin Cambiche, maistre maçon de Beauvais, auquel messrs. avoyent par plusieurs foys mandé qu'il voulsist venir par deça pour baillier et mettre ordre a commancer les fondemens desd. tours, lequel arriva en ceste ville le 23e. jour d'octobre l'an dessusd. et y demora par aucun temps tant a pourjecter et veoir le lieu ou on veult faire lesd. tours comme a aller visiter

1. To someone called Master Michel, master mason of Saint-Nicolas in Lorraine, and another master mason of the duke of Lorraine for having visited the place where it is necessary to build the towers or begin the new masonry, having seen the plans and articles made by Master Martin, mason from Beauvais, having visited the window toward the chapter which they found good . . . on June 5 . . . 20s. t.

1. To Grand Jehan the mason, Jehançon Garnache, Jehan Bailly, also masons, Jehan Carbonnier and Jehan de Dijon, carpenters, to whom the said Grand Jehan showed in chapter on the day of the Holy Cross in September a drawing/model that he had made of the 2 towers that they want to make in the said church . . . to go and dine together . . . 5s. t.

2. To the said Grand Jehan Gayde [Gailde], mason, for having made the said drawing/model and portrait of the said towers, shown and demonstrated by him, as has been said . . . £7 t.

3. Expense for roofing. . . . And for having placed lath and covered part of the big pillar and nearby where it is necessary to work for the foundations of the big tower to be built near the road. . . .

4. To uncover, remove lath, and heap up the tile and demolish the old wood that was on the big pillar [A 1] and on a bay of wall adjoining the house of the bell ringer. . . .

5. Expense to make the foundations of one of the two towers that my lords of the church of Troyes intend to build in the said church of Troyes, that is, the one toward the road.

6. To Master Martin Chambiges, master mason of Beauvais, whom my lords have ordered several times to come here to provide and to put order into the beginning of work on the foundations of the said towers, who arrived in this city on October 23 of the above-mentioned year and who stayed for some time to make plans and to see the place where they want to build the said

les perrieres du Ponts Humbert, Culoison et
Saincte Maure, et aussi a faire les memories de ce
qui est affaire pour faire les provisions et aultres
choses necessaires pour commancer a faire lesd.
fondemens . . . 22 l. t.

57 vº. . . . a faire ung crot de l'ordonnance dud.
maistre Martin prés du gros pillier joingnant
du pavey pour veoir les fondemens dudit pillier.
. . .

59 vº. . . . pour une charrette d'espine pour
mettre sur le pillier qui est auprés de la maison
du sonneur pour garder les enfans de monter
dessus payé 2s. 1d.

60 vº. A Grand Jehan le maçon, Jehançon Garnache, Jehan Bailly et Laurent Germain, perrier
de Tanlay, tous maçons, maistre Jehan Honnet,
Jehan de Dijon, Jehan Carbonnier, Jehan de
Grey et Jehan Oudot, charpentiers, lesquelz ont
estez appellez par l'ordonnance de messrs.
avecques aultres gens de bien de la ville, marchans
et autres, pour avoir leur adviz de ce qui estoit a
faire touchant les fondemens de la tourt qu'il
convient faire devers le pavey, et aussi de trans-
porter le beuffroy out sont les cloches, et aussi
d'abatre partie de l'ancienne tourt par devers led.
pavey . . . 30s.

64 rº. Aud. maistre Martin Cambiche pour sond.
voyaige et pour son retour, qui peullent bien
estre dix jours, comme dict est, cinq jours en ce
lieu pour monst[r]er ce qui estoit a faire touchant
lesd. fondemens . . . 18 l. 6s. 8d. t.

64 rº. A Colas Mathau pour avoir remené led.
maistre Martin jusques a Sens. . . 17s. t.

67 rº. A Colas Mathau pour ung voyaige faict a
Beauvaix par l'ordonnance de messrs. a la fin
du moys de jeuillet pour aller porter des lettres a
maistre Martin pour venir aleger les fondemens
par devers le pavey . . . 45s.

68 rº. A Jehançon Garnache, maistre maçon de
ceste eglise, pour ung voyaige faict a Aulnoy
et Savonnieres par l'ordonnance de messrs. au
commancement du moys de decembre . . . pour
porter aux perriers desd. lieux les patrons des

towers, and also to go and visit the quarries
of Pont Humbert, Culoison and Sainte-Maure
and also to make the memoirs on what is to be
done to make the provisions and other things
necessary to begin the said foundations . . . £22 t.

7. To make a hole on the orders of Master Martin
near to the big pillar adjacent to the road [A 1]
to see the foundations of the said pillar. . . .

8. . . . for a cart of thorns for placing on the
pillar [A 1] near the house of the bell ringer in
order to stop the children from climbing on
it, paid, 2s. 1d.

9. To Grand Jehan the mason, Jehançon Garnache, Jehan Bailly and Laurent Germain, quarry
man from Tanlay, all masons, Master Jehan
Honnet, Jehan de Dijon, Jehan Carbonnier, Jehan
de Grey, and Jehan Oudot, carpenters, who were
called on the orders of my lords together with
other people of substance from the city, merchants and others, to have their advice on what
was to be done concerning the foundations of the
tower to be made toward the road, and also to
transfer the belfrey where the bells are and to
demolish part of the old tower toward the said
road . . . 30s.

10. To the said Master Martin Chambiges for his
said trip and for his return, which could well
be 10 days, as has been said, 5 days here in order
to show what was to be done on the said foundations . . . £18 6s. 8d. t.

11. To Colas Mathau for having brought back the
said Master Martin as far as Sens . . . 17s. t.

12. To Colas Mathau for a trip made to Beauvais
on the orders of my lords at the end of the
month of July to go and carry letters to Master
Martin [asking him] to come to help [with] the
foundations toward the road . . . 45s.

13. To Jehançon Garnache, master mason of this
church, for a trip he made to Aulnois and to
Savonnières at the orders of my lords at the beginning of the month of December . . . to carry
to the quarry men of those places the templates

Appendix B. Selected Texts Relating to Construction

longue[u]rs et haulteurs des pierres qu'il convient
a la maçonnerie qui est affaire pour le commancement des pans de la tour, ainsi que maistre
Martin l'a ordonné . . . 29s. 6d. t.

111 v°. Despense et journees de maçons faictes
pour le commancement de la tour commancee a
faire du costé et par devers le pavey. . . . A Jehançon Garnache, auquel messrs. ont ordonné
baille[r] 5s. t. pour jour . . . 20s. t.

112 r°. A Jehan Bailly, maçon, pour avoir esté par
plusieurs foys toutes et quantes foys qu'on l'a
appellé a visiter ce qui est affaire pour les tours,
et avec ce par les deux derrenieres foys que
maistre Martin a esté par deça pour led. affaire
led. Bailly l'a tousjours acompaigné et a esté
presens a veoir la plate forme et a prandre les
mesures . . . 70s. t.

113 r°. A Jehançon Garnache et Jehan Bailly,
avecques de leurs serviteurs, qui furent une matinee a prandre les mesures des pilliers et les re-
traictes des murailles avecques Jehan de Dijon et
Ancelet . . . 5s. t.

123 v°. A Jehan de Dijon, Jaquot Berton, Jehan
Martin, Lyonnet . . . [blank] Estienne Peschat,
Thevenin Fallet et Didier Fallet son filz pour
cinquante journees d'eulx tous en la derreniere
sepmainne de juing, en la premiere, seconde
et tierce de jeuillet pour avoir abbatu tout le
pignon du grenier appellé le celier de l'eglise,
ouquel convient faire la chambre aux trectz. . . .

1507-8 F.A., Arch. Aube, G 1577.
396 r°. Despense pour le foretaige de ladicte
perriere de Tanlay. L'an mil cinq cens et sept, le
29e. jour de decembre Laurent Germain, me.
perrier de la perriere de Tanlay prés de Tonnerre,
a convenu et marchandé, . . . a messrs. de ceste
eglise de esquarrer et eschemiller chascun millier
de pierre du ban des cloz et du franc banc dur
en la maniere qui s'ensuit, c'est assavoir la
moindre haulteur de piece de pierre, que on
appelle communement ung bloc de douze peusses
de hault, l'aultre haulteur de 15 peusses et l'autre
haulteur de 18 peusses de hault, et de longueur

of the lengths and heights of the stones necessary
for the beginning of the bays of the tower, as
Master Martin has ordered . . . 29s. 6d. t.

14. Expense and days of masons to start work on
the tower that has been begun on the side toward
the road. . . . To Jehançon Garnache, to whom
my lords have ordained to be given 5s. t. per day
. . . 20s. t.

15. To Jehan Bailly, mason, for having been
several times, whenever he was called, to visit
the work on the towers, including the last two
times that Master Martin was here for the said
business the said Bailly always accompanied him
and was present to look at the model/plans and
to take the measurements . . . 70s. t.

16. To Jehançon Garnache and to Jehan Bailly
with their apprentices who spent a morning
in taking the measurements of the pillars and the
offsets of the walls together with Jehan de Dijon
and Ancelet . . . 5s t.

17. To Jehan de Dijon, Jaquet Berton Jehan
Martin, Lyonnet . . . [blank], Estienne Peschat,
Thevenin Fallet and Didier Fallet, his son, for 50
days of them all in the last week of June and
the first, second and third [week] of July for
having knocked down the entire gable of the
store chamber called the cellar of the church
where it is necessary to build the drawing chamber. . . .

1. Expense for quarrying at the said quarry of
Tanlay. The year 1507, on December 29, Laurent
Germain, master quarrier of the quarry at Tanlay
near Tonnerre has agreed and contracted with
my lords of this church to square and cut out
each *millier* of stone from the close bank and
from the free hard bank in the manner that follows, that is to say, the least height of the piece
of stone commonly called a block of 12 inches
high, the other height of 15 inches high and the
other height of 18 inches, and the length of
each of the said blocks 4 feet long, or whatever

chascun desd. blocz de quatre piedz de long, ou ainsi que led. bloc pourra contenir tous lesd. blocz de deux a trois piedz de large, et les plus estroictz de pied et demy. . . .

1508-9 F.A., Arch. Aube, G 1578.
103 r⁰. A Colas Mathau pour ung voiaige fait par l'ordonnance de messrs. au lieu de Beauvais pour aller querir maistre Martin Cambische et luy mener ung cheval pour le ramener . . . 32s. 6d.

103 v⁰. A maistre Martin Cambische, maistre maçon de Beauvais, . . . pour la despense dudit maistre Martin, ses deux varletz, ledit Mathau et cheval depuis ledit Beauvais jusques en ce lieu, ou ilz arriverent le sabmedi ensuyvant, dixᵉ. jour dud. mois . . . 100s. t.

104 r⁰. . . . pour le louaige d'une chambre . . . pour loger led. maistre Martin, Jehan de Damas, gendre dudit Martin, Pierre Cambische et autres maçons . . . 14 l. t.

104 v⁰. A Jehan Carbonnier pour le loiaige de son tumereau a deux chevaulx pour une demye journee a mener du maillon du gros pillier qu'on a derrenierement abbatu jusques devant la chambre aux traictz nouvellement faicte pource payé 3s. 4d. t.

105 v⁰. . . . a estaier ung grand pan de paroix, laquelle portoit sur le pillier derrenierement demolu par devers le pavey. . . .

110 r⁰. . . . pour une grant piece de boix a batir de 40 piedz de long et d'un pied a solle en tous sens pour faire une estaie pour soustenir le pignon que est sur la chappelle nouvellement faicte devers le pavey . . . 17s. 6d t.

140 v⁰. Autre despense pour le foretaige des perrieres d'Aulnay et Savonnieres . . . et le tout par l'ordonnance de maistre Martin Cambische, et lesquelz trois cens blocz doibvent faire les dessusdictz en trois haulteurs, c'est assavoir la premiere haulteur de douxe poussez, la 2e. de quinze poussez et la 3e. et derreniere haulteur de 18 poulcez, et doibvent lesd. blocz estre de longueur et largueur proporcionnez en façon qu'elles facent lison les unes sur les autres, dont les

the said block can reach, and all the said blocks at 2 to 3 feet wide and the narrowest at 1½ feet. . . .

1. To Colas Mathau for a trip made on the orders of my lords to the place of Beauvais to go and fetch Master Martin Chambiges and to take him a horse to bring him back . . . 32s. 6d.

2. To Master Martin Chambiges, master mason of Beauvais, . . . for the expense of the said Master Martin, his 2 apprentices, the said Mathau and horse from the said Beauvais to this place, where they arrived on the following Saturday, the 10th of the said month . . . 100s. t.

3. For the rent of a room . . . to lodge the said Master Martin, Jehan de Damas, son-in-law of the said Martin, Pierre Chambiges and other masons . . . £14 t.

4. To Jehan Carbonnier for renting his two-horse cart for half a day to take rubble from the big pillar that has just been demolished [A 1] to in front of the drawing chamber that has been recently made, for this paid 3s. 4d. t.

5. To prop up a great bay of screen [or wall] which was carried by the pillar just demolished toward the road. . . .

6. For a great piece of construction wood 40 feet long and 1 foot in width in all directions to make a prop to prop up the gable which is over the chapel recently made toward the road . . . 17s. 6d. t.

7. Other expense for quarrying of stone at the quarries of Aulnois and Savonnières . . . and everything according to the orders of Master Martin Chambiges, and the above-mentioned [quarriers] should make the said 300 blocks in 3 heights, that is to say the 1st height at 12 inches, the 2nd height at 15 inches and the 3rd and last height at 18 inches, and the said blocks should be of such a length and width that they fit one to another, and the smallest of the said blocks

Appendix B. Selected Texts Relating to Construction

maindres desd. blocz doibvent estre de huict a neuf piedz, les moyennes de 11 a 12 piedz, et les derrenieres et plus grandes de 14, 15 et 16 piedz. . . .

153 rº. Despense pour journees de maçons pour l'annee de ce present compte. Et premiers. En la 2e. sepmainne de feuvrier. . . . A maistre Martin Cambische, maistre maçon de ceste eglise, auquel messrs. ont ordonné baillier pour chascune sepmainne 40s. t. pource cy pour ceste presente sepmainne 40s. t. A Jehançon Garnache et Jehan Bailly, maçons de ladicte eglise, pour chascun 5 jours d'eulx a 5s. t. pour jour vallent 50s. t. A Legier Cambische et Symon de Sainct Homer, serviteurs dud. maistre Martin pour dix journees d'eulx deux a taillier pour la tour devers la pavey a 4s. 2d. t. pour jour vallent et paié 41s. 8d. t. 153 vº. A Alexandre le Blanc et Jaques Martellet, serviteurs de Jehan Bailly, et Guillaume Alexandre, pour 15 journees d'eulx trois, a 3s. 4d. t. pour jour, vallent 50s. t. A Colas Savetier, Colas Merlin, Symon Henry et Jehan Troucher, varletz de Jehançon, pour 20 journees d'eulx quatre a 3s. 4d. t. pour jour, vallent 66s. 8d. t. A Colleçon Fauchot pour quatre journees a 2s. 11d. t. pour jour, vallent 11s. 8d. t.

170 rº. A Jehan de Mussy, charpentier, pour quatre journees a remettre a poinct la grant grue, laquelle n'estoit pas faicte selon la devise de maistre Martin . . . 15s. t.

179 vº. Despense pour les molles des maçons. A Collet Godier, hucher, pour 21 molles collés et assemblés faictz de moians de quartier et tailliez selon l'ouvraige appartenant aux pourtaux et par l'ordonnance de maistre Martin. Item aud. Collot pour deux paneaux collez et assemblez, lesquelz ne sont point tailliez, pour avoir couroyé neuf moyens, lesquelz sont prest a coller, pource paié aud. Collot pour lesd. panneaux et lesd. 21 molles avec une escarre et deux regles payé par l'ordonnance de maistre Martin 7 l. 10s. t.

179 vº. Item aud. Collot pour avoir fourny de son bois deux grans molles contenans huict piedz de roy en tous sens pour servir aux arrechemens des pilliers par voies et aussi a ung pillier par voie de chascune tour avec une table de blanc

should be 8 to 9 feet, the middle ones 11 to 12 feet and the last and largest 14, 15 and 16 feet. . . .

8. Expense for the days of the masons for the year of this present account. And first, in the 2nd week of February. . . . To Master Martin Chambiges, master mason of this church, to whom my lords have ordered to be paid for each week 40s. t. for this, for the present week 40s. t. To Jehançon Garnache and Jehan Bailly, masons of the said church, for 5 days work of each of them at 5s. t. per day totals 50s. t. To Legier Chambiges and Simon de Saint Omer, apprentices of the said master Martin, for 10 of their days to cut for the tower toward the road at 4s. 2d. t. per day, totals and paid 41s. 8d. t. To Alexandre le Blanc and Jaques Martellet apprentices of Jehan Bailly and Guillaume Alexandre for 15 days of the 3 of them at 3s. 4d. per day totals 50s. t. To Colas Savetier, Colas Merlin, Simon Henry and Jehan Troucher, apprentices of Jehançon for 20 days of the 4 of them at 3s. 4d. t. per day, totals 66s. 8d. t. To Colleçon Fauchot for 4 days at 2s. 11d. t. per day totals 11s. 8d. t.

9. To Jehan de Mussy, carpenter, for 4 days to fix the great crane, which was not built according to Master Martin's specifications . . . 15s. t.

10. Expense for the masons' templates. To Collet Godier, joiner, for 21 templates glued and assembled, made to help quarter and cut the stones for the work on the portals and on the orders of Master Martin. Item, to the said Collet for 2 uncut panels glued and assembled, and for having planed 9 middle-sized ones which are ready to glue, for this paid to the said Collot for the said panels and the said 21 templates with a square and 2 rulers, paid on the orders of Master Martin £7 10s. t.

11. Item, to the said Collet, for having furnished 2 great templates of his own wood, containing 8 royal feet in all directions to serve for the enrichments [bases] of the free-standing pillars and also for a free-standing pier of each tower

bois estant en la petite chambre au bout des loges, laquelle table sert a coupper les molles, pource paié aud. Collot 40s. t.

1509–10 F.A., Arch. Aube, G 1579.
52 rº. A Pierre Cambiche, filz de maistre Martin, maistre maçon de ceste eglise, lequel partit de ce lieu le 3e. feuvrier de l'an present pour aller a Beauvaix querir son pere . . . 20s. Et arriva ledit maistre Martin en ce lieu le quinziesme dudit mois de feuvrier. . . .

53 rº. Despense pour ung angin que maistre Martin a ordonné estre fait pour asseoir devant la vielle tour auprés du pan de la nouvelle tour.

53 vº. Item pour avoir fait ung angin appellé pied de chievre divisé par ledit maistre Martin de trois pieces de bois pour mener au Pons Humbert pour lever les grosses pierres et chargier sur les cheriotz, pour ce que les perriers ne les sçavoient charger sur les cheriotz. . . .

55 vº. A Claude Bonjour pour deux boisseaux de ciment pour joincter le glacis de la formette de la chappelle nouvellement faicte jongnant du pan de la tour . . . 12d.

80 rº. Despense pour journees de maçons pour l'an de ce compte. Et premiers en la premiere sepmainne d'aoust. . . .
A Jehan de Damas, Jehançon Garnache et Jehan Bailly pour quinze journees d'eulx a 5s. t. pour jour, vallent 75s. t.
A Pierre Cambiche, Leger Cambiche, Pierre de Damas et Simon de Sainct Omer, pour 20 journees a 4s. 2s. pour jour, vallent 4 l. 3s. 4d. t.
A Colas Savetier, Lié Gilles et Colas Simart pour quinze journees d'eulx a 3s. 9d. t. pour jour, vallent 56s. 3d. t.
A Jehan Truchin, varlet de Jehançon, Alexandre le Blanc et Jaquet Martellot, varletz de Jehan Bailly, Colas Merlin, Marquet Riviere, Jehan Chasteau et Colleçon Fauchot, estans de present au Pons Humbert, pour 35 journees d'eulx a 3s. 4d. t. pour jour, vallent 116s. 8d.

98 vº. Despense pour journees de manouvriers a continuer le pan de la premiere tour par devers le pavey.

together with a sheet of white wood which is in the little chamber beside the masons' lodge, which sheet serves in the cutting of templates, for this paid to the said Collet 40s. t.

1. To Pierre Chambiges, son of Master Martin, master mason of this church who left here on February 3 this year to go to Beauvais to seek his father . . . 20s. And the said Master Martin arrived here on February 15. . . .

2. Expense for an engine that Master Martin ordered to be made to set in front of the old tower near the bay of the new tower.

3. Item, for having made an engine called a *pied de chievre* [goat's leg] devised by the said Master Martin out of 3 pieces of wood, for taking to Pont Humbert for lifting the big stones and loading them on the carts, because the quarriers did not know how to load them on the carts. . . .

4. To Claude Bonjour for 2 bushels of cement for pointing the weather moulding of the window of the chapel recently made adjacent to the bay of the tower . . . 12d.

5. Expense for days of masons in the year of this account. And first, in the 1st week of August. . . .
To Jehan de Damas, Jehançon Garnache, and Jehan Bailly for 15 of their days at 5s. t. per day totals 75s. t.
To Pierre Chambiges, Leger Chambiges, Pierre de Damas and Simon de Saint Omer for 20 days at 4s. 2d. per day totals £4 3s. 4d. t.
To Colas Savetier, Lié Gilles and Colas Simart for 15 of their days at 3s. 9d. t. per day totals 56s. 3d. t.
To Jehan Truchin, Jehançon's apprentice, Alexandre le Blanc and Jaquet Martellot, Jehan Bailly's apprentices, Colas Merlin, Marquet Riviere, Jehan Chasteau and Colleçon Fauchot, at present at Pont Humbert for 35 of their days at 3s. 4d. t. per day totals 116s. 8d.

6. Expense for the days of the laborers to continue the bay of the first tower toward the road.

Appendix B. Selected Texts Relating to Construction

1510–11 F.A., Arch. Aube, G 1580.
225 v°. A Thomas Fillet, manouvrier de ceste eglise, lequel partit de ce lieu le 29e. d'avril de l'an present pour mener le cheval de Robinet de Laage jusques a Beauvaix pour apporter maistre Martin, que messrs. envoyent querir pour l'affaire de leur maçonnerie, lequel retourna le 6e. de may qui sont huict jours qu'il a demoré sans avoir ramené ledit maistre Martin et a despensé oudit voiaige pour luy et ledit cheval qu'il a ramené la somme de 35 s. t.

244 r°. Despense pour journees de maçons a continuer le premier pan de la tour par devers le pavey. . . .

252 v°. A Jehan de Damas pour cinq journees a continuer la taille du pillier qui fait partie du petit portail a 5s. t. pour jour 25s. t.

1511–12 F.A., Arch Aube, G 1581.
43 v°. Pour ung voiaige faict par Jehan de Soissons pour aller querir maistre Martin a Beauvaix, lequel partit de ce lieu le derrenier jour d'auoust et revint avec led. maistre Martin et Martin Menart avec chascun ung cheval, et furent icy pour le retour le 13e. jour de septembre ensuivant 4 l. 15s.

43 v°. Audit maistre Martin, lequel partit de ce lieu le 22e. jour de septembre . . ., pour ce que son partement fut soudain . . . 18 l. 10s. t.

43 v°. A Pierre Cambiche, filz dud. maistre Martin, affin qui sollicitast son pere de retorner quant on le mandera luy baille ung escu souliel qui vault 37s. t.

44 r°. Item a elle pour certaine despense faicte en sa maison par ledit maistre Martin, Jehan de Soissons, Jehançon, Jehan Bailly, maistre Jehan Honnet et Jaques Boschet le jour des quatre temps d'aprés la saincte Croix, que les dessusds. furent appellez avec led. maistre Martin pour estre presens a oyr la conclusion qui fut prinse led. jour par monsr. de Troyes, monsr. le bailly, messrs. les doian et chapitre et plusieurs gens de bien de la ville pour faire les fondemens de la seconde tour par devers mond. sr. de Troyes et despenserent lesd. maistre Martin et ses consors pour le disner la somme de 12s. 6d. t.

1. To Thomas Fillet, laborer of this church, who left here on April 29 this year to take the horse of Robinet de Laage to Beauvais to carry Master Martin whom my lords ordered to be sought for the business of their masonry, who returned on May 6, making 8 days that he stayed without having brought back the said Master Martin, and on the trip he spent both for himself and for the said horse he brought back, the sum of 35s. t.

2. Expense for the days of the masons to continue the first bay of the tower toward the road. . . .

3. To Jehan de Damas for 5 days to continue to cut the pillar which is part of the little portal at 5s. t. per day 25s. t.

1. For a trip made by Jehan de Soissons to go and seek Master Martin at Beauvais who left here on the last day of August and returned with the said Master Martin and Martin Menart, each one with a horse, and their return here was on the following September 13, £4 15s.

2. To the said Master Martin, who left here on September 22 . . . because his departure was sudden . . . £18 10s. t.

3. To Pierre Chambiges, son of the said Master Martin, so that he would request his father to return when he is ordered, paid an *escu soleil* which totals 37s. t.

4. Item, to her [the widow of Henrion Sonnet] for certain expense made in her house by the said Master Martin, Jehan de Soissons, Jehançon, Jehan Bailly, Master Jehan Honnet, and Jaques Boschet the day of *Quatre Temps* [Ember Day] after the Holy Cross when the afore-mentioned were summoned with the said Master Martin to be present to hear the decision made on that day by my lord [the bishop] of Troyes, my lord the bailiff, my lords the dean and chapter, and several people of substance of the city to make the foundations of the second tower toward my said lord [the bishop] of Troyes, and the said Master Martin and his companions spent the sum of 12s. 6d. t. for the dinner.

44 vᵒ. Despense pour la couverture du premier pillier d'entre la grant porte et la petite par devers le pavey.

46 vᵒ. . . . pour deux grandes pieces de bois contenant chascune environ 37 piedz de longueur et cinq quars de pied de fourniture en tous sens pour estaier le pan de la vielle tour du costé que on veult presentement fonder l'autre tour par devers monsr. l'evesque . . . 65s. t.

49 rᵒ. Pour ung voiaige faict par Nicolas Mathau pour aller meney a maistre Martin le cheval de Pierre Cortillier au lieu de Beauvaix pour ramener led. me. Martin, ouquel voiaige il a vacqué par dix jours qui vallent a 2s. 6d. t. pour jour 25s. t.

49 rᵒ. Audit maistre Martin pour cinq jours qu'il a mis a venir et pour cinq autres jours qui luy faudra bien pour s'en retorner aud. Beauvaix, qui font ensemble dix jours. Item a luy pour dix autres jours qu'il fist l'annee que le roy estoit a Troyes, dont il ne fut poinct contentey, qui font ensemble vingt journees . . . 37 l. t.

52 vᵒ. A Jehan de Soissons, Jehançon, Jehan Bailly, me. Jehan Honnet et Bonaventure de Grez, lesquelz le 9e. jour de septembre furent assemblez entre eulx pour adviser la maniere de estaier ce qu'il convient faire et fonder ce ou estoit le petit portail de Droyn pour desjuner ensemble, payé 6s. t.

67 rᵒ-vᵒ. A maistre Martin Cambiche, lequel arriva en ceste ville le 7e. jour dudit mois de may, auquel a esté paié la sepmaine entiere pour ce qu'il estoit party de Beauvaix quatre jours devant, auquelz messrs. ont ordonné baille[r] chascune sepmaine 40s. t., pource cy 40s. t.

75 vᵒ. En la derreniere sepmaine de mars et premiere d'avril . . . on besongna ou pillier boutant qu'il a convenu faire dedans la chapelle Drouyn.

1512–13 F.A., Arch. Aube, G 1582.
132 vᵒ. Pour ung voiaige faict par Jehan de Soissons pour aller querir maistre Martin Cam-

---

5. Expense for the roofing of the first pillar [buttress] between the great portal and the little one toward the road. *Note*: this refers to the buttress to the left of the center portal.

6. For 2 great pieces of wood each containing about 37 feet in length and 1¼ feet in width on all sides to prop up the bay of the old bell tower on the side where they want to found the other tower toward my lord the bishop [the south side] . . . 65s. t.

7. For a trip made by Nicolas Mathau to go and take to Master Martin the horse of Pierre Cortillier at Beauvais to bring back Master Martin, on which trip he sent 10 days which, at 2s. 6d. t. per day totals 25s. t.

8. To the said Master Martin for 5 days that he spent to come and for 5 other days that were necessary for his return to the said Beauvais, which makes 10 days all together. Item, to him for 10 other days that he spent the year when the king was in Troyes, with which he was not at all content, making all together 20 days . . . £37 t.

9. To Jehan de Soissons, Jehançon, Jehan Bailly, Master Jehan Honnet, and Bonaventure de Grez, who on September 9 were summoned to give advice on the way to prop up the work to be made and founded, and this where the little portal of [the chapel of] Dreux used to be, to dine together, paid 6s. t.

10. To Master Martin Chambiges who arrived in this town on the 7th day of the said month of May, to whom has been paid for the entire week because he left Beauvais 4 days before, to whom my lords have ordered to be paid 40s. t. for this 40s. t.

11. In the last week in March and the first of April . . . work was done on the supporting buttress necessary inside the chapel of Dreux.

1. For a trip made by Jehan de Soissons to go and seek Master Martin Chambiges, on which trip

Appendix B. Selected Texts Relating to Construction

biche, ouquel voiaige il a demoré par quinze jours entiers ou mois de may . . . 6 l. 18s t.

132 v⁰. A maistre Martin Cambiche, lequel partit de Beauvaix pour venir en ce lieu le 26e. jour de may et y est demoré jusques au dixe. jour de juing ensuivant . . . 11 l. 5s. t.

135 v⁰. Despense pour journees de maçons a continuer la taille et maçonnerie de la seconde tour. Et premiers. En la troise. sepmaine de novembre, qui fut entiere et que on commança a tailler pour le pan de la 2e. tour par devers l'ostel episcopal en l'an de ce compte et que a ced. temps le fondement d'icelle tour a esté remply.

135 v⁰. A Jehan de Soissons pour six journees a 5s. t. pour jour paié 30s. t. A Jehançon Garnache pour six journees a 4s. 7d. pour jour paié 27s. 6d. t. A Colas Savetier et Colas Simart et Colin Royer pour dixhuict journees d'eulx a 2s. 11d. t. pour jour paié 52s. 6d. t. A Colleçon Fauchot pour six journees a 2s. 6d. t. pour jour paié 15s. t.

1513–14 F.A., Arch. Aube, G 1583.
287 r⁰. Despense pour journees de maçons a continuer la taille et maçonnerie de la seconde tour.

1514–15 F.A., Arch. Aube, G 1584.
60 r⁰. Despense tant pour charpenterie, couverture, reparations de verrieres et autres despenses qu'il a convenu et a esté necessité de faire a cause des Indulgences octroyees par notre sainct pere le Pape Leo Xe. de ce nom a la requeste du Roy François. . . .

71 v⁰. A Bonaventure de Grez [et al.] . . . a faire le cintre de la viz de la deuxieme tour . . . 7s. 6d.

71 v⁰. A Colas Marin pour ung voiaige faict par luy a Beauvaix par l'ordonnance de messrs. pour aller querir maistre Martin lequel ne sçeut venir avec se messaige a cause d'un fondement qu'il avoit commancé avant l'arrivey dud. messaige, ouquel voiaige a demoré par douze journees pour ce qu'il ramena avec luy la femme dudit maistre Martin et partit de ce lieu pour faire led. voiaige le 24e. jour de may et retourna le 4e. juing a luy payé 6os. t.

he spent 15 complete days in the month of May . . . £6 18s. t.

2. To the said Master Martin Chambiges, who left Beauvais to come here on May 26 and remained here until the following June 10, . . . £11 5s. t.

3. Expense for the days of masons to continue the cutting and laying [of stone] for the second [south] tower. And first. In the 3rd week of November which was [a] complete [week] and when work began on cutting for the bay of the 2nd tower towards the bishop's palace in the year of this account and at which time the foundation of this tower was filled in.

4. To Jehan de Soissons for 6 days at 5s. t. per day, paid 30s. t. To Jehançon Garnache for 6 days at 4s. 7d. per day paid 27s. 6d. t. To Colas Savetier and Colas Simart and Colin Royer for 18 of their days at 2s. 11d. t. per day paid 52s. 6d. t. To Colleçon Fauchot for 6 days at 2s. 6d. t. per day paid 15s. t.

1. Expense for days of masons to continue the cutting and laying [of stone] for the 2nd tower.

1. Expense for carpentry, roofing, repairs to windows and other expenses appropriate and necessary because of the indulgences granted by our Holy Father Pope Leo the 10th of this name at the request of King Francis. . . .

2. To Bonaventure de Grez [et al.] . . . to build the center of the staircase of the 2nd tower . . . 7s. 6d.

3. To Colas Marin for a trip made by him to Beauvais on the orders of my lord to go and seek Master Martin, who could not come, with this message: because of a foundation that he had begun before the arrival of the said message, and he [Marin] stayed for 12 days because he brought back Master Martin's wife, and he left here to make the said trip on May 24 and returned on June 4, paid to him, 6os. t.

71 vº. A la femme dudit maistre Martin, a laquelle je baillé a son partement de ce lieu, qui fut le 8e. jour de juing, la somme de sept livres tourn. pour son voiaige d'aller et venir, et pour autant qu'elle fist la despense dud. Marin au retour dud. Beauvaix, et avec ce affin qu'elle estee retournee aud. Beauvaix elle sollicite de venir ledit me. Martin pource que grande nécessité est qui vienne par deça . . . 7 l. t.

72 vº. A Jehan de Soissons pour ung voiaige faict par luy a Beauvaix par l'ordonnance de messrs. pour aller querir maistre Martin, ouquel voiaige il a demoré par douze journees dont les huict sont du mois de jeuillet et les autres quatre sont du mois d'aoust . . . 63s. 6d. t.

90 rº. Despense pour journees de maçons a continuer la taille et maçonnerie des tours et portaulx de ceste eglise.

90 rº. A Jehan de Soissons et Jehançon Garnache pour huict journees d'eulx deux a continuer la taille du gros pillier autrement dit le trumeau de la deuxe. tour par devers la maison episcopal a 5s. t. pour jour vallent et paié 40s. t.

1515–16; *lacuna.*

1516–17 F.A., Arch. Aube, G 1585.
63 rº. Despense pour la maçonnerie des tours et portaulx que messeigneurs de ceste eglise font faire en icelle.

63 rº. Pour ung voiaige faict par Jehan de Soissons par l'ordonnance de messeigrs. pour aller visiter les perrieres de Tonnerre et bailler aux perriers d'icelles les haulteurs et longueurs des pierres qui convient a present pour fermer et prandre les portaulx . . . 37s. t.

66 rº–66 vº. A Jehan Phelippon, menuysier, pour avoir refaict les mosles des gros doubleaux et des augyves c'est assavoir deux moles pour lesdictz gros doubleaux et deux pour lesd. augives

4. To the wife of the said Master Martin to whom I paid on her departure from here on June 8, the sum of £7 *tournois* for her trip to go and to come and because she rendered the expense of the said Marin on the return from Beauvais and so that when she had returned to Beauvais she would request Master Martin to come, because of the urgent necessity that he should come here . . . £7 t.

5. To Jehan de Soissons for a trip he made to Beauvais at the orders of my lords to go and seek Master Martin, on which trip he spent 12 days of which 8 were in the month of July and the other 4 in the month of August . . . 63s. 6d. t.

6. Expense for the days of masons to continue to cut and lay [the stones] of the towers and portals of this church.

7. To Jehan de Soissons and Jehançon Garnache for 8 of their days to continue to cut the big pillar otherwise called the *trumeau* of the 2nd tower toward the bishop's house at 5s. t. per day totals, and paid 40s. t. *Note*: it is clear from the usage of the word *trumeau* that it signified one of the great buttresses between the portals. In modern usage the word is applied to the support in the middle of a portal: this is called an *estanfiche* at Troyes.

1. Expense for the masonry of the towers and portals that my lords of this church are building in this [church].

2. For a trip made by Jehan de Soissons on the orders of my lords [the chapter] to go and visit the quarries of Tonnerre and to bring to the quarriers of the said [quarries] the heights and lengths of the stones which are necessary at present to close and finish the portals . . . 37s. t.

3. To Jehan Phelippon, joiner, for having redone the templates of the big transverse arches and the ribs, that is to say 2 templates for the said big transverse arches and 2 for the said ribs and

187

et ung autre mole pour les petiz portaulx par le dedans des tours a luy paié le 25e. juing l'an de ce compte 25s. t.

77 v⁰. Despense pour journees de maçons a continuer la taille des trumeaulx et pan de la deuxieme tour par devers monseigneur l'evesque de Troyes. . . . Et aussi l'estanfiche de la principalle porte desd. deux tours.

1517–18 F.A., Arch. Aube, G 1586.
60 r⁰. A Jehan Bertran, charpentier, pour six pieces de bois de 22 pieds de longueur et ung espan de largeur en tous sens pour faire les cintres de la principale porte des pourtaulx . . . 30s. t.

62 r⁰. A Jehan Briaix, painctre, pour avoir faict en papier de blanc et noir ung dieu pour l'estanfiche du principal portail, deux saincts Pierres et ung sainct Paul pour iceulx monstrer a messrs. pour savoir s'ilz seroient bons patrons pour sur iceaulx faire les ymaiges de la grandeur qu'il les convient pour les portaulx ou l'estanfiches pource a luy paié le penultime janvier 40s. t.

62 v⁰. Le 26e. jour d'avril l'an de ce compte donné a monsr. le doien de ceste eglise deux escuz souliel pour donner a Paris a Pierre Cambiche, filz de maistre Martin affin d'aller a Beauvaix par devers led. maistre Martin son pere pource 4 l. t.

99 r⁰. Despense pour journees de maçons a continuer la taille des portaulx, trumeaulx et pan de la deuxieme tour par devers monseigr. l'evesque. . . . Et aussi l'estanfiche de la principale porte. . . .

1518–19 F.A., Arch. Aube, G 1587.
67 v⁰. A Jehan Phelippon, menuysier, pour avoir faict deux grans mosles neufz pour la taille du maistre maçon et pour avoir retaillé cinq autres et raconstré les regles desdits maçons . . . 20s. t.

71 r⁰. A Pierre Cambiche filz de maistre Martin Cambiche auquel ay baillé par l'advis de monsr. le doien de Sainct Etienne et de monsr. Turquan la somme de dix escus souliel pour estre venu de Paris en ce lieu . . . pour venir visiter la maçonnerie et ouvraige de l'eglise pour en faire le rapport a messrs, 20 l. t.

another template for the little portals on the inside of the towers, paid to him on June 25 in the year of this account 25s. t.

4. Expense for days of masons to continue to cut the buttresses and bay of the 2nd tower toward my lord the bishop of Troyes. . . . And also the *estanfiche* [trumeau] of the main portal of the said 2 towers.

1. To Jehan Bertran, carpenter, for 6 pieces of wood 22 feet long and 1 span in width in all directions to make the centers of the main door of the portals . . . 30s. t.

2. To Jehan Briaix, painter, for having made on paper in black and white [an image of] God for the trumeau of the central portal, 2 Saints Peter and 1 Saint Paul to show them to my lords to know if they would be good cartoons to make the statues of the necessary size for the portals or trumeaux, for this paid on the penultimate day of January 40s. t.

3. On April 26 in the year of this account, given to my lord the dean of this church for 2 *escus soleil* to give to Pierre Chambiges in Paris, son of Master Martin, to go to Beauvais to the said Master Martin, his father, for this £4 t.

4. Expense for the days of masons to continue to cut the portals, buttresses, and bay of the 2nd tower toward my lord the bishop . . . and also the trumeau of the main portal. . . .

1. To Jehan Phelippon, joiner, for having made 2 great new templates for the cutting of the master mason and for having recut 2 others and for having remade the said masons' rulers . . . 20s. t.

2. To Pierre Chambiges, son of Master Martin Chambiges, to whom I have paid on the advice of my lord the dean of Saint-Etienne and my lord Turquan the sum of 10 *escus soleil* to have come here from Paris . . . to come and visit the masonry and the work on the church to make his report to my lords £20 t.

71 rº. A monsr. Turquan paié trois escus souliel pour pareille somme qu'il avoit declaree luy estant a Paris ou mois de may derreniere passé aud. Pierre Cambiche pour aller a Beauvaix par devers son pere maistre Martin Cambiche affin de l'admener ou faire venir en ce lieu pour visiter et veoir l'ouvraige de ceste eglise commant il est conduyt, ce que led. maistre Martin ne peut faire, obstant quelque greve maladie qu'il avoit . . . 6 l. t.

71 vº. Despense pour les cintres qu'il a convenu faire pour le petit portail de la deuxieme tour par devers monsr. l'evesque et aussi pour les cyntres de la chappelle Droyn.

95 vº. Despense pour journees de maçons a continuer la taille des portaulx, trumeaulx et pan de la deuxieme tour par devers monseigr. l'evesque. Et aussi continuer la taille du revestiere de la chapelle Droyn.

1519–20 F.A., Arch. Aube, G 1588.
182 vº. A Jehan Regnault [et al.] . . . pour avoir couvert tout le pan de maçonnerie de la deuxieme tour par devers monseigr. l'evesque ensemble les trois ars qui sont sur la chapelle Droyn . . . 7 l. t.

185 rº. Despense pour la plateforme qu'il a fallu asseoir sur le pavey pour besongner en la premiere tour par devers led. pavey avecquez la despense des engins qu'il a convenu monter sur ladicte plate forme.

214 vº. Despense pour journees de maçons a continuer la taille des portaulx, trumeaulx et pans des tours commancees en ceste eglise.

1520–21 F.A., Arch. Aube, G 1588.
304 vº. A Jehan de Soissons, maistre maçon, pour trois feuilles de papier colley pour faire des molles pour la viz par devers le pavey paié ou mois de septembre 6s. t.

312 rº. Aud. Simon Maurroy [et al.] . . . a descendre les cintres qui ont esté dressez en la chapelle Droyn pour la volter pour iceulx cintres recintrer, approprier et dresser en la chapelle joignant au pavey pour la volter comme est la chapelle Droyn . . . 75s. t.

3. To my lord Turquan, paid 3 *escus soleil* for an equal sum he has declared [as expense] while at Paris in the month of last May paid to Pierre Chambiges to go to Beauvais to his father, Master Martin Chambiges, to fetch him or bring him here to visit and see the work on this church [and] how it is conducted, but the said Master Martin could not do this because of some serious illness that he had . . . £6 t.

4. Expense for the centers necessary for the little portal of the 2nd tower toward my lord the bishop and also for the centers of the chapel of Dreux [chapel S 5].

5. Expense for the days of masons to continue to cut for the portals, buttresses, and bay of the 2nd tower toward my lord the bishop. And also to continue to cut for the vestry of the chapel Dreux.

1. To Jehan Regnault [et al.] . . . for having covered over the bay of masonry of the 2nd tower toward my lord the bishop together with the 3 arches which are over the chapel of Dreux . . . £7 t.

2. Expense for the platform which it has been necessary to set on the road to work on the 1st tower toward the said road, together with the expense of the engines which it was necessary to mount on the said platform.

3. Expense for the days of masons to continue to cut for the portals, buttresses, and bays of the towers [that have been] begun in this church.

1. To Jehan de Soissons, master mason, for 3 sheets of glued paper to make the templates for the staircase toward the road, paid in the month of September 6s. t.

2. To the said Simon Maurroy [et al.] . . . to take down the centers which have been erected in the chapel [of] Dreux [S 5] to vault it; to recenter, adjust, and erect them in the chapel adjacent to the road [N 5] to vault it like the chapel [of] Dreux . . . 75s. t.

189

331 vº. Despense pour journees de maçons a continuer la taille des portaulx, trumeaulx et pans des tours commancees a ceste eglise.

1521–22 F.A., Arch. Aube, G 1589.
73 rº. Despense pour la couverture du pan de la tour par devers le pavey . . . de couvrir tout ledit pan avec partie de la chapelle joignant led. pan qui convient volter. . . .

74 rº. A Jaquin Ancelot . . . a mener des terres descendues des deux voltes que on a derrierement volteez par devers le pavey joignant de la tour neufve . . . 10s. t.

98 vº. A Nicolas Halliz, tailleur d'imaiges, paié six escuz souliel sur ce qu'il a faict sur les histoires de la procession qui vallent 12 l. t.

1522–23 F.A., Arch. Aube, G 1589.
175 rº. A Nicolas Halins, ymager, demorant prés de la Licorne auquel ay paié la somme de 60s. t. de marché faict a luy par moy present Jehan de Soissons pour avoir une histoire de sainct Pierre pour asseoir au beau portail de ceste eglise pource cy 60s. t.

204 rº. Despense pour journees de maçons a continuer la taille des portaulx, trumeaulx et pans des tours commancees en ceste eglise.

1523–24 F.A., Arch. Aube, G 1589.
290 rº. A Pierre Damas, frere de Jehan de Soissons, auquel ay donné de l'ordonnance de monseigr. le doien de Sainct Estienne ou mois de janvier l'an de ce compte la somme de 20s. t. a cause qu'il estoit venu du lieu de Estarnay au mandement de messeigrs. de ceste eglise pour parler a sond. frere lequel estoit fort malade touchant la maçonnerie de ceste eglise cy 20s. t.

290 rº. A Nicolas Halins, ymagier, pour quatre histoires de la vie sainct Pierre qu'il a faictz pour asseoir ou premier portail devers la rue paié le 17e. mars, l'an de ce compte comme par quictance estant en mon manuel appert la somme de 12 l. t.

3. Expense for days of masons to continue to cut for the portals, buttresses, and bays of the towers begun in this church.

1. Expense for covering the bay of the tower toward the road . . . to cover the entire bay with part of the chapel adjoining the said bay, which has to be vaulted. . . .

2. To Jaquin Ancelot . . . to take away the earth brought down from the two vaults just erected toward the road adjacent to the new tower . . . 10s. t.

3. To Nicolas Halliz [Halins], carver of images [statues], paid 6 *escus soleil* for what he has done on the histories of the procession, which totals £12 t.
Note: the word "procession" should probably read "passion"—the theme of the sculptures of the central portal.

1. To Nicolas Halins, maker of images, living near the Licorne, to whom I have paid the sum of 60s. t. by contract made with him by me in the presence of Jehan de Soissons to have a history of Saint Peter to set in the Beautiful Portal [north transept] of this church, for this 60s. t.

2. Expense for days of masons to continue cutting the portals, buttresses, and bays of the towers begun in this church.

1. To Pierre Damas, brother of Jehan de Soissons, to whom I have given at the command of my lord the dean of Saint-Etienne in the month of January, the year of this account, the sum of 20s. t. because he came from Estarnay at the orders of my lords of this church to talk to his said brother who was seriously ill, on the subject of the masonry of this church. 20s. t.

2. To Nicolas Halins, maker of images, for 4 histories of the life of Saint Peter he has made to set in the 1st portal toward the road, for this paid on March 17 in the year of this account by quittance in my manual appears the sum of £12 t.

291 rº. Despense faicte pour faire le guect par les ouvriers de ceste eglise pour obvier aux dangiers de feu qui de present sont en ceste ville de Troyes affin de garder ceste eglise de nuyt desd. dangiers.

322 rº. Despense pour journees de maçons a continuer la taille des portaulx, trumeaulx et pans des tours commanceez en ceste eglise.

1524–25 F.A., Arch. Aube, G 1590.
62 rº. A Nicolas Halins, ymager, demorant a Troyes pour une histoire de la vie sainct Paul faicte par luy pour asseoir au portail neuf de sainct Paul pource a luy paié le 13e. jour d'aoust la somme de 60s. t.

82 rº. Despense pour journees de maçons a continuer la taille des portaulx, trumeaulx et pans des tours commancees a ceste eglise.

1525–26 F.A., Arch. Aube, G 1590.
204 vº. A Nicolas Halins, ymagier, demorant a Troyes auquel j'ay payé la somme de seize livres tornois pour ses peine et salaire d'avoir faict de son mestier deux anges tenans l'escu de France . . . assis sur le portal neuf de ceste eglise du costé de la rue . . . 16s. t.

230 rº. Despense pour journees de maçons a continuer la taille des portaulx, trumeaulx et pans des tours commancees a ceste eglise.

1526–27 F.A., Arch. Aube, G 1591.
79 rº-vº. A Nicolas Halins, ymagier, pour deux hystoires pour le grant portail du milieu, assavoir l'une comment nostre seigneur fu buffetté les yeux bandez et l'autre comment il fut coronné du chappeau d'espine, pource a luy payé le quinzieme de decembre l'an present 7 l. t.

109 vº. Despense pour journees de maçons a continuer la taille des portaulx, trumeaulx et pans des tours commancees a ceste eglise.

1527–28 F.A., Arch. Aube, G 1591.
281 vº. A Nicolas Halins, ymagier, payé la somme de seize livres tournois pour la façon des armoiries du daulphin, auquel messrs. en avoient marchandé, comme appert par quictance dudit Halins, cy 16 l. t.

3. Expense made in order to have the workers keep watch to guard against the dangers of fire which exist at present in Troyes in order to guard this church from the said dangers at night. *Note*: in this year a great fire swept through the western part of the city.

4. Expense for the days of masons to continue cutting for the portals, buttresses, and bays of the towers begun in this church.

1. To Nicolas Halins, maker of images, living in Troyes, for a history from the life of Saint Paul made by him to place on the new portal of Saint Paul, paid for this on August 13 the sum of 60s. t.

2. Expense for days of masons to continue cutting for the portals, buttresses, and bays of the towers begun in this church.

1. To Nicolas Halins, maker of images, living in Troyes, to whom I have paid the sum of £16 *tournois* for his efforts and salary for having made according to his profession 2 angels holding the shield of France, placed over the new portal of the church toward the road . . . 16s. t.

2. Expense for days of masons to continue cutting for the portals, buttresses, and bays of the towers begun in this church.

1. To Nicolas Halins, maker of images, for 2 histories for the great portal in the middle, that is one [showing] how Our Lord was buffeted, his eyes blindfolded, and the other how He was crowned with the crown of thorns, for this paid on December 15 this year, £7 t.

2. Expense for days of masons to continue cutting for the portals, buttresses, and bays of the towers begun in this church.

1. To Nicolas Halins, maker of images, paid the sum of £16 *tournois* for making the arms of the Dauphin, for which my lords had contracted, as appears in the quittance of the said Halins, £16 t.

Appendix B. Selected Texts Relating to Construction

313 v⁰. Despense pour journees de maçons a continuer la taille des portaulx, trumeaulx et pans des tours commancees a ceste eglise.

1528–30: *lacuna.*

1530–31 F.A., Arch. Aube, G 1592.
217 v⁰. A Nicolas Halins, ymagier, le 14e. jour de janvier, baillé la somme de six livres tournois sur et en deduction de la somme de 36 l. tournois, a quoy il a marchandé a messrs. le doyen et J. Huyart sen[ior] et moy de faire trois ymages assavoir Nostre Dame de Pitié, sainct Jehan et la Magdelene aux deux boutz, selon le volume et ordre que le maistre maçon de ceste eglise luy a donné, pour ce cy 6 l. t.

219 r⁰. . . . pour une poultre de vingt cinq piedz de longueur qu'ilz ont scyee en trois voyes pour l'arc boutant qui a esté rompu . . . 6s. t.

220 r⁰. Despense pour refaire l'arc boutant qui estoit ja faict et cheut le samedi d'aprés la Sainct Pierre et Sainct Paul en l'an 1531 par faulte des maçons, qui osterent trop tost la clef du scintre, pour quoy tout vint abas et fut tué Colin Millet, l'un desd. maçons.

230 r⁰. . . . pour quatrevingts voictures de sablon qu'ilz ont admenees en la 3e. sepmainne dud. moys de may pour les fondemens du premier piller par voye. . . .

259 r⁰. Despense pour journees de maçons a continuer la taille des portaulx, trumeaulx et pans des tours commancees a ceste eglise.

270 r⁰. . . . et a commancé de abbattre la vielle maçonnerie qui est entre les tours neufves de ceste eglise et a trie[r] la roche et la bonne pierre chascune apart et la divise[r] et mettre en monceaulx devant ceste eglise. . . .

2. Expense for days of masons to continue to cut for the portals, buttresses, and bays of the towers begun in this church.

1. To Nicolas Halins, maker of images, on January 14, paid the sum of £6 *tournois* to be deducted from the sum of £36 *tournois* for which he has contracted with my lords the dean and the elder J. Huyart and me to make 3 statues, that is, Notre Dame of Pity [with] Saint John and the Magdalene on each side according to the dimensions and the order that the master mason of this church gave to him, for this, £6 t.

2. . . . for a beam of 25 feet long that they have sawed on 3 sides for the broken flying buttress . . . 6s. t. *Note:* this was a provisional flyer springing from the masonry of the new towers and leaning against one of the western piers of the nave, C 1 or D 1.

3. Expense to rebuild the flying buttress that was already made and fell, on Saturday after Saint Peter and Paul 1531, through the fault of the masons, who removed the key of the center too quickly, for which reason everything came down, and Colin Millet, one of the said masons, was killed.

4. . . . for 80 carts of sand brought in the 3rd week of the said month of May for the foundations of the 1st free-standing pillar. . . .

5. Expense for the days of masons to continue cutting for the portals, buttresses, and bays of the towers begun in this church.

6. . . . and to begin to demolish the old masonry which is between the new towers of this church and sort the rock and the good stone and to divide it and set it in piles in front of this church. . . .

1531-32 F.A., Arch. Aube, G 1592.

73 v°. A Jehan Bailly, maçon, auquel messrs. le premier jour du mois de mars l'an de ce present compte, cinq cens trente et ung ont ordonné luy paye[r] la somme de seize livres tournois pour ses despens d'un voyage qu'il a faict a Paris et de la a Beauvais pour parler a maistre Pierre Chamiche, l'un des quatre maistre[s] maçons de Paris et a maistre Martin Chambiche, son pere, maistre maçon de Beauvais, pour consulter avec eulx touchant la besongne des tours de ceste eglise et principallement du pillier par voye que l'on veult presentement fonder . . . 16 l. t.

74 r°. A Jehan Gaillard, dict Marcaire, demorant a Vendheuvre, auquel a esté convenu et marchandé par l'ordonnance de messrs. et par l'advis de maistre Pierre Chambiche, l'un des quatre maistre[s] maçons de Paris de faire quatre pieces de bois de chascune de cinquante huict a soixante piedz de longueur ou environ, et d'un pied deux doigtz en quarré ou environ pour faire des estatz ou estansons pour estançonner et mettre lesd. pieces entre le pillier neuf qui est entre le grant portail et le portail sainct Paul audessoubz de l'arc boutant de pierre qui se prant aud. pillier en boutant contre le pignon de la nef de ceste eglise a cause que led. maçon a dict et raporté led. arc boutant n'estre suffisant . . . 23 l. t.

75 r°. A Jehan Roitin, dict du Bois, menusier demorant a Troyes, payé la somme de huict livres six solz huict deniers tournois pour cens pieces de bois de fente a les choisir par le maistre menusier de ceste eglise . . . pour faire les mosles des pilliers . . . 8 l. 6s. 8d.

75 v°. A maistre Pierre Chambiche, l'un des maistres maçons de Paris, que messrs. envoyerent querir tout exprés pour sçavoir de luy et avoir son oppinion sur la fondation des pilliers par voye et pour pourveoir d'un maistre maçon pour conduyre et avoir la charge de la maçonnerie de ceste eglise, actendu que puis nagueres feu Jehan de Damas, dict de Soissons, est allé de vye a trespas . . . 49 l. 10s. t.

102 r°. Despense pour journees de maçons a continuer la taille des portaulx, trumeaulx, pans des tours et fondemens des pilliers parvoye commancees a ceste eglise.

1. To Jehan Bailly, mason, to whom my lords on March 1 the year of this present account, 1531, have ordered to be paid the sum of £16 *tournois* for his expenses for a trip he made to Paris, and from there to Beauvais to talk to Master Pierre Chambiges, one of the 4 master masons of Paris, and to Master Martin Chambiges, his father, master mason of Beauvais, to consult with them on the work on the towers of this church and mainly on the free-standing pier that they want to found soon . . . £16 t.

2. To Jehan Gaillard, called Marcaire, living at Vendeuvre, with whom it has been agreed and contracted on the orders of my lords and on the advice of Master Pierre Chambiges, one of the 4 master masons of Paris, to make 4 pieces of wood, each of approximately 58 to 60 feet long and about 1 foot 2 fingers square, to make props or pillars to prop up and to put the said pieces between the new pillar which is between the great portal and the portal of Saint Paul below the stone flying buttress which leans against the said pillar butting against the gable of the nave of this church, because the said mason said and reported that the said flying buttress was not sufficient . . . £23 t.

3. To Jehan Roitin, called du Bois, joiner, living at Troyes, paid the sum of £8 6s. 8d. *tournois* for 100 pieces of split wood as a selection for the master joiner of this church . . . to make the templates for the pillars . . . £8 6s. 8d.

4. To Master Pierre Chambiges, one of the master masons of Paris, sought by my lords expressly to know from him his opinion on the foundation of the free-standing pillars and to provide a master mason to conduct and have charge of the masonry of this church since recently the late Jehan de Damas known as de Soissons has died . . . £49 10s. t.

5. Expense for the days of masons to continue to cut for the portals, buttresses, and bays of the towers and foundations of the free-standing pillars begun in this church.

Appendix B. Selected Texts Relating to Construction

127 vº. Le dix septme. jour de may messrs. ont
ordonné que Pierre Damas, l'esné et Jehan Bailly,
gendre de feu Jehan de Soissons, maçons, auront
chascun jour ouvrier entier qu'ils besongnerent
en l'atelier des maçons de ceste eglise la somme
de six solz huict deniers tournois. . . .

1532–33 F.A., Arch. Aube, G 1593.
52 vº. A . . . [blank] pour avoir fait ung pourtraict
pour l'ordonnance du grant portail, pource payé
40s. t.

103 rº. Despense pour journees de maçons a
continuer la taille des portaulx, trumeaulx et pans
des tours commancees a ceste eglise.

159 rº. Despense pour charpenterie pour la platte
forme et eschaffaulx pour les voltes de lad. eglise.

178 vº. C'est la despence qui a esté faicte pour
les journees des maçons a continuer de monter les
deux gros pilliers des tours de ceste eglise. . . . A
Jehan Bailly, maistre maçon, pour quattre journees de luy a 6s. 8d. t. par jour, payé 26s. 8d. t.

1533–34 F.A., Arch. Aube, G 1594.
73 rº-vº. A Yvon Bachot, tailleur d'ymages, pour
deux petites hystoires qu'il a faictes pour le grant
portal par marché faict a luy . . . 10 l. t.

87 vº. Despence commune pour les tours et
portaulx de ceste eglise a parfaire les eschaffaulx
et cintres du gros pillier des tours du costé de
monsr. de Troyes.

90 rº-vº. A Jehan Bailly pour avoir du grant
papier renforcy en grant volume pour faire des
mosles payé 4s. t.

151 rº. Despense pour journees de maçons a
continuer la taille des portaulx, trumeaulx et pans
des tours commancees a ceste eglise qui estoit a
la haulteur des retumbees quant je commancey a
exercier cest office, le premier dimenche aprés
la feste de la Magdelene.

1534–35 F.A., Arch. Aube, G 1594.
305 vº. Despense pour journees de maçons a
continuer la taille des portaulx, trumeaulx et pans
des tours commancees a ceste eglise.

6. On May 17, my lords ordered that Pierre
Damas the elder and Jehan Bailly, son-in-law of
the late Jehan de Soissons, masons, shall have the
sum of 6s. 8d. *tournois* for each complete day
that they shall work in the masons workshop.
. . .

1. To . . . [blank] for having made a portrait for
the layout of the great portal, for this paid 40s. t.

2. Expense for days of masons to continue the
cutting for the portals, buttresses, and bays of the
towers begun in this church.

3. Expense for carpentry for the platform and
scaffolding for the vaults of the said church.

4. This is the expense that has been made for
days of masons to continue to put up the 2 big
pillars of the towers of this church. . . . To Jehan
Bailly, master mason, for 4 of his days at 6s. 8d.
t. per day, paid 26s. 8d. t.

1. To Yvon Bachot, carver of images, for 2 little
histories that he made for the great portal
through contract made with him . . . £10 t.

2. General expense for the towers and portals of
this church to finish the scaffolding and centers
of the big pillar of the towers on the side toward
my lord [the bishop] of Troyes.

3. To Jehan Bailly for a large volume of large
[format] reinforced paper to make templates, paid
4s. t.

4. Expense made for masons' days to continue
cutting for the portals, buttresses, and bays of the
towers begun in this church, which were at the
height of the springers when I began to exercise
this office, the first Sunday after the feast of the
Magdalene.

1. Expense for masons' days to continue to cut
for the portals, buttresses, and bays of the towers
begun in this church.

1535–36 F.A., Arch. Aube, G 1595.
79 rº. Despense commune pour les tours et portaulx de ceste eglise.

79 rº. Pour ung voyage faict par moy a Sens avec maistre Jehan Bally et mon serviteur en la derniere sepmainne de febvrier pour visiter les osteaulx et tours neufves de l'eglise dudict Sens pour veoir principallement commant se deduisent les eaues desdiz osteaulx . . . 36s. t.

79 vº. . . . pour avoir livré a plusieurs foys ce pendent qu'on besongnoit a abbatre et redresser l'un des pilliers du cueur de l'eglise, qui fut trouvé malade a l'endroict de la chappelle saincte Marguerite, seize livres de chandelles pour allumer aux maçons en faisant lad. besonge . . .

80 vº. A Estienne Peschat, charpentier, en la derniere sepmainne de juillet que fut la feste de sainct Loup pour cinq journees de luy qu'il a vacqué lad. sepmainne a commancer a faire la plateforme pour asseoir entre les deux gros pilliers du portail de devant ceste eglise . . . 20s. 10d. t.

83 rº. . . . a abbatre premierement les cloches du clocher ou de la tour de bois estant devant le portal de l'eglise et aprés pour abbatre le beuffroy desd. cloches pour le retaller et asseoir sus la muraille neufve devers le pavey pour pandre lesd. cloches . . . 20s. 10d. t.

1536–37 F.A., Arch. Aube, G 1595.
243 rº. A Jehan Bally, maistre maçon de ceste eglise, pour avoir du gros papier pour faire des mosles, a luy payé a deux foys la somme de 8s. 4d. t.

244 rº. A Nicolas le Flament pour avoir faict ung entrepied ou pillier neuf du cueur de ceste eglise ou costé dextre pource payé 40s. t. A luy pour avoir blanchy et reparé les ymages de sainct Jaques et sainct Phelippe des deux pilliers neufz du cueur de ceste eglise a luy payé 25 s. t. A Michel Thays, paintre, pour avoir repainct les visages desd. deux ymages et pour le sainct Denis du portal de devant a luy payé pour tout 10s. t.

1. General expense for the towers and portals of this church.

2. For a trip made by me to Sens with Master Jehan Bailly and my servant in the last week of February to visit the windows and the new towers of the said church of Sens to see mainly how the water runs off the said windows . . . 36s. t.

3. . . . for having delivered on several occasions 16 pounds of candles during the work of demolishing and re-erecting one of the pillars of the choir of the church near the chapel of Saint Marguerite, which was found to be sick, in order to illuminate the masons as they did the said work. . . .

4. To Estienne Peschat, carpenter, in the last week of July, the feast of Saint Loup, for 5 of his days he spent the said week to begin to make the platform to set between the 2 big pillars of the portal in front of this church . . . 20s. 10d. t.

5. . . . first to take down the bells of the bell tower or tower of wood in front of the portal of the church and afterwards to take down the belfrey of the said bells to recut it and set it on the new wall toward the road in order to hang the bells . . . 20s. 10d. t.

1. To Jehan Bailly, master mason of this church, for having large [format] paper to make the templates, paid to him on 2 occasions the sum of 8s. 4d. t.

2. To Nicolas le Flamand for having made a pedestal in the new pillar in the choir of this church on the right side, for this paid 40s. t. To him for having whitened and repaired the statues of Saint James and Saint Philip on the 2 new pillars of the choir of this church, paid to him 25s. t. To Michel Thays, painter, for having repainted the faces of the said 2 statues and for the Saint Denis of the front portal, paid to him for everything 10s. t.

245 rº. . . . pour continuer a taller la plateforme pour le pillier qui fault copper devant la chappelle saincte Marguerite et pour commancer a taller lad. grue pour la tour devers le pavey . . . 4 l. t.

296 vº. Despense pour journees de maçons a continuer la talle des portaulx, trumeaulx et pans des tours commancees a ceste eglise.

1537–38 F.A., Arch. Aube, G 1596.
62 vº. A Estienne Peschat pour la façon des sainctres de la fenestre de la tour du costé de la rue qui regarde sur le cloistre payé 8 s. t.

62 vº. A luy pour cinq cintres pour les grandes fenestres de lad. tour du costé de Sainct Loup, 7s. t.

1538–39 F.A., Arch. Aube, G 1596.
340 rº. Despence pour journees de maçons a continuer la taille des portaulx, trumeaux et pans des tours commencees en ceste eglise.

1539–40: *lacuna.*

1540–41 F.A., Arch. Aube, G 1597.
26 vº. Payé pour vingt troys journees de louaige d'un cheval a 5s. t. chascun jour pour le maistre qui alloit a Paris avec monsr. pour consulter et communicquer a maistre Pierre Cambiche l'affaire des tours de l'eglise . . . 9 l. 15s. t.

51 rº. Despense pour journees de maçons a continuer la taille des portaulx, trumeaulx et pans des tours commancez en ceste eglise.

1541–42 F.A., Arch. Aube, G 1597.
112 rº. Despence pour journees de maçons a continuer la taille des portaulx, trumeaulx et pans des tours commancez en ceste eglise.

1542–43 F.A., Arch. Aube, G 1597.
355 vº-356 rº. Le 15e. septembre aprés avoir presenté a messrs. en leur chappitre la devise du boys qu'il failloit pour rehaulser le grand eschaffault d'entre les deux tours pour monter l'engin, me fut ordonné acheter led. boys et convenir avec marchans et faire le proffict de l'eglise.

3. . . . to continue to cut the platform for the pillar which it has been necessary to cut in front of the chapel of Saint Marguerite and to begin to cut the said crane for the tower toward the road . . . £4 t.

4. Expense for the masons' days to continue to cut for the portals, buttresses, and bays of the towers begun in this church.

1. To Estienne Peschat for making the centers of the window of the tower toward the road which looks out over the cloister, paid, 8s. t.

2. To him for 5 centers for the great windows of the said tower on the side toward [the abbey of] Saint-Loup, 7s. t.

1. Expense for the days of masons to continue cutting for the portals, buttresses, and bays of the towers begun in this church.

1. Paid for the rent for a horse for 23 days at 5s. t. per day for the master [Jehan Bailly] who went to Paris with my lord to consult and communicate with Master Pierre Chambiges [on] the matter of the towers of the church . . . £9 15s. t.

2. Expense for days of masons to continue cutting for the portals, buttresses, and bays of the towers begun in this church.

1. Expense for days of masons to continue cutting for the portals, buttresses, and bays of the towers begun in this church.

1. On September 15, after having presented to my lords in their chapter the bill for the wood necessary to heighten the great scaffold between the 2 towers to mount the engine, I was ordered to purchase the wood and to contract with merchants to the profit of the church.

196

379 v°. Despense pour journees de maçons a continuer la taille des portaulx, trumeaulx et pans des tours commancez en ceste eglise.

1543–44 F.A., Arch. Aube, G 1598.

1544–45 F.A., Arch. Aube, G 1598.
239 v°. Le neufiesme fevrier cinq cens quarante quatre pour ung voyage faict au lieu de Tonnerre par me. Jehan Bailly, me. maçon de ceste eglise et messire Edmon Colleçon, prestre, pour bailler les protraictz et visiter lesd. perrieres affin d'avoir pierres propres pour les grands doubleaux et cintre du portal de ceste eglise . . . 4 l. 18s. 8d.

246 r°. A Guillaume Baretel pour dix grans perches de tramble pour eschaffaulder a l'entour des cintres des doubleaux et aulteau de ceste eglise . . . 20s.

1545–46 F.A., Arch. Aube, G 1599.
25 r°. A maistre Jehan Bailly, me. maçon de ceste eglise, pour ung voyaige faict a la perriere le 6e. d'aoust avec Claude Damas pour faire amener les grandz pierres de l'auteau de ceste eglise . . . 7 l. 2s. 8d.

40 r°. A Henry Preudhomme, charpantier, pour deux jours de la 3e. sepmaine de septembre en l'an de ce compte qu'il a esté a oster les cintres du grand doubleau et de l'auteau payé pour chacun jour six solz tournois cy, 12s. t.

40 r°. A Estienne Pechat, charpantier demorant a Troyes, pour avoir transporté le beuffroy de ceste eglise, avec les cloches estant prés de l'une des tours de ceste eglise du costé de la grand rue sur l'autre tour du costé de la maison de l'evesché . . . 60 l. t.

41 r°. En la 4e. sepmaine de janvier commencent le 25e. du moys n'y a eu que cinq jours pour le Conversion sainct Paul, et en icelle a commancé ledit Pechat a faire les cintres de la grand croisee des voltes prés la cloison de bois.

2. Expense for the days of masons to continue to cut for the portals, buttresses, and bays of the towers begun in this church.

Note: work continues on the towers.

1. On February 9, 1544, for a trip made to Tonnerre by Master Jehan Bailly, master mason of this church, and by my lord Edmon Colleçon, priest, to bring the portraits and to visit the said quarries in order to have proper stones for the great transverse arch [over the west rose] and center of the portal of this church . . . £4 18s. 8d.

2. To Guillaume Baretel for 10 great planks of aspen for scaffolding around the centers of the arch and the window of this church . . . 20s.

1. To Master Jehan Bailly, master mason of this church, for a trip made to the quarry on August 6 with Claude Damas to fetch the great stones of the window [west rose] of this church . . . £7 2s. 8d.

2. To Henry Preudhomme, carpenter, for 2 days in the 3rd week of September in the year of this account that he spent to remove the centers of the great arch and the [rose] window, paid for each day 6s. *tournois*, for this, 12s. t.

3. To Estienne Peschat, carpenter, living in Troyes, for having moved the belfrey of this church with the bells from near one of the towers of this church toward the great road to the top of the other tower toward the bishop's palace . . . £60 t.

4. In the 4th week of January beginning on the 25th of the month there were only 5 [working] days because of the [feast] of the Conversion of Saint Paul, and in this [week] the said Peschat began to make the centers of the great crossing of vaults near the wooden screen [the westernmost vault of the central vessel]. . . .

Appendix B. Selected Texts Relating to Construction

71 v°. Despense pour la taille desd. pendans. Le 17e. de juillet 1546 a Jehan des Noes, maçon, pour la taille de huit cens ung quarteron de pendans, au pris de trois solz le cent, payé 25s. 2d. t.

1546–47 F.A., Arch. Aube, G 1599.
183 v°. Item le derrenier jour d'avril 1547, payé a Jehan des Portes, charretier, pour deux cens quatre vingts deux voictures de terre estans soubz le portal de ceste eglise, au pris de quatre deniers la voicture la somme de 4 l. 14s.

190 r°. Despence pour charpenterye. En la 4e. et derreniere sepmaine de juillet commancent le 26e. du moys, en la quelle n'y a heu que cinq jours pour la feste sainct Loup, et en icelle ont beisongné les charpentiers par quatre jours pour continuer les cintres des voltes du grand portal de ceste eglise.

191 r°. En la 4e. sepmaine de janvier 1546, en laquelle n'y a heu que quatre jours pour les festes de sainct Savinian et Conversion sainct Paul, et en icelle on a commencé a mettre bas les escharfolz et cintres estant soubz les haultes voltes du grand portal.

222 v°. Despence pour painctrerye. A Michel Thays, painctre demorant a Troyes, pour avoir painct dix clefz et icelles doreez d'or fin de la volte du grand portal de ceste eglise, ensemble les ogives et philatieres joingnantes ausdictes clefz, et pour ung protaict faict pour la verriere de l'auteu prés de ladite volte, payé la somme de vingt huict livres tournois, comme appert par les quictances dudit Thays, cy 28 l.

1547–48 F.A., Arch. Aube, G 1600.

1548–49 F.A., Arch. Aube, G 1600.

5. Expense for the cutting of the said vault stones [i.e., for the severies of the western vault]. On July 17, 1546, to Jehan des Noës, mason, for the cutting of 825 vault stones at the price of 3s. the hundred, paid 25s. 2d. t.

1. Item, on the last day of April, 1547, paid to Jehan des Portes, carter, for 282 carts of earth [delivered] below the portal of this church, at the price of 4d. per cart the sum of £4 14s. [the earth probably intended for use in the center of the last vault].

2. Expense for carpentry. In the 4th and last week of July, beginning on the 26th of the month, in which there were only 5 [working] days because of the feast of Saint Loup and in which the carpenters worked for 4 days to continue the centers of the vaults of the great portal of this church.

3. In the 4th week of January 1546 in which there were only 4 [working] days because of the feasts of Saint Savinien and the Conversion of Saint Paul, and in the same week they began to take down the scaffolding and centers below the high vaults of the great portal.

4. Expense for painting. To Michel Thays, painter, living in Troyes, for having painted 10 keystones of the vault of the great portal of this church and gilded them with fine gold together with the ribs and scrolls around the keystones, and for a portrait made for the glazing of the window near the said vault, paid the sum of £28 *tournois*, as appears in the quittances of the said Thays, for this, £28.

Note: work continues on the upper façade.

Same.

Appendix C
Analyses of the Workshop and Revenues

1. Masons' Workshops at Troyes Cathedral

The compilation of the accompanying six charts (Tables C-1–C-6) was made possible thanks to the unusually detailed recording system used by the *proviseurs* of the fabric of Troyes Cathedral. These *proviseurs* kept weekly wage sheets for all artisans employed in the workshop, as well as careful quittances for payments made to an artisan as the result of a contract. At the end of the year these wage sheets would be incorporated into a rough *manuel* (several of which survive) and the *manuel* itself would be tidied up and redrafted in the form of the fabric account. The fabric account was a carefully presented record, which had to bear the scrutiny of auditors. The accounting year, as can be seen in the accompanying charts, normally began at the feast of the Madeleine in late July, and ran for a whole year. If the *proviseur* rendering the account were to die, the account would be terminated and a new account begun by his successor.

In compiling the labor charts I have listed the artisans' names in the order in which they appear in the document: I have not rearranged them to reflect my own interpretation of the hierarchy of the workshop. Such a hierarchy is detectable through the salary scale. The salaries transcribed are the summer salaries, which were reduced through the winter months (though the master mason was generally exempt from such a reduction).

The total number of names listed for a particular year obviously does not necessarily express the size of the workshop: thus we find twenty two artisans listed for 1462–63, but many of them only made one appearance in the workshop. The intensity of work is reflected in man-days worked, and we see that 1494–95 saw the heaviest year's work of any of the years analyzed. The explanation for this heavy year's work was not financial confidence: on the contrary, the last decade of the fifteenth century was generally a bad period for the fabric. The explanation is rather to be found in the nature of the work in hand, on the southern flying buttresses of the nave. The decision was made in July 1494 to complete all of the flyers before starting to vault the central vessel, and some urgency was obviously felt.

Our charts reveal that during certain periods of construction, the masons' workshop was dominated by a team, such as Jehan Thierry, Michelin de Jonchery, and Michelin Hardiot (1366–67) or Henry de Bruisselles and Henry Soudan (1384–85). Such a team of masters, accompanied by their apprentices, was capable of providing the nucleus of the workshop. During other periods, however, this situation did not exist; for example, Jehançon Garnache came into the workshop as an individual, without bringing partners.

The master mason(s) at the head of the workshop were normally the only masons to enjoy the security of a contract. Such contracts are transcribed in Appendix B under the years 1365, 1366, and 1382–83. The terms of the contract would generally guarantee a fixed daily wage (sometimes reduced in winter months), the payment of a certain sum of money each year for a robe, the tenure of a house, and limited security of employment. In return, the master masons bound themselves to work diligently for a fixed number of hours per day, not to accept employment elsewhere without permission of the bishop and chapter, and (generally) to accept financial responsibility for any problems that might result from defective work.

The texts reveal that a variety of different titles were applied to a mason holding such a contract, including *magister fabrice* (1294), *masson de l'euvre* (1365), *maistre maçon* (1396–97), *maçon de l'eglise et maistre des maçons d'icelle et de l'ouvraige* (1462–63), and *maistre maçon de l'eglise* (1485–86).

When art historians employ the term "workshop" they tend to slip into the habit of thinking of a unified group of masons working under the direction of a powerful master mason who was able to provide leadership as far as structural and artistic decisions were concerned as well as decisions of a more administrative nature involving the overall planning of the work (what to build next), recruitment of new masons, and similar questions. A few such powerful master masons are found in the history of the construction of Troyes Cathedral, for example Martin Chambiges, who controlled all aspects of construction. Henry de Bruisselles was also such a powerful leader; an important text from the period of the latter master reveals that he was able to command the allegiance of the other artisans as a group: in 1392–93 we find that Henry has quit Troyes for Auxerre and he has taken with him "les autres ouvriers de la loge."

The word *loge* is used in a physical sense (it was located for much of the construction period in the area of the *gros clocher* at the west end of the nave). I have found no evidence for the political concept of the lodge as a self-governing entity. No references are ever made in the accounts to masons' guilds or any equivalent organization. The word "workshop" (*atelier*) is only found once in the texts transcribed in Appendix B (1531–32, 6). It is clear that on several occasions, however, the masons as a group were allowed to express their opinions on major problems of structure or style—for example, the decision over the priority of flyers or vaults. For considerable amounts of time, however, no powerful master masons commanded the builders of Troyes Cathedral, and the direction of the work must have lain in the hands of the clergy—in fact with the two canons designated as *proviseurs*. In this respect, it is important to note that these *proviseurs* were sometimes designated *maistre de l'euvre* (1382–83 and 1455). During certain periods a formally designated *maistre maçon de l'eglise* simply did not exist. This is true, for example, during the early 1450s, when work was resumed on the completion of the nave. Similarly, if major efforts were being concentrated upon carpentry work the overall direction would obviously be assumed by a master carpenter, for example Jehan de Nantes who supervised the construction of the crossing tower between 1410 and 1418.

Despite these reservations concerning the preconceptions that often accompany the use of the word "workshop" the term remains a useful one, and is employed here to express the idea of "les . . . ouvriers de le loge" (1392–93). The hierarchy implicit in the workshop was expressed primarily by salaries, and the accompanying charts suggest that a broadly tripartite structure existed. At the top were the master masons who enjoyed a contract with the bishop and chapter. Then came a second level of masons who earned somewhat less; for example, if the master earned 4s. 2d. *per diem* the second-rank masons would earn 3s. 4d. (1462–63). In one instance these second-rank masons had their own contract (1366, Jehan Thierry, Michelin de Jonchery, and Michelin Hardiot). The charts reveal considerable comings and goings on the part of these second-rank masons. Masons at this level would often serve as master mason in one of the parish churches of Troyes, as did Gerard Fauchot (Saint-Nicholas), Jehan Bailly (Saint-Pantaléon and Saint-Jean), and Jehan Gailde (La Madeleine). Then at the bottom of the heap came the unskilled laborers who were employed on an *ad hoc* basis as the occasion demanded for digging foundations and similar tasks. The wages of the latter group were subject to considerable fluctuation.

It would be possible to compile labor charts for every year in which a masons' workshop was in existence. A major interest in such a sequence of consecutive charts would be to watch the movements of individual masons up the hierarchy. Thus, by comparing the charts for 1470–71 and 1494–95, we can see that several names continue through this twenty-four-year period. Interestingly, however, I have found no examples of a case where a young mason worked his way up through the ranks to become master of the workshop. Masters were generally imported from elsewhere, Brussels, Paris, and especially Reims (Bleuet, Colas, Garnache) being the major centers drawn upon.

Appendix C. Analyses of the Workshop and Revenues

Were the great Gothic cathedrals of Chartres, Reims, and Amiens constructed by groups of artisans organized in a similar fashion? These earlier projects were almost certainly financed from the regular funds of the clergy, and the more copious flow of cash would be expressed in the presence of much larger groups of artisans. Troyes Cathedral took 350 years to construct, Chartres and Amiens only thirty to fifty years. On the other hand, the flexibility of the "workshops" of Troyes Cathedral may well have existed in an earlier era. In other words, rather than a tightly unified group of masons, under the leadership of a powerful master, it is probable that a thirteenth century "workshop" would have been a more loosely organized affair, with the clergy (the *proviseurs*) providing the main administrative framework, negotiating the contracts with the master masons, and hiring the other artisans on an *ad hoc* basis. I believe that the key decisions of a structural and stylistic nature that lay behind the evolution of Gothic architecture were taken in a context that involved an on-going dialogue between the leading master masons and their clerical patrons. These leading master masons probably enjoyed a status comparable with that of Henry de Bruisselles and Martin Chambiges at Troyes.

TABLE C-1.
1339–40: Work on Upper Transept and Eastern Bays of Nave

Days per week worked

#	Artisan	Daily Wage	JULY	AUG	SEPT	OCT	NOV	DEC	JAN	FEB	MAY	JUNE
1	Jacobus, lathomus	2s.	5	6 5 5	6 5 5	6 4 5 5	5 5 4 5	4 6 5	5 5 3 5	5 6 6	6 5 3 5 2 6	6 5 6 2 5 5 5
2	Johannes Niger, lathomus	2s.	5	6 2 2	6 4 6	4 5 4 2	3 4 6 5	5 5 3	4 6 4 6	6 6 5	6 6 3 5 2 6	2 6 4 5 5 5
3	Colinetus	1s. 8d.	5	6 5 5	5 3 6	5 3 5 5	2 3 5 6	4 5 4	3 5 3 5	6 6 6	6 6 2 3 5 6	2 6 4 5 5 5
4	Perinus Niger	1s. 6d.	5	6 5 5	6 5 6	5 2 5 5	5 5 4 6	4 6 4	6 5 3 5	6 6 6	6 6 5 5 5 2	5 6 4 5 5 5
5	Perinus Parvus	7d.	5	6 5 5	6 5 6	5 6 5 5	5 5 4 6	5 5 4	6 5 3 5	6 6 6	6 6 5 5 5 2	6 6 4 5 5 5
6	Dictus le Bergoingnat	10d.	5	6 5 5	6 5 6	5 6 5 5	4 5 4 5	6 5 5	4 6 4 6	6 6 6	6 6 5 6 3 5 2	5 6 4 5 5 5
7	Dictus Parigot, op. man.	1s. 1d.			4 6			5 4 6 4	5 5 3 5			
8	Guidimus, op. man.	1s.			2							
9	Dictus le Rousselant	10d.			3 5 5 5	5 6 5 5 4						
10	Dictus Vinant	10d.				4 1	4					
11	Jonannes de Dieneyo, lathomus	2s.				2 5 5 4	5 6 5	4 5 4 5	3 5 3 5	6 6 4 6	6 6 5 3 5 2 3 6 5 6	
12	Oudinus operarius	1s.				5 5 5	5					2 5 1 5
13	Henricus, lathomus	2s.				5 5 1	5 5 1					
14	Dictus le Borne, operarius	10d.					5 6 1	5 6 1				
15	Dictus Paleiz, lathomus	10d.							2 5 5 3	5 6 6 4	6 6 5 6 1 5 3 5 2 6	6 5 4 5 5 5
16	Michaelus le Mercerat, operarius	10d.									4	
17	Guillelmus le Henapier, operarius	10d.									4	
18	Dictus le Quiat	10d.									4	
19	Dictus Marcheant, operarius	1s.									2 5 1	
20	Johannes de Regiis, operarius	10d.									6	

203

TABLE C-2.

1366–67: Rebuilding Faulty Flyer of Choir; Work on New Nave Flyer, Division 4

Artisan	Daily Wage	JULY AUG	SEPT	OCT	NOV	DEC	JAN	FEB	MAR	APR	MAY	JUNE	JULY	
1 Johannes Thierrici	4s.	4 5 4 6	4 5 5	5 5 5 5	6 5 5	5 5 6 3	4 5 4 5	5 4 5	4 6 6	5 5	5 2 6	2 6 3 5	5 5 6 6 3	1
2 Michaelus de Joncheri	4s.	4 5 2 6	3 6 5 5	2 5 5	6 5 5	5 5 6 3	4 5 5 5	5 5 5	6 6 3	5 5	3 5 2 6	6 5 6 3 3	3 6 6 3	2
3 Michaelus Hardiot	4s.	4 5 4 6	3 6 5 5	4 5 5 5	6 5 5	5 5 6 3	4 5 5 5	5 5 5	6 4 6 6		1 3 5 2 6	2 6 3 5	5 6 6 3	3
4 Guiotus Maupronne operarius brachiorum	2s. 6d.	4 5 4 6	4 5	5 5 6 6 5 6 1								5		4
5 Petrus Ruffus op. brach.	2s.		4 5 6	5 5 6 6 5 5										5
6 Petrus de Lecherellis op. brach.	2s.		2 6					2 1						6
7 Stephanus de Billeta op. brach.	1s. 6d.									2				7
8 Oudinetus le Borne op. brach.	1s. 6d.											3		8
9 Johannes de Hugonis op. brach.	2s.												5 6 6 5	9

Notes

1. The three leading masons are working very much as a team. They maintain a daily wage of 4 sous throughout the year. Other wages are decreased in the winter, 2s. 6d. to 2s.; 2s. to 1s. 10d. or 1s. 6d.
2. From August 1366 to November 1366, the work is concentrated on a flyer against the choir.
3. In October 1366, work began on a *grossum pilerium* near the *grenier*, i.e., chapel S 3 of the nave.
4. In July 1367, work began on laying the stones for this *grossum pilerium*, doubtless a flying buttress upright. This explains the appearance of extra laborers in this month.

TABLE C-3.

1384–85: Work on the Choir Screen

Artisan	Daily Wage	JULY	AUG	SEPT	OCT	NOV	DEC	JAN	FEB	MAR	APR	MAY	JUNE	JULY
1 Henry Soudan	25s. week	*	* * * *	* * * *	* * * * *	* * * *	* * * *	* * * * *	* * * *	5 * * * *	* * * *	* * * * *	* * * *	* * * 5
2 Henry de Bruisselles	25s. week	*	* * * *	* * * *	* * * 2 1	2 * * *	* * * *	* * * * *	* * * *	5 * * * *	* * * *	* * * * *	* * * *	* * * 5
3 Marmet, vallet de H.S.	2s. 1d.	4	4 5 5	5 5 4 5	6 6 5	5 4 5	5 4 6 5	3 5 5	6 6 4	6 6 6	5 5 3 6	6 6 5 2 5	6 3 5 6	6 5 6 6 6 5
4 Colin, vallet de H. de B.	2s. 1d.	4	4 5 5	5 5 4 5	6 6 2 1 5	5 4 5	5 4 6 5	3 5 5	6 6 4	6 6 6	5 5 3 6	6 6 5 2 5	6 3 5 6	6 5 6 6 6 5
5 Jaquot Mignart, maçon	2s. 11d.	3	3 5 5	5 5 4 5	6 6 6 5	5 4 5	5 4 6 5	3 5 5	6 6 3	6 6 6	5 5 3 6	6 6 5 2 5	6 3 5 6	6 5 5 6 6 5
6 Conrot de Strambourc	4s. 2d.		3 5	3 5										
7 Anchier Daubruissel	2s. 1d.					1				3	3		6 3 5 6	6 5 6 6 6 6
8 Jehan de Couloigne, maçon	3s. 9d.						2 4 6	3 5 5	4 4 6	6 6 6	5 5 3 6	6 6 5 2 5	6 3 5 6	6 5 6 6 6 5
9 Jehan de Bruisselles, maçon	1s. 8d.						2 4 6	3 5 5	4 4 6	6 6 6	5 5 3 6	6 6 5 2 5	6 3 5 6	6 5 6 6 6 5
10 Jehan de Rameru, maçon	1s. 8d.						2 4 6	3 5 5	4 4 5 6 6					
11 Pierre Barbe, maçon	1s. 8d.						4							
12 Henry de Mez, maçon	2s. 1d.							5 5 4 4 5	6					
13 Henry de Mont en Allemanie	2s. 6d.									3				
14 Girardin de Mont en All.	2s. 6d.									3				
15 Jehan de Provins	5s.										2			
16 Jehan Fierabras	3s. 4d.										2			
17 Thevenin	3s. 4d.										2			
18 Jehan Verrouillot, ouvrier	1s. 8d.										2			
19 Jehan de Denemoine	1s. 8d.												6	

Notes

1. Henry Soudan and Henry de Bruisselles are paid 25 sous per week of 6 working days.
2. Other wages are subject to variations, for example Jehan de Couloigne, from 2s. 1d. to 3s. 9d.
3. Until April 1385 all the work is on stone-cutting.
4. In April 1385, the old jubé is torn down and the new foundations are dug. 15 laborers are hired in addition to the workshop shown above.
5. The artisans follow a fairly fixed rhythm in terms of the number of days per week worked.
6. Note the influx of Netherlandish and German artisans.
7. Conrot de Strambourc is a *tailleur d'images*.

TABLE C-4.

1462–63: Work on Vaults of Southern Aisle, Bay 2–3; a Great Pier at the Northwest End of the Nave; and the North Transept Portal

Artisan	Daily Wage	JULY AUG	SEPT	OCT	NOV	DEC	JAN	FEB	MAR	APR	MAY	JUNE	JULY	#
1 Anthoine Colas	4s. 2d.	5 5 5 5	4 5 6 5	4 5 5 5	4 5 5 5	4 6 6 5	4 3 5 5	6 6 4 5	6 6 6 5	5 5 5 6	2 6 5	4 4 5 5	6 6 5	1
2 Jaquet de la Bouticle	3s. 4d.	5 5 5 5		5 6 5 5	4 5 5 5	4 6 4 6	4 3 5 5	6 6 4 5	6 6 6 5	5 5 5 5	2 6 5	4 6 4 4	4 6 5	2
3 Alexandre Magot de Dijon	3s. 4d.	5	6 5 6 5	3 5 5 5	5 5 5 5	4 6 6 5	4 3 5 5	6 6 6 4	6 6 6 5	5 5 5 5	2 6 5	4 4 5 5	6 6 5	3
4 Gilet Louot (apprentice of Colas)	3s. 4d.	5 5	5 6 5 4	5 5 5 5	4 5 5 5	4 6 6 5	4 3 5 5	6 6 6 4	6 6 6 5	5 5 5 5	2 6 5	4 4 6 5	6 6 5	4
5 Pieret de S-Quentin	3s. 4d.	5 5	4 6 5 6	5 5 5 5	4 5 6									5
6 Nicolas Platot serviteur des maçons	2s. 6d.	5 4	5 5 6	5 5 6 4 5 4 3										6
7 Henry Tetel	2s. 6d.	5 4	5 4 1											7
8 Jehan de Channite	2s. 6d.	6 5	6 5 6 5 4 5 5 5 6 1											8
9 Jehan de Monstier, maçon	3s. 9d.		4											9
10 Jehan Jaqueton son manouvrier	2s. 6d.		4											10
11 Nicolas Bonne Chiere	2s. 1d.		4											11
12 Jehan Thiebault manouvrier	2s. 1d.		4											12
13 Simon Maistre Apart	2s. 1d.		4											13
14 Estienne Hundelot	2s. 1d.		5											14
15 Colin Colart	1s. 8d.			1 1										15
16 Thevenin Drouart	2s. 6d.			1 1										16
17 Tassin Jaquart														17
18 Thevenin le Menestrier					2									18
19 Jehan Martiau	3s. 4d.										2 6 5	4 6 5 5	5 6 6 5	19
20 Jehan Mathieu	3s. 4d.										2 4 5	4 6 4 4 5	5 1 3	20
21 Jaquet le Pointre														21
22 Coleçon de Chaslons	3s. 4d.												5 6 6 5	22

Notes

1. Anthoine Colas, unlike the other masons, receives the same wage winter and summer.

2. There is great diversity in the work under progress. It includes cutting stone for a great pier at the N.W. end of the nave; the reinforcement of the N. transept portal; the cutting of the ribs for the southern aisle vaults in bay 2–3; the masoning of the arches of these vaults; and the carving of capital and keystone.

3. After September 1462 Colas concentrates on the portal. Jaquet de la Bouticle sometimes is found assisting Colas, but sometimes leads a group of masons at work on the interior vaults and pier.

4. Pieret de S-Quentin, Nicolas Platot, and Henry Tetel were not employed through the winter, and when the workshop was enlarged again after the winter, their places were taken by Jehan Martiau and Jehan Mathieu. These two masons, and Colleçon de Chaslons, found a regular place in the workshop in the following year, 1463–64.

5. Lower echelon masons do not have a fixed salary. Informal agreements must have existed for each job: for example, in the 3rd week of October Nicolas Platot worked with Colin Colart and Thevenin Drouart to cart stones from Tonnerre. Although Platot had previously earned 2s. 6d. and 2s. 1d., he was reduced to the same wage as his companions, 1s. 8d.

6. Jaquet de la Bouticle's wage fell from 3s. 4d. to 2s. 11d. in November and returned to its original level in February. Gilet Louet's wage went from 3s. 4d. to 2s. 6d.

TABLE C-5.
1470–71: Work on Western Aisle Vaults and Upper Nave

Days per week worked

#	Artisan	Daily Wage	JULY	AUG	SEPT	OCT	NOV	DEC	JAN	FEB	MAR	APR	MAY	JUNE
1	Anthoine Colas	4s. 2d.	4	5 5 5	2 3 5	4 6 4 4	3 4 6 5	5 5 4 6	5 2 5 5	2 6 5 4	4 6 6	3 5 5	4 5 3	2 4 3
2	Pierre Roucelot	2s. 11d.	1	3 5 5	3 4	5 5 5	3 5 6 6	5						
3	Colleçon Fauchot de Chaalons	2s. 6d.	4	5 5 5	5 5 5	5 6 4 5	2 3 5 1	6 5 4 6	5 6 3 5	6 5 5 5	6 6 6	4 5 5	4 3 2 3	3 6 3 2
4	Jaquet de la Bouticle	2s. 11d.	1		4 5	4 6 3 5	6 2 2 3 6	1 5 6 3	5 4 5	6 4	1 4 4 1	4 3 4	2 4 1 2	
5	Jehan Thevenot	2s. 1d.	5	5 3	5 2 4 5 5						3 5	3 5 3	3 4 2 2	4 6 3 1 2
6	Henry Tetel	2s. 1d.		2	5 2 3 4 4		6 3			3 5		4 5 5	5 4 3 4 2 1	3 5 3 1
7	Gauthier Oudin	2s. 1d.		4	4 5 2 4 5 5	4 5 1								
8	Jehan le Fevre	2s. 11d.		1 2	4 5 1	1 5 6 3 5	4 6 4 4 6 5		2 5 4 5 3	5 6 5 4 5 6 6 6	6	4 5 5 5 4 5	3 4	2 4 4
9	Petit Pierre dit Gille	2s. 11d.			2 5 6 5 5	5 6 5 5 6 4	3 6 4							
10	Lambert Peletier	1s. 8d.				2	2 3 6 3					5 4 4		
11	Jaquinot Colart	1s. 8d.					1							
12	Gilet Lomme manouvrier	1s. 8d.									2			

Notes

1. All masons with the exception of Colas take a reduction in their wage during winter.
2. This is the last year for which receipt from the general pardon is recorded.
3. The work undertaken is again disparate, including the completion of the vaults of the inner aisles at the west end of the nave, and the commencement of work on the upper nave.
4. Some of the masons helping Colas had long careers in the cathedral workshop, especially Jaquet de la Bouticle and Colleçon de Chalons, also known as Colleçon Faulchot. His son Gerard also worked in the cathedral workshop in the late fifteenth century and was later to become master mason at the city church of Saint-Nicholas.

TABLE C-6.

1494–95: Work on Western Flyers of the Nave

#	Artisan	Daily Wage
1	Jehancon Garnache	4s. 2d.
2	Jaquet de la Bouticle	3s. 4d.
3	Denis Michel	3s. 4d.
4	Jehan le Semer	3s. 4d.
5	Guillaume Berthel	3s. 4d.
6	Regnault Perchet	3s. 4d.
7	Colas Aman	3s. 4d.
8	Philippe Colombe apprantis	2s. 6d.
9	Edmond Huguenot manouvrier	2s. 1d.
10	Thomas Girard manouv.	2s. 1d.
11	Jehan Nandot	3s. 4d.
12	Nicolas Savetier	3s. 4d.
13	Colleçon Faulchot	3s. 4d.
14	Martin des Molins	3s. 4d.
15	Pierre Gobin	3s. 4d.
16	Gerard Faulchot apprentis	2s. 1d.

Days per week worked — recorded by week across the months MAY, JUNE, JULY, AUG, SEPT, OCT, NOV, DEC, JAN, FEB, MAR, APR, MAY, JUNE, JULY (1494–1495).

Notes

1. This is a very large workshop in a year where expenses are only just covered by receipts. Even Garnache, master of the workshop, takes a salary cut in the winter (November–February).
2. Work undertaken concentrates upon flyer D E F 2 until July.
3. In July, the meeting takes place to determine whether to install the vault of the first bay.
4. It is decided to continue with the flyers. Between July 1494 and the end of the account work is on the three eastern flyers of the nave, on the south side.
5. It is possible that Jehan le Semer and Jehan Nandot are one and the same artisan. Jaquet de la Bouticle and Colleçon Faulchot have now been in the workshop for over 20 years.

2. Analysis of the Revenue of the Fabric

We present here two kinds of tabulation of the data from the income side of the fabric account. Firstly, the gross figures from the income and expense side of the account have been compiled in the form of a graph (see Fig. C-1). This shows the fluctuations of receipt and expense; the periods during which the expense exceeded the receipt (notably when the upper nave was under construction in the late fifteenth century); the inflationary movement of the late fifteenth century, and the prodigious cost of the west façade.

The detailed breakdown of the different sources of revenue (Figs. C-2–C-5) allows us to study the changing relationship between the various items of income (see conclusions given in each chapter). As far as possible, the totals given for each item of receipt have been transcribed directly into the chart in the order in which they are presented in the original. Some liberties have been taken in transcribing the figures for the sake of simplicity. All sums of money have been reduced to the nearest pound. Some of the entries in the original account have been run together, and some items have been detached from the section in which they were incorporated in order to express them separately. The following explanations will help define each item of income listed in the charts, and the extent to which the material has been simplified.

From the Previous Year. If income exceeded expense in any given year, the *proviseur* carried over the surplus into the following year as the first item of income. Sometimes details are given about money carried over from several previous years: when this happens I have added all the figures together into one total.

From the Present Year, sometimes rendered as *Ordinary Receipt.* Money from houses and other property belonging to the chapter and rented for the profit of the fabric. In the late fifteenth century a number of small houses were constructed by the fabric along the north side of the cathedral (the "logettes"). The rent from these new houses is expressed as a separate item in the fabric accounts: in our charts it has been added to the total from other rented property.

Quests in the Diocese of Troyes. This item is sometimes rendered as *Synod Boxes* in the fabric account, since the boxes used for collecting this money were opened on synod day. The income from this source constitutes one of the most important items of yearly revenue.

Quests Outside the Diocese. The office of quester for the fabric was farmed out to a layman at fixed rent. The geographical extent of the quests was wide, including Vienna, Chartres, Rome, and Jerusalem.

Revenue from the Relics (apport des reliques). The relics owned by the cathedral of Troyes included numerous sainted bishops of the diocese and several pieces of more universal interest, notably the relic of Saint Helen of Athyra (see articles by Geary and Constable listed in the Bibliography).

From the Relic Collecting Boxes (de l'escrin des reliques). This clearly implies money deposited into fixed collecting boxes placed in the proximity of relics on display. Collecting boxes were also placed in the nave and the choir, but these latter boxes did not account for much of the income.

From the Churches of Troyes. The collecting boxes placed in the city churches yielded, for the most part, a pitifully small income.

Anniversaries. Payments made for the annual remembrance of the donor in the form of prayers or a mass. Payments in cash and in kind (grain) are listed separately in the fabric accounts: here the two sums have been added to form a single total. The payments were derived from an initial gift of rents made by a pious donor on the condition that he or she should be remembered each year. Normally the income was administered by the Great Chamber and handed out to the clergy as distributions, but after c. 1300 some was diverted to the fabric.

New Canons. In the fourteenth century the sum of money paid by a newly appointed canon for his cope was diverted towards the fabric fund.

Funerals. Payment of five pounds for the privilege of a funeral with pomp.

Legacies. Money willed to the fabric by persons now deceased. We have conflated cash legacies with legacies in kind (robes).

Masses of the Holy Spirit. A mass said once a week where the collection was given to the fabric fund.

General Chapters. A small payment made at general chapter meetings for the benefit of the fabric. An insignificant source of income.

Confraternities. Money raised by organizations of layfolk in the city of Troyes. The most important confraternities were those of Saint-Savinien and SS. Pierre et Paul. A new confraternity was set up at the end of the fifteenth century to help finance the completion of the nave and the construction of the west façade.

Manumissions, mortmain, and feudal dues. This source, derived from the legal rights of the bishop and chapter, occurs very rarely in the fifteenth century, and was not of any great profit.

Common. Money collected at various services and processions throughout the year.

Extraordinary. Casual gifts, often made for a specific purpose, for example for the reconstruction of the upper nave after the 1389 collapse, or for the work on the new bell tower in the early fifteenth century. In the accompanying charts, substantial gifts from the Duke of Burgundy, the king, the bishop and chapter, or the people of Troyes have been separated from this category, since they are of high historical interest.

General Pardon. After the granting of the general pardon by Pope Nicholas V in 1451, a special category was set up for this substantial source of income. Receipts continue until 1471. One quarter of the total to be paid to the Apostolic Chamber.

Figure C-1. Receipts and Expenses of the Fabric

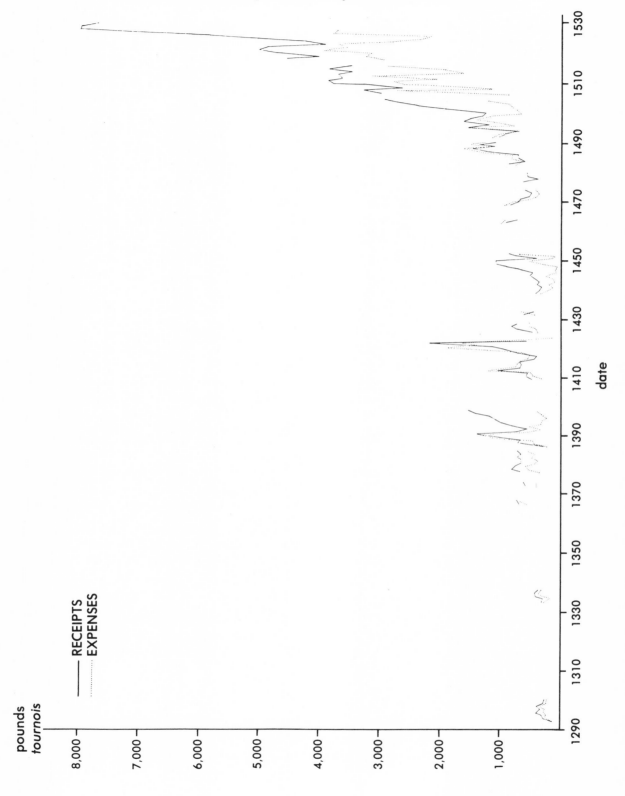

Appendix C. Analyses of the Workshop and Revenues

Figure C-2. Revenue of the Fabric, 1296-1390

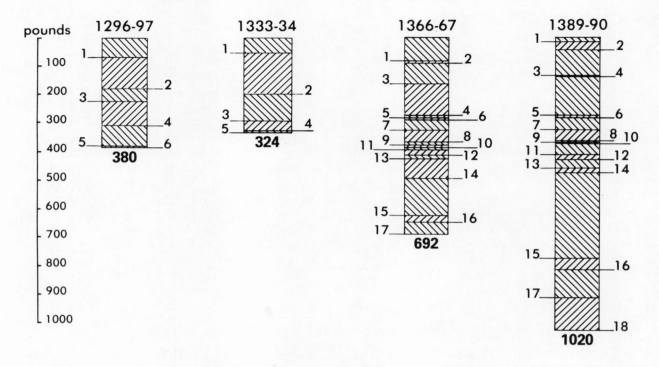

1 previous year	65	1 previous year	50	1 previous year	80	1 previous year	18
2 quests in diocese	112	2 quests	148	2 present year	8	2 present year	26
3 external quests	42	3 box in choir	92	3 relics	75	3 relics	95
4 collecting boxes	88	4 legacies	32	4 quests in diocese	113	4 box in church	1
5 legacies	72	5 present year	2	5 boxes in city		5 quests in diocese	136
6 present year	1		324	churches	17	6 boxes in city	
	380			6 box in choir	3	churches	10
				7 external quests	30	7 external quests	40
				8 anniversaries	42	8 anniversaries	36
				9 receipt of grain	12	9 general chapters	1
				10 common	9	10 funerals	2
				11 general chapters	1	11 legacies	44
				12 new canons	27	12 mass of Holy	
				13 legacies	12	Spirit	16
				14 mass of Holy		13 confraternities	29
				Spirit	65	14 rent from house	21
				15 from King		15 from chapter	300
				Charles V	128	16 from bishop	40
				16 gift of prebend	21	17 from Duke of	
				17 extraordinary	49	Burgundy	100
					692	18 extraordinary	105
							1020

Figure C-3. Revenue of the Fabric, 1390-1450

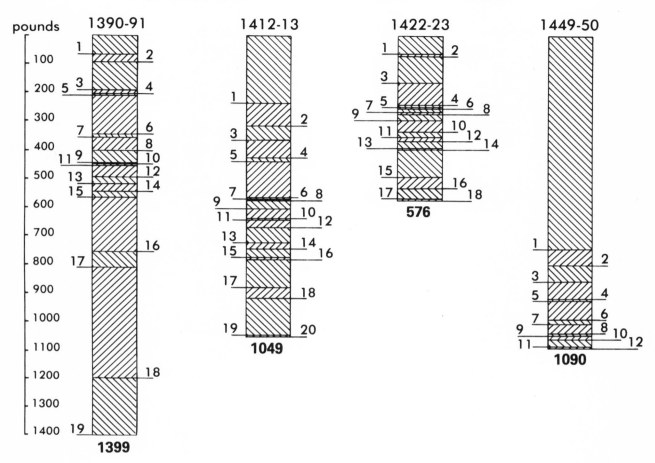

1	new canons	67	1	previous year	236	1	previous year	65	
2	present year	26	2	new canons	80	2	new canons	7	
3	relics	98	3	present year	48	3	present year	93	
4	relic boxes	12	4	relics	63	4	relics	78	
5	box in church	1	5	relic boxes	12	5	box in church &		
6	quests in diocese	141	6	quests in diocese	125		altar of relics	6	
7	boxes in city		7	box in choir	1	6	box in choir	1	
	churches	10	8	boxes in city		7	quests in diocese	16	
8	external quests	45		churches	2	8	boxes in city		
9	anniversaries	40	9	external quests	35		churches	7	
10	general chapters	1	10	anniversaries	34	9	external quests	18	
11	funerals	5	11	general chapters	1	10	anniversaries	43	
12	legacies	51	12	funerals	31	11	legacies	22	
13	mass of Holy		13	legacies	54	12	mass of Holy		
	Spirit	19	14	mass of Holy			Spirit	11	
14	confraternities	26		Spirit	16	13	confraternities	22	
15	rent from house	21	15	confraternities	33	14	manumissions etc	4	
16	from King		16	manumissions etc	8	15	from Duke of		
	Charles V	200	17	from chapter	100		Burgundy	100	
17	from the Pope	50	18	from inhabitants		16	from inhabitants		
18	from the			of Troyes	40		of Troyes	40	
	inhabitants of		19	extraordinary	122	17	extraordinary	35	
	Troyes	386	20	common	8	18	common	8	
19	extraordinary	200			1049			576	
		1399							

1	previous year	749
2	new canons	53
3	present year	58
4	relics	61
5	relic boxes & box	
	in nave	4
6	quests in diocese	69
7	external quests	15
8	legacies	33
9	mass of Holy	
	Spirit	7
10	confraternities	12
11	extraordinary	27
12	common	2
		1090

Appendix C. Analyses of the Workshop and Revenues

Figure C-4. Revenue of the Fabric, 1462-1499

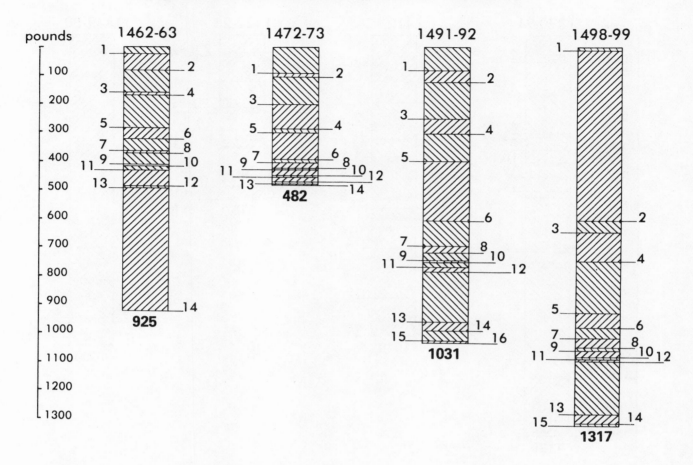

	1462-63			1472-73			1491-92			1498-99	
1	new canons	27	1	previous year	95	1	previous year	85	1	previous year	12
2	present year	57	2	new canons	13	2	new canons	40	2	present year	591
3	relics	74	3	present year	94	3	present year	128	3	relic boxes & box in nave	43
4	relic boxes & box in nave	9	4	relics	86	4	relic boxes & box in nave	50	4	relics	100
5	quests in diocese	119	5	box in nave	13	5	relics	95	5	quests in diocese	180
6	boxes in city churches	37	6	quests in diocese	96	6	quests in diocese	207	6	external quests	51
7	external quests	40	7	boxes in city churches	10	7	external quests	88	7	anniversaries	34
8	anniversaries	8	8	external quests	19	8	anniversaries	24	8	legacies	35
9	legacies	40	9	anniversaries	3	9	legacies	25	9	mass of Holy Spirit	8
10	mass of Holy Spirit	5	10	legacie	22	10	mass of Holy Spirit	6	10	confraternities	25
11	confraternities	15	11	mass of Holy Spirit	3	11	confraternities	21	11	alms	8
12	extraordinary	57	12	confraternities	18	12	alms	17	12	*foire des vierges*	5
13	common	5	13	extraordinary	6	13	new confraternity	173	13	new confraternity	183
14	general pardon	432	14	common	4	14	from inhabitants of Troyes	30	14	extraordinary	32
		925			482	15	extraordinary	36	15	common	9
						16	common	5			1317
								1031			

Figure C-5. Revenue of the Fabric, 1501-1507

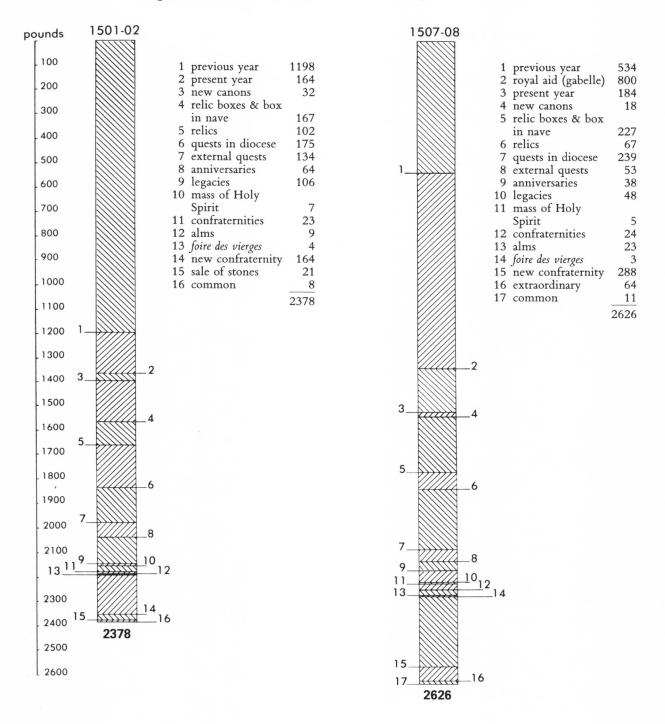

pounds

1501-02

1	previous year	1198
2	present year	164
3	new canons	32
4	relic boxes & box in nave	167
5	relics	102
6	quests in diocese	175
7	external quests	134
8	anniversaries	64
9	legacies	106
10	mass of Holy Spirit	7
11	confraternities	23
12	alms	9
13	*foire des vierges*	4
14	new confraternity	164
15	sale of stones	21
16	common	8
		2378

1507-08

1	previous year	534
2	royal aid (gabelle)	800
3	present year	184
4	new canons	18
5	relic boxes & box in nave	227
6	relics	67
7	quests in diocese	239
8	external quests	53
9	anniversaries	38
10	legacies	48
11	mass of Holy Spirit	5
12	confraternities	24
13	alms	23
14	*foire des vierges*	3
15	new confraternity	288
16	extraordinary	64
17	common	11
		2626

Appendix C. Analyses of the Workshop and Revenues

Appendix D

Description and Chronology of the Flying Buttresses of the Nave

1. *Review of the Chronology of the Nave Flyers*

Phase I, 1340s–1362, directed by Jehan de Torvoie. One bay (4-5) completed, including vaults and attendant flyers. Torvoie was in the process of working on the second nave vault when the work was interrupted by the expertise of 1362. He thus had constructed two flyers and was in the process of constructing a third one. His upper flyers had a simple supporting arch with chambered edges; vertical tracery panels, and an upper rim with no gutter. His three flyers were taken down, modified, and reinstalled along the north side of the nave at 5, 4, and 3.

Phase II, 1362–1370s. Pierre Faisant, in his expertise of 1362, had reported that the new flyers had been placed too high, and should be rebuilt, using the old masonry as far as possible. He offered his own services for this reconstruction, but was not hired; instead, we find a contract first with Master Thomas (1365) and later with Michelin de Jonchery, Michelin Hardiot, and Jehan Thierry (1365). These masons took down both flyers which had been installed by Torvoie, and modified them, reducing the height of the upper part of the flyer—hence we see how the upper rim cuts into the vertical panels in the three upper flyers on the north side of the nave (the third flyer had been prepared, but not yet installed by Torvoie). The upper flyer at 5 on the south side (D E 5, Fig. 58) was entirely rebuilt, with its angle tilted downward to achieve a lower point of abutment. The distorted main piers at C 5 and D 5 were rebuilt. The adjacent piers C 4 and D 4 were brought up to their full height and the second high vault was installed in bay 4-5. The workshop then began work to proceed to the third vault in bay 3-4, but although the flyers were prepared for this vault, it was never installed. The foundation of pier C 2 formed part of a campaign to lay out the lower parts of the fourth bay (arcade level) to provide a prop for the third high vault, but this work was interrupted by structural difficulties in the late 1380s, and the collapse of the two high vaults in 1389.

Phase III, 1390s. After the collapse, the fabric accounts reveal that a part of the masons' workshop was assigned to work on the upper nave, and that certain parts of the buttressing system were demolished, and certain upper piers were brought up to the height of the provisional roof. We can see evidence of this work of heightening piers in C 5, D 5, C 4, and D 4. Because high vaults no longer existed, the full weight of the upper flyers was no longer necessary. These were therefore dismantled, modified, and the supporting arches were put back into position, with a light cover on top of them—this cover was left in place as the middle strut of the flyers as they exist now. The piers of the central vessel at bay division 3 were brought up to the height of the provisional roof, and also were buttressed by reduced flyers as described.

Phase IV, 1470s–1490s, the work of masters Anthoine Colas, Jaquet le Vachier, and Jehançon Garnache. We have very full documentation for the work on the nave roof, flyers, vaults, and clerestory window tracery, and we can reconstruct the sequence of the work on a monthly basis, as shown in Table D-1.

TABLE D–1.

Phase IV, the Final Operations

YEAR	MONTH	FLYERS	VAULTS	WINDOWS
1492	Sept.	Templates made. Cutting begins.		
	Oct.	Cutting.		
	Nov.	Cutting.		
	Dec.	Cutting.		
1493	Jan.	Cutting.		
	Feb.	Cutting.		
	Mar.	Starts to mason pillar A 2.		
	Apr.	Masons A 2.		
	May	Starts to mason pillar B 2.		
	June	Cutting stones for arches. Centers installed.		
	July	Stone cutting for arches.		
	Aug.	Masons arches of A B C 2. *This flyer is completed.*		

Appendix D. Description and Chronology of the Flying Buttresses of the Nave

	Sept.	Starts cutting for D E F 2 (pillars).	
	Oct.	Cutting.	
	Nov.	Cutting.	
1494	Jan.	Cutting.	
	Feb.	Cutting.	Man sent to quarry to start cutting stones for high vaults. First center is prepared.
	Mar.	Cutting.	
	Apr.	Starts to mason pillars.	
	May	Cuts and masons pillars. Centers installed.	
	June	Cuts and masons.	
	July	Cuts and masons. *This flyer is completed.* Next flyer on S. side is begun.	Meeting to review priority: vaults or flyers?
	Aug.	Cutting, S. side.	
	Sept.	Cutting, S. side.	
	Oct.	Cutting, S. side.	
	Nov.	Cutting, S. side.	
	Dec.	Cutting, S. side.	
1495	Jan.	Cutting, S. side.	
	Feb.	Cutting, S. side.	
	Mar.	Starts to mason, S. side.	
	Apr.	Cuts and masons, S. side.	
	May	Cuts and masons, S. side.	
	June	Cuts and masons, S. side.	
	July	Cuts and masons, S. side. D E F 5 is said to be finished.	
	Aug.	Masons, S. side.	
	Sept.	Man sent to quarry to cut for flyers on N. side. *The S. flyers are finished.* Cutting begins for flyers on N. side.	
	Oct.	Cutting, N. side.	
	Nov.	Cutting, N. side.	
	Dec.	Cutting, N. side.	
1946	Jan.	Cutting, N. side.	Decision to erect first center for high vault at east end of nave.

218

	Feb.	Cutting, N. side.	
	Mar.	Cutting, N. side.	
	Apr.	Begins to mason.	
	May	Masons, N. side.	
	June	Masons, N. side.	Garnache goes to quarry to show how ribs and arches of vaults are to be cut.
	July	Masons, N. side.	
	Aug.	Masons, N. side.	
	Sept.	Masons, N. side.	
	Oct.	*The N. flyers* are finished.	
	Nov.		Garnache and men celebrate commencement of work on vaults.
	Oct.		Work on vault 1.
	Nov.		Work on vault 1.
	Dec.		*Completion of vault* 1, Garnache paid 50 pounds.
1497	Jan.		Vaulting (2).
	Feb.		Vaulting (2).
	Mar.		Vaulting (2).
	Apr.		Vaulting (2), Garnache given an extra 10 pounds for vault 1.
	May		*Completion of vault* 2.
	June		Vaulting (3).	Garnache goes to quarry to instruct men on cutting of window tracery. Works on the windows at 60 pounds for first 2; 70 pounds for each subsequent one.
	July		*Completion of vault* 3.
	Aug.		Vaulting (4).
	Sept.		*Completion of vault* 4.
	Oct.		Vaulting (5).
	Nov.		*Completion of vault* 5.
	Dec.		Removal of last center.
1498	Jan.		
	Feb.		
	Mar.		
	Apr.		
	May		
	June		
	July		3 windows on S. side now complete.
	Aug.		
	Sept.		
	Oct.		
	Nov.		
	Dec.		

Appendix D. Description and Chronology of the Flying Buttresses of the Nave

1499   Jan.
Feb.
Mar.
Apr.
May   2 more windows on
June   S. side now com-
July   plete. 3 windows on
Aug.   N. side now com-
Sept.   plete.
Oct.
Nov.
Dec.
1500   Jan.
Feb.
Mar.   2 more windows on
Apr.   N. side complete.
May
June
July

TABLE D-2.

The Nave Flyers: Structural Description

BAY DIVISION 5.

Outer upright, A 5 (Fig. 54). Exterior pinnacle has straight gables; rounded mouldings; foliage of same generation as interior high capital at 5. Moulding on upright set very high; it does not engage with upper rim (cover) of flyer.

Outer flyer, A B 5 (Fig. 55a). Lower arch with simple champfered edges; tracery with simple uncusped O and soufflet in tail; upper rim (cover) with no gutter. This upper rim does *not* engage on mouldings of outer or intermediary uprights.

Intermediary upright, B 5 (Fig. 55a). Receives flyers for transept and central nave. Terminates in 4-way straight-sided gable and pinnacle. West side strengthened in 19th century.

Inner flyer, B C 5 (Fig. 55b). Supporting arch with simple champfered corners. Some dislocation between this supporting arch, and upper parts. Middle strut continues down into solid tail. 4 vertical panels with Flamboyant element in tail; the pointed arches of the vertical panels are cut through by the upper rim. Upper rim with no gutter, except at head. Dislocation at junction with pier of central nave occurs between the middle strut and the upper rim.

Inner upright, C 5 (Fig. 56). Rectangular block with shafts on corners and on outer surface to receive head of flyer. Lower parts of pier clearly *set against* the window mouldings (up to height of c. 2.60m. above passage). Above this, pier coursed in with mouldings. Lower pier with slant outwards, corrected in upper part. Dislocation where upper head of flyer meets pier.

Inner upright, D 5 (Fig. 57). Rectangular block with shafts on corners and on outer surface to receive head of flyer. Lower parts of pier clearly *set against* the window mouldings (up to a height of c. 2.60m. above passage). Above this point, mouldings continue, and are coursed with pier. Lower window mouldings lean outward: they are not parallel with shaft on pier. Same kind of cursive masons' marks found throughout upper part, into springers for window enclosing arches.

INTERPRETATION

Constructed early 1300s.

Unit is Phase I, or earlier, and has been reset at a lower level in Phase II (1360s).

Phase I, or earlier.

Originally constructed Phase I. Reconstructed at a lower level in Phase II: hence the rim cutting the vertical panels. Supporting arch and middle strut reassembled after 1389 collapse (Phase III). Upper tracery and rim installed Phase IV.

Window mouldings are Phase I, distorted because of badly placed flyers and rebuilt after the 1362 expertise. Upper part is Phase III, 1390s, when piers brought up to level of provisional roof.

Window mouldings are Phase I, reinforced in Phase II rebuild (1360s). Upper part is Phase III, 1390s, when pier brought back up to level of the provisional roof.

221

Inner flyer, D E 5 (Fig. 58b). Supporting arch with concave moulding; dislocation evident at springing of this arch. Middle strut is fully detached from the supporting arch. 5 vertical panels with delicate moulding, innermost unit with ogee head. Upper rim has a gutter. The inner and outer flyers are not in alignment: inner unit is tilted downward.

Belongs to 1360s, Phase II rebuild. Tilted to achieve lower level of abutment. Upper tracery panels and upper rim reassembled by Jehançon Garnache (Phase IV): hence the ogee arch.

Intermediary upright, E 5 (Fig. 58a). As on north side, C 5.

Phase I, or earlier.

Outer flyer, E F 5 (Fig. 58a). Supporting arch with simple champfered edge; tracery with 4-cusped O and soufflet in tail; upper rim with gutter. Upper rim engages with prominant mouldings on outer and intermediary uprights.

Phase I, or earlier, not reset.

Outer upright, F 5. Much as on north side.

Constructed early 1300s.

BAY DIVISION 4.

Outer upright, A 4. Mouldings on sides of upright have concavities. Exterior pinnacle has gables formed of inverted curves; sharpened mouldings.

Phase II, 1360s.

Outer flyer, A B 4. Lower arch with simple champfered edges; tracery with simple uncusped O; upper rim with no gutter does not engage on mouldings of uprights.

Phase II, 1360s.

Intermediary upright, B 4. Concave, sharpened mouldings; gables at top in form of inverted curves, pinnacle thinner than in B 5.

Phase II, 1360s.

Inner flyer, B C 4. Forms are much the same as B C 5: supporting arch with champfered edges; middle strut continues down into solid tail; 4 vertical panels; Flamboyant element in the tail; upper rim without gutter cuts into the arches of the vertical panels.

Unit prepared in Phase I, 1350s as the 2nd flyer for the first vault (to be used at D E 5). Transferred to present location and upper rim reduced in height in Phase II; rebuilt by Garnache in Phase IV.

Inner upright, C 4 (Fig. 52). The pillar has the same form as C 5. A break in the window mouldings occurs at 2.60m above the passage: below this level mouldings are simple flat surfaces; above, they comprise 2 concave scoops. Some dislocation between pillar and lowest window mouldings, but evidence harder to read than in C 5. Dislocation is evident between stones of upper part of flyer head and the pier. Lower part of pillar leans outwards.

Lower part is Phase II, 1360s rebuild. Upper part, up to canopy is Phase III, with some use of older window jamb mouldings.

Inner upright, D 4 (Fig. 53). Same form as D 5. Lowest level of pillar set against window mouldings; mouldings are simpler than D 5, here with only 2 orders. No breaks in window mouldings; above the level of the 2nd stone, window mouldings coursed in.

Basically Phase II (1360s).

Inner flyer, D E 4 (Fig. 53b). Lower arch with concave mouldings; middle strut merges into solid tail; tracery with 5 pointed panels with simple moulding forms. Some Flamboyant work at the head. Top rim has a gutter.

Phase II, modified in Phases III and IV.

Intermediary upright, E 4. Straight gables, sharpened mouldings.

Phase II.

Outer flyer, E F 4. Supporting arch with champfered edges; tracery with uncusped O; soufflet in the tail; upper rim with gutter.

Phases I and II.

Outer upright, F 4. Sharpened mouldings; gables with concave curves; exterior pinnacle with tree-trunk decoration.

Phases I and II, pinnacle is 16th century.

BAY DIVISION 3.

Outer upright, A 3. Similar to A 4, but the decoration is richer. A fleur-de-lys on west face.

Phase II, 1360s.

Outer flyer, A B 3. Similar to A B 4.

Phase II, 1360s.

Intermediary upright, B 3. Similar to B 4.

Phase II, 1360s.

Inner flyer, B C 3. Similar to B C 2.

Phases I and II. This is the third upper flyer with a simple supporting arch and tracery panels cut through by upper rim. Thus, Phase I had involved flyers for one bay, with a second bay under preparation.

Inner upright, C 3 (Fig. 49). Pillar is more substantial in thickness, and is designed around a system of rotated squares.

Phase III, 1390s, the work of Henry of Brussels.

Inner upright, D 3. Similar to C 3.

Phase III.

Inner flyer, D E 3. Similar to D E 4.

Phase II, 1360s, reset 1390s and 1490s.

Intermediary upright, E 3. Similar to E 4.

Phase II, 1360s.

Appendix D. Description and Chronology of the Flying Buttresses of the Nave

Outer flyer, E F 3. Similar to E F 4.   Phase II, 1360s.

Outer upright, F 3. Similar to F 4.   Phase II, 1360s, with details added in 16th c.

BAY DIVISION 2.

Outer upright, A 2. Gables of exterior pinnacle are   Phase IV, Jehançon Garnache.
slightly curved, foliage decoration is much dryer
than in work to the east.

Outer flyer, A B 2. Supporting arch with champ-   Phase IV, Jehançon Garnache.
fered edges; tracery includes O with trefoil cusps
and double soufflet in the tail. Upper rim has a
gutter.

Intermediary upright, B 2. Capped by straight-sided   Phase IV, Jehançon Garnache.
gable enframing trefled arch. Pinnacle is very
slender.

Inner flyer, B C 2 (Fig. 50). Supporting arch has   Phase IV, Jehançon Garnache.
concave mouldings. Middle strut is very massive,
and merges into the supporting arch of the flyer,
rather than sitting on top of it. Tracery includes
two roundels and heavy flamboyant elements.
Upper rim has gutter along top. No signs of
dislocation.

Inner upright, C 2. Designed around system of   Phase IV, Anthoine Colas.
rotated squares.

Inner upright, D 2. Same as C 2.   Phase IV, Anthoine Colas.

Inner flyer, D E 2. (Fig. 51). Supporting arch with   Phase IV, Jehançon Garnache.
concave mouldings; heavy middle strut merges
into supporting arch; tracery panels not vertical,
but aligned with middle strut; gutter along upper
rim.

Intermediary upright, E 2. Straight gables enframe   Phase IV, Jehançon Garnache.
awkwardly depressed trefled arches. Capped by
slender pinnacle with dry foliage sprigs.

Outer flyer, E F 2. Supporting arch with champ-   Phase IV, Jehançon Garnache.
fered edges; tracery with roundel having 3 cusps
and Flamboyant element in the tail; upper rim
with gutter.

Outer upright, F 2. Exterior pinnacle with tree-   Phase IV, with 16th c. pinnacle.
trunk decoration.

BAY DIVISION I.

North side, B C 1. A solid spur topped by an openwork "flyer" built against a pier which is similar to C 2 and C 3.

Phase IV, the spur added by Jehançon Garnache against pillar by Colas.

South side, D E 1 (Fig. 47). Same as north side, but with inscription, "Le premier pillier de la tour."

Same.

Appendix D. Description and Chronology of the Flying Buttresses of the Nave

Notes

Abbreviations used in Notes and Bibliography

Ann. Aube	Annuaire de l'Aube
Arch. Aube	Archives départementales de l'Aube
Art Bull.	Art Bulletin
Bibl. Ecole Chartes	Bibliothèque de l'Ecole des Chartes
Bibl. Dép. Aube	Le Bibliophile du département de l'Aube
Bull. arch.	Bulletin archéologique
Bull. mon.	Bulletin monumental
Cong. arch.	Congrès archéologique
Gaz. B.-A.	Gazette des Beaux-Arts
Jour. Brit. Arch. Assoc.	Journal of the British Archaeological Association
JSAH	Journal of the Society of Architectural Historians
Mém. Soc. acad. Aube	Mémoires de la Société académique de l'Aube

I. Introduction

1. These dates are approximate. The beginning date cannot be fixed with complete certainty. By 1550 the cathedral was complete except for the west towers. The northwest tower, finished in the latter part of the sixteenth century, falls outside the scope of this book. The southwest tower was never built. An excellent survey of previous writings on Troyes Cathedral is given by J. Roserot de Melin, *Bibliographie commentée des sources d'une histoire de la cathédrale de Troyes*, 2 vols., Troyes, 1966 and 1970. For a brief chronology of the construction, see V. de Courcel, "La cathédrale de Troyes," *Cong. arch.*, CXIII, 1955, 9–28. For the Late Gothic campaigns on the cathedral, see L. Pigeotte, *Etude sur les travaux d'achèvement de la catédrale de Troyes*, Troyes, 1870. A sketch of the history of construction was attempted by S. Murray and N. Bongartz, "Chronologie abregée des étapes de construction de la cathédrale de Troyes," *Vie en Champagne*, 22e. année, 235, 1974, 6–16. Most recently, see N. Bongartz, *Die frühen Bauteile der Kathedrale in Troyes, Architekturgeschichtliche Monographie*, Stuttgart, 1979.

2. Valuable contributions to our knowledge of the working practice of medieval masons have been made by Lon Shelby; for example, L. R. Shelby, "Medieval Masons' Templates," *JSAH*, XXX, 1971, 140–54; idem, "The Geometrical Knowledge of Medieval Master Masons," *Speculum*, XLVII, 1972, 395–421; idem, *Gothic Design Techniques*, Carbondale, 1977. See also P. Booz, *Der Baumeister der Gotik*, Munich, 1956; P. Knoop and G. P. Jones, *The Medieval Mason*, Manchester, 1967; L. F. Salzman, *Building in England down to 1540*, Oxford, 1952; J. Harvey, *The Mediaeval Architect*, London, 1972.

3. For example see R. Branner, "Jean d'Orbais and the Cathedral of Reims," *Art Bull.*, XLIII, 1961, 131–33; idem, "The Labyrinth of Reims Cathedral," *JSAH*, XXI, 1962, 18–25.

4. The word "fabric" is used to convey both the envelope of the cathedral as a physical entity and the organizational structure created by the bishop and chapter in order to maintain the existing building and its contents (including liturgical objects and vestments) and to undertake new construction. Historians of Troyes have been aware of the importance of the fabric accounts of the cathedral since the early nine-

teenth century, but little attempt has been made to correlate the evidence from the accounts with the study of the building itself. The following authors have worked with the accounts: P. J. Grosley, *Ephémérides*, 2 vols., Paris, 1811; J. Quicherat, "Notice sur plusieurs registres de l'oeuvre de la cathédrale de Troyes," Paris, 1848, extract from *Mémoires de la Société royale des antiquaires de France* XIX, 1848; J. F. Gadan, "Comptes de l'église de Troyes, 1375–1385," *Le Bibliophile Troyen* I. Troyes, 1851; A. F. Arnaud, *Voyage archéologique et pittoresque dans le département de l'Aube*, Troyes, 1837 (this author is said to have used Gadan's notes rather than consulting the original texts); A. Assier, "Comptes de l'oeuvre de l'église de Troyes avec notes et éclaircissements, ou nouvelles recherches sur la construction des églises et sur les usages au moyen-âge." Troyes, 1855, extract from *Bibl. Dép. Aube*, X, 1855. idem, *Les arts et les artistes dans l'ancienne capitale de Champagne*, 1250–1680, 2 vols., Paris, 1876; H. d'Arbois de Jubainville, "Documents relatifs aux travaux de construction faits à le cathédrale de Troyes," *Bibl. Ecole Chartes*, 23e. année, Paris, 1862, 214–47 and 393–423; F. André, *Inventaire-sommaire des Archives départmentales de l'Aube antérieures à 1790*, II, Paris et Troyes, 1896; L. Pigeotte, *Etude*; J. Roserot de Melin, *Bibliographie*, I and II; J. Harvey, *The Mediaeval Architect*, esp. 218–20.

5. The problems addressed by the chapter in their meetings were by no means confined to administrative or budgetary matters, but also included questions pertaining to structure and decisions of an aesthetic nature. See entries in Appendix B under 1362, 1365, 1494.

6. The fiscal year generally ran from the Sunday after the feast of the Magdalene, July 22nd, to the same day in the following year.

7. This information can be summarized in the form of statistical charts, see Appendix C.

8. The comparable accounts of Sens Cathedral, for example, do not provide such a wealth of information; see Archives de l'Yonne, G 1141–1143. Similarly, the accounts of Westminster Abbey and Exeter Cathedral offer considerably less information than the Troyes accounts, see H. Colvin, *Building Accounts of King Henry III*, Oxford, 1971; A. M. Erskine, "The Accounts of the Fabric of Exeter Cathedral 1279–1353," *Devon and Cornwall Record Society*, New Series, XXIV and XXVI, 1981 and 1983.

9. Thus, A. Assier commented, "les comptes sont donc trop nombreux pour que jamais éditeur

en entreprenne la publication," *Comptes de l'oeuvre*, viii.

10. The height of the keystone of the easternmost nave vault is 28.85m. The span of the central vessel is 13.94m.

11. For Braine see J. Bony, *French Gothic Architecture of the 12th and 13th Centuries*, Berkeley, 1983, 172.

12. The northern rose window was rebuilt in the years around 1400 and the southern window dates entirely from the nineteenth century.

13. In the hemicycle the moulding of the triforium sill continues around these shafts.

14. It is not possible to circulate through this passageway in all parts of the building. Structural difficulties caused the Late Gothic builders of the cathedral to block existing passageways through the upper piers and to construct the nave without such openings. Access to each bay of the triforium is thus gained through a small door let into the stained glass of the triforium.

15. The original roofs were in the form of a series of pyramids, see pre-restoration model of the cathedral, Fig. 38. In the nineteenth century this roof was completely rebuilt in its present form, Fig. 44.

16. The original choir flyers had openwork tracery. For a general discussion of the nineteenth century restorations see N. Bongartz, *Die frühen Bauteile*.

17. The northern tower, the *Tour Saint Pierre*, was finished only in the first half of the seventeenth century and will not be studied in this book. For a brief bibliography, see J. Roserot de Melin, *Bibliographie*, I, 229–34.

18. One pier (C2) and one arch in the northern arcade of the choir were actually left protruding outside the provisional wall.

19. L. Pigeotte, "Le grand clocher de la cathédrale de Troyes," *Mem. Soc. acad. Aube*, XLI, 1877, 149–210.

20. For example, P. Knoop and G. P. Jones, *The Medieval Mason*.

21. The word "school" is perhaps inappropriate when applied to Champenois Gothic, since many characteristics (diagonally placed chapels, for example) were shared with contiguous areas, especially the Ile-de-France. For a recent discussion of the problem, see A. Prache, "L'art dans la Champagne du nord," *Cong. arch.*, CXXXV, 1977, 9–15.

22. S. Murray, "Bleuet and Anthoine Colas, Master Masons of Troyes Cathedral. Artistic Personality in Late Gothic Design," *JSAH*, XLI, 1982, 7–14.

23. P. Piétresson de Saint-Aubin, "La fourniture de la pierre sur les grands chantiers troyens du moyen-âge et de la Renaissance," *Bull. arch.*, 1928–1929, 569–601.

24. S. Murray, "Master Jehançon Garnache (1485–1501) and the Construction of the High Vaults and Flying Buttresses of the Nave of Troyes Cathedral," *Gesta*, XIX, 1980, 37–49; J. Harvey, *The Mediaeval Architect*, 107.

25. P. J. Grosley, *Ephémérides*, II, 192.

26. The outward thrust of an arch may be illustrated by means of the following demonstration: if a person raises his hands and places them against a wall forming half an arch and pushes, then his feet will tend to slip outward and away from the wall. In the same way arches tend to push their supports outward, and these supports, if of inadequate cross-section, may bend or may rotate around a fulcrum at the base.

27. For the Gothic Cathedral as Idea, see O. von Simson, *The Gothic Cathedral*, New York, 1956.

28. This chalk was quarried just outside the city walls and was infinitely less expensive than the hard limestone which had to be carted over considerable distances.

29. The nineteenth-century restorations at Troyes affected the choir and transept much more deeply than the nave or the west façade. For the reconstruction of the choir and the south transept in the nineteenth century, see N. Bongartz, *Die frühen Bauteile*. In the nave the restoration work included the re-shaping of the roofs of the aisles, the finishing of unfinished details and the replacement of worn stones. All this work is fully documented in the memoirs of the successive architects of the cathedral, kept in the office of the *Agence des Bâtiments de France*, Troyes. An impression of the pre-restoration state of the Cathedral can also be gained from the cork model in the *Musée Vauluisant*, Troyes (Fig. 38).

30. An expansive effect accompanies the freezing of water. If water penetrates into crannies in the masonry and subsequently freezes, these crannies will be enlarged and dislocation of stones will ensue.

31. The decision to glaze the triforium was essentially an aesthetic one—although the stained glass in the triforium carried figurative subject matter adding to the iconographic programs of the cathedral's interior. This aesthetic decision resulted in serious maintenance problems which, because of neglect, translated into structural problems.

32. Other options for the roof included a flat terrace of stone (as at Clermont-Ferrand Cathedral) or a continuous double-pitched roof, as was actually built by the nineteenth century restorers of Troyes Cathedral.

33. The collegiate church of Saint-Urbain in Troyes is a similar case. Construction was begun in 1262, but progress was delayed on account of the violent opposition of the abbess and nuns of the nearby house of Notre-Dame-aux-Nonnains. By 1300 work had advanced as far as the west portals but the entire upper nave was left incomplete. It was finished only in the nineteenth century, see F. Salet, "Saint Urbain de Troyes," *Cong. arch.*, CXIII, 1955, 96–122. Beauvais Cathedral was another major project, begun in 1225, where political difficulties and a collapse delayed work. The transept was only finished in the sixteenth century and the nave not at all, see S. Murray, "The Choir of the Church of Saint-Pierre, Cathedral of Beauvais," *Art Bull.*, LXII, 1980, 533–51. At Tours Cathedral we have a case very similar to Troyes: a choir from the early thirteenth century and a nave and western frontispiece finished only in the fifteenth to sixteenth centuries.

34. J. H. Pirenne, *Medieval Cities, Their Origins and the Revival of Trade*, Princeton, 1969. For a review of the relationship between urban politics and cathedral construction, see A. Mussat, "Les cathédrales dans leur cités," *Revue de l'Art*, LV, 1982, 9–22.

35. Useful introductions to the topography of Troyes can be found in E. Chapin, *Les villes de foires de Champagne, des origines au début du XIVe. siècle*, Paris, 1937, and P. Piétresson de Saint-Aubin, "La formation de Troyes," *Vie en Champagne*, 17e. année, 177, 1969, 5–11, especially 9, "It is necessary to underline the particular characteristics of the formation [of the city of Troyes]. Dominant role for the central power, the count of Champagne. He constructs the walls, he channels the waters of the Seine through the suburbs in new canals, the *Clos du Comte* develops thanks to the privileges conceded by its proprietor. The religious establishments, whose role was so remarkable in other cities, were of little importance over the extension of the city" (translated by author). See also M. Bur, *La formation du comté de Champagne v. 950–v. 1150*, Nancy, 1977, and R. Kaiser, *Bischofsherrschaft zwischen Königtum und Fürstenmacht*, Bonn, 1981.

36. It is to be presumed that the earliest cathedral in Troyes was on the same site. Sources on the subject of the previous cathedrals are

very vague—it is known that an early cathedral was destroyed in the Viking invasion of the ninth century. See N. Bongartz, *Die frühen Bauteile*, 40

37. E. Chapin, *Les villes*, 17–18.

38. On the history of the counts of Champagne, see H. d'Arbois de Jubainville, *Histoire des ducs et des comtes de Champagne*, 7 vols., Paris and Troyes, 1859–1869. For Anségise, see vol. I, 140–41. A useful summary of the circumstances attending the formation of the county of Champagne is given by E. Chapin, *Les villes*, 239–240. Until the late Carolingian period the duchy of Burgundy extended to the Aube and included Troyes. Champagne became a separate county under the control of the Vermandois counts in the first half of the tenth century.

39. M. Bur, *La formation du comté de Champagne*, 495. The episcopal seigneurie within the walls of the city of Troyes was created in the eleventh century by counts Eudes and Hugues.

40. The counts helped render the marshy area to the southeast of this new suburb habitable through the construction of a drainage system.

41. On the fairs of Champagne see E. Chapin, *Les villes*; F. Bourquelot, *Etudes sur les foires de Champagne, Mémoires présentés par divers savants à l'Académie des Inscriptions et Belles Lettres de l'Institut impériale de la France*, IIe. série, V, Paris, 1865; R.-H. Bautier, "Les foires de Champagne, recherches sur une évolution historique," *Recueils de la Société Jean Bodin*, V, Brussels, 1953, 97–147.

42. We have no evidence as to the value of the fairs at their peak of prosperity in the twelfth century. By the late thirteenth century the revenue from the fair of Saint Jean was around 1,000 pounds and Saint Remi about 700 pounds. Moreover, a total of about 2,000 pounds was produced through various kinds of tolls levied on industrial and commercial activity in Troyes, the most important source being from the production and sale of pieces of woolen cloth—the production rate was about 48,000 pieces per year, see E. Chapin, *Les villes*, 87 and 170–71. The revenues of the county of Champagne for the six months from July to December, 1288, are given in the account published by A. Longnon, *Documents relatifs au comté de Champagne et de Brie, 1172–1361*, III, Paris, 1914, 71–101. Receipts from the city of Troyes (including the fairs) totalled 4,308 pounds and total receipts (including the bailiwicks of Troyes, Meaux, Provins, Vitry, and Chaumont) were 22,377 pounds for the six-month period.

43. For Henry the Liberal, see H. d'Arbois de Jubainville, *Histoire des ducs et des comtes*, III.

44. Count Henry the Liberal established the college of Saint-Etienne in 1157. He endowed the college most generously and an attempt was made to free the establishment from the jurisdiction of the bishops of Troyes. The college disposed of seventy-two prebends at the time of its foundation. The church was intended to serve as seigneurial chapel and necropolis for the counts. See J.-C. Courtalon-Delaistre, *Topographie historique de la ville et du diocèse de Troyes*, 3 vols., Troyes, 1733–1734, esp. II, 136–150. Henry the Liberal was also most generous toward the powerful house of Notre-Dame-aux-Nonnains. This house of Benedictine nuns was among the oldest and best endowed in the region, holding important prerogatives such as the right of presentation in several of the key parishes of Troyes; high, middle, and low justice in several parts of the city of Troyes; and certain symbolic rights over the newly appointed bishop at the time of his entry into his city. The bishop was obliged to give his horse to the abbess and nuns. See J.-C. Courtalon-Delaistre, *Topographie historique*, II, 170–76.

45. H. d'Arbois de Jubainville, *Histoire des ducs et des comtes*, III, 81.

46. M. Bur, *La formation du comté de Champagne*, 495–96. It is possible that Bishop Henri de Carinthie initiated a major construction campaign on the episcopal palace, see J.-M. Roger, "Note sur la construction du palais épiscopal de Troyes à l'époque romane," *Vie en Champagne*, 32e. année, 341, 1984, 11–13.

47. M. Bur, *La formation du comté de Champagne*, 496.

48. E. Chapin, *Les villes*, 146–61. Count Thibaut IV, under the pressure of the invasion of his county, conceded communal privileges to Troyes and Provins in 1230. The bourgeois of Troyes were exempted from the *taille* in exchange for *la jurée*, a tax of 2 pence in the pound on immovable property, and 6 pence on movable property. These taxes could be bought off for 20 pounds per annum. Important rights were retained by the count, including high justice *ost*, and *chevaunchée*, and the inhabitants of Troyes were still required to grind their flour at the count's mills and to bake in his ovens.

49. I am particularly indebted to John Benton for bringing to my attention the estimate of c. 1300. This figure comes from an estimate of church revenues in the Archives Nationales, J 206 no. 3. The document was published by A. Longnon, who omitted the key item relating to

the income of the bishops of Troyes; see *Documents relatifs au comté de Champagne*, III, 124–33. John Benton noticed this omission, and was kind enough to share his own transcription of the document with me.

50. *Gallia Christiana*, XII, Paris, 1770, 483.

51. Similar great western towers were found at Reims Cathedral, Châlons-sur-Marne, and the abbey of Saint-Thierry. See A. Prache, "L'art dans la Champagne du nord," 18–19. The foundations of the older cathedrals on the site were exposed in an excavation undertaken in the 1973 Indiana University Summer School in Troyes. The excavation was directed by N. Bongartz; see *Die frühen Bauteile*, 311–17.

52. R. Branner, "Les débuts de la cathédrale de Troyes," *Bull. mon.*, CXVIII, 1960, 111–22.

53. N. Bongartz, *Die frühen Bauteile*, 122.

54. Ibid., 202, 251. This conclusion is based upon the many similarities between the organization of the interior walls of the radiating chapels at Troyes and Châlons-sur-Marne and on the general resemblance of the plan type to the choir at Meaux.

55. J. Bony, *French Gothic Architecture*, 172 and 255.

56. This took place during the regency of Blanche of Navarre, discussed later in this chapter.

57. R. Branner, *Saint Louis and the Court Style*, London, 1965; N. Bongartz, *Die frühen Bauteile*, 234–36; C. Bruzelius, *The Thirteenth Century Church at Saint-Denis*, Yale University Press, New Haven, 1985. Bongartz maintains the priority of the work at Troyes, arguing that construction of the upper choir followed directly after the 1228 collapse. Bruzelius, on the other hand, believes that Troyes followed after Saint Denis.

58. For a recent discussion of the linkage of clerestory with triforium by means of continuous mullions, see P. Kurman, "L'église Saint-Jacques de Reims," *Cong. arch*, CXXXV, 1977, 109–21. Such linkage existed in a number of churches in the region including Orbais, Essommes, and the hemicycle of Reims Cathedral.

59. N. Bongartz, *Die frühen Bauteile*, 233.

60. In the choir at Amiens several different campaigns of restoration on the flyers were necessary, as is attested by the variety of tracery types. In the nave of Troyes the same type of flyer was found to be placed too high (in 1362); these were subsequently rebuilt with an additional strut in the middle, see Chapter II.

61. This rebuilding was directed mainly toward the reduction of the height of the upper rims of the flyers. Such adjustments are evident in the flyers flanking the transept arms, and the nave flyers were rebuilt after an expertise in 1362.

62. J. Roserot de Melin, *Le diocèse de Troyes*, Troyes, 1957, J.-C. Courtalon-Delaistre, *Topographie historique*, I, 353–65.

63. J.-C. Courtalon-Delaistre, *Topographie historique*, II, 111–20. This author states that the chapter formerly disposed of forty prebends and twelve dignitaries. The most powerful dignitary in the twelfth century was the provost, who was nominated by the bishop. In 1167 this position was suppressed, however, and the dean, elected by the chapter, assumed dominance. The chapter appointed its administrative officers on a year-by-year basis, including a *compteur*, a receiver of rents, a *syndic* for the maintenance of discipline, a recorder, and a *fabricien* or *proviseur* to administer the fabric of the cathedral. Each *proviseur* drew a salary from the fabric fund. In the period around 1300 this salary was twenty pounds per annum.

64. In 1228 the canons of Saint Peter agreed to set aside one sixth of their prebends for the restoration of Saint Helen's shrine, which had been smashed in the collapse of the upper choir. A prebend in the fourteenth century was worth about twenty pounds per annum. However, it is possible that the money was never actually collected, since the work on the shrine was still not complete in the following century, see G. Constable, "Troyes, Constantinople, and the Relics of Saint Helen in the Thirteenth Century," *Mélanges René Crozet*, II, Poitiers, 1966, 1035–41. When, in the eighteenth century, a major campaign of embellishment was undertaken to transform the choir, the canons agreed to give from their annual income "une somme proportionnée à ce que chacun d'eux pouvoit consacrer." The bishop promised an annual sum of 600 pounds; see J.-C. Courtalon-Delaistre, *Topographie historique*, II, 125.

65. For the most recent discussion of these indulgences, see N. Bongartz, *Die frühen Bauteile*, 258–259, and Documents 10, 11, 16, 17, 19, and 20.

66. Ibid., Document 10, "Hinc est, quod cum venerabilis frater noster episcopus et capitulum Trecensis circa reparationem ecclesie Trecensis curam adhibeant et operam efficacem, nec facultates habeant. . . ." Ibid., Document 11, ". . . miro ac sumptuoso opere reedificari ceperit. . . ."

67. Ibid., Document 16, "Cum igitur ecclesia beati Petri Trecensis, quam nuper repentine casus ruine deiecit, nobili opere ac sumptuoso consurgat, nec ad eius reedificationem proprie suppetant facultates, nisi fidelium elemosinis adjuvetur. . . ." Ibid., Document 17, "Cum igitur Trecensis ecclesia nuper tenebroso turbine convoluta, concussis quatuor angulis, ab imis corruerit fundamentis. . . ."

68. T. Evergates, *Feudal Society in the Bailliage of Troyes under the Counts of Champagne, 1152–1284*, Baltimore, 1975, provides a useful summary of the history of the Counts.

69. H. d'Arbois de Jubainville, *Histoire des ducs et des comtes*, IV, part I, especially 1–72. Henry II died under rather curious circumstances—he fell from an upper window in his lodgings in Acre.

70. Ibid., 73–100. Thibaut III married Blanche, daughter of the king of Navarre.

71. Ibid., 101–97.

72. Ibid., 121–23. The treaty of 1213, for example, cost Blanche 20,000 pounds. The regent raised the money by means of aids; for example, we are told that the village of Chaource contributed 400 pounds.

73. Ibid., 198–265.

74. The relics of Troyes Cathedral included the body of Saint Mastida (Mâthie), a little-known virgin saint of local origin; Saint Savinien, martyr and evangelist of Troyes; also a set of objects acquired from Constantinople, including not only the relics of Saint Helen of Athyra, but also a fragment of the True Cross, the skull of Saint Philip, the arm of Saint James the Greater, as well as a dish used at the Last Supper. See J.-C. Courtalon-Delaistre, *Topographie historique*, II, 120–22, and P. J. Geary, "Saint Helen of Athyra and the Cathedral of Troyes in the Thirteenth Century," *Journal of Medieval and Renaissance Studies*, VII, 1977, 149–68; G. Constable, "Troyes, Constantinople, and the Relics of Saint Helen in the Thirteenth Century."

75. Ibid., 1040.

76. P. J. Geary, "Saint Helen of Athyra"; see also P. Héliot and M.-L. Chastang, "Quêtes et voyages de reliques au profit des églises françaises du moyen âge," *Revue d'histoire ecclésiastique*, LIX, 1964, 789–822; LX, 1965, 5–32.

77. P. J. Geary, "Saint Helen of Athyra," 159–60.

78. E. Viollet-le-Duc, *Dictionnaire raisonné de l'architecture française*, II, Paris, n.d., 341.

II. Conservatism and Innovation, Mistakes and Disaster

1. See especially R. H. Bautier, "Les foires de Champagne," 97–147.

2. F. Bourquelot, *Etudes sur les foires*, 199, provides a graph showing taxation levied on the fairs between 1275 and 1340. The sum recorded for the *foire de Saint Jean* was 1,300 pounds for 1275 and 180 pounds for 1340–1341.

3. H. d'Arbois de Jubainville, *Histoire des ducs et des comtes*, IV, 438. Henri had two children, Thibaut and Jeanne, but the son had fallen or been dropped from a high battlement of the château at Estellas to his death.

4. Ibid., IV, 456.

5. T. Boutiot, *Histoire de la ville de Troyes et de la Champagne méridionale*, 4 vols., Troyes and Paris, 1870–1875, esp. II, 134.

6. Ibid., 123–34.

7. A. Rigault, *Le procès de Guichard, évêque de Troyes (1308–1313)*, Mémoires et documents publiés par la Société de l'Ecole des Chartes, I, Paris, 1896; A. Pétal, "Documents inédits concernant Guichard, Evêque de Troyes," *Mém. Soc. acad. Aube*, LXVII, 1903, 199–213.

8. T. Boutiot, *Histoire de la ville de Troyes*, II, 111–21. See also F. Bibolet, "Le rôle de la guerre de cent ans dans le développement des libertés municipales à Troyes," *Mém. Soc. acad. Aube*, XCIX, 1939–1942, 295–315, esp. p. 305 where it is noted that the city walls were primarily of timber before the 1350s.

9. T. Boutiot, *Histoire de la ville de Troyes*, II, 139–46; F. Bibolet, "Le rôle de la guerre de cent ans," 306.

10. T. Boutiot, *Histoire de la ville de Troyes*, II, 237–38; F. Bibolet, "Les métiers à Troyes au XIVe. et XVe. siècles," *Actes du 95e. Congrès national des Sociétés savantes*, Reims, 1970, 113–32. Bibolet estimated that the population of Troyes fell from around 10,000 in the thirteenth century to around 6,000 in 1406. See also P. H. Denifle, *La désolation des églises, monastères et hôpitaux en France pendant la guerre de cent ans*, 2 vols., Paris, 1897–1899, esp. II, 240–41 and 370, where the author discussed the destruction of the countryside around Troyes in the period between 1359 and the 1370s, the damage done to the monastery of Montier-la-Celle, and the sale of several reliquaries by the clergy of the cathedral.

11. T. Boutiot, *Histoire de la ville de Troyes*, II, 262.

12. Income in these years ranged from 136 pounds (1294) to 1,398 pounds (1389–90). See Appendix C.

13. A *proviseur* might hold office for many years. Thus, from 1294 to 1301 Johannes Cantor, archdeacon of Sainte-Margerie, and Odo de Toriaco, canon, occupied the positions. Similarly, in the 1330s (between 1333 and 1340) the positions were held by Johannes de Auxeyo, cantor, and Obertus de Placentia, canon. Between 1366 and 1368 we find Guido de Virduno, archdeacon of Arcis, and Guillelmus de Creneyo, canon, as *proviseurs*. Guido still held the position in 1372-73, when his name was linked with that of Petrus de Arbosio or Pierre d'Arbois the younger, a canon. In 1377-78 Pierre d'Arbois served with Pierre d'Arcis, a canon, but in the following year a new team appeared, Jaques Cousin and Thomas Belle, described as *marreglier, presbytre*. The account for 1386-87 records the deaths of both Cousin and Belle, and for several years Pierre d'Arbois served alone as *proviseur*. He is described as being commissioned by the bishop and chapter. In the following year, he was joined by Erart de Vitel, and d'Arbois was described as being commissioned by the bishop and Vitel by the chapter. This arrangement provided the format used throughout the rest of the Middle Ages, with the exception of a brief period in the early fifteenth century when a third *proviseur* was added to report to the townspeople of Troyes. Vitel and d'Arbois worked together as a team for a period of about fifteen years.

14. S. Murray, "The Choir of the Church of Saint-Pierre, Cathedral of Beauvais." What the bishops of Beauvais gained in income they certainly lost in terms of the goodwill and support of the inhabitants of the city. It is no coincidence that the tenures of the two most enthusiastic building bishops of the thirteenth century, Miles de Nanteuil and Guillaume de Grez, were accompanied by violent urban uprisings. In Troyes, on the other hand, relations between the clergy and *bourgeois* were generally amicable, see F. Bibolet, "La participation du clergé aux affaires municipales de la ville de Troyes aux XIVe. et XVe. siècles," *Mém. Soc. acad. Aube*, C, 1943-1945, 51-70.

15. H. d'Arbois de Jubainville, *Pouillé du diocèse de Troyes redigé en 1407*, Paris, 1853. The chapter disposed of about forty prebends, see C. Lalore, *Cartulaire de Saint-Pierre de Troyes. Collection des principaux cartulaires du diocèse de Troyes*, V, Paris and Troyes, 1880, I-LXXIV, and A. Prévost, *Le diocèse de Troyes*, 3 vols., Domois, 1923-1926, esp. I, 132-48.

16. P. Geary, "Saint Helen of Athyra."

17. The arrangement of the first account in this series, 1294, differs from the others, evidently resulting from the fact that the *proviseurs*, Johannes and Odo, had just assumed office on the death of the previous agent, Johannes de Toriaco. The term of the account runs from Easter 1294 to July 1294.

18. For example, in 1300-1301 Arcis contributed 37 pounds and Troyes only 13; in 1299-1300 Arcis contributed 35 pounds and Troyes 12; in 1298-99, Arcis 32, Troyes 11, etc., etc.

19. References to the boxes opened on synod day in later accounts suggest that these boxes were placed in parish churches of the diocese.

20. In other words, the clergy refrained from commiting a fixed percentage of their regular income for the construction of the cathedral.

21. The sum involved was ten pounds; see Bibl. nat. lat. 9111, fol. 217 v°.-218 r°.

22. Ibid., 219 v°.

23. Bibl. nat. nouv. acq. lat. 1949, fol. 14 r°.

24. Each new canon paid a sum of money for his cope. In 1363 it was decided to assign these moneys to the fabric fund, see deliberations of the chapter, Arch. Aube, G 1273, fol. 10 r°. The assignment of the anniversaries is recorded, ibid., 12 r°. Another example of income normally received by the chapter being diverted to the fabric is recorded for the year 1365 when Pierre d'Arbois, *proviseur*, diverted 60 francs (pounds) to the fabric, "pour le fait de l'euvre il convient de l'argent," ibid., 24 r°. On September 11, 1365, the chamberlain was ordered to refrain from distributing money to those canons who owed money to the fabric, including the great archdeacon, ibid., 24 r°. On October 1, 1365, the *estat* (state) of the fabric was reviewed in a meeting of the chapter. It was noted that the receipts totalled 480 l. 2s. 7d. and expenses 471 l. 16s. 4d., ibid., 24 r°. Other examples of moneys diverted from the great chamber or from distributions are recorded, ibid., 27 v°. and 28 r°.

25. Arch. Aube, G 1273, fol. 4 r°.

26. F. Bibolet, "Le rôle de la guerre de cent ans," 300-308.

27. J. Roserot de Melin, *Bibliographie*, I, 92-97 and 109-14. The author is entirely negative concerning the use by previous historians of heraldic evidence as a means of dating the construction of the choir and transept. The arms of France and Navarre were once visible on the crossing vault, but Roserot pointed out that these arms were used by several different French kings.

28. L. Pigeotte, *Etude*, Preface, note 1, remarked that he was unable to extract any useful information from these accounts.

29. The upper parts of the transept were dated by N. Bongartz to the last decades of the thirteenth century (1280/85–1300/10); see *Die frühen Bauteile*, 175. I believe that the completion of the transept may have been somewhat more protracted, with the vaults only installed in the 1330s. The roof and tower would have been constructed before the vaults.

30. Payments to the glaziers are recorded twelve times in 1295–96 and twenty-nine times in 1296–97, but with no indication of which windows were being glazed.

31. For the original dedication of the nave chapels, see C. Lalore, *Collection des principaux obituaires et confraternités du diocèse de Troyes. Collection de documents inédits relatifs à la ville de Troyes et la Champagne méridionale*, Troyes, 1882, 205; A Prévost, *Le diocèse de Troyes*, I, 278; J. Roserot de Melin, *Bibliographie* I, 110; ibid, II, fig. 12; L. Pigeotte, *Etude*, VI-VIII. The chapels were known under the following designations:

North 1 (east end) Saint Michael, Saint John the Evangelist, station of Saint Jean de Latran, founded by Jaques de Basson, 1325.

North 2, Saint Fiacre, Trinity, Purification, "La Belle Chapelle."

North 3, Conception, Madeleine, founded by Jacques and Girard de la Noue, 1326.

North 4, Maurice du Gýe (1556); the chapel was built in the 1450s and 1460s.

North 5, Saint John Baptist, Hennequin, chapel of the archdeacon of Margerie.

South 1 (east end) Annunciation, Saint James the Greater.

South 2, Nativity, Assumption, Saint Jacques à la Lanterne, founded by Henri de la Noue, 1305.

South 3, Saint Louis, Saint Lazare, posthumous foundation by Denis de Champguion, 1309.

South 4, Saint Claude, Chapelle Pion.

South 5, Dreux (also Droin, Drouin, etc.) de la Marche, Assumption, later became baptismal chapel.

32. C. Lalore, *Collection des principaux obituaires*, 54 and 160–64; the original charters are in Arch. Aube, G 2659.

33. L. Pigeotte, *Etude*, XI.

34. Arch. Aube, G 2661. References to the generosity of Dean Henri de la Noue abound in the obituaries of Troyes Cathedral, see index in Lalore, *Collection des principaux obituaires*.

35. Ibid., 63, "Oct. 22, ce jour est mort, en 1270, M. Denis de Champguion, doyen, qui a fondé un anniversaire et les deux chapelles [read chaplains] de Saint Louis. Pour laquelle fondation des executeurs de son testament donnerent 2,000 livres. . . ." J. Roserot de Melin, *Bibliographie*, I, 110, provided a useful commentary on the charter of foundation of 1309, Arch. Aube, G 3757. It was only well after the death of the dean that his executors endowed the chaplaincies at the altar of Saint Louis (charter of March, 1309). Some confusion exists over the date of the death of Denis de Champguion. We thus find an obit with the date of his death given as 1270, another with 1295, while J. Roserot de Melin refers to his testament dated 1299. It was during this period (1270s to 1290s) that the decision was made to add chantry chapels. The chapels and aisles were receiving their vaults in the 1290s.

36. Arch. Aube, G 3761. Jacobus de Baacono also founded an anniversary (in 1325) for Bishop Nicolas, see C. Lalore, *Collection des principaux obituaires*, 35.

37. Ibid., 73, "Dec. 8, la feste de la Conception fondee annuelle par M. Pierre d'Arbois, chanoine at prebstre. . . . Elle estoit double de la fondation de Jacques de la Noe, qui est inhumé dans la chapelle de la Conception avec sa femme: leur tombeau estoit au milieu et fut relevé en 1619 quand M. Vestier fit bastir la dicte chapelle." For the foundation of the feast of the Conception in 1326, see A. Prévost, *Le diocese de Troyes*, II, 130. The knight Jacobus de la Noa is named as *garde des foires* between 1326 and 1335, see F. Bourquelot, *Etudes sur les foires*, 228–29.

38. H. d'Arbois de Jubainville, "Documents," XI and XII. See also J. Roserot de Melin, *Bibliographie*, I, 101–108.

39. Another passage in a fabric account of the same period places the archdeacon's house near the staircase turret of the north transept. There is every reason to believe that the two faulty choir flyers were in the bay immediately to the east of the transept.

40. The description of the rebuilding of Canterbury Cathedral is conveniently available in T. G. Frisch, *Gothic Art, 1140–c.1450, Sources and Documents in the History of Art*, Englewood Cliffs, 1971, 14–22.

41. J. Roserot de Melin, *Bibliographie* I, 104.

42. The word "forme" can have many meanings. "Forma" in ancient Latin could be used both as "shape" and "form" or to designate the moulds used in casting metal. In the fabric accounts we find "forme" applied both to the framework or center of an arch, and to the arch itself. It is frequently used to designate the arch of a window, hence "formette," a small

234

window, and "formeret," a window arch. The context of the word here makes it quite clear that a window is involved, since we read of a buttress inside a "forme" ("un pillier de croye qui est dedans la forme," B, 1389–90, 2). For "ferme" as a beam in the roof, see J. Roserot de Melin, *Bibliographie*, I, 134.

43. Piers C 5 and D 5 were originally pierced by a passage at triforium level. This passage was subsequently blocked and all the later piers of the nave were built without a passageway through them, access to the triforium being provided by means of a panel in each window, see N. Bongartz, *Die frühen Bauteile*, 169.

44. His disappearance from the cathedral workshop was not the result of his death since his name recurs several times in the following years in the records of the deliberations of the chapter, Arch. Aube, G 1273, 35 r⁰., 1365, discussion of a visit by Jehan de Torvoie to a house owned by the cathedral chapter.

45. H. d'Arbois de Jubainville, "Documents," XII.

46. Arch. Aube, G 1559, fol. 18 r⁰. fabric account for 1366–67 records the death of Master Thomas. An additional kind of remuneration was made available to this master mason: the deliberations of the chapter for 1363 record the decision to set aside the first available benefice for Master Thomas's son, Arch. Aube, G 1273, 10 r⁰.

47. H. d'Arbois de Jubainville, "Documents," XIV.

48. L. Pigeotte, *Etude*, X.

49. For a discussion of this account, see J. Quicherat, "Notice sur plusieurs registres de l'oeuvre de la cathédrale de Troyes," where the author, having noticed the more modern forms in the windows to the west of the transept arms adjacent to the crossing piers, suggests that the pier founded in 1372–73 was in this area. This suggestion is clearly quite out of the question.

50. The pillar was constructed by Michelin de Jonchery, Jehan Thierry, and Michelin Hardiot, each of whom earned 3s. per day. Jehan Thierry went on to undertake a number of other small projects in the 1370s. In 1378–79 he was thrown into the royal tower in Troyes in connection with the theft of a piece of iron from one of the cathedral bell towers, but his stay in prison was a short one, see Bibl. nat. lat. 9113, fol. 42 r⁰.

51. J. F. Gadan, "Comptes de l'église de Troyes."

52. A. de Champeaux and P. Gauchery, *Les travaux d'art, d'architecture et de sculpture exécutés pour Jean de France, Duc de Berry*, Paris, 1894; F. Lehoux, *Jean de France, Duc de Berri, sa vie, son action politique (1340–1416)*, 4 vols., Paris, 1966–1968. See also N. Canat de Chizy, "Etude sur le service des travaux publics et spécialement sur la charge de maître des oeuvres en Bourgogne sous les ducs de la race des Valois," *Bull. mon.*, LXIII, 1898, 245–72, 341–57, and 439–73.

53. This operation is also summarized in Appendix D.

54. J. Lafond, "Les vitraux de la cathédrale Saint-Pierre de Troyes," *Cong. arch.*, CXIII, 1955, 29–62.

55. For the earlier work at Troyes, see N. Bongartz, *Die frühen Bauteile*. For Saint-Urbain see F. Salet, "Saint-Urbain de Troyes." For Notre-Dame, M. Aubert, *Notre-Dame de Paris, sa place dans l'architecture du XIIe au XIVe siècle*, Paris, 1920.

56. The fact that the crowns of the vaults of the outer aisles are higher than those of the inner aisles contributes to the difficulty experienced in evacuating the rain water.

57. I am grateful to Caroline Bruzelius for sharing her unpublished manuscript on Saint-Denis with me. For Beauvais, see S. Murray, "The Choir of the Church of Saint-Pierre." The author is preparing a new study of Pierre de Montreuil.

58. The tracery of the clerestory windows on the east side of the transept arms was entirely replaced around 1506, see Appendix B.

59. These mouldings are not coursed into the masonry of the piers behind the front surfaces of the triforium and it is possible that some changes were introduced into the work in the course of execution. The relationship of the mullions of the triforium with the mullions of the clerestory is particularly uncomfortable. G. Russell kindly shared her ideas with me on the complex tracery pattern with interlocking lancets which was probably developed in the mid-thirteenth century on French soil and used at Westminster Abbey and Durham Cathedral; see G. Russell, "The North Window of the Nine Altars Chapel, Durham Cathedral," reprinted from *Medieval Art and Architecture at Durham Cathedral*, British Archaeological Association, 1980, 87–89.

60. A. F. Arnaud, *Voyage archéologique et pittoresque*, 158.

61. The unity of style in the first three bays of the nave is quite formidable, suggesting firm

direction and adequate funding. Some of the exterior details of the chapels on the north and south sides differ, suggesting that the southern chapels may have been constructed first.

62. Pier F 6 at the east end of the south aisles was entirely rebuilt at this time.

63. When the chapels were built no balustrade had been intended. The present balustrade was added by Master Anthoine Colas in the mid fifteenth century.

64. See note 37 above. Dean Henri de la Noue was buried in his chapel, the second from the east on the south side.

65. An identical window was placed in the eastern angled wall of each of the first two nave chapels, but these windows have been blocked with a thin screen of stone.

66. R. Branner, *Saint Louis and the Court Style*, fig. 76.

67. J. Lafond, "Les vitraux de la cathédrale Saint-Pierre de Troyes," 54. He remarked on the paradox that this provincial resistance to the acceptance of the dominance of grisaille should have taken place in the city of Troyes, where Saint-Urbain had been such an important pioneer in the use of grisaille. We might echo Lafond's comments as far as the architecture of Saint-Urbain and the cathedral is concerned.

68. The flanking pilasters, the gable, and trefoil are all present in the glass of the third chapel on the north side. We also note the absence of a balustrade in the architectural images of the stained glass and in the actual architecture of the chapel.

69. Such a square-nosed fillet can be found in the arcade on the west side of the transept arms of the cathedral. The matching arcade on the east side has almond shaped mouldings.

70. See Chapter IV.

71. Three distinct arrangements can be seen in the bases of the outermost mullions of the triforium bays. Attached to C6, D6, C5 and D5 we see tall flat-sided plinths, topped with a flattened moulding. Attached to C4 and C3 the base has been eliminated altogether. Attached to D4 and D3 can be seen bases that resemble the first type, with an additional moulding half way up. A very similar base is used at C2.

72. Thus, Henri de la Noue gave 4,000 pounds, a very substantial sum, and Denis de Champguion gave 2,000 pounds.

73. C. Lalore, *Collection des principaux obituaires*, from the Obituaire de Saint Pierre (fourteenth century) "Recommandises qui se faisaient tous les dimanches a la cathedrale de Troyes

devant la chapelle du Saint Sauveur apres la procession. . . . Pour l'ame le dean Henry de la Noe." He was considered such an important patron of the cathedral that he was allowed a tomb in his chapel and a prominant inscription in the window, ibid., 131.

III. *Maintenance, Repair, and Embellishment, 1390–1450*

1. For a recent survey of the artistic climate of the period see *Les fastes du gothique, le siècle de Charles V*, Paris, 1981.

2. T. Boutiot, *Histoire, de la ville de Troyes*, II, 426. The preliminary agreement between Henry V, Charles VI and the Duke of Burgundy was formalized in the cathedral. The wedding took place in Saint-Jean since Henry V was lodged in this parish.

3. T. Boutiot, *Histoire de la ville de Troyes*, II, 309, 314, 350.

4. H. d'Arbois de Jubainville, *Inventaire-sommaire des Archives départementales antérieures à 1790, Aube*, I, Paris, 1872, Introduction, esp. v, provides a useful analysis of the balance of political power and the Duke's efforts to gain support in the city of Troyes. Thus, in these years he made several substantial gifts to the cathedral fabric.

5. T. Boutiot, *Histoire de la ville de Troyes*, II, 464–65, quotes from the accounts from the episcopal estates. Collectors reported that they did not dare to venture into certain villages or that "la ville de Méry a esté destruite par la guerre et n'y demeure aucun des hommes ou femmes dud. eveché." A useful discussion of the effects of the war on the estates of the bishop of Troyes was provided by H. d'Arbois de Jubainville, *Inventaire-sommaire des Archives*, I, x–lxviii. He found that revenues of all kinds were sharply reduced or entirely eliminated through the damage caused by rival armies, with the worst periods directly after the murder of the Duke of Burgundy (1419) and in the 1430s, after the return of Troyes to loyalty to Charles VII.

6. T. Boutiot, *Histoire de la ville de Troyes*, II, 485–86. See also A. Prévost, *Le diocèse de Troyes*, II, 34.

7. The sources recording the consecration are indirect (obituaries, for example) and late, see J. Roserot de Melin, *Bibliographie*, I, 190.

8. Municipal support for the construction of the crossing tower may be explained in terms of practical considerations—the tower would

provide a look-out point commanding the surrounding countryside and could be used to hang bells. A tower would also assume a certain symbolic importance as the visual expression of the municipality. Thus, the meetings of the bourgeois for the annual election of the *voyeur* of the city took place at the *Beffroi*, a fortified gate; see F. Bibolet, "Le rôle de la guerre de cent ans," 300–301. It is important to note that the contributions from the municipality began well before the construction of the tower was taken in hand. In 1390–91, in the wake of the collapse of the upper nave, a sum of 386 pounds was received; in 1391–92, 40 pounds; in 1394–95, 40 pounds; in 1396–97 a similar sum was promised but not paid; in 1402–1403, 40 pounds, in 1409–10, 40 pounds, and in 1410–11 the same sum. It is possible that the citizens of Troyes were not happy with the way in which their contributions were being spent, and that this dissatisfaction lay behind the discussions that took place in 1412–13.

9. F. Bibolet, "La participation du clergé," 52.

10. H. d'Arbois de Jubainville, "Documents," XXV.

11. A. Prévost, *Le diocèse de Troyes*, II, 18; R. Vaughan, *Philip the Bold*, London, 1979; H. David, *Claus Sluter*, Paris, 1958; G. Troescher, *Claus Sluter und die burgundische Plastik um die Wende des XIVten Jahrhunderts*, Freiburg, 1932.

12. G. Durand, *Monographie de l'église Notre-Dame, cathédrale d'Amiens*, 2 vols., Paris, 1901–1903.

13. The bibliography for this provisional roof is very limited, and is summarized by J. Roserot de Melin, *Bibliographie*, I, 126–36.

14. This well, covered by a slab of stone, still exists at the foot of pier D3.

15. P. Piétresson de Saint-Aubin, "L'église de Saint-Jean-au-Marché à Troyes," *Cong. arch.*, CXIII, 1955, 85–95; F. Salet, "Saint-Urbain de Troyes," 114.

16. The choir buttresses have been transformed as a result of restoration work in the nineteenth century. However, the buttresses around the transept are original, and it can be seen that on the east side of the transept arms they had originally been pierced by a passageway which has subsequently been blocked.

17. The interior panelling is referred to as "chambril." F. Godefroy, *Dictionnaire de l'ancienne langue française*, II, Paris, 1883, cites a fifteenth century usage of the word "chambril" to indicate such a wooden barrel vault.

18. Roserot, in the many references he makes to the western wall, tends to confuse the "parois" or lateral screens with this provisional western wall; J. Roserot de Melin, *Bibliographie*, I, 159–65.

19. On the screen, see J. Roserot de Melin, *Bibliographie*, I, 146–56; A. Babeau, "La décoration intérieure de la cathédrale de Troyes," *Ann. Aube*, LXXIV, 1900, 37–39; A. F. Arnaud, *Voyage archéologique et pittoresque*, 158–59.

20. Arnaud specified that the depth of the arcade and the passageway surmounting the screen projected out to the east of the supports, which had angular fillets continuing into the arches. The five arched openings thus had some considerable depth—this depth was treated as a series of small ribbed vaults.

21. The career of Drouet de Dammartin is sketched in *Les fastes du gothique*, 430.

22. J. Roserot de Melin, *Bibliographie*, I, 258.

23. Ibid., 172, where the author is unnecessarily negative on the possibility of locating the pier in question.

24. H. d'Arbois de Jubainville, "Documents," XXI, gives the contract for the glazing of this rose;" see Appendix B, 1408.

25. L. Behling, *Gestalt und Geschichte des Masswerks*, Halle, 1944. See also P. Frankl, *Gothic Architecture*, 114–15.

26. J. Vallery-Radot, "Saint-Germain d'Auxerre"; idem, "La cathédrale de Saint-Etienne, *Cong. arch.*, CXVI, 1958, 26–39 and 40–59. See also C. Porée, *La Cathédrale d'Auxerre*, Paris, 1926, 16. A new monograph on Auxerre Cathedral is currently being prepared by Harry Titus.

27. F. Bibolet, "Le rôle de la guerre de cent ans," esp. 307. When after the disaster of Poitiers (1356) it was necessary to raise 3,750 pounds for the construction of city walls, the governer, Bishop Henri de Poitiers, asked for the advice of "les plus souffisans personnes et sages de touz les estaz de ladicte ville, tant d'église comme nobles, bourjois, monnoiers frans et autres." The accounts of the tax to be levied would be rendered in the presence of the bailiff and a delegation of the inhabitants of the city. Similar levies made in the following years helped to foster the development of the *conseil municipal*.

28. For a useful discussion of Gothic steeples, see E. Viollet-le-Duc, "Flèche," *Dictionnaire*, V, 426–72. See also L. Pigeotte, "Le grand clocher."

IV. The Late Gothic Masters of the Nave

1. T. Boutiot, *Histoire de la ville de Troyes*, III, 167–68. The Raguier family originated in

Bavaria and had come to France with Queen Isabella. They became wealthy through ecclesiastical benefices and financial speculation. Louis Raguier was abbot of Montier-la-Celle and Jacques, his nephew, of Montiéramey. The generosity of the Raguiers toward the fabric of Troyes Cathedral was made possible only through their considerable private fortune.

2. F. Bibolet, "Les métiers à Troyes," 115.

3. A useful summary of economic conditions and patronage in Troyes around 1500 can be found in R. Koechlin and J. J. Marquet de Vasselot, *La sculpture à Troyes et dans la Champagne méridionale au seizième siècle* (reprint), Paris, 1966, 21–43. See also R. Boutruche, "The Devastation of Rural Areas during the Hundred Years War and the Agricultural Recovery of France," *The Recovery of France in the Fifteenth Century*, ed. P. Lewis, London, 1971, esp. pp. 26–41 where the author provides illustrations of the destruction of the countryside and a discussion of Louis XI's policy of encouraging the revival of commerce and industry through the creation of a class of wealthy bourgeois.

4. The opening of the collecting boxes for the general pardon is recorded in a series of documents in Arch. Aube, G 2593.

5. Troyes was represented by Odard Hennequin, Simon Hennequin, Jean Pinette, Etienne Huyard, and Pierre de Brabant; see A. Prévost, *Le diocèse de Troyes*, II, 51.

6. The makeshift device referred to here is the support of the western bay of the nave by means of a battery of flying buttresses against the old bell tower and adjacent chapel.

7. Arch. Aube, G 1567.

8. Arch. Aube, G 1568.

9. The rather rigid format used in the receipt section of the accounts tends to make the process seem simpler than it actually was. The year of the account generally ran from July to July, and the accountant was supposed to declare all transactions made within that fiscal year. The flow of cash from the various sources of income was a continuous and disorderly one and it seems that additional gifts could generally be procured to meet a crisis situation, such as the collapse of the upper nave in 1389. A *proviseur* could always meet a small deficit in a particular year's account by applying some of next year's income. No examples of loans can be found.

10. Martin Chambiges, the master of the western frontispiece, was described as *supremus artifex* in the records of the deliberations of the chapter (B 1502). Masters such as Jaquet le Vachier, Anthoine Colas, or Jehançon Garnache were simply called "mason" or "master mason." Such masters were able to design and construct units such as pillars, arches, vaults, windows, etc., but needed constant direction as far as the overall planning was concerned. Martin Chambiges, on the other hand, assumed direction of the entire process of planning and construction, including control of details such as the design of lifting gear at the quarry, and he did not need to be told what to do next.

11. A. F. Arnaud, *Voyage archéologique et pittoresque*, 140, remarked, "on peut suivre progressivement la décadence du goût. . . ."

12. A fillet is a moulding form with a rounded body and a square-shaped front edge; see Fig. 22.

13. The five piers were A 2, B 2, D 2, E 2, and F 2. C 2 had been built in the fourteenth century.

14. L. Benoist, *Notre-Dame de l'Epine*, Paris, 1933; A Villes, "Notre-Dame de l'Epine, sa façade occidentale," *Cong. arch.*, CXXXV, 1977, 779–862. At Notre-Dame de l'Epine pier forms similar to those favored by Bleuet can be found in the choir screen.

15. This master had first been identified as Master "B," see S. Murray, "The Completion of the Nave of Troyes Cathedral," *JSAH*, XXXIV, 1975, 121–39. The discovery of new documents allowed the identification of Master "B" as Bleuet; see S. Murray, "Bleuet and Anthoine Colas, Master Masons of Troyes Cathedral."

16. For the use of the rotated square in Late Gothic, see F. Bucher, "Design in Gothic Architecture," *JSAH*, XXVII, 1968, 49–71 and L. Shelby, *Gothic Design Techniques*.

17. It is hard to give a precise date for the end of this master's tenure, since Martin Chambiges, who first arrived in Troyes in 1502, directed as an absentee master from Beauvais, only visiting Troyes from time to time.

18. It is evident that the bundles of shafts attached to the piers at C 3 and D 3 were only brought up to the level of the capitals of the main arcade in the early campaigns of construction on the nave. Below this level the mortar joints gape somewhat, suggesting that the piers have been subject to weathering.

19. J. Fitchen, *The Construction of Gothic Cathedrals*, Oxford, 1961, esp. 139. A roof was, of course, necessary to protect the unfinished vaults from the rain. The timbers of the roof might also serve to support lifting gear used in the installation of the vaults.

238

20. These spurs were restored in 1889 by the architect Selmersheim, who fortunately left us a sketch of the southern spur prior to restoration (Fig. 23). At the outer edge of the spur, a wall was to have joined at 90 degrees: this would have been the northern wall of the south tower. The inscription "The First Pillar of the Tower," was originally situated at the angle where the spur joined the wall of the tower, but it was removed and set in its present location on the west side of the southern spur.

21. The gable and the roof to the west of the gable were heavily reworked in the nineteenth century. Prior to this restoration, much of the gable had been hidden by a steeply pitched roof. By reducing the pitch of the roof the restorers of the cathedral were able to expose the gable. The original disposition is visible in the pre-restoration lithograph, Fig. 33.

22. Stone flyers against a structure without vaults can be seen at Saint-Pantaléon, Troyes.

23. Although Garnache would have to find the wages of his apprentices who would help him with the installation of the vaults. One reason why the vaults were built under contract related to fund-raising. Thus, it was convenient to have a round sum to propose to potential donors. The vaults of the nave were given by the great archdeacon, the city of Troyes, the bishop, and the king. The great archdeacon was Pierre de Refuge, archdeacon of Arcis, counsellor in the parlement and licensed in law.

24. R. Sanfaçon, L'architecture flamboyante en France, Quebec, 1971, 118–19.

25. Each clerestory window in the nave was given by a different donor. Among these donors we find the confraternity of Saint Sebastian; three widows; two merchants; two lawyers; two ecclesiastics, one person of seigneurial rank, and two persons with no designation of rank; see C. Fichot, Statistique monumentale du départemente de l'Aube, II, Troyes, 1884, 209–45; P. Biver, L'Ecole troyenne de peinture sur verre, Paris, 1935. Biver characterizes the glass of the nave in terms of the absence of architectural frames, the audacity of the deeply saturated colors, the signs of mass production and the forceful, almost savage quality of the figure style. The return to deeply saturated colors in the revival of stained glass in the decades around 1500 allowed Troyes Cathedral to retain a wonderful unity in the glass of the clerestory.

26. S. Murray, "The Completion of the Nave."

27. R. Branner, Saint Louis and the Court Style, figs. 48 and 140.

V. Martin Chambiges

1. The word "artifex" means master of any art, but it also carries the additional meaning of artist, maker, or contriver.

2. For the political events of the period see E. Lavisse, Histoire de France, V, Paris, 1903, 67–83. The period coincides with the end of the war in Italy.

3. H. Reinhardt, La cathédrale de Reims, Paris, 1967, 207–209.

4. The quittance for the visit of Martin Chambiges to Senlis in 1504 is conserved in the Archives Départementales de l'Oise, G 2717, titres généraux. Chambiges signed with a mark. E. Couard-Luys, "Note sur une mission de Martin Chambiges à Senlis en 1504," Bulletin archéologique du Comité des travaux historiques et scientifiques, 1884, 470–73, concluded that Chambiges was illiterate. However, a full signature can be found in a document dated 1502, recording a visit to the river Merdenson in Beauvais; see V. Leblond, L'art et les artistes en Ile-de-France au XVIe siècle (Beauvais et Beauvaisis) d'après les minutes notoriales, Paris and Beauvais, 1921, Plate I.

5. The escalation of income and expenses also reflects a sharp inflationary movement; see Y. Labande—Mailfert, Charles VIII et son milieu (1470–1498), Paris, 1975, esp. p. 522. The same author (p. 511) also provides a useful discussion of the extraordinary taxation that had been developed in the fourteenth century under the pressure of war, including the salt tax (gabelle). With the end of the war it was now possible to apply this wealth to building. For a useful study of the strong economic revival in Troyes, see P. Leroy, "Histoire économique et sociale des églises de la Champagne méridionale à la fin du moyen âge et au début des temps modernes," Diplôme d'études supérieures d'histoire, n.d.

6. A.-S. Det, "La Belle-Croix de Troyes, Ann. Aube, LVIII, 1884, 83–134.

7. R. Koechlin and J. J. Marquet de Vasselot, La sculpture à Troyes, 27.

8. The fabric accounts for the work on the Sens transept are in the Archives Départementales de l'Yonne at Auxerre, G 1141-1143. See also the excellent study by C. Porée, "Les architectes et la construction de la cathédrale de Sens," Cong. arch., LXXIV, 1907, 559–598. Cuvelier worked at Sens as second-in-command, interpreting

the plans of Martin Chambiges during that master's absences.

9. For "false templates" see Appendix B, 1452–53, 3.

10. Jehan Gailde is also sometimes called "Big John" (Grand Jehan) in the contemporary written sources. He is well known as the architect of the choir screen of the Madeleine in Troyes; see F. Salet, "la Madeleine de Troyes," *Cong. arch.*, CXIII, 1955, 139–52. The choir of the church of the Madeleine was rebuilt in the last years of the fifteenth century and the fabric accounts of the cathedral allow us to establish the identity of Jehan Gailde as master mason, since we find several instances of purchases of stones from the cathedral fabric for the construction of the choir of La Madeleine. These purchases were negotiated by Jehan Gailde, named as master mason of la Madeleine (for example, Arch. Aube, G 1514, 329 v⁰.). Gailde also worked on the city fortifications, especially the gates known as the Beuffroy and Comporte; see T. Boutiot, *Histoire de la ville de Troyes*, II, 222–23 and idem, "Des anciennes fortifications et de l'ancien beffroi de la ville de Troyes," *Ann. Aube*, XLVIII, 1894, 77–110; see also the *Archives de la Ville de Troyes*, series B and D. Gailde also worked on the Belle-Croix of the city of Troyes, see R. Koechlin and J. J. Marquet de Vasselot, *La sculpture à Troyes*, 63.

11. Jehan Bailly assumes considerable importance in the workshop in these years, but I have not been able to ascertain his background. In 1499 he was listed together with Jehançon Garnache in the context of a visit to inspect the city walls, see *Archives de la Ville de Troyes*, B 57. He went on to work at the churches of Saint-Jean and Saint-Pantaléon, Troyes; see *Arch. Aube*, G 19 and G 15. His son, Jehan II Bailly, became master of the cathedral workshop in 1532.

12. The size of these blocks of stone is unprecedented, as is the very detailed nature of the instructions. P. Piétresson de Saint-Aubin associated this with a change in the relationship between the cathedral workshop and the quarry placing more responsibility for the preliminary cutting upon the quarriers; see Chapter I, note 23.

13. The bulk of the figurative sculpture was located in the voussoirs: there were twelve "histoires" in the voussoirs of each of the side portals and thirty-four in the center portal (eighteen in an outer order, and sixteen in an inner one). Most of the "histories" for the voussoirs were carved by the Flemish artist, Nicolas Halins; see E. Gavelle, *Nicolas Halins dit le Flamand, tailleur d'images à Troyes (vers 1470–après 1541)*, Lille, 1924, and R. Koechlin and J. J. Marquet de Vasselot, *La sculpture à Troyes*. The work was spread over a fourteen-year period, and the execution of sculptures for the three portals overlapped to a considerable extent, as can be seen in the following table:

LEFT PORTAL	CENTER PORTAL	RIGHT PORTAL
Life of St. Peter	Passion of Christ	Life of St. Paul
1517–18 Cartoons made for figures of Peter, Paul, and Christ, to serve in the trumeaux		
1521–22	Passion cycle begun (Scenes unnamed)	
1522–23 1. Scene from the life of St. Peter.		
1523–24 2–5. Four unnamed scenes from the life of St. Peter. *Note*: these scenes were made for the north transept façade, presumably as *essais* for the west façade.		

1524–25	1. Scourging of Christ.	1. Unnamed scene from the life of St. Paul.
6. Simon Magus breaks his neck.	2. Job beaten by the devil.	2. Paul baptized by Ananias.
7. Dogs tear Simon Magus.		3. Paul decapitated by Nero.
8. Peter unleashes the dogs.		4. Paul preaches to the Jews in prison.
		5. Paul receives letters from the bishop of Jerusalem.
		6. Entombment of Paul.
1525–26	3. Resurrection.	7. Paul lowered over the city wall.
Arms of France.	4. Jonah and the whale (a "figure" of the resurrection).	8. Paul raises Patriocle.
		9. Paul converts St. Denis.
		10. Paul preaches the name of Jesus to him.
		11. Paul beaten by the Jews.
		12. Paul casts devil out of woman.
1526–27	5. Christ blindfolded and buffeted.	
	6. Crowned with crown of thorns.	
	7. Shown by Pilate to the Jews.	
	8. Pilate judges Christ and washes his hands.	
	9. God (Christ) carries his cross to Calvary.	
	10. Descent into hell.	
	11. Entombment.	
	12. Notre Dame de Pitié holds Christ on her lap.	
	13. Descent from the cross.	
	14. Christ raised on cross.	
	15. Hanging on the cross.	
1527–28		Arms of the Dauphin, perhaps intended for the south portal.
1530–31	Pieta, John, and Madeleine for the gable of the central portal.	

The succession of "histoires" in the voussoirs recalls the sequence of scenes in a mystery pageant, and similar sequences can also be seen in numerous retables from the early sixteenth century, see R. Koechlin and J. J. Marquet de Vasselot, *La sculpture à Troyes* and C. Avery, *Sculpture from Troyes in the Victoria and Albert Museum*, London, 1974.

14. The vaults under the towers were left unfinished, presumably to allow material to be hoisted up inside the towers to facilitate the completion of the upper parts. These vaults were only completed in the late eighteenth century,

thanks to the initiative of the canon Bouczo; see the *Almanach de Troyes*, 1783, 188, and 1789, 196–97.

15. The date 1554 is carved on a scroll held by a bearded man sometimes identified as Jehan II Bailly, see J. Roserot de Melin, *Bibliographie*, II, 55.

16. The west façade can be seen at a variety of angles from the ample space of the *Place Saint-Pierre*. The north side of the north tower can be seen from the *Rue de la Cité*, although the south flank of the south tower is somewhat hidden by the buildings of the former episcopal complex.

17. This organ tribune was installed after 1806; see J. Roserot de Melin, *Bibliographie*, I, 267.

18. The sculptural decoration of these niches provides an amusing commentary upon the arrival of Italianate taste in France: in the Gothic niches we find chubby *putti* and cockleshells. The towers were to have housed spacious chambers with octopartite vaults and lavish sculptural details, but the vaults were never installed, and the vast interior spaces of the towers were left to serve as a meeting spot for the masons at work on the cathedral. Generations of such masons have left their graffiti.

19. A. F. Arnaud, *Voyage archéologique et pittoresque*, 131, cited by J. Roserot de Melin, *Bibliographie*, I, 224.

20. A. F. Arnaud, *Voyage archéologique et pittoresque*, 140.

21. H. d'Arbois de Jubainville, "Documents," 214. The author assured the potential visitor that once through the west portal they would see a splendid program of architecture and stained glass, constructed over many centuries.

22. L. Pigeotte, *Etude*, 67.

23. P. Frankl, *Gothic Architecture*, 200.

24. R. Sanfaçon, *L'architecture flamboyante en France*, 109.

25. M. Vachon, *Une famille parisienne d'architectes maistres maçons, les Chambiges, 1490–1643*, Paris, 1907, 76; V. de Courcel, "La cathédrale de Troyes," 26.

26. A. Blunt, *Art and Architecture in France; 1500–1700*, Harmondsworth, 1970, 3.

27. H. K. Kunze, *Das Fassadenproblem der französischen Früh- und Hochgotik*, Leipzig, 1912.

28. F. Bucher, "Design in Gothic."

29. S. Murray, "An Expertise at Beauvais Cathedral," *Jour. Brit. Arch. Assoc.*, CXXX, 1977, 135–44.

30. The best existing survey of the work of Martin Chambiges is still M. Vachon, *Une famille parisienne*. An unsigned note on "Chambriche ou Chambige" appeared in *Magasin Pittoresque*, 1856, 339–40, in which the author (perhaps M. Vallet de Viriville) suggested that the master's name signified "from Cambrai." See also A. Berty, *Les grands architectes français de la Renaissance*, Paris, 1860. See also the *Histoire générale de Paris; topographie historique du vieux Paris*, I, Paris, 1885, 263–64, where Martin Chambiges is treated as "un des architectes les plus éminents que la France ait produits." L. Gonse, *L'art gothique*, Paris, 1890, p. 280, added several nondocumented attributions to M. Chambiges' already prolific

oeuvre. See also C. Bauchal, *Nouveau dictionnaire biographique et critique des architectes français*, Paris, 1887; unpublished Ph.d. dissertations on Martin Chambiges were done by R. J. Nelson for Johns Hopkins University and S. Murray for the University of London.

31. C. Porée, "Les architectes"; P. Kurman and D. von Winterfeld, "Gauthier de Varinfroy, ein 'Denkmalpfleger' im 13. Jahrhundert," *Festschrift für Otto von Simson zum 65. Geburtstag*, Berlin, 1977, 101–59.

32. The motif was derived from late thirteenth-century prototypes.

33. E. Gavelle, *Notice architecturelle sur l'église de Rumilly-les-Vaudes (Aube)*, Arcis, 1896; R. J. Nelson, "A Lost Portal by Martin Chambiges," *JSAH*, XXXIII, 1974, 155–57; L. Gonse, *L'Art gothique*, 280; L. Brochard, *Saint-Gervais. Histoire du monument d'après de nombreux documents inédits*, Paris, 1938.

34. J. Meurgey de Tupigny, *Saint-Jacques de la Boucherie et la Tour Saint-Jacques*, Paris, 1960.

35. Many examples can be found of the most characteristic motif employed by Martin Chambiges—namely the penetration of two or more straight lines through the curving lines of a portal or niche canopy: for example, in the portal of Saint-Benoît, Paris, now conserved in the garden of the Musée de Cluny; in the fragments of woodwork in the same museum; in the niche canopies of Saint-Nicolas-des-Champs, in the work of Jehan de Beausse at Chartres, namely the *clôture* of the choir and the northwest tower. In Paris, the work which most resembles that of Martin Chambiges can be seen in the sculptured fragments of the Hôtel le Gendre now conserved at the Ecole des Beaux-Arts and Musée de Cluny (Fig. 107), see A. Chastel, "Les vestiges de l'Hôtel le Gendre et le véritable Hôtel de la Trémoïlle," *Bull. mon.*, CXXIV, 1966, 129–65.

36. F. Bonnardot, *Registres des délibérations du Bureau de la Ville de Paris*, I, 1499–1526, Paris, 1883, I–LXXVIII.

37. A. Barrault, *L'église Saint-Aspais de Melun*, Meaux, 1964. Jean de Felin's work at Melun was criticised by contemporaries as too decorative and too expensive.

38. G. Durand, *Monographie de l'église Notre-Dame, cathédrale d'Amiens*.

39. G. Desjardins, *Histoire de la cathédrale de Beauvais*, Beauvais, 1865; V. Leblond, *La cathédrale de Beauvais*, Paris, 1956; idem, "Les artistes de Beauvais et du Beauvaisis au XVIe siècle et leurs oeuvres," *Mémoires de la Société académique de*

242

l'Oise, XXIV, 1923; 85–138; idem, *L'art et les artistes*.

40. The evidence for this chronology is derived from the so-called Bucquet–aux Cousteaux Collection, a series of texts copied in the eighteenth century from the lost archives of the cathedral, coupled with an analysis of the changing forms of the pier bases. See S. Murray, "The Choir of Saint-Etienne at Beauvais," *JSAH*, XXXVI, 1977, 111–21.

41. The piers of Saint-Etienne, which are very similar to those in the cathedral, cannot be considered copies since they embody variations on the same design theme; a similar change affects the bases of the piers in both monuments presumably at the same time, and the earliest bases in Saint-Etienne embody a similar design to that used by Martin Chambiges at Sens Cathedral.

42. Thus, if we start with the main circle used to locate the center points of the eight shafts and inscribe hexagons inside this main circle, we find that the sixth such hexagon gives us the size of the plinths used for the main shafts and the ninth hexagon gives us the size of the plinths used for the diagonals. This system works for the smaller piers of the Beauvais Cathedral transept, but not for the great crossing piers.

43. In the piers attached to the lateral walls of the west towers at Troyes, we see that the center points for the main shafts and the diagonals do not lie upon a single master circle, thus placing this design in relationship with the piers in the choir of Saint-Etienne, where we also find that two different main circles are used.

44. M. Dumoulin and G. Outardel, *Les églises de France. Paris et la Seine*, Paris, 1936, 35; A. Boinet, *Les édifices réligieux: moyen âge—Renaissance*, Paris, 1910, 75–87; A. Demy, "Essai historique sur l'église Saint-Séverin," *Librairie des Archives nationales de la Société de l'Ecole des Chartes*, Paris, 1903; Abbé Y. Moubarac, *Guide de l'église Saint-Séverin*, Paris, 1964. The church of Saint-Germain l'Auxerrois offers us another example of a Parisian church where successive campaigns of construction took place in the fifteenth century, but the dating of the nave and porch is difficult to establish: see works by Lesort and Troche cited in the Bibliography. The porch is usually dated in the 1430s and attributed to Jean Gaussel,

but even the most cursory study of the porch will indicate that while this date is feasible for the two outer bays (Fig. 109), the three inner bays, with their complex piers and star vaults are closer to 1500.

45. Bucquet–aux Cousteaux Collection, XXVIII 221–40.

46. M. L. Régnier, *La renaissance dans le Vexin et dans une partie du Parisis*, Pontoise, 1886; idem, *Quelques mots sur les monuments de Gisors*, Gisors, 1909. For Saint-Antoine, Compiègne, and Allonne, see *Dictionnaire des églises*, IV D2 and IV D55. For Senlis, see M. Aubert, *Monographie de la cathédrale de Senlis*, Paris, 1910.

47. Vachon suggested that Martin Chambiges retained control over the workshop using his son-in-law Jehan de Damas as local director. Given the latter's full-time role in the construction of the Troyes façade, this seems most unlikely.

48. The presence of Pierre Chambiges as master at Senlis is documented. See Afforty's handwritten *Notes sur Senlis*, microfilm, Archives départementales de l'Oise, vol. 24, p. 30.

49. P. Piétresson de Saint-Aubin, "L'église Saint-Jean," F. Salet, "L'église Saint-Pantaléon."

50. See note 11 above.

51. The accounts for Saint-Jean are in the Archives de l'Aube, G 15.

52. C. Lalore, *L'église de l'abbaye de Montier-la-Celle*, Troyes, 1882.

53. The workshops of both churches were visited by the master mason of the cathedral, but it is clear that the master involved was Jean de Damas and not Martin Chambiges.

54. E. Lefèvre-Pontalis, "L'architecture gothique dans la Champagne méridionale au XIIIe et au XVIe siècles," *Cong. arch.*, LXIX, 1902, 273–349; Mgr. A. Marsat, *Les églises de l'Aube*, 2 vols., Art et Tourism, n.d.

55. See note 10 above. The accounts for Saint-Jean-au-Marché reveal the existence of quite a tug-of-war between Gailde and the Chambiges' men for influence over the workshop.

56. E. Poulle, "L'église Saint-Nicolas de Troyes," *Cong. arch.*, CXIII, 1955, 71–84.

57. L. Neagley studied Brienne for her Master's Essay at Indiana University.

58. M. Vachon, *Une famille parisienne.*

Selected Bibliography

Ackerman, J. S., "Ars Sine Scientia Nihil Est,"
  Art Bull., XXXI, 1949, 84–111.
Almanach de Troyes, 1783 and 1789.
André, F., *Inventaire-sommaire des Archives départe-
  mentales antérieures à 1790, Aube*, II, Paris and
  Troyes, 1896.
Arbois de Jubainville, H. d', *Pouillé du diocèse de
  Troyes redigé en 1407*, Paris, 1853.
————, *Répertoire archéologique du département de
  l'Aube*, Paris, 1861.
————, "Documents relatifs aux travaux de
  construction faits à la cathédrale de Troyes,"
  Bibl. Ecole Chartes, 23e. année, Paris, 1862,
  214–47 and 393–423.
————, *Histoire des ducs et des comtes de Champagne*,
  7 vols., Paris and Troyes, 1859–1869.
————, *Inventaire-sommaire des Archives départemen-
  tales antérieures à 1790, Aube*, I, Paris and
  Troyes, 1872.
Arnaud, A. F., *Antiquités de la ville de Troyes*,
  Troyes, 1822.
————, *Voyage archéologique et pittoresque dans le
  département de l'Aube*, Troyes, 1837.
Assier, A., "Comptes de la fabrique de l'église
  Sainte-Madeleine de Troyes," *Bibl. Dép.
  Aube*, VIII, Troyes, 1854.
————, "Comptes de la fabrique de l'église
  Saint-Jean de Troyes," *Bibl. Dép. Aube*, IX,
  Troyes, 1855.
————, "Comptes de l'oeuvre de l'église de
  Troyes avec notes et éclaircissements ou
  nouvelles recherches sur la construction des
  églises et sur les usages au moyen-âge,"
  Troyes, 1855, extract from *Bibl. Dép. Aube*,
  X, 1855.
————, *Les arts et les artistes dans l'ancienne capitale
  de la Champagne 1250–1680*, 2 vols., Paris,
  1876.
Aubert, M., *Monographie de la cathédrale de Senlis*,
  Paris, 1910.
————, *Notre-Dame de Paris; sa place dans l'archi-
  tecture du XIIe au XIVe siècle*, Paris, 1920.

Aufauvre, A., *Album pittoresque et monumental du
  département de l'Aube*, Troyes, 1852.
Avery, C., *Sculpture from Troyes in the Victoria and
  Albert Museum*, London, 1974.
Babeau, A. "L'église Saint-Pantaléon de Troyes,"
  Ann. Aube, LV, 1881, 33–74.
————, "La décoration intérieure de la cathédrale
  de Troyes," *Ann. Aube*, LXXIV, 1900, 31–
  59.
Barrault, A., *L'église Saint-Aspais de Melun*, Meaux,
  1964.
Bauchal, C., *Nouveau dictionnaire biographique et
  critique des architectes français*, Paris, 1887.
Baurit, M., *Saint-Germain l'Auxerrois. Son histoire
  et ses oeuvres d'art*, Paris, 1952.
Bautier, R.-H., "Les foires de Champagne, re-
  cherches sur une évolution historique,"
  Recueils de la Société Jean Bodin, V, Brussels,
  1953, 97–147.
Bégule, L., *La cathédrale de Sens, son architecture,
  son décor*, Lyon, 1929.
Behling, L., *Gestalt und Geschichte des Masswerks*,
  Halle, 1944.
Benoist, L., *Notre-Dame de l'Epine*, Paris, 1933.
Berty, A., *Les grands architectes français de la
  Renaissance*, Paris, 1860.
Bialostocki, "Late Gothic, Disagreements about
  the Concept," *Jour. Brit. Arch. Assoc.*, XXIX,
  1966, 76–105.
Bibolet, F., "Le rôle de la guerre de cent ans
  dans le développement des libertés munici-
  pales à Troyes," *Mém. Soc. acad. Aube*, XCIX,
  1939–1942, 295–315.
————, "La participation du clergé aux affaires
  municipales de la ville de Troyes aux XIVe.
  et XVe. siècles," *Mém. Soc. acad. Aube*, C,
  1943–1945, 51–70.
————, "Les métiers à Troyes au XIVe. et XVe.
  siècles," *Actes du 95e. Congrès national des
  Sociétés savantes*, Reims, 1970, 113–32.
Biver, P., *L'Ecole troyenne de peinture sur verre*,
  Paris, 1935.

Blunt, A., *Art and Architecture in France; 1500–1700*, Harmondsworth, 1970.

Boinet, A., *Les édifices réligieux: moyen âge—Renaissance*, Paris, 1910.

Bongartz, N., *Die frühen Bauteile der Kathedrale in Troyes, Architekturgeschichtliche Monographie*, Stuttgart, 1979.

Bonnardot, F., *Registres des délibérations du Bureau de la ville de Paris, I, 1499–1526*, Paris, 1883.

————, and Lespinasse, R. de, *Les métiers et corporations de la ville de Paris, XIIIe. siècle. Le livre des métiers d'Etienne Boileau*, Paris, 1879.

Bonnenfant, G., *La cathédrale d'Evreux*, Paris, n.d.

Bony, J., *French Gothic Architecture of the 12th and 13th Centuries*, Berkeley, 1983.

Booz, P., *Der Baumeister der Gotik*, Munich, 1956.

Bourquelot, F., *Etudes sur les foires de Champagne. Mémoires présentés par divers savants à l'Académie des Inscriptions at Belles Lettres*, IIe. série, V, Paris, 1865.

Boutiot, T., "Fouilles de la cathédrale de Troyes opérées en juin 1864," *Mém. Soc. acad. Aube*, XXX, 1866, 5–11.

————, *Histoire de la ville de Troyes et de la Champagne méridionale*, 4 vols., Troyes and Paris, 1870–1875.

————, "Des anciennes fortifications et de l'ancien beffroi de la ville de Troyes," *Ann. Aube*, XLVIII, 1874, 77–110.

Boutruche, R., "The Devastation of Rural Areas during the Hundred Years War and the Agricultural Recovery of France," in *The Rural Recovery of France in the Fifteenth Century*, ed. P. Lewis, London, 1971.

Branner, R., "Les débuts de la cathédrale de Troyes," *Bull. mon.*, CXVIII, 1960, 111–22.

————, "Jean d'Orbais and the Cathedral of Reims," *Art Bull.*, XLIII, 1961, 131–33.

————, "The Labyrinth of Reims Cathedral," *JSAH*, XXI, 1962, 18–25.

————, "Le maître de la cathédrale de Beauvais," *Art de France*, II, 1962, 78–92.

————, *Saint Louis and the Court Style*, London, 1965.

Brochard, L., *Saint-Gervais. Histoire du monument d'après de nombreux documents inédits*, Paris, 1938.

Bruzelius, C., *The Thirteenth Century Church at Saint-Denis*, New Haven, 1985.

Bucher, F., "Design in Gothic Architecture, a Preliminary Assessment," *JSAH*, XXVII, 1968, 49–71.

Bur, M., *La formation du comté de Champagne, v. 950–v. 1150*, Nancy, 1977.

Cali, F. *L'ordre flamboyante et son temps*, Paris, 1967.

Camusat, N., *Promptuarium*, Troyes, 1610.

Canat de Chizy, N., "Etude sur le service des travaux publics et spécialement sur la charge de maître des oeuvres en Bourgogne sous les ducs de la race de Valois," *Bull. mon.*, LXIII, 1898, 245–72; 341–57 and 439–73.

Champeaux, A. de and Gauchery, P., *Les travaux d'art, d'architecture et de sculpture exécutés pour Jean de France, Duc de Berry*, Paris, 1894.

Chapin, E., *Les villes de foires de Champagne, des origines au début du XIVe. siècle*, Paris, 1937.

Chastel, A., "Les vestiges de l'Hôtel le Gendre et le véritable Hôtel de la Trémoïlle," *Bull. mon.*, CXXIV, 1966, 129–65.

Christ, Y. *Eglises parisiennes actuelles et disparues*, Paris, 1947.

————, "Les vestiges de l'ancien Musée des Monuments français à l'Ecole des Beaux-Arts et leur sort," *Gaz des B. A.*, LXVI, 1965, 167–74.

Colombier, P. du, *Les chantiers des cathédrales*. Paris, 1953.

Colvin, H., *Building Accounts of King Henry III*, Oxford, 1971.

Constable, G., "Troyes, Constantinople, and the Relics of Saint Helen in the Thirteenth Century," *Mélanges René Crozet*, II, Poitiers, 1966, 1035–41.

Couard-Luys, E., "Note sur une mission de Martin Chambiges à Senlis en 1504," *Bulletin archéologique du Comité des travaux historiques et scientifiques 1884*, 470–73.

Courcel, V. de, "La cathédrale de Troyes," *Cong. arch.*, CXIII, 1955, 9–28.

Courtalon-Delaistre, J.-C., *Topographie historique de la ville et du diocèse de Troyes*, 3 vols., Troyes, 1733–1734.

Coyecque, E., "Le transept de la cathédrale de Beauvais 1499–1500," *Nouvelles archives de l'Art français*, VII, 1891, 101–103.

Crozet, R., "Les églises rurales de la Champagne orientale et méridionale du XIIIe. au XVIe. siècle," *Bull. mon.*, LXXXIX, 1930, 355–79.

David, H., *Claus Sluter*, Paris, 1958.

Demoy, P., and Mangue, E., *La cathédrale de Troyes*, Colmar, 1976.

Demy, A., "Essai historique sur l'église Saint-Séverin," *Librairie des Archives nationales de la Société de l'Ecole des Chartes*, Paris, 1903.

Deneux, H., *L'évolution des charpentes du XIe. au XVIIIe. siècle*, Paris, 1927.

Denifle, P. H., *La désolation des églises, monastères et hôpitaux en France pendant la guerre de cent ans*, 2 vols., Paris, 1897–1899.

Desjardins, G., *Histoire de la cathédrale de Beauvais*, Beauvais, 1865.

Det., A.-S., "La Belle-Croix de Troyes," *Ann. Aube*, LVIII, 1884, 83–134.

Dorez, L., *Dominique de Cortone et Pierre Chambiges*, Paris, 1904.

Dufourcq, N., *L'église Saint-Merry*, Paris, 1947.

Dumoulin, M., and Outardel, G., *Les églises de France. Paris et la Seine*, Paris, 1936.

Durand, G., *Monographie de l'église Notre-Dame, cathédrale d'Amiens*, 2 vols., Paris, 1901–1903.

Enlart, C., "Origine anglaise du style flamboyant," *Bull. mon.*, LXX, 1906, 38–81 and 511–25; LXXIV, 1910, 125–47.

Erskine, A. M., "The Accounts of the Fabric of Exeter Cathedral, 1279–1353," *Devon and Cornwall Record Society*, New Series, XXIV and XXVI, 1981 and 1983.

Evergates, T., *Feudal Society in the Bailliage of Troyes under the Counts of Champagne, 1152–1284*, Baltimore, 1975.

Les fastes du gothique, le siècle de Charles V, Paris, 1981 (exhibition catalogue).

Fichot, C., *Statistique monumentale du département de l'Aube*, 5 vols., Troyes, 1884–1900.

Fitchen, J., "A Comment on the Function of the Upper Flying Buttress in French Cathedral Architecture," *Gaz. des B.-A.*, XLV, 1955, 69–90.

———, "The Erection of French Gothic Nave Vaults, a Study of Thirteenth Century Building Practices," *Gaz. des B.-A.*, LV, 1960, 281–300.

———, *The Construction of Gothic Cathedrals*, Oxford, 1961.

Frankl, P., *The Gothic*, Princeton, 1960.

———, *Gothic Architecture*, Harmondsworth, 1962.

Frisch, T. G., *Gothic Art, 1140–c. 1450. Sources and Documents in the History of Art*, Englewood Cliffs, 1971.

Gadan, J. F., "Comptes de l'église de Troyes, 1375–1385," *Le Bibliophile Troyen*, I, Troyes, 1851.

Gallia Christiana, XII, Provincia Ecclesiastica Senonensis, Paris, 1770.

Gavelle, E., *Notice architecturelle sur l'église de Rumilly-les-Vaudes (Aube)*, Arcis, 1896, extract from *Revue de Champagne et de Brie*.

———, *Nicolas Halins dit le Flamand, tailleur d'images à Troyes (vers 1470–après 1541)*, Lille, 1924.

Geary, P. J., "Saint Helen of Athyra and the Cathedral of Troyes in the Thirteenth Century," *Journal of Medieval and Renaissance Studies*, VII, 1977, 149–68.

Gebelin, F., *La Sainte-Chapelle et la Conciergerie*, Paris, 1931.

Geldner, F., *Matthäus Roriczer. Das Buchlein von der Fialen Gerechtigkeit*, Wiesbaden, 1965.

Gimpel, J., *Les bâtisseurs des cathédrales*, Paris, 1958.

Godefroy, F., *Dictionnaire de l'ancienne langue française et de tous ses dialectes du IXe. au XVe. siècle*, 10 vols., Paris, 1880–1902.

Gonse, L., *L'art gothique*, Paris, 1890.

Grodecki, L. *La Sainte-Chapelle*, Paris, 1962.

Grosley, P. J., *Ephémérides*, 2 vols., Paris, 1811.

———, *Mémoires historiques et critiques pour l'histoire de Troyes*, 2 vols., Paris and Troyes, 1811–1812.

Gross, W., *Die abendländische Architektur um 1300*, Stuttgart, 1948.

Harvey, J., *The Mediaeval Architect*, London, 1972.

Héliot, P., and Chastang, M.-L., "Quêtes et voyages de reliques au profit des églises françaises du moyen âge," *Revue d'histoire ecclésiastique*, LIX, 1964, 789–822, LX, 1965, 5–32.

l'Huillier, V., *La paroisse et l'église Saint-Etienne de Beauvais*, Beauvais, 1896.

Kaiser, R., *Bischofsherrschaft zwischen Königtum und Fürstenmacht*, Bonn, 1981.

Knoop, P., and Jones, G. P., *The Medieval Mason*, Manchester, 1967.

Koechlin, R. and Vasselot, J. J. Marquet de, *La sculpture à Troyes et dans la Champagne méridionale au seizième siècle*, Paris, 1900, reprinted Paris, 1966.

Koepf, H., *Die gotische Planrisse des Wiener Sammlungen*, Vienna, 1969.

Kraus, H., *Gold Was the Mortar*, London, 1980.

Kubler, G., "A Late Gothic Computation of Rib Vault Thrusts," *Gaz. des B. A.*, XXVI, 1944, 135–48.

Kunze, H. K., *Das Fassadenproblem des französischen Früh- und Hochgotik*, Leipzig, 1912.

Kurman, P., *La cathédrale Saint-Etienne de Meaux*, Geneva, 1971.

———, "L'église Saint-Jacques de Reims," *Cong. arch.*, CXXXV, 1977, 109–21.

Labande-Mailfert, Y., *Charles VIII et son milieu (1470–1498)*, Paris, 1975.

Laborde, L. de, *Les comptes des bâtiments du roi, 1528–1571*, 2 vols., Paris, 1877–1880.

Lafond, J., "Les vitraux de la cathédrale Saint-Pierre de Troyes," *Cong. arch.*, CXIII, 1955, 29–62.

Lalore, C., *Incendie de la cathédrale de Troyes le 8e. octobre 1700*, Troyes, 1876.

———, *Cartulaire de Saint-Pierre de Troyes. Collection des principaux cartulaires du diocèse de Troyes*, V, Paris and Troyes, 1880.

————, *Collection des principaux obituaires et confraternités du diocèse de Troyes. Collection des documents inédits relatifs à la ville de Troyes et la Champagne méridionale*, Troyes, 1882.

————, *L'église de l'abbaye de Montier-la-Celle*, Troyes, 1882.

Lasteyrie du Saillant, R. C. de, *L'architecture réligieuse en France à l'époque gothique*, 2 vols., 1926–1927.

Leblond, V., *L'église et la paroisse Saint-Etienne de Beauvais au XVe. siècle d'après les comptes des marguilliers et des chanoines*, Beauvais, 1913.

————, *L'art et les artistes en Ile-de-France au XVIe. siècle (Beauvais et Beauvaisis) d'après les minutes notariales*, Paris and Beauvais, 1921.

————, "Les artistes de Beauvais et du Beauvaisis au XVIe. siècle et leurs oeuvres," *Mémoires de la Société académique de l'Oise*, XXIV, 1923, 85–138.

————, *L'église Saint-Etienne de Beauvais*, Paris, 1929.

————, *La cathédrale de Beauvais*, Paris, 1956.

Lefèvre-Pontalis, E., "L'architecture gothique dans la Champagne méridionale au XIIIe. et au XVIe. siècles," *Cong. arch.*, LXIX, 1902, 273–349.

Lehoux, F., *Jean de France, Duc de Berri, sa vie, son action politique (1340–1416)*, 4 vols., Paris, 1966–1968.

Lenoir, A., *Statistique monumentale de Paris*, 3 vols., Paris, 1867.

Leroy, P., "Histoire économique et sociale des églises de la Champagne méridionale à la fin du moyen âge et au début des temps modernes," Diplôme d'études supérieures d'histoire, n.d.

Lesort, A., and Verlet, H., *Saint-Germain l'Auxerrois. Epitaphier du vieux Paris*, V, Paris, 1974.

Lewis, P. S., *The Recovery of France in the Fifteenth Century*, London, 1971.

Longnon, A., *Documents relatifs au comté de Champagne et de Brie, 1172–1361*, III, Paris, 1914.

Marsat, A., *Les églises de l'Aube*, 2 vols., Art et Tourisme, n.d.

Meurgey de Tupigny, J., *Saint-Jacques de la Boucherie et la Tour Saint-Jacques*, Paris, 1960.

Mortet, V., *Recueil des textes relatifs à l'histoire de l'architecture et à la condition des architectes en France au moyen âge, XIe.–XIIe. siècles*, Paris, 1911.

Morel-Payen, L., *Troyes et l'Aube*, Troyes, 1929.

Moubarac, Y., *Guide de l'église Saint-Séverin*, Paris, 1964.

Murray, S., "The Completion of the Nave of Troyes Cathedral," *JSAH*, XXXIV, 1975, 121–39.

————, "La chronologie des arcs boutants de la nef de la cathédrale de Troyes," *Vie en Champagne*, 24e. année, 256, 1976, 9–15.

————, "An Expertise at Beauvais Cathedral," *Jour. Brit. Arch. Assoc.*, CXXX, 1977, 135–44.

————, "The Choir of Saint-Etienne at Beauvais, *JSAH*, XXXVI, 1977, 111–21.

————, "The Choir of the Church of Saint-Pierre, Cathedral of Beauvais," *Art Bull.*, LXII, 1980, 533–51.

————, "Master Jehançon Garnache (1485–1501) and the Construction of the High Vaults and Flying Buttresses of the Nave of Troyes Cathedral," *Gesta*, XIX, 1980, 37–49.

————, "Bleuet and Anthoine Colas, Master Masons of Troyes Cathedral. Artistic Personality in Late Gothic Design," *JSAH*, XLI, 1982, 7–14.

————, and Bongartz, N., "Chronologie abrégée des étapes de construction de la cathédrale de Troyes," *Vie en Champagne*, 22e. année, 235, 1974, 6–16.

A. Mussat, *Les cathédrales dans leurs cités*, *Revue de l'Art*, LV, 1982, 9–22.

Nelson, R. J., "A Lost Portal by Martin Chambiges," *JSAH*, XXXIII, 1974, 155–57.

Panofsky, E., *Gothic Architecture and Scholaticism*, New York, 1958.

Pétal, A., "Documents inédits concernant Guichard, Evêque de Troyes," *Mém. Soc. acad. Aube*, LXVII, 1903, 199–213.

Pevsner, N. "Terms of Architectural Planning in the Middle Ages," *Journal of the Warburg and Courtauld Institutes*, V, 1942, 232–37.

Piétresson de Saint-Aubin, P., "La fourniture de pierre sur les grands chantiers troyens du moyen-âge et la Renaissance, *Bull. arch.*, 1928–1929, 569–601.

————, "L'église Saint-Jean-au-Marché à Troyes, *Cong. arch.*, CXIII, 1955, 85–95.

————, "La formation de Troyes," *Vie en Champagne*, 17e. année, 177, 1969, 5–11.

Pigeotte, L., "Notice sur l'incendie de Troyes en 1524," *Ann. Aube*, XXXII, 1858, 41–66.

————, *Etude sur les travaux d'achèvement de la catédrale de Troyes*, Troyes 1870.

————, "Le grand clocher de la cathédrale de Troyes," *Mém. Soc. acad. Aube*, XLI, 1877, 149–210.

Pirenne, J. H., *Medieval Cities, Their Origins and the Revival of Trade*, Princeton, 1969. First published 1946.

Poinsignon, M., *Histoire générale de la Champagne et de la Brie*, 3 vols., Paris, and Châlons-sur-Marne, 1885–1886.

Selected Bibliography

Porée, C., "Les architectes et la construction de la cathédrale de Sens," *Cong. arch.*, LXXIV, 1907, 559–98.

———, *La cathédrale d'Auxerre*, Paris, 1926.

Poulle, E., "L'église Saint-Nicholas de Troyes," *Cong. arch.*, CXIII, 1955, 71–84.

Prache, A., "L'art dans la Champagne du nord," *Cong. arch.*, CXXXV, 1977, 9–15.

Prévost, A., *Le diocèse de Troyes*, 3 vols., Domois, 1923–1926.

Quantin, R., *La cathédrale de Troyes*, Troyes, 1953.

Quicherat, J., "Notice sur plusieurs registres de l'oeuvre de la cathédrale de Troyes," Paris, 1848, extract from *Mémoires de la Société royale des antiquaires de France*, XIX, 1848.

Régnier, M. L., *La renaissance dans le Vexin et dans une partie du Parisis*, Pontoise, 1886.

———, "Une particularité architectonique du choeur de Saint-Etienne de Beauvais," *Cong. arch.*, LXXII, 1905, 530–34.

———, *Quelques mots sur les monuments de Gisors*, Gisors, 1909.

Reinhardt, H., *La cathédrale de Reims*, Paris, 1967.

Rigault, A., *Le procès de Guichard, évêque de Troyes (1308–1313). Mémoires et documents publiées par la Société de l'Ecole des Chartes*, I, Paris, 1896.

Roger, J.-M., "Note sur la construction du palais épiscopal de Troyes à l'époque romane," *Vie en Champagne*, 32e. année, 341, 1984, 11–13.

Rondot, N., *Les sculpteurs de Troyes au XIVe. au XVe. siècle*, Paris, 1887.

Roserot, A., *Dictionnaire historique de la Champagne méridionale (Aube)*, 3 vols., Langres and Troyes, 1942–1948.

Roserot de Melin, J., *Bibliographie commentée des sources d'une histoire de la cathédrale de Troyes*, I, *Construction*, Troyes, 1966; II, *Décoration, ameublement*, Troyes, 1970.

———, *Le diocèse de Troyes*, Troyes, 1957.

Russell, G., "The North Window of the Nine Altars Chapel, Durham Cathedral," reprinted from *Medieval Art and Architecture of Durham Cathedral*, British Archaeological Association, 1980, 87–89.

Saint-Paul, A., "Les origines du gothique flamboyante en France," *Bull. mon.*, LXX, 1906, 483–510.

———, "L'architecture française et la guerre de cent ans," *Bull. mon.*, LXXII, 1908, 5–40, 269–302 and 388–436.

Salet, F., "Saint-Urbain de Troyes," "La Madeleine de Troyes," "L'église Saint-Pantaléon de Troyes," *Cong. arch.*, CXIII, 1955, 96–122, 139–52 and 153–65.

Salzman, L. F., *Building in England down to 1540*, Oxford, 1952.

Sanfaçon, R., *L'architecture flamboyante en France*, Quebec, 1971.

Shelby, L. R., "Medieval Masons' Templates," *JSAH*, XXX, 1971, 140–54.

———, "The Geometrical Knowledge of Medieval Master Masons," *Speculum*, XLVII, 1972, 395–421.

———, *Gothic Design Techniques*, Carbondale, 1977.

Simson, O. von, *The Gothic Cathedral*, New York, 1956.

Tamir, M. H., "The English Origin of the Flamboyant Style," *Gaz. des. B. A.*, VI. series, XXIX, 1946, 257–68.

Thibout, M., *Saint-Médard*, Paris, 1946.

Troche, M., Mémoire historique et critique sur le portail, le porche et les peintures du porche de l'église royale et paroissiale de Saint-Germain l'Auxerrois à Paris," *Revue archéologique*, 1846.

———, *La tour de Saint-Jacques-de-la-Boucherie*, Paris, 1857.

Troescher, G., *Claus Sluter and die burgundische Plastik um die Wende des XIVten Jahrhunderts*, Freiburg, 1932.

Vachon, M., *Mémoire à la commission du vieux Paris sur l'origine français de l'ancien Hôtel de Ville de Paris*, Paris, 1911.

———, *Une famille parisienne d'architectes maistres maçons, les Chambiges, 1490–1643*, Paris, 1907.

Vale, M. G. A., *Charles VIII*, London, 1974.

Vallery-Radot, J., "La cathédrale Saint-Etienne d'Auxerre," *Cong. arch.*, CXVI, 1958, 40–59.

———, "Saint-Germain d'Auxerre," *Cong. arch.*, CXVI, 1958, 26–39.

Vaughan, R., *Philip the Bold*, London, 1979.

Velte, M., *Die Anwendung des Quadratur und Triangulatur bei des Grund- und Aufrissgestaltung der gotischen Kirchen*, Basel, 1951.

Villes, A., "Notre-Dame de l'Epine, sa façade occidentale." *Cong. arch.*, CXXXV, 1977, 779–862.

Viollet-le-Duc, E., *Dictionnaire raisonné de l'architecture française du XIe. au XVIe. siècles*, 10 vols., Paris, 1854–1868.

Vroom, W.H., *De financiering van de Kathedraalbouw*, Maarsen, 1981.

Wiggishof, J. C., "L'affaire Boccador-Chambiges," *Archéologie parisienne*, 1912.

Index

Agincourt, battle of, 45, 48, 49, 59
Aigremont, quarry of, 146–147
Aix-en-Othe, 20
Alexandre le Blanc, apprentice of Jehan Bailly, 182–183
Alexandre Magot de Dijon, 206
Allonne, 107
Amiens Cathedral, 2, 7, 49, 101, 104, 149, 150, 201
Ancelet la Can(n)e, carpenter, 174, 177, 180
Anchier Daubruissel, mason, 205
Angy, quarry of, 28
Anjou, duke of, 44
anniversaries, 25, 26, 210, 212–215
Anségise, bishop, 11
Anthoine Colas, master mason, 7, 41, 50, 52, 56, 66, 67, 69–75, 77–78, 82, 85–86, 89, 100, 108, 111–112, 150–158, 201, 206–207, 217, 224–225
Apostolic Chamber, 62, 157
Archa reliquarium, 24
Arcis-sur-Aube, 23, 108; archdeacon of, 121
Armagnacs, 44, 45, 59
Arras, treaty of, 46
artistic personality, 7
Aulnois, quarry of, 8, 89, 177, 179, 181
Auxerre: Cathedral of, 14, 55, 59, 135; Saint-Germain, 55, 59, 135
Auxon, 108

Balthazar, glazier, 174
Balustrades, 30, 121, 164–165
Bar-sur-Seine, 8, 146
Beauvais: cathedral of, 12, 21, 37, 89, 90–92, 96, 104–105, 107, 183, 185–187, 189; Saint-Etienne, 104–105, 106–107

Bedford, duke of, 45
Bells, 27–28, 118–120, 154, 195, 197
Berry, duke of, 34, 44, 59–60
Bertrand du Guesclin, 44
Black Death, 20
Blanchart, roofer, 119
Blanche d'Artois, 20
Blanche de Navarre, 16, 20
Bleuet, master mason of Reims Cathedral, 7, 64, 67–69, 71–75, 85–86, 89, 100–101, 112, 149–151, 201
Bonaventure de Grez, mason, 185–186
Boniface VIII, pope, 20
Boulogne, 10
Bourges: cathedral of, 2, 59; city of, 45, 59, 141; pragmatic sanction of, 62
Bourguignons, quarry of, 8, 146
Braine, Saint-Yved, 4, 13
Brétigny, treaty of, 21
Brienne-le-Château, 108–109
Briars, 9, 179
Brokars de Fenestrange, 20
Brussels, 9, 201
Buckingham, duke of, 21
Building campaigns, interpretation of, 5–6, 34, 42, 50, 64
Burgundians, 8, 20, 44–45, 59
Burgundy, dukes of (see also individual dukes by name), 21–22, 27, 44, 47–48

Calais, treaty of, 44
Cayel de Pont-Sainte-Marie, 173
Centers (for vault construction), 79, 81, 84, 119, 139, 155–156, 163, 165, 167–173, 186, 188–189, 196–198

Chalk, used a building stone, 8–10, 42, 56, 138, 154
Châlons-sur-Marne, 11, 12; Notre-Dame-en-Vaux, 13
Champagne: counts of (see also individual counts by name), 1, 11, 43; fairs of, 1, 11–12, 19
Champmol, charterhouse of, 48, 56
Charles V, king, 21, 26, 30, 34, 44, 122, 212–213
Charles VI, king, 44, 46
Charles VII, king, 45–46, 62
Charles VIII, king, 89, 103
Charles the Rash, duke of Burgundy, 61
Chartres, cathedral of, 2, 13, 40, 83, 202
Chavanges, 108
Claude Bonjour, 183
Claude Bourgeois, laborer, 162
Claude Damas, mason, 197
Claus Sluter, sculptor, 55
Colas Aman, mason, 208
Colas Marin, 186
Colas Mathau, 179, 181
Colas Merlin, mason, 182–183
Colas (Nicolas) Savetier, mason, 170, 172, 182–183, 186, 208
Colas Simart, mason, 183, 186
Colerne, mason, 139
Colin, apprentice of Henry de Bruisselles, 205
Colin Colart, laborer, 206
Colin Guignon, mason, 138–139
Colin Millet, mason, 9, 92, 192
Colin Noot, 143
Colin Royer, mason, 186
Colinetus, mason, 203
Colleçon Faulchot (de Châlons), mason, 169–170, 172, 174, 182–183, 186, 206–208
Collecting boxes, 24, 209–210, 212–215
Collet Godier, joiner, 182
Compiègne, 107
Confraternities, 26, 63, 88, 210, 212–215
Conrot de Strambouc, 48, 205
Constantinople, conquest of, 16
Copes, 26, 210, 212–215
Cranes, lifting gear, 9, 118–120, 144, 149, 156, 161, 182–183, 189, 196
Crusade, 15
Culoison, quarry of, 179

Denis, apprentice of Jaquet le Vachier, 147
Denis Aubert, mason, 160
Denis de Champguion, canon, 234, 236
Denis Michel, mason, 168–169, 172, 208
Denisot, pointer, 127
Didier Fallet, laborer, 180
Dijon, 55
Dorigny, family of, 62
Drawings, architectural, 55, 59, 67, 89, 127, 129, 138, 141, 142–143, 150, 170, 177–178, 194, 197
Dreux (Droin) de la Marche: canon, 29; chapel of, 29, 73, 76, 86, 92, 149, 151, 155–158, 163, 185, 189, 234
Droin de Mantes, sculptor, 127, 129
Drouet de Dammartin, master mason, 34, 56, 127

Edmon Colleçon, 197

Edmond Huguenot, laborer, 208
Edward I, king of England, 19
Elision, 13
Emery, carpenter, 161
Entablatures, 30, 120
Episcopal revenues, 12
Erart de Vitel, proviseur, 43, 136
Ervy-le-Châtel, 59, 140
Etienne Audigier, plumber, 137
Etienne de Givry, bishop, 45, 47, 56
Etienne Gillebert, canon, 122
Etienne Hundelot, laborer, 206
Etienne Peschat, carpenter, 180, 195–197
Eudes IV, duke of Burgundy, 20
Eustache d'Aubrecicourt, 20–21
Expertise of 1362, 10, 26, 30–33, 43, 52, 120–121, 216

Fabric, 15, 21, 26, 43, 45–46, 87, 135, 209–215; accounts, 2–3, 21–22, 27–28, 33–35, 80; use of Latin and French, 3; audited, 3
Felin, de, brothers, master masons, 103–104
Felisot Clement, 145
Felisot Jaque, mason, 132, 136
Felisot, roofer, 137
Fierabras, carpenter, 131, 133–134, 136–137, 205
Flamboyant, 48, 58, 64–65, 68, 71, 78, 83, 89, 95, 102
Fleur-de-Lys, 71
Forme, center or frame, especially for windows, 32, 126, 131, 133
Formeret, window arch, 56–57, 80, 138
Foundation (endowment) of altars and chapels, 29–30, 36
Foundations (masonry footings) 9–10, 34, 125, 176, 178–179
François I, king, 89
Frost damage, 10, 30, 32, 56–57, 131–132, 138
Funerals, 26, 210, 212–215

Gabelle, salt tax, 88, 177, 215
Gabriel Favereau, master mason, 93
Gallicanism, 62
Gargoyles, 120, 145, 163
Garnier de Trainel, bishop, 15–16
Garno, smith, 118
Gauthier Oudin, mason, 207
General Pardon, 62, 146, 150–151, 157, 210
Gerard Faulchot, master mason, 108, 201, 208
Gerart de Prague, mason, 48
German artisans, 48–49
Gilet du Pont, plasterer, 145
Gilet Lomme, laborer, 207
Gilet Louot, apprentice of Anthoine Colas, 206
Gillot de Lessart, 170
Girard de la Noue, 30, 234
Girard le Noquat, glazier, 159–160
Girardin de Mont en Allemagne, 48, 205
Girart de Han (Ham), sculptor, 129
Girart d'Aubeterre, roofer, 132
Gisors, 107
Glazed triforium, 4, 10, 13

Grenier, storechamber, 33, 34, 124–125, 148, 180
Grisaille glass, 40, 126, 134, 140
Guerart, 135
Guichard, bishop, 20, 24, 28
Guichart, canon, 175
Guidimus, laborer, 203
Guienne, 46
Guillaume Alexandre, mason, 182
Guillaume Baretel, 197
Guillaume Belin, 140
Guillaume Berthel, mason, 208
Guillaume, brother, 128
Guillaume de Creney, canon, 122, 129
Guillaume Huyart, lawyer, 84
Guillaume le Cur, 138
Guillaume Méchin, bishop, 20
Guillelmus, carpenter, 119–120
Guillelmus le Henapier, laborer, 203
Guillelmus, questor, 24
Guiot Brisetour, glazier, 54, 126, 131, 134–135, 140
Guiotus Maupronne, laborer, 204
Gutters, 10, 30, 33, 118, 120–121, 124

Hance de Couloigne (Cologne), 48
Hatton, bishop, 11
Helen of Athyra, Saint, 16, 22, 24, 209
Hemart de Saint Oulph, 122
Hennequin, family of, 45, 62
Hennequin, laborer, 131
Hennequin de Bruisselles (Brussels), 48
Henri de Carinthie, bishop, 11
Henri de la Noue, dean, 30, 43, 234, 236
Henri de Poitiers, bishop, 20, 26, 47
Henricus, mason, 203
Henricus, master mason, 28, 35–37, 118
Henrion d'Arcis, canon, 46
Henrion Sonnet, tavern-keeper, 176, 184
Henry I, the Liberal, count of Champagne, 11, 16
Henry II, count of Champagne, 16
Henry III, count of Champagne, 19
Henry V, king of England, 45
Henry de Bruisselles (Brussels), master mason, 22, 35, 43, 48, 53, 55, 56, 74, 76–77, 128–130, 132–137, 200, 202, 205
Henry de Mez (Metz), 46, 205
Henry de Mont en Allemagne, 48, 205
Henry Preudhomme, carpenter, 197
Henry Soudan, master mason, 43, 55, 129–130, 200, 205
Henry Tetel, mason, 206–207
Herveus, bishop, 15
Hexagons in Gothic design, 40, 65–66, 72, 96–97, 103–104
High Gothic, 7, 14–15, 36, 64, 68, 83
Hugues Cuvelier, master mason, 89, 101, 175–176
Hugo, master carpenter, 119
Huguenin Viremignot, laborer, 166
Hundred Years War, 1, 20, 46, 101
Huyard, family of, 62, 84

Ile-de-France, 7, 13

Indulgences, 15, 22
Inscribed squares in Gothic design, 52–53, 70–71, 74, 93–94, 96, 99

Jacobus, master mason, 28, 35–37, 119, 124, 203
Jacobus de Noa, Jacques de la Noue, 30, 124, 234
Jacomardus, smith, 119
Jacquerie, 20
Jacques Boschet, 184
Jacques Cousin, proviseur, 43, 122, 129
Jacques de Basson, archdeacon, 30, 234
Jacques Raguier, bishop, 61, 63
Jaques Guichart, 177
Jaques le Fuzelier, messenger, 177
Jaques Martellet, apprentice of Jehan Bailly, 182
Jaques Robelin, organist, 173
Jaquet Berton, mason, 180
Jaquet de la Bouticle, mason, 70, 75, 153, 156–157, 159–160, 206–208
Jaquet le Pointre, 206
Jaquet le Vachier, master mason, 7, 65–67, 69–71, 73, 75–76, 86, 100, 111, 147–151, 159, 217
Jaquet Martellot, apprentice of Jehan Bailly, 183
Jaquin Ancelot, laborer, 190
Jaquinot Clivet, mason, 139
Jaquinot Colart, laborer, 207
Jaquinot Ladvocat, locksmith, 145
Jaquot de Pouant (Pouan), mason, 128
Jaquot Mignart, mason, 136, 205
Jaquoti, 176
Jay, mason, 132
Jean Braque, bishop, 29
Jean d'Aubigny, bishop, 20
Jean d'Auxois, bishop, 20
Jean II d'Auxois, bishop, 20
Jean de Cherchemont, bishop, 20
Jean de Nanteuil, bishop, 24, 28
Jean d'Orbais, master mason of Reims Cathedral, 2
Jean Leguisé, bishop, 45–47
Jeanne, 19
Jehan Aubelet, master mason, 56, 138–139
Jehan Babelin, 163
Jehan Bailly, master mason, and Jehan II Bailly, his son, 90–93, 108, 175, 177–181, 183–185, 193–197, 201
Jehan Bertran, carpenter, 188
Jehan Blanche, *proviseur,* 143
Jehan Briaix, painter, 188
Jehan Carbonnier, carpenter, 77, 81, 158–159, 163–164, 167, 171–174, 177–179, 181
Jehan Chasteau, mason, 183
Jehan Cheuriat, *proviseur,* 149–150
Jehan Chevallier, mason, 65, 147
Jehan Colombe, carpenter, 50, 133, 139
Jehan de Bruisselles (Brussels), mason, 48, 205
Jehan de Couloigne (Cologne), mason, 48, 205
Jehan de Damas ("de Soissons"), master mason, 91, 93, 108, 181, 183–187, 189–190, 193–194
Jehan de Denemoine, 205
Jehan de Dijon, carpenter, 177–180

Jehan de Dijon, master mason of Reims Cathedral, 56, 139
Jehan de Fontainnes, mason, 136
Jehan de Grey, carpenter, 177, 179
Jehan de Monstier, mason, 153, 206
Jehan de Mussy, carpenter, 182
Jehan de Nantes, master carpenter, 59–60, 138–139, 141–144
Jehan de Provins, 205
Jehan de Rameru (Ramerupt), mason, 131, 205
Jehan de Torvoie, master mason, 31–35, 37, 42–43, 52, 54, 77, 121, 131–132, 216
Jehan des Noës, mason, 198
Jehan des Portes, carter, 198
Jehan Doce, mason, 139
Jehan du Bois, laborer, 170, 172–173, 176
Jehan Fremault, carpenter, 154
Jehan Gailde, master mason, 90, 108–109, 177–179, 201
Jehan Gaillard, 193
Jehan Gaillart, 137, 138
Jehan Gilot, mason, 136, 138
Jehan Girart, carter, 156
Jehan Guerart, master of the works for the duke of Berry, 143
Jehan Honnet, carpenter, 179, 184–185
Jehan Huyart, canon, 84
Jehan Jaqueton, laborer, 206
Jehan l'Abbé de Lusigny, 167
Jehan le Fevre, mason, 157, 207
Jehan le Semer, mason, 208
Jehan le Valeton, roofer, 165–166
Jehan Lescaillon, slater, 128
Jehan Martiau, 206
Jehan Martin, 180
Jehan Mathieu, 206
Jehan Michel, joiner, 148
Jehan Nandot, mason, 208
Jehan Oudot, carpenter, 179
Jehan Phelippon, joiner, 187–188
Jehan Poignant, 140
Jehan Prevost, master mason, 56, 138
Jehan Raoulin, laborer, 131
Jehan Regnault, 189
Jehan Roitin, joiner, 193
Jehan Thevenot, laborer, 207
Jehan Thiebault, laborer, 206
Jehan Thierry, master mason, 33, 36–37, 48, 52, 54–56, 77, 122–123, 125–129, 200–201, 204
Jehan Troucher (Truchin), apprentice of Jehançon Garnache, 182–183
Jehan Verrat, glazier, 174
Jehan Verrouillot, laborer, 205
Jehan and Colart Neveu, roofers, 50, 132–133
Jehançon Garnache, master mason, 41–42, 50, 52, 74–86, 89–91, 100, 108, 111–112, 160–187, 200–201, 208, 217–219, 222, 224–225
Jehanin du Bechot, carpenter, 154
Jehanin Fajot, mason, 147
Jehanin Gilot, mason, 138
Jehanin Loriot, carpenter, 145

Jehanin and Gatherin de Vitel, joiners, 135
Jerusalem, queen of, 16
Joan of Arc, 45
Johannes, archdeacon of Sainte-Margerie, 23
Johannes de Auxeyo, *proviseur*, 24
Johannes de Dieneyo, mason, 203
Johannes de Hugonis, laborer, 204
Johannes de Regiis, laborer, 203
Johannes de Villeta, questor, 24
Johannes Niger, mason, 203
John Chrysostom, 17
John the Fearless, duke of Burgundy, 44, 45

Knights Templar, 20

Lambert Peletier, laborer, 207
Lancaster, Henry of, 45
Lancastrians, 20
Langres, 11
Late Gothic, 7, 14–15, 36, 41, 50–52, 63–65, 67–68, 70, 76, 86–87, 97, 107, 112
Laurent de la Hupperoye, vicar, 157
Laurent Germain, quarry man, 83, 179, 180
Laurent Herault, carpenter, 148, 154, 156
Le Bergoingnat, laborer, 203
Le Borne, laborer, 203
Le Quiat, laborer, 203
Le Rousselant, laborer, 203
Legacies as a source of income, 23, 210, 212–215
Legier Chambiges, mason, 182–183
Leo X, pope, 186
Léon Cathedral, 85
Lezinnes, quarry of, 8
Lié Gilles, mason, 183
Linkage, 13
Lisignes, quarry of, 136
Logettes, rental houses belonging to the fabric, 63
Louis VII, king, 12
Louis X, king, 19–20
Louis XI, king, 61–62
Louis XII, king, 88–89
Louis Raguier, bishop, 47, 61–63, 146, 163
Low Countries, 48–49
Lyon, 10
Lyonnet, 180

Macelinus, carpenter, 125
Marcheant, laborer, 203
Marguerite of Burgundy, 20
Marquet Riviere, mason, 183
Marissel, 107
Marmet, apprentice of Henry Soudan, 205
Martin Chambiges, master mason, 7–8, 75, 84, 86, 87–109, 112, 175–189, 193, 200, 202
Martin de Vaux, master mason, 108
Martin des Molins, mason, 169, 208
Martin Menart, 184
Masoning earth, 8–9, 81, 153, 156, 170–171, 190, 198
Masons' lodge, 154–156
Mastidia, Saint, 24

Mathieu, bishop, 11–12
Maurice de Gyé, 233
Maurice Favereau, master mason, 108
Meaux, 11–13
Mehun-sur-Yèvre, 59, 141
Melun, Saint-Aspais, 104
Méry-sur-Seine, 12
Mesgriny, family of, 45, 62
Michaelus le Mercerat, laborer, 203
Michau, apprentice of Jaquet le Vachier, 147
Michau de Loches, *proviseur,* 141
Michel, master mason of Saint-Nicolas in Lorraine, 90, 178
Michel Thays, painter, 195, 198
Michelin de Jonchery, master mason, 32–33, 36–37, 48, 52, 54, 77, 122–123, 125–126, 200–201, 204, 216
Michelin Hardiot, master mason, 32–33, 36–37, 48, 52, 54–56, 77, 122–123, 125, 127–129, 200–201, 204, 216
Michiel de Bruisselles (Brussels), mason, 48
Milo, bishop, 12
Molé, family of, 45, 62
Money changing, 11
Montgueaux, hill of, 9
Montereau, 45
Montier-la-Celle, 20, 108
Mouchettes, 58, 68, 74, 83, 102
Moulins, 83

Navarre, 20, 59, 140
Niches in Gothic design, 93–96, 103, 105–106
Nicholas V, pope, 22, 48, 62, 146
Nicolas, carpenter, 161
Nicolas Bonne Chiere, mason, 206
Nicolas Cochart, clerk, 140
Nicolas Halins (Halliz, etc.) "le Flamand," sculptor, 190–192, 195
Nicolas Ladvocat, carpenter, 141
Nicolas Lombart, 150
Nicolas Ludot, paper maker, 166, 172
Nicolas Matan, 139
Nicolas Matau, 185
Nicolas Platot, apprentice/laborer, 206
Nicolas Savetier, mason, *see* Colas Savetier
Nicolas Solacium, canon, 175
Nicolas (also Nicole) Tetel, canon, 63, 146, 150–151
Nicole Coiffart, *proviseur,* 164
Nicole Meurgey, warden, 157
Noffo-Dei, 20
Nogent-sur-Seine, 20
Normandy, 46
Notre-Dame de l'Epine, 67, 148, 150

Obertus de Placentia, *proviseur,* 24
Octagons in Gothic design, 65–66, 72
Odo de Toriaco, *proviseur,* 23
Ogees, 39, 58, 68–70, 82, 92, 95
Orbais, 13
Orléans: council of, 62; duke of, 44
Oudinus, laborer, 203
Oudinetus le Borne, laborer, 204

Paleiz, mason, 203
Pamplona, 19
Parigot, laborer, 203
Paris: city of, 24, 60, 77, 85, 137, 143, 177, 201; Jacobins, convent of, 103; Notre-Dame, 7, 36, 38–40, 61, 85, 94, 101, 103, 105, 111, 149–150; Pont Notre-Dame, 103; Saint-Etienne du Mont, 105; Saint-Jacques de la Boucherie, 103; Saint-Merry, 105; Saint-Séverin, 105; Sainte-Chapelle, 57, 103; SS. Gervais and Protais, 103
Parisian Rayonnant, 15
Perinot Calon, 132
Perinus Niger, mason, 203
Perot de Fromgnicourt, 132
Perrin Loque, master carpenter, 60, 143
Petit Pierre dit Gille, mason, 207
Petrus, master carpenter, 119
Petrus de Lecherellis, laborer, 204
Petrus Ruffus, laborer, 204
Phelippot, 48, 55
Philip Augustus, king, 16
Philip III, king, 19
Philip IV, king, 19–20
Philip the Good, duke of Burgundy, 45
Philippe Colombe, apprentice, 208
Picardy, 7
Piecework/daywork, 80–81, 84, 133, 135
Pieret de Saint-Quentin, mason, 206
Pieret, sculptor, 137
Pierre, apprentice of Thomas Michelin, 142
Pierre Barbe, mason, 205
Pierre Chambiges, master mason, 91, 93, 107, 109, 181, 183–184, 188–189, 193, 196
Pierre Damas, mason, 190
Pierre d'Arcis, bishop, 46, 48, 54
Pierre d'Arbois, canon, *proviseur,* 21, 26, 43, 122, 127, 129, 132, 135–137
Pierre de Damas, mason, 183, 194
Pierre de Montreuil, master mason, 37, 39–40
Pierre de Refuge, 239
Pierre de Villiers, bishop, 48
Pierre de Verdun, 26
Pierre Faisant, visiting expert, 30–33, 43, 52, 120
Pierre Gobin, mason, 208
Pierre Guiot, carter, 153, 166
Pierre Hardouyn, mason, 157
Pierre Jacoti, 177
Pierre Prevost, laborer, 172
Pierre Robin, laborer, 160
Pierre Roucelot, mason, 207
Pierre Tarissel, master mason of Amiens Cathedral, 104
Pierre Trubert, 150
Pierre Vatat, carpenter, roofer, 158
Pilier cantonné, 13, 40
Pinnacles, 31, 120, 121
Plaster, 118, 133–134, 142, 161
Poitiers: battle of, 20, 43; city of, 45
Polisot, quarry of, 8
Pont Humbert, quarry of, 148–149, 179, 183
Pont-Sainte-Marie, 8, 108

Pont-sur-Seine, 20
Provins, Saint-Ayoul, 20
Proviseurs, masters of the works, 2–3, 21, 24–25, 43, 47, 59, 64, 111, 199, 201–202

Quarries, 7–8, 28, 79, 90, 118, 130
Quests, 22–24, 46, 48, 62–63, 88, 209, 212–215

Rayonnant Gothic architecture, 14, 18, 36–37, 42, 56, 58, 64, 96
Regionalism in Gothic architecture, 7, 14
Regnault Perchet, mason, 208
Reims: cathedral of, 2, 7, 13, 31, 67, 75, 88, 101, 149–150, 201; city of, 77, 85, 160, 201; Saint-Anthoine, 24
Relics, 16–17, 23, 88, 209
Remon (Remond) Pienne, carpenter, 138–139, 141
Remond, master of the king's works, 137
Renaust de Langres, canon, 122
Rental property belonging to the fabric, 62–63, 87, 209, 212–215
Richard, brother, 46
Richard the Locksmith, 126, 137
Rimaucourt, seigneur of, 59
Robert, count of Champagne, 11
Robert de Luzarches, 2
Rome, 24
Rouen Cathedral, 94
Rumilly-les-Vaudes, 108

Saint-Denis, abbey church of, 13, 37, 85
Saint-Denis, bourg of, 11
Saint-Germain-en-Laye, 57
Saint-Loup-du-Naud, 24
Saint-Parres-aux-Tertres, 108
Saint-Phal, 108
Saint-Quentin, 13–14
"Saint-Urbain master," 38, 68
Sainte-Margerie, archdeacon of, 122
Sainte-Maure, quarry of, 8, 108, 179
Savonnières, quarry of, 8, 179, 181
Scaffolding, 3, 73, 79, 84, 118, 124–125, 132, 153–154, 156, 158–159, 161, 170, 189, 194–196, 198
Seine river, 10
Senlis, cathedral of, 88, 93, 107
Sens: cathedral of, 24, 95–96, 101–104, 107, 179, 195; archbishop of, 45
Simon de Saint Omer, mason, 182–183
Simon Felix, carpenter, roofer, 158
Simon Henry, apprentice of Jehançon, 182
Simon Maistre Apart, 206
Simon Maurroy, carpenter, 189
Simon, smith, 118
Snails, use of in capital sculpture, 70–71
Soissons Cathedral, 2, 13, 31
Soufflets, 58, 68, 71, 74, 82–83, 182
Spherical triangles and squares, 58–59
Stephanus de Billeta, laborer, 204
Style, neo-Platonic definition of, 2, 9
"Super-Gothic," 88, 91, 112

Symon Jehanine, rip-saw operator, 142

Tanlay, quarry of, 8, 168–169, 179–180
Tassin Jaquart, laborer, 206
Templates, 75, 77, 79, 90–91, 93, 132, 142–143, 148, 151, 154, 159, 166–167, 172, 180, 182, 187–189, 193–194
Templates, "false" (paper), 65, 83, 89, 147, 171–172, 174, 176
Thassin, joiner, 151
Theobaldus, questor, 24
Thevenin, mason, 205
Thevenin Drouart, mason, 206
Thevenin Fallet, 180
Thevenin le Menestrier, 206
Thibaut III, count, 16, 20
Thibaut IV, count, 16
Thomas, master mason, 32–33, 36–37, 52, 122, 216
Thomas Belle, *proviseur,* 43
Thomas Fillet, laborer, 184
Thomas Girard, laborer, 208
Thomas le Chat, blacksmith, 54, 134
Thomas Michelin, master mason, 56–59, 138–142
Tie beams, 155, 164
Tonnerre, quarry of, 8, 28, 56, 83, 128, 159, 171, 173, 187, 197
Tracing chamber, 56, 60, 138, 142, 153, 161, 165, 180–181
Troyes, cathedral of: cellar, 25; chamber, great, 25, 210; chapter, distributions, 21–22, 25, 29; chapter, prebends, 15, 21; choir, 5–6, 12–13, 37; choir flying buttresses, 5, 13–14, 30–31, 34, 42, 120; choir screen (*jubé*), 22, 34–36, 43, 47, 49–50, 54–56, 75, 86, 127–135, 160; choir triforium, 13; collapse in 1228, 9, 13, 15, 40; collapse in 1365, 9, 18, 26, 30, 33, 36, 54; collapse in 1389, 9, 18, 23, 27, 30, 32, 35–36, 41–43, 46, 49, 52–53, 64, 132; collapse in 1700, 9, 38, 50, 60; consecration of, 46; crossing, 35, 54, 133; crossing tower (*grand clocher*), 6, 9, 18, 27, 30, 33, 36, 47, 49, 59–60, 121, 123–124, 133, 140–145, 162, 164, 174; crossing vault, 27, 37–38, 50, 133, 162, 164; description of, 4; design faults, 10, 56; nave aisle capitals, 66, 69, 71, 151–152; nave aisle piers, 40, 65–68, 72–74, 85–86, 90–91, 147, 150, 152–153, 177; nave aisle roof, 35, 125, 174; nave aisle vaults, 41, 66, 69–74, 86, 153, 155–156; nave chapels, 4–5, 30, 33, 36, 38–43, 66, 68, 71, 74, 82, 86, 90–92, 124–125, 148, 150–151, 158, 160, 181; nave clerestory, 4, 35, 42, 50–51, 54, 76, 82, 161, 163–164, 170, 172–174; nave flying buttresses, 5, 9–10, 31–34, 41–42, 50–51, 53, 77–79, 121, 124, 166–170, 216–225; nave gable, 77, 79, 85, 165, 166–167; nave high capitals, 41, 50, 74, 76, 155, 157; nave high vaults, 50, 78–82, 150, 168–169, 171–173; nave main piers, 6, 34, 36, 38, 40, 43, 50, 53, 55, 64–66, 68–69, 72–73, 85–86, 133, 136, 147–149, 159; nave roof, 35, 50, 77, 119, 164; nave triforium, 4, 41–42, 50–51, 54, 73–74, 82, 154, 156, 158, 165; nave upper piers, 51–53, 73–77, 92, 134, 156–162; pavement, 55, 135, 136; provisional flying buttresses, 9, 35, 54, 57, 72–74, 76, 86, 89,

92, 131–133, 154–155, 157, 162–164, 166, 192–193; provisional props, 9, 75, 137–138, 159, 163–164, 181, 184–185, 192–193; provisional roof, 9, 35, 49, 50–54, 63, 73, 75–76, 133–135, 137, 159; provisional screens (parois), 9, 49, 53–54, 63, 84, 133, 135, 159, 161, 173; provisional west wall, 6, 34, 54, 73, 75, 125, 133, 136, 159; restorations (nineteenth century), 9, 14; transept, 4–5, 14, 18–19, 27, 31, 34, 35–39, 42, 49–50, 52, 57, 89, 125, 177; transept flying buttresses, 19; transept, north façade and portal, 69, 86, 136, 153; transept, north, rose window, 18, 35, 49, 50, 56–59, 131–132, 134–136, 140; transept, south, rose window, 127; treasury complex, 4, 33, 62, 124; well, 7, 125, 133, 152, 155; west tower (gros clocher), 6, 12, 27, 30, 49, 56, 72, 85–86, 89, 92, 124, 127, 144, 148–150, 152, 154–157, 160, 164, 179, 184; western frontispiece, 5, 63, 67–69, 75, 77, 84–109, 149–151, 160, 167, 175, 178–180, 184–192, 194–197; western frontispiece, figurative sculpture, 92, 188, 190–191
Troyes, city of: Belle Croix, 89; Rue de la Cité, 4, 6–7, 10, 57
Troyes: commune of, 12; Roman city of, 10; municipality, 26, 46–47, 59, 139
Troyes: La Madeleine, 90; Saint-Etienne, 11, 12; Saint-Jean-au-Marché, 45, 50, 107–108; Saint-Jean-en-Chastel, 11; Saint-Loup, 11, 137; Saint-Nicholas, 107–108; Saint-Nizier, 109; Saint-Pantaléon, 107–108; Saint-Remi, 109; Saint-Urbain, 36, 38–39, 41, 50, 57, 70, 111; Treaty of, 45, 59; urban development of, 88–89

Urban IV, pope, 17

Valeton, carpenter, 158, 160
Vault construction, 8, 9, 27–29, 35, 41, 50, 106, 118, 120
Vault stones (pendans), 3, 81, 118, 124, 198
Vendeuvre, 59
Veluz, de, canon, 175
Venlay, de, canon, 175
Vinant, laborer, 203

Whitewash, 118, 127, 133
William of Sens, master mason of Canterbury Cathedral, 31
Wooden piles (pilotis), 89, 147–148
Workshop, analysis of, 3, 199–208

Yvon Bachot, sculptor, 194

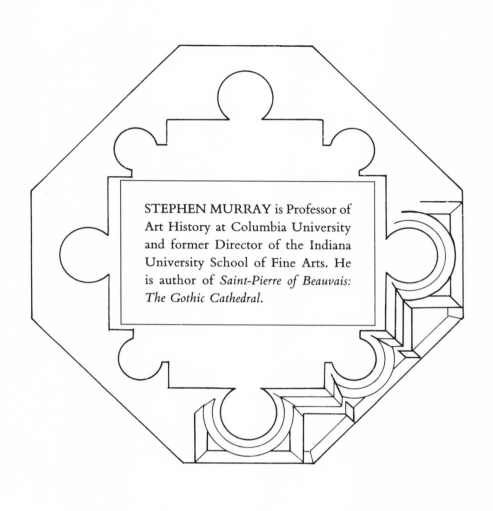

STEPHEN MURRAY is Professor of
Art History at Columbia University
and former Director of the Indiana
University School of Fine Arts. He
is author of *Saint-Pierre of Beauvais:
The Gothic Cathedral*.

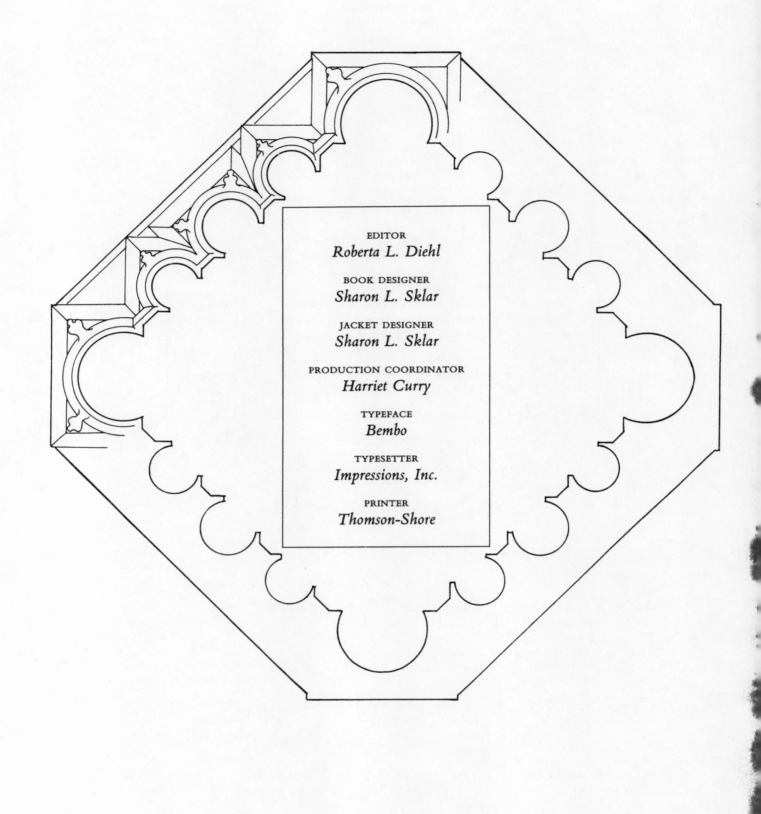

EDITOR
Roberta L. Diehl

BOOK DESIGNER
Sharon L. Sklar

JACKET DESIGNER
Sharon L. Sklar

PRODUCTION COORDINATOR
Harriet Curry

TYPEFACE
Bembo

TYPESETTER
Impressions, Inc.

PRINTER
Thomson-Shore